Politics in
WEST GERMANY

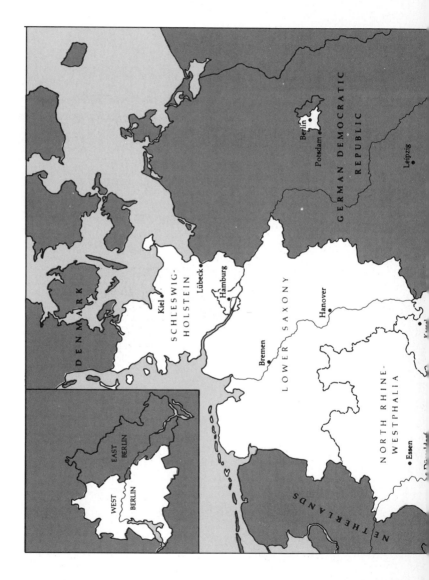

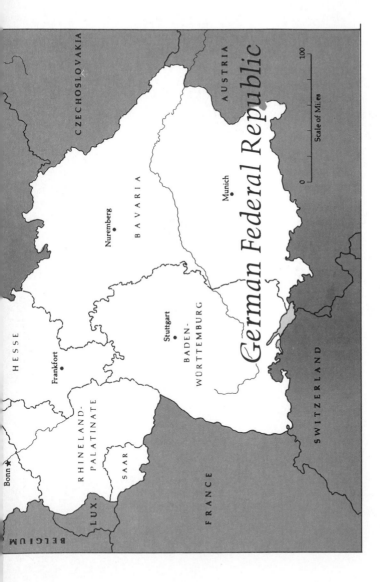

German Federal Republic

CZECHOSLOVAKIA

AUSTRIA

BAVARIA

Nuremberg

Munich

HESSE

Frankfort

BADEN-
WÜRTTEMBURG

Stuttgart

RHINELAND-
PALATINATE

SAAR

Bonn ★

LUX.

BELGIUM

FRANCE

SWITZERLAND

Scale of Miles

0   100

Scott, Foresman/Little, Brown Series
in Comparative Politics

Under the Editorship of

GABRIEL A. ALMOND

LUCIAN W. PYE

A COUNTRY STUDY

Politics in
WEST GERMANY

Russell J. Dalton
Florida State University
Tallahassee

Scott, Foresman/Little, Brown Series in Political Science
SCOTT, FORESMAN AND COMPANY
Glenview, Illinois   Boston   London

Library of Congress Cataloging in Publication Data

Dalton, Russell J.
  Politics in West Germany / Russell J. Dalton.
     p.   cm. — (The Little, Brown series in comparative politics.
  A Country study)   (Scott, Foresman/Little, Brown series in
  political science)
     Bibliography: p.
     Includes index.
     ISBN 0-673-39887-0
     1. Germany (West)—Politics and government.   I. Title.
  II. Series.   III. Series: Little, Brown series in comparative
  politics.   Country study.
  JN3971.A2D28   1989
  320.943—dc19   88-25162
                                                                 CIP

1 2 3 4 5 6 7 8 9 10 — KPF — 94 93 92 91 90 89 88

Printed in the United States of America

For PENN

Preface

Nearly a century ago, the philosopher Friedrich Nietzsche observed that "it is characteristic of the Germans that the question: 'What is German?' never dies out among them." This observation still holds true today. The question of the German identity and Germany's role in world affairs continues to thwart attempts at a simple answer because of the complexity of the nation and its people. For me, the attempt to answer this question is what makes the study of German politics challenging and intriguing, and one of the primary goals of this book is to share with students the progress we have made in unraveling the complexities of German politics.

One of the factors that makes Germany a challenge to study is the dynamic aspect of German politics. Forty years ago, when the Federal Republic of Germany was first created, many observers doubted that the newly formed West German government would last this long. But the Federal Republic has not only endured, it has prospered economically, socially, and politically. To recount the story of postwar Germany, therefore, is to describe how political development created a stable socio-economic system and well-functioning democracy, all in the span of the first postwar generation.

The process of change did not end with the construction of a new social and political order, however. The Federal Republic rapidly developed the characteristics of an advanced industrial society, which redefined the content and style of politics. The student movement of the 1960s, the participatory revolution of the 1970s, and the new social movements of the 1980s place the Federal Republic at the forefront of political and social change in Western Europe. The West German Green party (*Die Grünen*) is a focal point for the alternative, anti-establishment movement in Europe.

Because these trends seem to be accentuated in the German case, the Federal Republic provides a unique setting to explore the political changes affecting other advanced industrial democracies.

The lessons of German history and politics are also an important part of this book. I once read that the history of happy nations is boring to read; German history is anything but boring. German history and politics often involve fundamental questions of the nature of man presented in the starkest examples. The political horrors of the Third Reich are so extreme that they sometimes defy description; can anyone adequately explain why political elites would initiate a world war that results in the death of 60 million individuals or why a society would allow the state to persecute and then exterminate the Jews? Having sunk to these depths, how was Germany able to remake its society and political culture in a single generation to become the success story of Europe? One of the major goals of modern social science in Western Europe and North America has been to answer these questions. I try to share these inquiries with the reader, without oversimplifying the diversity and complexity of the German political experience. This is a difficult task, which might explain why Germans even today talk of their "undigested past." Perhaps the greatest challenge in writing this book was the attempt to digest Germany's past, drawing out these lessons of history to give the reader an understanding of the origins of contemporary German politics.

Gabriel Almond's invitation to write this book and share my interest in German politics with students was an offer I could not refuse. Frankly, I learned of German politics from Almond's early writings and those of Lewis Edinger. I hope that this book continues the tradition that they began.

I depended on the counsel and advice of several people throughout this project. Many of my fundamental views of German politics were formed in writing a book on German political development with Kendall Baker and Kai Hildebrandt; the ideas expressed here are often our ideas. I also want to express my special thanks to Manfred Küchler who took the time to review the first draft of this manuscript in extensive and critical detail; every reader benefits from the improvements he encouraged me to make. Gabriel Almond, Thomas Rochon, and Don Schoonmacher criticized the revised manuscript, and their comments helped me to rethink some important points and thus improve the book still further.

A long list of people furnished other very valuable help along the way. Kendall Baker, Samuel Barnes, Earl Beck, Ursula Hoffmann-Lange, and Andrei Markovits commented on selected portions of the book and freely gave me the benefit of their expertise. Wolfgang Gibowski granted me access to the extensive survey research findings of the Forschungsgruppe Wahlen; Max Kaase and Hans-Dieter Klingemann generously provided intellectual support and empirical data; Jens Alber shared his treasure trove of research and data on the German welfare state. Most of the public opinion data used in this study (Eurobarometer surveys, the West German election studies, and the published polls of Allensbach and Emnid) were made available by the Interuniversity Consortium for Political and Social Research or the Zentralarchiv für empirische Sozialforschung. Neither the archives nor the original collectors of the data bear any responsibility for the interpretations presented here. Erwin Rose of the Zentralarchiv was always willing and able to find the data and reports that no one else could. The staffs of the German Consulates in Atlanta and Miami, the German Information Center in New York, and Internationnes in Bonn were invaluable sources of information. Several classes of my West European politics course at Florida State University (CPO 3103) helped me refine this manuscript with their hands-on experiences. And throughout this all, Robert Rohrschneider served as a valuable research assistant and critic. The help of all of these friends is what made this book possible.

Finally, I would like to thank John Covell and the other talented people at *Scott Foresman-Little Brown* and *Editing, Design and Production* for their skill and professionalism in producing this book. A publisher's quiet support is always appreciated, even if the expression of appreciation sometimes waits until the preface is written.

Contents

Illustrations

Tables

Introduction

AFTER HIS SECOND VICTORY AT WIMBLEDON, German tennis star Boris Becker gave an interview to an American journalist. In the interview Becker explained his maturity and well-mannered behavior in a sport sometimes known for its exhibitionists. I am a German, he said, and Germans must behave differently because of what happened in earlier times. It seems odd that the behavior of a young tennis star should be shaped by political events that occurred before his birth, and with which he has no direct connection. But "what happened in earlier times" is crucial to understanding German politics and society today.

This is a book about contemporary West German politics, but it—like Boris Becker—views the present in the context of Germany's past. Throughout the following chapters we will see how the structure and institutions of the political process were shaped in reaction to their historical antecedents. The constitutional form of the West German political system, for example, was deliberately engineered to avoid the institutional weaknesses of the Weimar Republic. The development of the party system intentionally charted a new course. Even the political culture was systematically remade to change the political beliefs inherited from the Third Reich. Indeed, I was initially surprised by how often I was drawn to historical materials in order to explain the development of postwar West German politics. One can describe modern political institutions and the workings of the political process without resort to historical precedent, but without history one cannot understand the nature of German politics and society. Still, rather than a historical study, this is an examination of how a nation has tried to rise above parts of its history.

Most of the major problems that preoccupied West German politics during its first generation were distinctly German, reflecting the legacy of German history. The various aspects of the "German question" focused on whether West Germany could escape the negative aspects of its political inheritance. Political analysis focused on what was exceptional about Germany, why it differed from other Western nations, and what steps were necessary to lessen this exceptionality.

There were three major challenges that initially confronted Germany and upon which the fate of post–World War II German politics would ultimately be decided. One of these concerns was the problem of nation building. Germany had lost a substantial quantity of land as a result of the war. In 1949 the remaining German territory was further divided into two states. A parliamentary democracy, the *Federal Republic of Germany* (FRG), was created in the western portion of the country, and the communist *German Democratic Republic* (GDR) was created by the Soviet Union in the eastern zone. The Western Allies retained the right to intervene in the domestic affairs of West Germany even after 1949. Thus, to become an independent nation the Federal Republic had to regain its sovereignty and develop a sense of national identity. This would be a difficult task, because Germany was an outcast among the international community of nations, and opposition to the rebuilding of any German state was considerable.

West German policy makers, especially Chancellor Konrad Adenauer, placed a high priority on attaining national sovereignty and rehabilitating West Germany's image in international affairs. These goals were achieved by integrating the Federal Republic into the Western Alliance. By cooperating with its Allies, West Germany was slowly able to improve its national image. Moreover, the Western powers were willing to grant greater autonomy to the Federal Republic if it was exercised within the framework of an international body. For example, economic redevelopment was channeled through the European Coal and Steel Community (ECSC) and the Common Market, and military rearmament occurred within the North Atlantic Treaty Organization (NATO). Full national sovereignty finally was gained in 1955, and the Federal Republic gradually reached a position of formal equality and respectability within the Western Alliance.

Another pressing challenge was the economic condition of postwar Germany. Most of the West German public struggled to survive during the years immediately after the war. Despite the progress made by 1949, the economic picture was still bleak. Unemployment remained high and the average wage earner received less than $60 a month. In 1950 almost two-thirds of the public felt they had been better off before the war, and severe economic hardships were still common for much of the population.

The nation achieved remarkable success in meeting this economic challenge. Relying on the Social Market Economy (*Soziale Markt-wirtschaft*), which was basically a free-enterprise system, the country experienced a period of sustained and unprecedented economic growth. By the early 1950s, incomes reached the prewar level, and growth had just begun. Over the next two decades, per capita wealth increased nearly fivefold, and average incomes grew nearly sevenfold. By almost all economic indicators the people became several times more affluent than at any time in prewar history. Furthermore, other social indicators followed the same developmental pattern, and in doing so changed the structure of society. The labor force shifted from a concentration in the traditional agricultural and industrial sectors to employment in the service sector and government. Access to education grew rapidly and educational levels rose dramatically. This phenomenal economic record came to be known as West Germany's Economic Miracle (*Wirtschafts-wunder*).

The Federal Republic's third major challenge was to develop support for the new institutions of democratic government. The new regime was born with many of the handicaps that led to the collapse of the Weimar Republic in the 1930s. German democracy lacked the historical tradition common to other West European nations. Moreover, the new political institutions were not solely the product of German efforts; they came from wartime defeat and were imposed by occupying powers. Thus many feared that the Federal Republic would share the same fate as Weimar.

It may have been this omnipresent image of Weimar, the trauma of the Third Reich, the negative example of East Germany, or the economic and political successes of the new system that prevented the Federal Republic from following the same course as the Weimar Republic. From the beginning, widespread support for a democratic political system existed among the leaders of the major political parties and other political elites. This consensus in support of democratic ideals led to conscious efforts to reeducate the public to adopt these values. Gradually public opinion was changed, and extensive public support developed for the democratic institutions and procedures of the Federal Republic. Social and political tolerance grew more commonplace.

The changing political culture was paralleled by a growing institutionalization and stabilization of the political system. A broad social consensus developed on the basic principles of the welfare state and Germany's role within the Western Alliance. The party system stabilized as the number of parties in the Parliament declined from ten in 1949 to only three in 1961. The political system was transformed into an effective parliamentary democracy and the political vitality of Germany rivaled many of the more established European democracies. By the 1972 election, one party claimed that West Germany had become the model for other European democracies to follow (*Modell Deutschland*).

West Germany's progress in meeting these challenges made it the political success story of postwar Europe, but this progress also led to a second period of political development. As the "German question" was gradually addressed, West Germany's political process— its institutions and policy concerns—began to resemble those of other advanced industrial democracies. The Federal Republic had, in a sense, "caught up" with the other nations of Western Europe and begun to share many of the same political and social concerns as these other nations. West German politics is still unique, but no longer is it a clear exception to the norm for Western democracies.

One aspect of this new phase in the development of the culture was a shift away from the traditional concerns of the past to the *New Politics* issues facing the Federal Republic and other advanced industrial democracies. Demands for reforms in education and social programs were first voiced in the late 1960s. Soon other groups demonstrated for environmental protection and policies aimed at improving the quality of life. The women's movement became a vocal advocate for sexual equality. More recently, an active peace movement has led many people to question the basis of West German foreign policy. In other words, political interests have broadened beyond the traditional economic and security issues of the past to a group of issues that reflect the new policy concerns of advanced industrial societies.

After these new political orientations had spread among the young and better educated, traditional economic and security issues began to reappear in a new form. During the last decade the previous trend of almost ever-increasing affluence was replaced by slow and unsteady economic progress. The rate of economic growth in the 1970s, for example, was one-third the 1950s rate of increase. Even a slight economic upturn in the early 1980s has left unemployment at nearly 10 percent of the labor force. Foreign policy developments also worked to renew old concerns. The spirit of détente that guided East-West relations for a large part of the 1970s gradually weakened in the face of a continuing Soviet military buildup in Eastern Europe and Soviet aggression in Afghanistan. West Germany is again a pressure point in East-West tensions. International terrorism emerged as an internal and external threat to the nation. Business leaders, government offices, military installations, and public facilities are terrorist targets. The Federal Republic, like other Western democracies, is experiencing renewed concerns about the public order and the security of the nation.

It is notable, however, that a partial renewal of traditional economic and security concerns has neither created widespread fears about the viability of the political system nor undermined support for the New Politics. Rather, contemporary politics is characterized by a mix of old and new concerns and increasing political tensions between these alternative social viewpoints. The political consensus of the past is facing challenges from several directions. For instance, a citizen group might protest against an economic development project aimed at promoting jobs and growth because it threatens the quality of the environment. Alternatively, neoconservatives decry the state's extensive social programs in a time when the government's resources are overtaxed. The young and the old frequently speak different languages and have different ideas about what the nation's goals should be. The clash of these two cultures is visible in the restructuring of the party system, the changing pattern of interest-group activity, and other aspects of the contemporary political process.

Another product of West Germany's sociopolitical transformation is a change in the pattern of citizen action. As democratic norms have taken root, the public has increased its involvement in the political process. Voting turnout has always been high, but citizen action is shifting toward more sophisticated and assertive forms of participation. Perhaps the most dramatic change in political participation is the growth of citizen action groups (*Bürgerinitiativen*). Interested citizens form ad hoc groups to articulate their political demands and influence decision makers. Some groups even use such direct actions as protests and demonstrations. These kinds of participation overturn all stereotypes of the German public as quiescent or unmotivated. A new style of citizen politics has been introduced into the political process.

Although this new style of citizen politics is not unique to the Federal Republic, these changes are often more apparent in West Germany than in other Western democracies, perhaps because the social transformation of West German society was proportionally greater. For instance, the student movement of the 1960s was one of the most extensive and politically organized in Europe. The advocates of New Politics issues, such as the environmental movement and peace groups, are a more potent political force in West Germany than in most other European nations. In 1980 a new political party, the Greens, was formed to represent these alternative political views. The Greens are one of the few environmental parties in Western Europe that have won seats in a national parliament. West Germany thus provides a very rich example of the new sociopolitical trends affecting other Western industrial democracies.

If only because of its international stature, West Germany is also an important country to study and understand. The Federal Republic now is a mainstay of the Western European economic system through its participation in the Common Market. It is both a leading European contributor to the Western military alliance and a valuable diplomatic bridge between East and West. West Germany also is a major trading partner of most industrial societies and many less-developed nations.

At the same time, German politics has its special lessons to teach. One goal of this book is to describe the Federal Republic's phoenix-like rebirth from the ashes of World War II. At the end of the war, virtually no one could have imagined the social and political transformation that Germany quickly experienced. Chapter I describes the historical legacy inherited by postwar German politics, focusing on the factors that contributed to the collapse of the democratic Weimar Republic in the 1930s and the horrors of the Third Reich. Chapter II details the creation of the Federal Republic as a sovereign nation and the political institutions of the new state. Chapter III describes the socioeconomic transformation that restructured the basis of German society, as well as the new social forces that are shaping the Federal Republic's future. Chapter IV documents the consequences of this process in the creation of a democratic political culture and, later, the development of new social values. The processes of cultural change and social learning are also discussed in Chapter

V, which examines the methods of political socialization and communication.

A second goal is to describe the operation of the contemporary political system and consider how the system addresses the new challenges facing an advanced industrial democracy. Chapter VI discusses how citizen participation in the political process has grown over the years and how participation has broadened to include more assertive activities, such as citizen-action groups, protests, and demonstrations. Chapter VII examines the role of political elites within the policy process. Chapter VIII looks at the established interests in West German politics—business, labor, agriculture, and religious associations—and how these groups are being joined by new political interests. Chapter IX examines change within the German party system, as the established parties attempt to respond to new political conditions and the Green party challenges the political establishment. Chapters X and XI focus on the policy-making process and the major policy issues now confronting the political system.

Perhaps no other nation in Western Europe has experienced the same degree of social, economic, and political change during the past thirty years. Thus, the cultural and political tensions within West German society are often more pronounced versions of what other nations are experiencing. In one sense this means that the Federal Republic is still an exceptional case among other Western nations. But in another sense, West Germany may provide an ideal setting to explore the impact of social trends that are affecting most other Western democracies.

CHAPTER I

The Legacy of History

THE POLITICS OF EVERY NATION IS SHAPED, to some extent, by its history. This is especially true for German politics. Germans often display an intense conviction about their nation's "place" in history, and frequently use historical precedents to judge current political problems. In addition, the lessons of German political history are drawn in stark terms. Germany is the site of some of the highest and lowest points in the history of mankind.

The German experience differs substantially from those of most other West European democracies, however. The social and political forces that modernized the rest of Europe came much later in Germany and possessed a less certain effect. For some time after most national borders were relatively well defined, Germany was still divided into dozens of political units. Although a dominant national culture had evolved in most European states, Germany was torn by the Reformation and continuing conflicts between Catholics and Protestants; sharp regional and economic cleavages also polarized society. Industrialization generally was the driving force behind the modernization of Europe, but German industrialization came late and did not overturn the old feudal and aristocratic order. German history thus represents a difficult and protracted process of nation building.

Once national unification was achieved, the new German state followed a course in domestic politics that limited political development and perpetuated the traditional feudal order. In international affairs, German policies directly contributed to the outbreak of World War I. The horrors of that war shocked the world, but they were soon outdone by the fanaticism of Adolf Hitler and the Third Reich. Hitler's regime combined political oppression at home with aggressive international adventurism. The culmination was a second world war, which overshadowed the first in its death and destruction.

The political legacy of the last century thus contains many negative lessons. Indeed, because of their importance, the questions derived from the German historical experience have been a central concern of social scientists throughout the world for nearly half a century. First, how could the failures of the democratic Weimar Republic be explained? Second, could there be any possible explanation for the horrors of the Third Reich? And finally, could the new, postwar Federal Republic of Germany rise above the historical legacy it inherited? To answer these questions we need to look more closely at the historical record.

THE FORMATION OF THE SECOND GERMAN EMPIRE

In the middle of the nineteenth century the future German state was still a collection of dozens of autonomous political units. In the north, Prussia was the dominant political force, controlling an area from west of the Rhine to the east coast of the Baltic sea. In the south, Vienna was the center of the Hapsburg empire, which included the multinational region of the Danube valley. Between and within these two nations were numerous smaller states: kingdoms, duchies, city-states, and principalities. These political entities were united by a common language, cultural tradition, and history, but they also jealously guarded their political independence.

The social forces of industrialization first began to be felt in the 1830s and 1840s. The growth of an industrial sector created a new class of business owners and managers, the *bourgeoisie,* who pressed for the modernization of society and the extension of political rights. In comparison to the rest of Europe, however, the German bourgeoisie wielded less political influence. Industrialization came to Germany only after it had already developed in most of the rest of northwestern Europe. This delay in industrialization retarded the development of many factors normally identified with a modern society: urbanization, widespread literacy, extensive communication and transportation networks, and an industrial infrastructure. More important, German industrialization followed a course quite different from that of the rest of Europe. German industry was integrated into the old feudal political structure. The control of economic and political development by the landed aristocracy attenuated the influence of the new industrial class.

As a result of this developmental pattern, the democratic tide that swept across Europe from 1848 to 1849 did not represent a serious threat to the established political order in Prussia or most other German principalities. A series of small revolutionary actions occurred throughout Germany, and an assembly of representatives met in Frankfurt to debate proposals for constitutional reform and national unification. This group of largely middle-class reformers lacked the revolutionary zeal and influence necessary to change the political system. Moreover, they suffered from a problem that would weaken democratic forces in Germany for the next century: Military conflict between Prussia and Denmark divided the delegates to the Frankfurt assembly along nationalist lines and undercut attempts to develop a consensus on political reforms. While the assembly bickered, Friedrich Wilhelm IV reestablished his control over the Prussian government and a conservative backlash developed in Vienna and Berlin. The Prussian government functioned by the motto *Gegen Demokraten helfen nur Soldaten* (only soldiers are helpful against democrats). When the Frankfurt assembly finally offered the crown of emperor (and a constitutional monarchy) to Friedrich Wilhelm, he was again secure enough to claim the divine right of kings and refused. Germany's first encounter with democracy had passed with little effect, and in subsequent years liberal influences would weaken further.

THE BISMARCK ERA

The course of history changed again when Otto von Bismarck became chancellor in 1862. The conditions of Bismarck's appointment typified his career. When the Prussian monarch faced an impasse with liberal forces in Parliament, Bismarck was appointed to defend the established political order. By manipulating the issue of German unification he divided and defeated the liberal challenge. Over the next decade Bismarck enlarged the territory of Prussia in the northern half of Germany through a combination of military victories and diplomatic skill. Finally, in 1870 Bismarck maneuvered France into declaring war on an obviously stronger German-led alliance. Military victories and the nationalist sentiments stirred by war led to the incorporation of the southern German states into the North German Confederation. In 1871, a unified Second German Empire was formed, and the Prussian monarch was crowned as emperor (*Kaiser*).[1]

The new empire was a federal system, with representation of the state governments in the upper legislative house, the *Bundesrat,* and direct representation of the public in the lower house, the *Reichstag.* The structure of the federal system ensured that Prussia would indirectly control the development of the empire; this protected the status and influence of the Prussian landed aristocracy, the *Junkers.* The constitution was a fairly complex construction of formal checks and balances, but in practice, power was exercised by the Kaiser and his representative, the Chancellor. There was universal male suffrage for Reichstag elections, but the constitution did not transfer significant political influence to the populace. In fact, the government's directives were quite clear. Citizens had three responsibilities: to pay taxes, to serve in the army, and to keep their mouths shut.

Bismarck was concerned primarily with protecting the traditional political order and extending the influence of the empire as the guarantor of this order. These goals led to him to attack enemies of the Reich wherever they were found. One of the first victims was the Catholic church. In the 1870s the church attempted to reassert its influence throughout Europe in order to oppose liberal reforms that threatened church interests. Bismarck viewed these activities as a challenge to the authority of the state, and reacted against such political expressions of church views as the newly formed Center party. With the support of liberals, the government limited the church's role in society and then openly attacked Catholic institutions (*Kulturkampf*). The government moved against Catholic schools, initiated civil (nonreligious) marriage procedures, and expelled all priests from government positions. The infamous May laws attempted to control the appointment of new priests and expel uncooperative clergy. By 1876 all the Catholic bishops in Prussia were imprisoned or expelled, and a third of the Catholic parishes in Prussia lacked pastors.

Bismarck's next target was the growing political consciousness of the working class. When a new Social Democratic party (SPD) began to win a few seats in the Reichstag, Bismarck perceived another dire threat to the state. In 1878 the government passed anti-socialist laws that banned all meetings and publications by Social Democrats, Socialists, or Communists.[2] Hundreds of political activists were imprisoned or exiled over the next twelve years. The formal institutions of the SPD were destroyed and the socialist movement was forced underground.

Through these actions Bismarck attempted to hold back the forces
of political change in a rapidly developing society. In the end, however, even he could not prevent all change from occurring. The Kulturkampf lasted for only a few years; within a decade most antichurch legislation ended and the Catholic Center party became a
large and fairly stable element in the Reichstag. The suppression of
the Social Democrats initially weakened the working-class movement, but it also created a stronger bond among the remaining
members of the movement. When the antisocialist legislation was
softened under Kaiser Wilhelm, the SPD's vote totals began to grow
again. Furthermore, these attacks on the political opposition alienated a large segment of society and undercut the process of building citizen identification with the new political system. How could
Catholics and members of the working class develop an attachment
to the new empire when they were treated as enemies of the state?
Neither the Center party nor Social Democrats represented an
immediate threat to the social and political order of the empire.
Rather, they represented dissent and potential change—neither of
which was tolerated by government leaders.

In overall terms, the formation of the empire marked the weakening of German liberalism and the growth of conservative and reactionary political forces. The chancellor strengthened the Conservatives in the Reichstag and shifted the government's basis of
parliamentary support away from the National Liberals, who had
played a significant role in the creation of the empire. In addition, a
new economic order was established, which united capitalism and
the traditional aristocracy. The government protected the Junker's
agricultural interests with high trade tariffs. Other laws catered to
the demands of the new conservative industrial elites.

WILHELMINE POLITICS

When Wilhelm II became Kaiser, a new era began—Germany
without Bismarck. Bismarck left office in 1890, and his successors
lacked the Iron Chancellor's political insights and pragmatic skills
in balancing contending forces. Although the economic situation
began a dramatic upturn in 1895, the slow spiral of social and political decay continued. The government's reliance on conservative
and reactionary support in the Reichstag further alienated a large
segment of society. After the 1910 election, the SPD was the largest

party in Parliament, and tensions between the conservative government and social/liberal opposition continually worsened. The German sociologist, Max Weber, described the dilemma Germany faced: Rule by the Junkers was undesirable, the liberal middle class was politically inept, and the socialists were immature.

Internationally, conditions were even worse. One of Bismarck's major accomplishments was the protection of Germany's foreign policy interests through a delicate balancing of international alignments. Under Bismarck, Germany was a major force for stability and peace in Europe. The country's international status declined steadily without the master statesman at the helm. Political leaders fed the public a steady stream of expansionist dreams, advocating a policy of *Weltpolitik* intended to make Germany a world power.[3] Instead, an ill-conceived foreign policy succeeded in alienating almost all of Europe. In the background, the military kept pushing the country toward war with a xenophobic view of other nations and optimistic war plans. The political system was out of control; the nation seemed to face the sobering choice of civil war or international conflict.

In the end, the crisis at Sarajevo was only the match that sparked a waiting tinderbox of European politics. Germany gave Austria a "blank check" of support in its conflict with Serbia, French hostility fanned the flames of war, and the Russian army went to full mobilization status. A complex chain of events culminated in the German invasion of Belgium and France and the start of World War I (1914–1918). The conflict aroused feelings of nationalism among all the participants. Government propaganda led the German public to view the war as an act of national defense and an opportunity for Germany to establish its hegemony in Europe and become a world power. By encouraging these feelings, the government raised public expectations even higher.

Optimistic predictions of early victory and territorial expansion soon became mired in the fields of Flanders, as German and Allied troops confronted each other in bloody trench warfare. At home, the war effort began to take its toll in shortages of supplies, manpower, and even food. Over 700,000 Germans died of starvation in the winter of 1916–1917, and the war continued for nearly two more years. As the government's legitimacy eroded, the military exercised greater control over the course of the war. The unrealistic (and imperialistic) attitudes of such generals as Erich Ludendorff and Paul von Hindenburg sabotaged every possibility for an early peace agreement.

Germany was not prepared for or able to endure a long war on such a scale. The nation was devastated by the costs of war. Almost three million German soldiers and civilians lost their lives, the economy was strained beyond the breaking point, and the government of the empire collapsed under the weight of its own incapacity to govern. In late 1918, the generals called for an armistice to avoid the complete collapse of the nation; two weeks later the Kaiser was forced to abdicate his throne. The SPD majority in Parliament, which had only grudgingly supported the war, faced the task of making peace and guiding the postwar reconstruction of the society and political system. V.R. Berghahn notes that the transfer of power from the Kaiser to Parliament was not based on altruistic motives:[4]

> After years of military-dominated government, it was now for the civilian politicians . . . to sign the armistice and hence shoulder the burden of defeat. Even in the hour of bankruptcy, the generals showed a remarkable ability to uphold the self-interest of the Prussian military state. As Ludendorff put it at the meeting of 29 September, as many people as possible were to be held responsible for the humiliation of defeat—with the exception of those who had been instrumental first in unleashing war and then in conducting it uncompromisingly.

In short, having led Germany into a catastrophic war, the military and the political establishment of the empire were eager to escape responsibility by yielding power to the Reichstag.

The Second Empire left behind an uncertain legacy. The process of industrialization changed the economic and social system, but it did not result in political reform and modernization. The Prussian Junkers retained their positions of influence, even after the fall of the empire. The growth of industry also followed a distinctly German pattern. Control of industry was concentrated in the hands of a relatively few institutions, and individual firms were further organized into cartels, which limited free trade and retarded the development of economic liberalism. Together, the aristocracy and the conservative industrial elite formed an alliance to preserve their positions of privilege and limit the democratization of Germany. The new political order was integrated with the old.

The political system of the empire also failed to modernize. Democratic reforms were successfully thwarted by an authoritarian state strong enough to resist the political demands of a weak middle class. The state remained supreme; its needs took precedence over those of individuals and society. Politics was marked by an intolerance of potential opposition, seen most clearly in the government's attacks on Catholics and Socialists. Society also displayed this intolerance in periodic surges of anti-Semitic feelings. Germans were taught to be good subjects of the state, but not participants in the political process—especially if they disagreed with the government. The public itself held divided political loyalties, and these differences were exacerbated by the intolerance of the political process. In short, the empire had united Germany in geographic terms and built a strong economy, but it did not build a nation of shared political values. According to Ralf Dahrendorf, what emerged from the Industrial Revolution in Germany was an "industrial feudal society."[5] Modernization and democratization were still to come.

THE WEIMAR REPUBLIC

In 1919, a popularly elected constitutional assembly established the new democratic system of the Weimar Republic. The constitution created a parliamentary democracy based on a directly elected *Reichstag* and a *Reichsrat* of state government representatives. The new system attempted to redress some of the structural problems of the Second Empire. It provided constitutional guarantees of basic citizen rights, granted universal suffrage, gave more power to the Reichstag, and lessened the political influence of the state governments. Political parties organized across the full spectrum of political interests and became legitimate actors in the political process. Belatedly, the Germans had their first real exposure to democracy.

The constitution, however, also contained provisions that ultimately weakened the Weimar government. The popularly elected president was to serve as a national representative, but, during the later stages of the Republic, the office evolved into a substitute for the authoritarian Kaiser (*Ersatzkaiser*). The electoral procedures of referendums and proportional representation were significant democratic innovations, but in the end they put heavy strains on a political system that lacked a popular consensus. The federal system of Weimar also failed to solve the continuing problems of reconciling differences between the state and national governments. And finally, the new constitution included a provision, Article 48, that granted "emergency" powers to the government; these powers were greatly abused during the later years of the Republic. Many historians believe that the structural features of the Weimar constitution contributed to the problems the political system eventually faced.

From the outset, the Weimar government was plagued by severe problems. The most persistent difficulties involved the consequences of World War I. Many Germans did not believe that their country had lost the war. The armistice was signed while German troops were still occupying French and Belgian territory, and the armies were welcomed home as unconquered heroes. The peace treaty of Versailles thus came as a shock to many people. Germany lost all of its overseas colonies and a substantial amount of European territory including Alsace-Lorraine in the west, and parts of Prussia in the east. There was a forced demilitarization of Germany, with severe limits on the size and type of forces that could be maintained. Finally, Germany was burdened with very large reparation payments to repay the war-related expenses of the Allied powers. Conservative politicians exploited popular disdain for the treaty and created the myth that Germany had been "stabbed in the back." These politicians maintained that the nation's defeat and subsequent emasculation did not come from losses on the battlefield, but from the betrayal of those groups who revolted against the empire, forced the armistice upon the military, and founded the Weimar Republic: Socialists, Liberals, and Jews.

Another continuing challenge came from the elite class of the old empire. The constitution guaranteed the status of the civil servants who had worked under the empire, which ensured the presence of many government officials who opposed the democratic system of Weimar. Many judges blatantly gave preferential treatment to right-wing radicals who attacked the Weimar government, while dealing harshly with leftists. Universities often were centers of antidemocratic thought. In responding to a series of radical uprisings, the military showed that it would defend the republic from leftist attacks, but not necessarily against conservative or reactionary forces that wished to restore the empire.

The early years of the Weimar Republic were ones of perpetual political instability. In 1919, there were radical uprisings from both left and right extremists; in the following year, the *Kapp Putsch* attempted to overthrow the government. Government representatives reacted to the Versailles treaty with self-defeating exhibitions of defiance, and Germany's international position deteriorated. Resistance to the Allies' reparation plans led to France's occupation of the Ruhr in January 1923, which further incited extremists and destabilized the political system.

These political problems worsened the already ill economic health of the nation.[6] The Kaiser had financed Germany's actions in World War I through loans rather than increased taxes. The burden of these loans, the instability of the economy, the pressure of reparation payments, and the consequences of France's occupation of the Ruhr gradually eroded all confidence in the economy. Total industrial production in 1923 was only 55 percent of the prewar level. Government printing presses kept the nation afloat on a sea of inflated currency, and a brewing inflation problem finally exploded in 1923. In less than a year the inflation rate was an unimaginable 26 billion percent; German currency became worthless. For example, a kilogram of potatoes that cost a Berlin housewife 20 marks in January carried a price tag of 90 billion marks by October.[7] A single Berlin streetcar ticket that already cost 100 thousand marks in August cost 150 million marks in November. Some workers were paid twice a day, then given time off from work to rush out and spend their money before the daily price rates were revised. Many self-employed small-business people were forced out of work. Families that had saved for a retirement saw their life savings become worthless overnight; bonds and savings accounts had virtually no value. Those who were already retired on a fixed income often became wards of the state. The middle class suffered economic hardships even greater than the experiences of World War I.

This period of hyperinflation contributed to social disintegration, rising crime rates, and disillusionment with the political system. Army units planned coups against the government; signs of imminent leftist revolts also surfaced. A little-known radical, Adolf Hitler, attempted to mobilize nationalist forces in Bavaria into a *Putsch* against the government. This time Hitler failed and was sentenced to a short prison term. In the end, the government was able to resist these attacks and stabilize prices before the end of the year. Still, the severe economic losses of the middle class could not be restored, and many citizens saw the inflation crisis as another example of the failures of the Weimar democracy.

By the mid-1920s, the political tensions that eventually tore apart the Weimar Republic were becoming visible. The parties that had formed the Weimar Republic—Socialists, Liberals, and the Center party—lacked cohesion and lost support at the polls (see Table I.1). The Social Democrats would not look beyond their narrow Marxist viewpoints, and thus could not work effectively with the other political parties. The liberal parties lost influence and voting strength. The moderate Centrist party gradually moved toward the right. The prodemocratic parties were attacked by radicals on the left (the

TABLE I.1 *Reichstag Election Results (percentage), 1919–1933*

Party	1919	1920	May 1924	Dec 1924	1928	1930	July 1932	Nov 1932	1933
Left									
Communists (KPD)	—	2.1	12.6	9.0	10.6	13.1	14.3	16.9	12.3
Indep. Socialists (USPD)	7.6	17.9	.8	—	—	—	—	—	—
Socialists (SPD)	37.9	21.7	20.5	26.0	29.8	24.5	21.6	20.4	18.3
Center									
Center (Zentrum)	19.7	13.6	13.4	13.6	12.1	11.8	12.5	11.9	11.3
Liberals									
German Democrats (DDP)	18.6	8.3	5.7	6.3	4.9	3.8	1.0	.9	.8
People's party (DVP)	4.4	13.9	9.2	10.1	8.7	4.5	1.2	1.9	1.1
Nationalists									
German Nationals (DNVP)	10.3	15.1	19.5	20.5	14.2	7.0	5.9	8.3	8.0
Nazis (NSDAP)	—	—	6.5	3.0	2.6	18.3	37.3	33.1	43.9
Other									
Other parties	1.6	7.4	11.8	11.5	17.1	17.0	6.2	6.5	4.3
TOTAL	100.0	100.0	100.0	100.0	100.0	100.0	100.0	100.0	100.0
Turnout rate	82.7	79.2	77.4	78.8	75.5	82.0	84.0	80.6	88.7

Communists) and the right (the nationalist parties). Government leaders reverted to Bismarck's strategy; they used foreign-policy initiatives to distract attention from the government's domestic problems.

THE BEGINNING OF THE END

The fatal blow to the Weimar Republic came with the Great Depression in 1929. The nation was caught in the grasp of a worldwide economic downturn, and its already fragile economy was especially vulnerable. Employment rates began to decline and business failures spread. Nearly one sixth of the labor force was out of work by 1930, and millions more were underemployed. These economic problems were compounded by Germany's dependence on foreign loans and investments and the continuing drain of reparation payments. Moreover, as tax revenues decreased, growing demands for unemployment benefits and social assistance strained the government's diminishing resources. The public was frustrated by the government's inability to deal with this latest crisis. Political tensions increased, and parliamentary democracy began to fail. In 1930 the government of Chancellor Heinrich Brüning tried to generate political support for a program of economic reform, but the parties in the Reichstag seemed irreconcilably divided. Brüning dissolved Parliament and called for new elections. In the midst of this political void, the government bypassed the parliamentary process and implemented its reform package by presidential decree. This event marked the government's first significant break with the democratic principles of the Weimar Republic, and opened the door to further erosion in the constitutional process.

In the crisis environment of 1930, turnout at the polls increased and many voters succumbed to calls for radical change. Adolf Hitler and his National Socialist Workers' Party (NSDAP), *Nazis*, were the major beneficiaries (Table I.1). The Nazi vote increased from a mere 2 percent in 1928 to 18 percent. At the other extreme of the political spectrum, the Communists also improved their showing at the polls. Together the antisystem parties—Nazis, Communists, and Nationalists—controlled nearly half the seats in the Reichstag and were able to block any prospects for moderate policy reform.

The economic situation continued to deteriorate in 1931 and 1932. During the worst periods of 1932, nearly one out of every three workers was unemployed; the unemployment rolls swelled to over 6 million. Political violence and street battles between rival political groups threatened the social order. The presidential election in 1932 reflected the darkening mood of the German public. President Paul von Hindenburg, the former World War I general, and Adolf Hitler faced each other in a runoff election for the presidency. Hindenburg grudgingly tolerated the democratic process and Hitler was dedicated to its overthrow. That these two were the final candidates demonstrated the vulnerability of the Weimar Republic, and Hitler's strong second-place finish represented an ominous sign of the future. In subsequent state elections the Nazi vote continued to increase. The public was looking for radical solutions to their worsening situation.

To maintain some semblance of political order, the Brüning government turned further and further away from the democratic process, ruling by presidential decree and relying on the emergency powers of Article 48. Nevertheless, conservative leaders in industry, government, and the military felt that the government was still too democratic and thereby limited in its ability to take the strong measures they felt necessary to solve the nation's economic and political problems. Many of these elites favored restoration of an authoritarian state and began working toward that goal. In May 1932, Brüning was forced from the chancellorship by von Hindenburg; Franz von Papen and a nationalist cabinet took control of the government. Von Papen was a nobleman and a former military officer; he was also a reactionary monarchist who wanted to restore the empire of the Kaiser. The historian, Hajo Holborn, maintains that "with Brüning's resignation, democracy in Germany . . . was dead."[8]

Papen's government quickly moved against its democratic opponents. The government functioned by presidential decrees instead of the legislative process. The legal bans against the Nazi paramilitary organizations, the SA and SS, were removed. The SPD-led government of Prussia was overturned by decree. In the July federal elections, the Nazis made major gains, winning 37 percent of the votes and emerging as the largest party in the Reichstag. When the new Reichstag opposed the government's program, another round of elections were planned for November. These were the last free elections of the Weimar democracy. Although the Nazis lost votes in the election, Parliament was still deadlocked. Political violence was increasing, and the country again seemed on the verge of civil war. In a final attempt to restore public and political order, President Hindenburg appointed Hitler Chancellor of the Weimar Republic in January 1933. The collapse of the Weimar democracy was complete.

WHY WEIMAR FAILED

Weimar's failure opened the door to a Nazi regime that would corrupt Germany and begin a worldwide conflagration. Thus, social scientists have invested a great effort to understand what led to Weimar's demise.[9] There is no single explanation or simple prescription to avoid a similar catastrophe in the future. Rather, Weimar's collapse resulted from interaction among a complex set of factors.

A basic weakness of the Weimar Republic was its lack of support from political elites and the general public. From its birth, the republic was unable to develop a popular consensus behind the democratic institutions and procedures of the new political system. The elite class of the empire retained control of the military, the judiciary, and the civil service. Democracy depended on an administrative elite that often longed for a return to a more traditional political order. Gordon Craig maintains that:[10]

> The Republic's basic vulnerability was rooted in the circumstances of its creation, and it is no exaggeration to say that it failed in the end partly because German officers were allowed to put their epaulets back on again so quickly and because the public buildings were not burned down, along with the bureaucrats who inhabited them.

Many political leaders also opposed the Weimar system. Even before the onset of the Depression, a number of well-known political figures were working for the overthrow of the Weimar system. These antirepublican forces gained strength when the economy faltered; what was worse, the Nazis eventually established themselves as the vanguard of the antidemocratic movement.

Criticism of Weimar by the elites was shared by many average citizens and encouraged by the rhetoric of elites. Many people felt that the creation of the republic at the end of World War I contributed to Germany's wartime defeat; from the outset the regime was stigmatized as a traitor to the nation. Large portions of the public retained strong emotional ties to the Second Empire and questioned the basic legitimacy of the Weimar Republic. Germans still had not developed a common political identity, a political culture, that could unite and guide the nation.

The fledgling democratic state then faced a series of major crises:

repeated leftist and rightist coup attempts, political assassinations
and violence, the inflation of the 1920s and the Depression of the
1930s. Such strains might have overloaded the ability of any system
to govern effectively.

The political system was never able to create a reservoir of popular support that could sustain it through these crises. Consequently,
the dissatisfaction created by the Great Depression dangerously
eroded public confidence in the political system. Nazis, Nationalists, and Communists argued that the democratic political system
was at fault, and many more Germans lost faith in the republic.
Even the actions of the so-called Weimar parties (Socialists, Liberals, and the Center) contributed to the undemocratic mentality of
the times. Party leaders too often placed ideological purity and partisan self-interest above the national interest. Politicians were hesitant to negotiate and compromise, and frequently displayed an
intolerance of divergent points of view. These attitudes led to a
fragmentation and radicalization of the party system. Instead of
showing the public how democrats *should* act, politicians often
furnished negative role models. As the situation worsened, the leadership of several moderate and conservative parties displayed more
concern in protecting the power and authority of the state than in
protecting democracy. In many senses, Weimar was crippled by the
legacies of intolerance and weak democratic values that it inherited
from the authoritarian system of the empire.

The political institutions of Weimar also contributed to its
vulnerability. Political authority was not clearly divided between
Parliament and the president. The infamous Article 48 granted the
president broad emergency powers to protect the constitution that
eventually were instrumental in the overthrow of democracy. As the
government's reliance on emergency decrees expanded (from five in
1930 to fifty-seven in 1932) the basis of parliamentary democracy
was eroded. The decrees forced a series of unpopular policies on the
public, such as reducing wages and social services while increasing
taxes. Moreover, the decrees did not solve the economic problems of
the Depression; instead, they stimulated opposition to the government, and the Nazis led the assault.

Finally, most Germans drastically underestimated Hitler's ambitions, intentions, and political abilities. Industrial leaders dis-
counted his policies as political rhetoric, and eventually supported
him in exchange for promises of political and economic stability.
Political moderates who read Hitler's writings and listened to his

speeches still convinced themselves that his anti-Semitism and excessive nationalism only existed for political show. Even at the end of Weimar, conservative politicians thought he could be controlled as chancellor by the nationalist parties in his cabinet. Everyone, it seems, tried to ignore the true nature of Hitler and his policies. This, perhaps, was Weimar's greatest failure.

HITLER AND THE THIRD REICH

The Nazis' rise to power was incredibly quick. Hitler first announced the formation of the NSDAP in 1920, and thirteen years later he was chancellor. Admittedly, the party's fortunes had fluctuated widely. After the abortive coup in 1923, the party attracted little public attention for several years. The Nazis' phenomenal growth in electoral support in the early 1930s was a crucial factor in their rise to power. To understand the origins of the Third Reich we need to understand why Hitler's party appealed to so many voters.

There was never any question that Hitler was a demagogue. He preached anti-Semitism and theories of racial superiority, he advocated the destruction of democracy and the construction of a Nazi dictatorship, and he championed ultranationalist policies that could only lead to war. These views were clearly spelled out in his book, *Mein Kampf*, and in innumerable Nazi publications. How could so many Germans vote for such a man?

A large part of the NSDAP's success can be traced to the creation of a new political model that overwhelmed its opponents when crisis befell the Weimar Republic. One hallmark of the NSDAP was its organizational efficiency. The central party office commanded an extensive network of closely coordinated regional and local branches. On any given day the party headquarters could direct an impressive nationwide propaganda campaign that was faithfully repeated in almost every German region and city. Another feature of the party was its paramilitary units, the SA and SS. These units furnished a military air at political rallies and intimidated the party's opponents through acts of violence. During election campaigns the NSDAP could produce more leaflets, amass more supporters at rallies, out-battle its opponents in street fights, and out-campaign most other parties.

Another source of the Nazi appeal was their unprincipled propagandizing. Hitler was a charismatic leader and a dynamic speaker who could capture an audience's imagination. Party political meetings and rallies were elaborately staged to create a mood that Hitler could exploit. Martial music and rousing speeches combined with mass marches and military drills to stir the participants into an emotional fever—culminated by Hitler's dramatic arrival and demagogic oratory. Such propaganda shows were an important component of the Nazi movement, but the appeal of the NSDAP went deeper.

Popular support for the NSDAP can be traced to the party's attempt to transcend traditional social divisions and develop into a party of national integration. Rather than appealing just to farmers, workers, or one religious group, the party tried to attract support from all sectors of society. One source of this broad appeal was a vehement nationalistic policy. The Nazis nurtured the "stab in the back" myth and attacked the Versailles treaty as an unjust international conspiracy against Germany. The party argued that Germany was being deprived of its rightful role in the world, and the public proved all too receptive to such nationalistic sloganeering.

The party also developed electoral campaigns targeted to different social groups based on a two-pronged tactic of lofty promises and accusations against the group's purported enemies. To the middle class of small farmers and merchants, the party promised government aid at the same time that it attacked the supposed enemies of the German middle class: Jewish financiers and the Marxist welfare state. The Nazis appealed to blue-collar workers by promising full employment and the true socialism of a united *Volk*, while also castigating capitalists and Marxists as the oppressors of the working class. Pensioners were told that the government's cuts in retirement benefits were unnecessary and only the Nazis could rescue them from destitution. In short, Hitler sought to be all things to all people.

Contemporary voting research indicates that people generally vote "against" the failures of the government, rather than "for" the program of the opposition. Clearly, Weimar had many failures, and the Nazis were the loudest non-Marxist critics of the Weimar system. At the nadir of the Depression the German people were desperate, and many succumbed to the Nazis' impossible promises. They overlooked the contradictions and extremism of the Nazi program and focused on their own self-interest. The core of Nazi support came from three areas: non-Catholic rural districts, the upper class, and the petite bourgeoisie.[11] At the same time, a significant share of the Nazi vote came from conservative members of the working class and lower middle class. A study of NSDAP members testified to the diversity of the party's appeal: 34.4 percent of the members who joined before the mid-1930s came from the self-employed middle class, 28.1 percent were from the working class, and 25.6 percent were salaried white-collar employees.[12] The Nazis were a socially diverse party of antis—antidemocracy, anti-Versailles, anticapitalist, anti-Jewish, or anti-Marxist—but it is unclear whether these same voters agreed on Nazism as the alternative.

TAKING CONTROL

Once Hitler gained the chancellorship, he began to consolidate his hold on political power. Against the wishes of the other parties, Hitler called for new Reichstag elections in March 1933. The elections occurred under a shadow of Nazi threats and violence. Hitler used a presidential decree to suppress the Communist party and severely restrict campaigning by the SPD. The Nazis' control of the Prussian police enabled the SA to attack political opponents with official sanction. The state-run radio was turned to Hitler's use. Public expression of opposition was reduced to a minimum.

Even in the oppressive environment of the elections, the Nazis failed to win a majority of the popular vote. Many citizens still resisted Hitler's appeal. Nevertheless, NSDAP gains in the election led to the collapse of opposition to Hitler by most political elites. With the support of the other nationalist parties Hitler moved to revise the constitution and end the democratic era of the Weimar Republic. The Reichstag met on March 23. Hitler's decree excluded newly elected Communist party deputies, and the ring of Nazi stormtroopers surrounding Parliament prevented several SPD deputies from attending. The other political parties had already comes to terms with Hitler. Only the SPD opposed the Enabling Act, which granted Hitler dictatorial powers. The Weimar Republic was replaced by the Third Reich, and the black, red, and gold flag of democratic Germany was replaced by the swastika on the black, white, and red colors of imperial Germany.

Hitler then moved to create the new National Socialist order. The Nazis destroyed all potential bases of internal opposition through a process of "coordination" (*Gleichschaltung*). Social and political groups that might challenge the government were destroyed, taken over by Nazi representatives, or coopted into accepting the Nazi regime. Learning from the lesson of Weimar, Hitler moved against the civil service within a month of coming to power. Hitler

removed officials sympathetic to democracy or the SPD from
government service, along with civil servants of Jewish descent.
Nearly one third of the civil servants in Prussia, for example, were
purged in this manner. As a result, Hitler assured that the remaining government officials would obey Nazi directives.

Socioeconomic groups were the next targets of "coordination."
To assure the working class of the Nazis' good intentions, the Nazis
declared May 1 a national workers' holiday. On May 2, the Nazi SA
troops broke into labor union headquarters and forcibly took control of the union movement. Within a few weeks the Nazis had
created a new labor organization in the National Socialist image.
Next in line were the farmers. Hitler's representative gained control
of the leading agricultural association and then became agricultural
minister in the Nazi government. The associations of various small
businesses suffered a similar fate over the next several months. The
only significant economic interest group to resist the Nazis domination was the Federation of German Industry. Hitler did not have to
control industry by force, however; he only had to guarantee
enough profits to buy their support.

The political parties faced escalating pressure as soon as the Nazis
assumed power. The SPD was divided on how to deal with the
NSDAP. Some SPD leaders pursued a course of fundamental opposition from exile, while other party leaders tried to oppose the Nazis
within the legal channels of the Third Reich. Hitler resolved this
quandary by outlawing the SPD in June 1933 and imprisoning
many of the remaining SPD leaders in Germany. Once the largest
partisan challenger was removed, the other parties provided little
resistance to the Nazi onslaught. Over the next few weeks the German People's party, Bavarian People's party, and Democratic party
quietly dissolved. When the Vatican reached a concordat with the
Nazis that assured the rights of the Catholic church in Nazi Germany, the Center party also disbanded.[13] On July 14, the government declared that the NSDAP was the only legal party acknowledged by the Third Reich and party competition came to an end.

The Nazi coordination drive moved with such speed that most
potential sources of political opposition to Hitler were destroyed
within the first year of the Reich. The most significant criticisms of
Hitler then came from within the ranks of the NSDAP itself. The
head of the SA troops, Ernst Röhm, pressed for a greater role within
the Nazi government for himself and his troops. Hitler's solution to
this challenge was simple. On the night of January 30, 1934 ("The

night of the long knives"), Hitler's elite SS corps assassinated Röhm, dozens of other SA leaders, and other opponents of the Reich. The brutality of the Third Reich was clear for all who wished to see.

The Nazis total consolidation of political power came after the death of President Hindenburg in mid-1934. Hitler assumed the political authority and responsibilities of the office of president, but chose a new title to signify his role in the new Germany. Hitler became the *Führer* (leader) of his people as well as Reichschancellor of the government. The dual structures of the Nazi party and the Nazi state were united under Hitler's control. Führer-power (*Führergewalt*) became the ultimate source of political authority. The armed forces had to swear their allegiance to Hitler as their commander-in-chief. With the military's formal oath of "unconditional allegiance to the Führer," the Nazis' coordination process was essentially complete.

Just before Hitler became chancellor, Von Papen had predicted that Hitler would last only a few months before being forced from office. The Nazis, after all, controlled only two government ministries and were no match for the skillful political leaders of the conservative parties. He predicted that after Hitler was brought under control, the conservative parties could then create their own political revolution. These predictions, like many more to follow, disastrously underestimated Hitler. In actual fact, within only eighteen months of becoming chancellor, Hitler assumed nearly total control of society and politics.

HITLER'S DOMESTIC POLICIES

The Nazi state used its extensive power to restructure the economy. Reducing the vast numbers of unemployed workers was a first priority. The economic recovery program emphasized government investment in capital development projects that would create jobs. The German highway system (*autobahnen*) was the centerpiece of a program that included public works, large housing projects, and other heavy construction. Another aspect of the recovery program, and more important to Hitler, was the rearmament of Germany. At first secretly and then boldly violating the Versailles treaty limits on German military strength, Hitler began a military buildup greater than any nation had ever pursued in peacetime.

The health of the economy quickly improved. Unemployment

decreased from about six million in January 1933 to four million in 1934, and to only two million in 1935. The situation of the average worker was noticeably improved by higher employment levels and a stable or slightly increasing standard of living. In addition, the government's optimistic propaganda and the decrease in social strife improved the economic climate. Rebounding business confidence further stimulated a reviving economy. By 1936, full employment was achieved and industrial production surpassed the pre-Depression levels.

Most historians credit Hitler with successfully restoring the German economy, even while most Western democracies were still suffering from the effects of the Depression. In many ways, however, Hitler's was a false success. The government's economic program boosted employment, but the costs of these advances were not as immediately obvious.[14] The economic advances were very uneven; farmers actually suffered from Nazi agricultural policies. The social costs of Nazi policies were often overlooked; women, for example, were pressured to leave the labor force and assume traditional social roles as wives and mothers.[15] Government spending reached unsustainable levels. Government expenditures accounted for a larger share of the national economy than in Britain or France. The government increased taxes to finance these expenditures, but even these new revenues were inadequate. Government debt skyrocketed, quadrupling in six years. In the long term, the government's polices would lead toward economic collapse, but Hitler's plan focused on building the infrastructure for war. By 1940, Germany must be winning a war of conquest, or the long-term effects of the government's economic program would become obvious. Germany was racing toward a precipice.

INTERNATIONAL CONQUEST

Hitler charted Germany's course toward war long before the actual outbreak of hostilities. First, he insisted that Germany throw off the burden of Versailles and renounce the treaty's limits on Germany. Second, he called for an expansion of German territory to the east, which would provide the living space (*Lebensraum*) for future agricultural and economic growth. These two foreign policy goals guided the actions of the Third Reich.

Hitler's style was to challenge the international status quo directly and then depend on the inaction of other European powers or their willingness to compromise. Regrettably, almost every one of his initial foreign policy adventures was successful, emboldening him still further. In 1935 Hitler renounced the Versailles limits on German military forces, and the Allies did little. A year later he remilitarized the Rhineland. His advisors feared that this risky policy would fail; its success weakened any remaining sense of caution. Austria was merged into the Reich in 1938. When Germany threatened Czechoslovakia over the status of German-speaking border areas, the British Prime Minister responded by offering the territory to Hitler. In March 1939, German troops marched into Prague. The Third Reich was the most powerful state in Europe.

The other European nations finally realized the true scope of the Nazi threat, but it was almost too late. Britain and France quickened the pace of their military buildup. Meanwhile, Hitler had obtained a mutual nonaggression treaty with the Soviet Union. This removed the threat of a two-front war as in World War I. Hitler was hopeful that the Allies would remain neutral as he moved to expand German territory into Poland, but he was also prepared for full-scale war. On September 1, 1939, German troops invaded Poland. Britain and France came to Poland's defense and declared war on Germany—World War II had begun.

What started as a localized conflict progressively widened as the Axis powers—Germany, Italy, and Japan—displayed their imperialistic intentions. German mechanized armor and dive bombers overwhelmed the Polish defenses in a few weeks. In April 1940, Hitler's troops occupied neutral Denmark and Norway. Germany invaded Belgium and the Netherlands and defeated both in May. The army moved on to France, and by mid-June the French government capitulated. Only England remained to battle the Nazi advance in Western Europe. The incredibly rapid pace of German victories added a new term to the vocabulary of warfare, *Blitzkrieg* (lightning war).

The war continued to expand in 1941. The Nazis invaded the Balkans in the spring and quickly brought them under control. In June, Hitler began his most ambitious campaign, the invasion of the Soviet Union, violating the nonaggression treaty signed two years earlier. German troops raced across the steppes of Russia, but an early winter halted their advance on the outskirts of Moscow. Japan's surprise attack on Pearl Harbor in December brought the United States into the conflict and made the war truly worldwide in scope.

Germany had now overextended its resources, and hopes for rapid victory faded. During 1942, the Allies developed air and naval superiority over German forces in Western Europe. Allied troops in North Africa forced the Germans from the region in early 1943 and then invaded Italy. In the east, the German defeat at Stalingrad in January 1943 began a long retreat that would eventually end in Berlin; the turning point in the war had been reached.

War is always violent and harsh, but many actions of the Nazi state in conquering the territories in the East displayed a brutal disregard for humanity. Hitler's concept of a German *Lebensraum* called for the expulsion of millions of Poles and Russians from the eastern territories destined to be new German colonies. Poland was to become a nation of slave laborers, with only rudimentary education and minimal living standards. As German troops invaded Russia, special SS squads (*Einsatzkommandos*) terrorized the population and sought out and murdered over a million Soviet political activists and Jews. The conquerors relocated millions of foreign workers to Germany and forced them into the production lines of German factories. The Nazis considered the Slavs subhuman, and considered virtually any actions against them to be justified.

The inhumanity of the Nazi regime is most clearly seen in its actions toward the Jews.[16] Germany, as many other European nations, had experienced recurring periods of anti-Semitism, often associated with such national crises as the depression of 1873 and the collapse of the empire in 1918. The Nazis, however, made Aryan racial superiority and virulent anti-Semitism central themes of the party's program. Hitler attacked the Jews as symbols of everything that was wrong with the Weimar Republic and found a receptive audience among many people. Hitler unabashedly stated that his goal was to rid Germany and Europe of Jewish influences. The Third Reich followed this policy consistently, with steadily more oppressive measures. One of Hitler's first actions in 1933 was to purge Jews from the civil service. In 1935, the Nuremburg laws stripped citizenship rights from Jewish citizens and strengthened the racist aspects of Nazi ideology by prohibiting intermarriage with Jews. Nazis used outright violence and oppression of the Jews to force them to emigrate. In 1938, during the infamous *Kristallnacht* ("crystal night," for the shattered glass of Jewish-owned stores), SA troops attacked Jewish-owned businesses and destroyed Jewish synagogues; the government later confiscated the Jews' insurance payments as compensation for the disruption caused by the

Jews! The Nazis systematically excluded Jews from economic and social activity simply because of their religious heritage.

When German war hopes began to fade, the Third Reich began a top-secret program to exterminate all Jews in German-occupied territory. Dozens of concentration camps were established throughout Europe. Germans rounded up Jews from the conquered territories and sent them in railway freight cars to the camps. At Auschwitz, Treblinka, Bergen-Belsen, and the other camps, the Third Reich brutally exterminated Jews, Socialists, Communists, Democrats, and others the regime found socially undesirable. In the end, six million European Jews were murdered.

The war ended as it had begun—with all eyes focused on Hitler. As Soviet troops surrounded Berlin and the Allies rapidly advanced through Western Germany, Hitler directed the last final desperate defense of his Third Reich. When all hope was lost, he committed suicide and left Germany to suffer the consequences of his leadership. On May 8, 1945, Germany surrendered unconditionally to the victorious Allied forces. Sixty million lives were lost worldwide in the war. Germany lay in ruins: its industry and transportation systems destroyed, its cities in rubble, and millions left homeless and with little food. Hitler's grand designs for a new German Reich instead had destroyed the nation in a Wagnerian *Gotterdämmerung*.

NOTES

1. The first Empire was formed in the ninth century through the partitioning of Charlemagne's empire. The Reich expanded to become the Holy Roman Empire and lasted until 1250. See Kurt Reinhardt, *Germany: 2000 Years* (New York: Ungar, 1986).

2. See the discussion in Chapter XI of Bismarck's attempt to buy the support of the working class through a package of social insurance programs.

3. Fritz Fischer, *Germany's Aims in the First World War* (New York: Norton, 1967).

4. V. R. Berghahn, *Modern Germany* (Cambridge: Cambridge University Press, 1982), p. 58.

5. Ralf Dahrendorf, *Society and Democracy in Germany* (New York: Doubleday, 1967), p. 61.

6. David Abraham, *The Collapse of the Weimar Republic* (Princeton: Princeton University Press, 1981).

7. Thomas Childers, *The Nazi Voter* (Chapel Hill: University of North Carolina Press, 1983), p. 50.

8. Hajo Holborn, *A History of Modern Germany* (New York: Knopf, 1969), p. 695.

9. Karl Dietrich Bracher, *The German Dictatorship* (New York: Praeger, 1970); Rainer Lepsius, "From Fragmented Party Democracy to Government by

Emergency Decree and the National Socialist Takeover," in *The Breakdown of Democratic Regimes,* ed. Juan Linz and Alfred Stephen (Baltimore: Johns Hopkins University Press, 1978).

10. Gordon Craig, *Germany, 1866-1945* (New York: Oxford University Press, 1978), p. 396.

11. Richard Hamilton, *Who Voted for Hitler?* (Princeton: Princeton University Press, 1982); Childers, *The Nazi Voter.*

12. Martin Broszat, *The Hitler State* (New York: Longman, 1981), p. 31.

13. Throughout the Third Reich, the Catholic and Protestant churches were virtually the only entities that retained some independence from the government. See Chapter VIII and the discussion of church activities in Ernst Helmrich, *The German Churches under Hitler* (Detroit: Wayne University Press, 1979).

14. Holborn, *A History of Modern Germany,* pp. 750-759.

15. Detlev Peukert, *Inside Nazi Germany* (New Haven: Yale University Press, 1987).

16. Yehuda Bauer, *A History of the Holocaust* (New York: Franklin Watts, 1982); Sarah Gordon, *Hitler, Germans, and the "Jewish Question"* (Princeton: Princeton University Press, 1984).

CHAPTER II

The Formation of the Federal Republic

MAY 1945 IS GENERALLY considered the "zero point" in the development of postwar German politics. Hitler had insisted that Germany battle until the bitter end, even after all hope of victory was lost. Thus the cost of defeat soared much higher than in World War I. The nation suffered massive social, economic, and political destruction. The economy was shattered, citizens were destitute, and politics became a denigrated activity.

The country faced a long road back to social and national recovery. Moreover, at the war's end no one knew where that road would lead, and almost all believed that it would be a long journey. Opinion surveys conducted more than a year after the war ended showed that many Germans expected the military occupation by the Allies to last half a century!

The rebirth of postwar Germany is thus a truly amazing story. Eventually a new, affluent, independent, and democratic nation would rise from the ashes of war. Within a single generation, Germany changed from an international outcast to a respected member of the Western Alliance, from a defeated and impoverished society to one of the richest nations in the world, and from an inhuman totalitarian state to a vibrant democracy. West Germany's success in meeting all these challenges makes it the political success story of postwar Europe.

THE OCCUPATION PERIOD

Even before the end of World War II, the Allied powers began to plan the fate of postwar Germany. One of the first decisions was to divide the territory of the former Reich in order to dismantle the Nazi state and simplify public administration. Germany was to be partitioned into three occupation zones, each under the control of a separate military commander. Southern Germany would be administered by the United States, northern Germany by Great Britain, and the eastern region by the Soviet Union. Later, France joined the Allied powers and occupied a zone drawn from the American and British sectors. The conquered German capital of Berlin, which was over 100 kilometers within the Soviet occupation zone, would be administered by a joint Four-Power commission.

The Allies also agreed on a set of broad goals to guide the administration of occupied Germany. Policies of demilitarization and denazification, which would immediately remove the Nazi threat to world peace, received top priority. For instance, war-related industries were to be seized by the occupation forces and dismantled or converted to other production. The principles of administrative decentralization and economic deconcentration also received Allied endorsement.

Beyond these general goals, however, the views of the Allies often failed to converge. Questions about the details of administration, economic reconstruction, and political reform remained unresolved at the war's end. A series of Allied summits failed to reach agreement on the conditions of peace and the intended structure of postwar Germany. Even while the Allies celebrated their imminent victory, fundamental divisions existed in their political orientations.

Policy differences among the Allies arose for several reasons. Each of the Allied governments sought different goals from the defeat of the Third Reich.[1] The Soviet Union pressed for large reparation payments (to recover a portion of its wartime losses) and territorial concessions to Poland (to compensate Poland for its territorial losses to the Soviet Union). In order to lessen the possibility of another German threat on its eastern border, France favored the dismemberment of Germany and cession of the Saar and a portion of the Rhineland to France. The policy of the United States was ambiguous. The U.S. goal was to remove Germany as a military and political threat to the world, but U.S. policy makers were divided on how best to carry out this objective. Many leading foreign policy officials advocated reform and democratization of postwar Germany, in order to avoid the popular resentment and hostility that accompanied the harsh terms of Versailles. President Roosevelt, however, favored a Carthaginian peace that would destroy Germany as an economic and political force once and for all. In the spring of 1944, Roosevelt officially adopted the *Morgenthau Plan,* which called for returning Germany to a nonindustrial, agrarian society. Britain preferred a solution closer to the American reformist program.

The Allied governments also disagreed in their perceptions of the causes of Nazism, and hence the steps necessary to remove this influence from German society. Many French authorities saw National Socialism as an extension of Prussian nationalism and authoritarian values; they therefore favored the destruction of Prussia and eradication of these attitudes from the German culture. The Soviets viewed the Third Reich as stemming from the excesses of Western capitalism; only a social revolution on the Soviet model could correct this situation. The British saw Hitler's ascent to power as a failure of political leadership, and consequently emphasized the removal of Nazi sympathizers from leadership positions. American sentiments were divided between those who viewed the Third Reich as a unique, abnormal failure of the political process and those who considered Hitler an inevitable consequence of the German pattern of political development.

When the Allied occupation forces took control of Germany in May 1945, the magnitude of the problems they faced temporarily overshadowed their differences. Germany presented a gloomy picture. The casualties of war personally affected millions of German families and virtually all personal savings had been lost with the collapse of the Nazi government.[2] In addition, nearly a quarter of Germany's prewar territory, encompassing all lands east of the Oder-Neisse rivers, was under Polish or Soviet administration. Several million ethnic Germans were expelled from these territories and the other nations in Eastern Europe and forced to Germany. These expellees, having left all their property to flee for their lives, settled in refugee camps and added to the burden of postwar reconstruction. A later wave of refugees from the communist nations of Eastern Europe swelled the number of relocated persons to over 10 million.

The German economy was unable to match the demands forced upon it.[3] Much of the country's productive capacity was either destroyed, idle, or being dismantled by the victors. Estimates suggest that industrial production in 1946 was only 33 percent of the 1936 level, and that national income reached only 40 percent of its prewar level. The transportation system lay in ruins; railways and waterways had been blocked by Allied bombs or by the retreating German troops. Almost 50 percent of prewar housing units were destroyed or damaged, and the number of homeless was swelled by the expellees from the east. Agricultural production, especially in the more industrialized western occupation zones, could not feed this large population. Shortages of food and basic necessities created a thriving black market, where some goods sold for 50 to 100 times their official price. It was estimated that even with the help of American food donations the average daily food intake over the years 1945 to 1947 was only 1300 calories per person. Not until December 1947 did the American military command conclude that the German people had sufficient food to avoid malnutrition.

The Western Allies initially followed the general strategy of the Morgenthau Plan. Economic recovery proceeded slowly, and the expropriation of resources for reparation payments further narrowed the economic base necessary to restore the economy. Adherence to this policy and the efficiency of its administration varied sharply across the occupation zones. The French rapidly moved to extract reparation compensation from their occupation zone, while the British acted much more slowly. The Soviet Union was most ambitious in expropriating reparation payments, either by seizing plants and equipment in the eastern zone or by the forced labor of German prisoners of war in Soviet factories.

Denazification was another cornerstone of the reconstruction program.[4] The program's goal was to remove Nazi influences from German society and politics as a necessary first step in creating a liberal, democratic state. These efforts began with the International Military Tribunal at Nuremberg. The principal surviving leaders of Nazi Germany were placed on trial for war crimes and crimes against humanity, such as the mass murders in the concentration camps. To some extent the German nation also stood in the docket and was forced to confront, often unwillingly, the horrors of the Third Reich. The court returned guilty verdicts against the Nazi leadership and the institutions of the Nazi state (the SA, SS, SD, Gestapo, and Nazi party).

A second phase of denazification gradually expanded the scope of the program to the broader spectrum of German society. Because Nazi institutions were judged illegal by the Nuremberg court, the military governors arrested several thousand individuals who held posts in these institutions. There were also mass expulsions of individuals with Nazi ties from government and professional positions. Finally, the denazification program was expanded to the public at large. Every adult in the American occupation zone had to fill out a questionnaire detailing past political activities. These questionnaires (over 13 million) provided a basis for taking further action against individuals who were closely involved with the Nazi movement.

Many contemporary historians criticize the denazification program. Beyond removing the top level of Nazi leadership, the program had mixed effects in truly ridding Nazi influences from German society. The application of guidelines was imprecise and varied greatly across occupation zones. The practical need for experienced people to run the government and economy often conflicted with denazification guidelines. Moreover, most Germans wanted to forget the experiences of the Third Reich, and the Allies' stress on the collective guilt of the Germans created discontent and increased hostility toward the occupation forces. In the end, the administrative task of screening all Germans became impossible to manage, and the Allies deemphasized the program. Yet, given the inhumanity of the Third Reich, it would have been a graver error if the Allies had done nothing and let the world forget. If not a sense of collective guilt, the Germans (and the world) felt a sense of collective shame over what had happened during the Third Reich.

As soon as the immediate crises of postwar Germany were addressed, tensions between the Allies resurfaced. Political and social developments within each occupation zone followed diverging courses. The Potsdam conference had called for decentralization, local self-government, and representative institutions. Each of the Allies interpreted these goals differently. The Americans quickly established local political institutions. By the end of 1945, a network of local, county, district, and state (*Länder*) governments already existed, and democratic institutions were far advanced. In addition, the Americans restructured the economy along free-market lines; they broke up large industrial conglomerates and bank cartels. Similar developments occurred in the British and French zones, albeit at a slower pace. The major disparity separated the three western zones from the Soviet occupation zone. The Russians openly displayed their intentions to Sovietize the eastern zone. A large proportion of industry was nationalized or reorganized as Soviet-owned cooperatives. Even before the war had ended, Walter

Ulbricht, the future East German leader, traveled from his exile in Moscow to Berlin and began molding the political system into the Soviet image.

Political differences among the Allies also grew. The Western powers became increasingly concerned with the Soviet's creation of satellite states in Eastern Europe. Open conflict arose between democratic and communist forces in Greece. As the Western media became more critical of Soviet actions, the Soviet Union reacted with attacks on the "capitalist and imperialist press." Slowly and steadily, the gap between East and West widened.

THE DIVISION OF GERMANY

In March 1947, the four Allied foreign ministers met in Moscow to continue earlier planning talks concerning the administration of postwar Germany. Soon after the conference began, U.S. President Truman announced a new doctrine of opposition to further communist expansion. In a climate of tension and distrust, the meeting broke down and accomplished nothing. Alfred Grosser maintains that the failure of the Moscow conference "marked the beginning of the Cold War and the splitting of the world into two parts."[5]

The attitude of the Western Allies toward Germany underwent a fundamental transformation over the next several months. Rather than cripple the German state, they wanted to create an economically strong and politically sound Germany as an ally in the West's emerging conflict with the Soviet Union. The Western Allies replaced harsh treatment of Germany with serious attempts at economic and political reconstruction. The economic base of the American and British occupation zones was strengthened by the merger of their economies in May 1947 (the *Bizone*) and the creation of a joint import/export program. During the summer, the Marshall Plan of American aid for European reconstruction was proposed and implemented. Soviet-controlled East European nations, however, rejected the aid offer.

The Cold War had begun. In October 1947, the Cominform was established. A communist-led coup in Czechoslovakia in February 1948 removed any remaining Western doubts about Soviet intentions for Eastern Europe. The communist seizure of Czechoslovakia was a sharp blow for the West, because its loss to Hitler in 1939 had displayed the weakness of Western governments and prefaced the outbreak of World War II. As a result of events in Czechoslovakia, the French policy toward the Soviet Union moved closer to the Anglo-American position.

Economic reforms in the western occupation zones widened this breach between East and West. The Western occupation powers established the Economic Council in 1947 to administer a common economic policy in the three western zones. The Council was the first German national administrative unit and provided the training ground for many future political leaders. Under the directorship of Ludwig Erhard, the Economic Council advocated policies leading to a Social Market Economy (*Soziale Marktwirtschaft*). Following liberal theories of capitalist economics, this model was premised on free-enterprise initiative. The state's role was limited to stabilizing the economy as a whole, ensuring competitive markets, and protecting the socially disadvantaged. The prerequisites of the Social Market Economy were the establishment of a sound currency as the base of the free market and the removal of economic constraints such as rationing, price and wage controls, and high taxation levels.

The Currency Reform of June 1948 constituted the first major step in this new economic program. By establishing a new currency and abolishing many economic controls, Erhard created public trust in the new *Deutsche Mark* (DM). Display windows that were empty one day filled overnight. The economy quickly began to grow within a basically capitalistic framework. Using official figures, Werner Kaltefleiter reported that "from July to December 1948, the industrial production index climbed at *monthly rates* which later were achieved only in full years."[6]

The currency reform also further institutionalized the division between the eastern and western zones. The east was structured upon a socialist economy, while the west had a capitalist system with a different currency. The Soviet Union responded to the currency reform by obstructing American, British, and French access to Berlin in June 1948. The Berlin blockade served as a test of Western resolve; a massive Allied airlift of supplies was necessary to sustain a city of over 2 million. The Berlin blockade marked another turning point in postwar German history. It changed German attitudes toward the United States from that of a occupying power to the protector from Soviet aggression. In addition, it changed the world's image of Berlin from the capital of the Nazi Reich to the symbol of democratic freedom. Most important, the blockade solidified the East-West division of Germany. As the airlift to Berlin continued for nearly a year, Allied preparations for the creation of a separate German state in the West went forward.

THE CREATION OF THE FEDERAL REPUBLIC

In 1948, the London conference of Western Allies called for the establishment of an independent West German state in the three western occupation zones. The conference directed the Länder governments to select representatives for a *Constituent Assembly* to draft a democratic constitution based on a federal government structure. At the same time, the Allies would control this process. The occupation powers reserved certain areas of political responsibility, and required that the new constitution be approved by the military governors.

The heads of the Länder governments were hesitant to institutionalize the break with the eastern part of the former nation. They insisted that a less formal-sounding *Parliamentary Council* be established; rather than draft a constitution, the Council would prepare a *Basic Law (Grundgesetz)* for the governing of the western zones. The representatives to the Parliamentary Council were selected by the state governments, roughly in proportion to the population of each Land and the distribution of parties within the Land government.

In Bonn, a small university town along the banks of the Rhine that would become the capital, the Germans began their second attempt at democracy. In September 1948, the Parliamentary Council met to draft a constitution to organize West German politics until the entire nation should be reunited.

The content of the Basic Law reflects the convergence of several forces affecting the political development of postwar Germany.[7] The Allied occupation authorities held veto powers over the contents of the final document; the drafting was done under their watchful eyes and with their occasional intervention. The leaders of the state governments and heads of the newly established political parties had a vested interest in the structure of government. Administrative, judicial, and economic elites shared a concern about the form of the new government. Of course, the people of West Germany had the largest stake in the creation of a new political system, but their direct involvement was kept to a minimum. Essentially, the Allied and West German elites framed the Basic Law.

In this context, the members of the Parliamentary Council set out to create the formal institutions upon which a democratic system could be based. Maintaining some historical continuity in political institutions was one major objective. The starting point was a parliamentary system of democracy, similar to that used in the Weimar Republic. Most Germans were familiar with the workings of a parliamentary system, as were the British and French authorities. A general consensus also existed in support of a federal system of government. Both the Second Empire and the Weimar Republic had contained federal structures. The Allies further saw federalism as a means of preventing the emergence of a strong centralized German government that again might marshal the power of Hitler's Reich.

A second objective was to deal with the lack of democratic values in the German public. Many German elites displayed open disdain for the average citizen, which was well-rooted in German political tradition. Peter Merkl wrote that "the framers of the Basic Law were motivated by a deep distrust of the common man, who, in their opinion, by his support of Hitler had convincingly demonstrated his inability to control his own affairs."[8] This harsh view of the public conveniently overlooked the role of political elites in orchestrating Weimar's collapse, but it was a view shared by the Allies. The Basic Law would therefore create institutional structures to restrain the excesses of the popular will and mediate the direct influence of the public on the political process.

A third general objective was to design a political system without the structural weaknesses that contributed to the collapse of the Weimar Republic. The framers of the Basic Law wanted to establish clearer lines of political authority and responsibility. At the same time, the new political system should contain more extensive checks and balances, to avoid the usurpation of power that occurred in the Third Reich. Finally, an obvious need existed for institutional limits on extremist and antisystem forces that might attempt to destabilize and subvert the democratic political order.

The Parliamentary Council completed the drafting of the Basic Law by early May 1949. The occupation powers approved the document after a few slight modifications. The state governments (except Bavaria) ratified the Basic Law and it was promulgated on May 23, 1949. The *Federal Republic of Germany* (FRG), or West Germany, was established as a parliamentary democracy. The Soviet responded almost immediately by creating the *German Democratic Republic* (GDR), East Germany, as a communist-led system. Germany became two states within one nation.

The wheels of this new political system starting turning in August 1949 with the first national elections. The Allied forces had been very cautious in constructing the party system of the Federal Republic. Only political parties that were free of Nazi ties and committed to democratic procedures were allowed to form, and early party activity was limited to the local or Land level. In 1949, therefore, the party system was fairly fragmented, with more than a dozen parties competing in the election. Most political observers expected the Social Democratic Party (SPD) to be victorious, because it had inherited the legacy of the prewar SPD and was the best organized of the major political parties. Instead, the conservative Christian Democratic Union (CDU) emerged from the election as the largest party. Under the leadership of Konrad Adenauer, the first West German chancellor, the CDU formed a coalition government to take control of the new West German state.

INSTITUTIONS AND STRUCTURE OF GOVERNMENT

The style of the Basic Law reflects a fundamental characteristic of the political culture. German political norms emphasize strong respect for legal principles and a taste for legal details. Clearly delineated rules of law are necessary in order for a political system to function smoothly. Legal precepts also possess special legitimacy (a *Rechtsstaat* orientation). To guarantee basic human rights, therefore, the first seventeen articles of the Basic Law define them as legal entitlements. To strengthen the authority of the state, the Basic Law defines the workings of the political system with unusual precision. The formal institutions and procedures of the political system are described in detail uncommon for a constitution. Consequently, despite its supposedly provisional nature, the political institutions of the Federal Republic were carefully designed in the articles of the Basic Law.

A FEDERAL SYSTEM.

Germany has a strong tradition of regional government, and one of the first steps of political reconstruction by the Allied occupation forces was to create state governments (*Länder*). A few of the states maintained their historical tradition as prewar regions; however, in most instances the new states were constructed by the occupation forces to facilitate administration of postwar Germany. After further consolidation, the Federal Republic is now organized into ten Lander.[9] West Berlin is unofficially considered the eleventh Land, but it is still administered by the wartime powers (the United States, Britain, France, and the Soviet Union) and remains outside the formal jurisdiction of the Federal Republic. The Federal Republic is a relatively small nation by American standards, but the states vary considerably in their cultural, economic, and political tendencies (see Chapter III).

The Länder provided the focal point for much of the early political activity in the western occupation zones. Political parties and the mass media were first organized and licensed at the Land level, and restoration of local self-government was one of the first political reforms of the Allies. By late 1947, all the Länder had conducted elections to select their governments. The heads of the Länder served as the formal representatives of the German people before a national government was formed. Given the historical and practical importance of the state governments, it was inevitable that they would become central institutions in the political system framed by the Basic Law.

The Basic Law created a federal system of government, which divides political power between the federal government (*Bund*) and the state governments (see Figure II.1). The structure of state governments is based on a parliamentary system modeled after the

FIGURE II.1 *The Structure of Government*

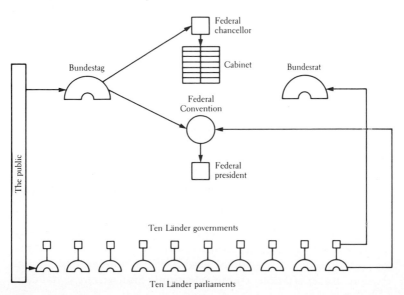

national government. Most states have a unicameral legislature, normally called a *Landtag*, which is directly elected by popular vote.[10] The party or coalition of parties that controls the legislature selects a minister president to head the state government. The minister president appoints a cabinet to administer the state agencies and perform the executive functions of the state government.

The minister presidents are important national figures in West German politics. The federal system of government enables them to wield influence at both the state and national levels. The position also serves as a stepping stone to national office, either as federal chancellor or a member of the federal cabinet. Three of last four chancellors, including the present incumbent and his opponent in the last election, were former heads of state government.

Even though the political system is structured along federal lines, the nature of this federal arrangement is substantially different from the American form of federalism. The separation of powers assigns greater legislative responsibility to the Bund and greater administrative responsibility to the state governments. This continues a pattern of policy making inherited from earlier German political systems. German federalism is thus based on functional division of legislative and administrative responsibility as well as exclusive policy domains.

The Basic Law seemingly gives primary political authority to the Länder. Article 30, for instance, maintains that "the exercise of government powers and the discharge of governmental functions shall be incumbent on the Länder insofar as this Basic Law does not otherwise prescribe or permit." In another section the states are given "the right to legislate so far as this Basic Law does not confer legislative power on the federation." In both cases, however, similar clauses limit Länder power, because other articles specify the federal government as the principal legislative authority.

The legislative mandate of the federal government is divided into three categories:

1. Exclusive powers (Articles 71, 73)
2. Concurrent powers (Articles 72, 74, 74a)
3. Framework powers (Article 75)

The federal government possesses exclusive legislative responsibility in matters that concern the national security interest or require policy coordination on a national level. Defense, foreign trade, immigration, transportation, communications, and currency standards are the types of policies that are workable only on a national scale and therefore are exclusive powers of the Bund. In several other policy areas the states and federal government share concurrent powers, although in case of conflict federal law takes priority. About two dozen areas of concurrent powers are now specified by the Basic Law, including civil law, refugee and expellee matters, public welfare, land management, consumer protection, public health, nuclear energy, traffic regulations, and the collection of vital statistics (births, deaths, and marriages). In their concern for detail, the framers of the Basic Law even specified the protection of forest seedlings, plants, and animals as a concurrent power justifying constitutional treatment.

Framework legislation limits the federal government to providing broad policy guidelines, which are subsequently implemented by detailed legislation at the Land level. These federal legislative directives are limited to the areas of the mass media, nature conservation, regional planning, and public service regulations. Another category of "joint tasks" was added to the Basic Law in 1969 (Article 91a, 91b); it provides for joint federal-state action in areas of broad social concern, such as improving higher education, developing regional economic structures, and improving rural conditions.

After these federal government "exceptions" are taken into account, the remaining policy areas are the legislative authority of the state governments. The Länder exercise jurisdiction in education (especially at the primary and secondary levels), law enforcement, regulation of radio and television, and cultural activities. Furthermore, the states retain residual powers to legislate in any area of concurrent responsibility where the federal government has not acted.

Despite a concerted effort to specify the relationship between Bund and Länder in clear terms within the Basic Law, the relationship is a continuing source of conflict and competition between the two levels of government. On the one hand, the federal government often finds itself confronted with important issues of national scope that it feels are not being adequately met by the states. On the other hand, the Länder governments jealously protect the principles of states' rights elaborated in the Basic Law. Education policy is one example of continuing controversy. The Basic Law explicitly treated education as a Land responsibility, to destroy the propagandizing educational system of the Third Reich by decentralizing educational policy making. When severe inadequacies in the educational system became apparent in the mid-1960s, however, this structure of fragmented, state-level policy making thwarted systematic reform. In 1969 a constitutional amendment finally authorized the federal government to set a legislative framework for educational reform and improving university education through joint projects with the states. Subsequent federal legislation, such as the Higher Education Law of 1976, expanded the role of the federal government in this area previously reserved for the states. This pattern has been repeated in other policy areas. The Federal Republic, like many other Western democracies, is following a trend toward the nationalization of political issues and political decision making that is slowly eroding the influence of the states.

Although the federal government is the major force in the legislation of policy, the states hold primary responsibility for the implementation and administration of policy. The states enforce their own regulations and most of the domestic legislation enacted by the federal government. The Länder governments also oversee the operation of the local governments within their respective control. As one indicator of the states' central administrative role, more civil servants are employed by the state governments than by the federal and local governments combined.

This delegation of administrative responsibility substantially increases the bargaining power of the states in making and actually implementing policy, even if legislation is initiated by the federal government. A federal law setting general policy guidelines must be implemented by legislation at the state level and then is administered by state officials. The states' ability to use this division of responsibility to maintain their autonomy is evident in education policy. Despite federal education guidelines, individual states vary significantly in how rapidly and extensively reforms have been implemented. The administrative strength of the states thus partially counterbalances their legislative limitations.

The political powers of the state governments extend beyond their legislative and administrative roles at the state levels. One house of the federal legislature, the *Bundesrat* (see below), is comprised solely of representatives appointed by the state governments. Länder officials also comprise half the members of the Federal Council, which meets every five years to elect a federal president, and the state governments participate in selecting justices of the major federal courts.

In addition to these formal constitutional arrangements, extensive informal or semiofficial channels for policy consultation exist between state and federal officials. Intergovernmental committees and planning groups coordinate the different interests of federal and state governments. The growth of these coordinating committees is described as a third level of the federal system, bridging the gap between the Länder and the Bund. These organizations practice a style of "cooperative federalism" whereby Länder governments can coordinate their activities at a regional level or work together with federal officials.[11] Surveys of elites find that state and federal officials are in frequent personal contact.[12] Dialogue and voluntary cooperation are essential factors in the smooth functioning of this federal system. Informally, at least, considerable overlap exists between the federal and state governments.

PARLIAMENTARY GOVERNMENT

Germany has had a parliament since national unification, but the tradition of parliamentary authority was still weakly developed in 1949. Under the second empire, Parliament was often little more than a political club disdained by the real holders of power, the Kaiser and his chancellor. Through a combination of suppression and manipulation, the government escaped most legislative control. The Kaiser and chancellor left no doubts that they felt Germany would be better off without politicians and Parliament.

The experience of parliamentary government during the Weimar Republic was also negative. Weimar was based on a parliamentary system: a popularly elected parliament selected the chancellor and held substantial legislative powers. The Weimar parliament, however, often ignored its responsibilities and became a forum for partisan bickering and conflict. The inability of the parliamentary system to produce a stable governing majority severely sapped the strength of the Weimar Republic.

Despite these negative experiences, the framers of the Basic Law favored a parliamentary system for the Federal Republic. Most citizens were familiar with the mechanics of parliamentary democracy; a parliamentary system would also fulfill the military governors' guidelines for the new government; and while past experiences with national parliaments were largely negative, parliaments at the state level had earned a better record.

The Basic Law thus created a parliamentary democracy for the Federal Republic. The central institution of the federal government is a bicameral parliament consisting of the *Bundestag* and *Bundes-*

rat. It passes legislation, elects the federal chancellor and president, debates government policies, and oversees the activities of the federal ministries. To avoid the problems of the past, however, the parliamentary system has an extensive set of checks and balances to both strengthen and control government action.

The Bundestag. The *Bundestag,* or *Federal Diet,* is the primary legislative body of the Parliament, comparable to the American House of Representatives or the British House of Commons. Its members are the only government officials directly elected by the West German public, its support is required for the passage of all laws, and its members select the chief executive of the government. Despite these lofty responsibilities, the Bundestag began from very humble beginnings. Early parliamentarians worked in Spartan conditions, with limited staff and resources. For nearly the first four decades of its existence, its meetings took place in the remodeled auditorium of a former teachers' college in Bonn, chosen as the site of parliament because it was one of the few large buildings left standing in Germany at the end of the war. The setting was devoid of the monumental status of the U.S. Congress or the political history of Britain's Westminster.

As the Bundestag has grown in status and political responsibility, so have its resources. The original parliament was finally replaced in 1989 and is flanked by a twenty-story office building for deputies that dominates the Bonn skyline. Bundestag salaries are among the highest in Europe, and the size of the legislative staff exceeds most other European parliaments.

The Bundestag is composed of 496 full deputies, who represent the voters of the Federal Republic. An additional 22 members, with nonvoting observer status, represent West Berlin. The 496 deputies are selected in national elections every four years, unless the Bundestag is dissolved prematurely. In order to avoid the political intransigence and narrow vision of parliaments in past regimes, the formal principles of the Bundestag encourage deputies to evaluate issues from a national perspective. The Basic Law states that deputies serve as representatives of the whole people, subject only to their conscience. These norms are very different from many other parliamentary systems, where legislators are often expected to represent only the voters in their district or the special-interest groups that helped their election. In practice, however, the behavior of West German deputies also reflects their group ties.

Within the Bundestag, deputies are organized into strict party groupings (*Fraktionen*).[13] In organizational and political terms, the Bundestag is structured around these Fraktionen rather than the individual deputies. The key legislative posts and committee assignments are restricted to members of a party Fraktion. The size of a Fraktion determines its representation on legislative committees, its share of committee chairmanships, and its participation in the executive bodies of the legislature. Most government funding for legislative and administrative support is distributed to the Fraktionen and not the deputies. It is said that a deputy without a Fraktion cannot be whole.

Each Fraktion is headed by a parliamentary party leader, several deputy leaders, and an executive committee. It is the responsibility of the leadership to represent the Fraktion, direct party activities in parliament, and maintain party discipline. The members of each Fraktion are divided into specialized working groups dealing with specific policy issues. For instance, the SPD Fraktion includes working groups dealing with foreign affairs, economics, social policy, and other themes. The working groups include the party's deputies on the Bundestag committees relevant to this policy area and other party members interested in the issue. Much of the actual decision making in Parliament occurs at the weekly Fraktion meetings, where pending legislation is discussed and the party's position is decided. On the whole, Fraktion activities account for a large share of the deputies' average work week (see Figure II.2). The Green party rejects the hierarchical structure and bureaucratic organization of the other party Fraktionen in favor of a more decentralized party grouping; this means that party meetings constitute an even more important activity for Green deputies.

The leadership of the Bundestag and the Fraktion representatives coordinate their activities through the *Council of Elders*. The council is the steering committee of the Bundestag; it is responsible for scheduling of debates, setting the legislative agenda, and making committee assignments. Many of the negotiations among parties occur in this forum, as party leaders press the position of their party on pending legislation and the procedural matters of the Bundestag. The council is headed by the Bundestag president, who also presides over legislative sessions. This is normally an honorific position for an elder deputy, who is expected to keep above party politics. The Bundestag president and vice-presidents also constitute a second executive body, the *Praesidium*, which is responsible for the routine administrative matters of the parliament.

A unique aspect of the West German parliament is the heavy

FIGURE II.2 *Weekly Activities of Bundestag Deputies*

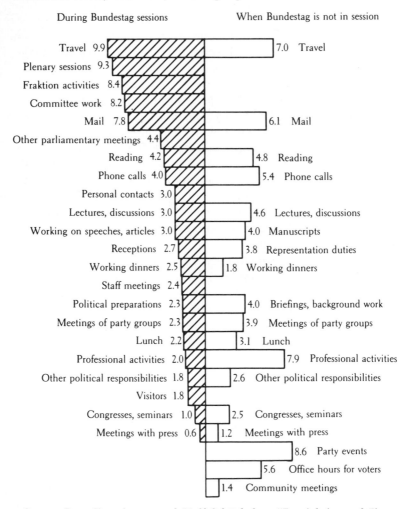

During Bundestag sessions   When Bundestag is not in session

During Bundestag sessions		When Bundestag is not in session
Travel	9.9	7.0 Travel
Plenary sessions	9.3	
Fraktion activities	8.4	
Committee work	8.2	
Mail	7.8	6.1 Mail
Other parliamentary meetings	4.4	
Reading	4.2	4.8 Reading
Phone calls	4.0	5.4 Phone calls
Personal contacts	3.0	
Lectures, discussions	3.0	4.6 Lectures, discussions
Working on speeches, articles	3.0	4.0 Manuscripts
Receptions	2.7	3.8 Representation duties
Working dinners	2.5	1.8 Working dinners
Staff meetings	2.4	
Political preparations	2.3	4.0 Briefings, background work
Meetings of party groups	2.3	3.9 Meetings of party groups
Lunch	2.2	3.1 Lunch
Professional activities	2.0	7.9 Professional activities
Other political responsibilities	1.8	2.6 Other political responsibilities
Visitors	1.8	
Congresses, seminars	1.0	2.5 Congresses, seminars
Meetings with press	0.6	1.2 Meetings with press
		8.6 Party events
		5.6 Office hours for voters
		1.4 Community meetings

Source: Peter Kevenhorster and Wulf Schönbohm, "Zur Arbeits- und Zieto-
konomie von Bundestagsabgeordneten," *Zietschrift für Parlamentsfragen* 4
(1973): 18–37. Figure entries are hours spent on each activity. Used by
permission.

reliance on a system of specialized committees, much like the U.S. Congress but unlike other parliamentary systems, such as the British House of Commons or the French National Assembly. Most of the formal work of the Bundestag takes place in these committees.[14] The overall committee structure generally follows the divisions of the federal ministries, such as transportation, defense, labor, and agriculture. The tenth Bundestag (1983–1987) had twenty such committees. Committees are composed of deputies who normally possess a special expertise or interest in the subject matter of the committee. Committee assignments are divided among the Fraktionen in proportion to their sizes. In addition, the committee chair positions are also distributed proportionately among the Fraktionen. In the tenth Bundestag, the CDU/CSU chaired ten committees, the SPD eight, and the FDP and the Greens one each. This means that a large number of legislative committees are always directed by representatives of the opposition parties, another example the system's extensive checks and balances.

By most objective measures, the Bundestag is an exceptionally active parliamentary body (Table II.1). The Bundestag meets nearly all year round, except for long summer and holiday recesses. The rhythm of parliamentary life follows a four-week cycle, with plenary sessions held during the first two weeks of each cycle. During the period with plenary sessions, members devote the first two days of the week to Fraktion activity, set Wednesday aside for committee work, and hold plenary sessions on Thursday and Friday. Outside meetings and taking care of constituents' needs add to this already full schedule. It is easy to see why the average deputy has 60–70-hour workweeks when Parliament is in session.

The Bundestag's is most active in its legislative function, which deputies feel is their most important task.[15] The initiative for most legislation, though, lies in the executive branch. The bulk of the bills considered by the legislature are proposed by the executive (see Chapter X). Like most modern parliaments, the Bundestag focuses on evaluating and amending the government's legislative program. Much of this work occurs in committee, where deputies study the government's proposal and suggest amendments.

Another function of the Bundestag is to provide a forum for public debate. The plenary sessions of the Parliament consider the legislation before the chamber. All party Fraktionen receive debating time according to their size; both party leaders and back benchers usually participate. Because party members already have caucused

TABLE II.1 *Activities of the Parliament, 1949-1986*

Activity	1949–1953	1953–1957	1957–1961	1961–1965	1965–1969	1969–1972	1972–1976	1976–1980	1980–1983	1983–1986
Bundestag										
Plenary sessions	282	227	168	198	247	199	259	230	142	256
Party meetings	1774	1777	675	727	802	529	718	674	400	900
Committee meetings	5474	4389	2493	2986	2692	1449	2223	1955	1099	2305
Public information committee hearings	0	1	1	6	58	80	76	70	42	162
Investigative-committee meetings	174	34	0	37	101	26	77	52	5	209
Enquete-commission hearings	—	—	—	—	—	52	89	47	83	84
Oral/written questions	392	1069	1536	4786	10,733	11,073	18,497	23,467	14,384	22,864
Grosse Anfragen	160	97	49	35	45	31	24	47	32	175
Kleine Anfragen	355	377	411	308	488	569	480	434	297	1066
Current hours	—	—	—	2	17	8	20	9	12	117
Bundesrat										
Plenary sessions	116	69	54	50	56	43	55	51	28	52
Committee meetings	1092	887	718	705	803	650	820	796	436	828

Source: *Statistiches Jahrbuch für die Bundesrepublik Deutschland, 1987*, p. 92; *Datenhandbuch zur Geschichte des Deutschen Bundestages 1949 bis 1982*. Note that premature elections in 1972 and 1983 shortened the length of the two respective parliaments. Procedures implementing current hours were first introduced during the 1969-1972 parliament.

and agreed on their voting positions, these plenary sessions primarily serve as a means of expressing the party's views. These sessions command a large share of a deputy's workweek, although attendance is normally sparse unless important issues are under consideration (Figure II.2). The Bundestag now televises important plenary sessions, thus expanding the public audience for these policy debates. The increasing importance attributed to this educational function is also seen in the growing use of public hearings by the Bundestag committees. These hearings provide the committees with an opportunity to obtain testimony from experts in the field and focus public attention on an issue.

The Bundestag also carries responsibility for the selection of the government. In parliamentary democracies, the head of the executive branch is elected by the parliament; it is as if the U.S. president were elected by the House of Representatives. This makes Bundestag elections nearly winner-takes-all contests; the party coalition that wins controls of the legislature also heads the executive branch. Bundestag deputies also constitute half of the Federal Convention (the other half is drawn from the state governments), which elects the Federal President every five years.

As well as selecting the executive, the Bundestag is charged with scrutinizing the actions of the executive branch on both policy and administrative issues. Next to the passage of legislation, deputies consider this the Bundestag's most important function. The most commonly used method of government oversight is the question hour (*Fragestunde*) adopted from the British House of Commons. An individual deputy can submit a written question to a government minister; questions range from broad policy issues to the specific needs of one constituent. Government representatives answer these queries during the question hour, and deputies can raise supplementary questions at that time. The use of the question hour has grown almost steadily; more than 20,000 such questions were posed during the 1983–1986 term of the Bundestag (Table II.1).

Another method of government oversight is the written question (*Grosse Anfragen* or *Kleine Anfragen*) submitted to the government, which requires a more formal written or oral reply. Several deputies must sign such requests, and 400 to 500 questions are submitted during an average Bundestag session. In addition to submitting questions to the government, a group of deputies can petition for a special debate on a contemporary policy problem (*Aktuelle Stunde*). These policy debates tend to be more genuine than those at the plenary sessions, perhaps because debate is not limited to a specific legislative proposal. Over the last decade, topics have varied from discussions of human rights, to NATO defense policies, to East Germany's restrictions on travel from the Federal Republic. Finally, the individual committees of the Bundestag may also conduct public information hearings or investigative meetings to shed light on policy issues within their area of specialization.

The opposition parties normally make greatest use of the question and oversight activities of the Bundestag, because these methods provide an opportunity to cross-examine government representatives and expose government errors. For instance, during the last few parliaments, about two-thirds of the inquiries during question hour were posed by members of the opposition parties. The use of these techniques has also increased dramatically since the entry of the Green party into the Bundestag.[16] The Greens presented about 70 percent of the written questions submitted in the last Bundestag session, even though they are only about 5 percent of the deputies. In order to emphasize their antiestablishment tendencies, the Greens do not hesitate to challenge the CDU-led government or the SPD opposition. Government ministers are summoned before the Bundestag to explain to a Green deputy, who is often dressed in jeans and baggy sweater, what the government is doing to halt environmental pollution, end the arms race, or promote social equality. The exchanges between Green deputies and government representatives often are quite animated, as the following example from a debate on domestic security measures illustrates:

> *Zimmermann (Interior Minister)*: We need to arrive at balanced conclusions when considering this subject. We have to be aware of the fact that the protection of individual rights may collide with the goal of maintaining public order. . . . [But] it is the security of the citizens that led us to discuss these issues, isn't it?
> (Applause from CDU/CSU and FDP)
> *Fischer (Greens)*: The contrary is true!
> *Zimmermann*: The citizen is not afraid of your bleak outlook that you, Herr Fischer, developed here unnecessarily! Citizens are not afraid of a new passport either. They are only afraid of you!
> *Fischer*: If somebody develops a bleak outlook then it is you!
> *Zimmermann*: But only for you. And I am proud of it!
> *Fischer*: At least you have something left to be proud of!
> *Zimmermann*: If you loved me, I would be afraid, Herr Fischer!
> *Fischer*: I love you, Herr Zimmermann, I love you!

Probably the greatest difference between the Bundestag and the U.S. Congress is in constituency service. Because of the structure of the electoral system (see Chapter IX), half of the West German deputies do not represent a specific geographic constituency. Moreover, neither the public nor the deputies stress constituency service as part of the legislator's role. In comparative terms, relatively few German voters know the name of their deputy or are likely to contact the deputy about a political problem. On the other side, the personal staff of individual deputies is modest, and the tradition of U.S. constituency branch-offices or British surgeries is underdeveloped in the Federal Republic. The Bundestag emphasizes political representation through party representation, rather than through the intercession of individual deputies.

When all these various functions are taken into account, the Bundestag wields considerable political power, especially for a legislature in a parliamentary system. Although it mainly reacts to government proposals rather than taking the legislative initiative, the Bundestag's review and amendment process often produces substantive changes in legislation. At the same time, in its oversight activities, the Bundestag displays an unusual parliamentary autonomy from the executive branch. The Bundestag is often described as a body that blends the independent policy role of the U.S. Congress with the debating function of the British House of Commons. The organization of the Bundestag—especially the political structure of party Fraktionen and institutional structure of committees—is a key factor in its independence. More than just organization is involved, however. The Basic Law intended to create an institution that possessed more autonomy than Weimar's parliament, which could serve as a check on the excesses of the government. The Bundestag has developed as it has because these objectives are identified as part of the institution.

The Bundesrat. The second chamber of Parliament, the *Bundesrat*, is a clear example of West Germany's federal system of government. Its forty-one members are appointed by the state governments to represent their interests in Bonn. Bundesrat seats are allocated to each state roughly proportionate to the state's population. Those Länder with over six million inhabitants each receive five seats: Northrhine-Westphalia, Bavaria, Lower Saxony, and Baden-Württemberg. The middle-size Länder have four seats each: Rhineland-Palatinate, Schleswig-Holstein, and Hesse. The smallest states, with less than two million residents are assigned three seats each: the Saar, Hamburg, and Bremen. Because a delegation represents its Land as a whole, the votes of each state delegation are cast in a block according to the instructions of the state government.

The Bundesrat is substantially smaller than the Bundestag and therefore lacks much of the formal organizational structure that accompanies larger legislative bodies. The Bundesrat normally schedules only about a dozen plenary sessions in a year, in comparison to roughly fifty plenary sessions for the average Bundestag. Most of the Bundesrat's legislative activity takes place in committees; an even higher proportion than in the Bundestag.

The state governments regularly appoint members of the state cabinet to serve jointly in the Bundesrat. This has led some observers to ask whether the Bundesrat should be considered a house of parliament or a permanent conference of minister presidents. In fact, the Bundesrat's role in popular representation and government oversight is fairly modest. At the same time, however, the Bundesrat plays a vital role in the federal system.

The Bundesrat is directly involved in the passage of federal legislation, though its legislative authority is secondary to the Bundestag. The federal government is required to submit all legislative proposals to the Bundesrat before forwarding them to the Bundestag. Bundesrat approval of legislation is required in policy areas where the Basic Law grants the states concurrent powers or where the states will administer federal regulations.

The political role of the Bundesrat was one of the most hotly contested issues in the drafting of the Basic Law. The Social Democrats favored a strong national government, while many conservative politicians preferred granting more power to the states. The status of the Bundesrat has changed over time, but this debate is still unresolved. Because the states administer most federal laws, Bundesrat approval conceivably could be required on nearly all legislation. Instead of claiming this possible, wide jurisdiction, the Bundesrat chose a narrow scope during the early years of the Federal Republic. The chamber focused on the administrative aspects of federal legislation. Civil servants from the state governments examined the technical language of proposals and their potential effect on the states.

Beginning in the 1960s, the Bundesrat broadened its definition of state-related policy. More and more often, too, the chamber's deliberations are guided by political considerations rather than administrative details. This was especially true for the period when the CDU/CSU controlled the Bundesrat, while the SPD-FDP coalition held a majority of the Bundestag (1969–1982). Only the constitutional limits on the Bundesrat's authority and agreement among West German policy makers avoided a debilitating deadlock between the Bundestag and Bundesrat. The Federal Constitutional Court restricted the Bundesrat's legislative ambitions in 1974 by ruling that Bundesrat approval was not required for bills which merely revised existing programs. Moreover, since 1982 both chambers of Parliament have been controlled by the same party coalition and so interparliamentary disagreements have decreased. Still, this expansion of the Bundesrat's involvement means that about two-thirds of legislative proposals now require Bundesrat approval.

Despite its secondary role to the Bundestag in most legislative functions, the Bundesrat is still a vital part of the West German political system. The formal representation of the states in the federal government provides an important opportunity for closer policy coordination between the Bund and Länder. Furthermore, the gradual nationalization of political issues has increased the role of the Bundesrat as a representative of the states at the national level. The Bundesrat serves as a national forum for state government officials and their points of views. When all of these activities are considered, the Bundesrat wields more political influence than most second chambers in other parliamentary systems, such as the French Senate or British House of Lords.

THE FEDERAL CHANCELLOR AND CABINET

The German tradition of executive power presented an unclear model for the authors of the Basic Law. Earlier political systems based on a strong executive—the Second Empire and Third Reich—were authoritarian regimes. The Weimar Republic divided executive authority between the president and chancellor, and this fragmentation of executive power contributed to the ineffectiveness of government and the ultimate collapse of democracy. As in many other cases, the ghosts of Weimar were more visible in the Parliamentary Council.

The Basic Law concentrates executive authority in the office of the federal chancellor (*Bundeskanzler*). Moreover, the incumbents of this office have dominated the political process and symbolized the federal government by the force of their personalities. The chancellor plays such a central role in the political system that some observers describe the West German system as a "chancellor democracy."

A parliamentary system implies a fusion of the executive and legislative branches of government, and this is generally true for the Federal Republic. After nomination by the federal president, the chancellor is elected by a majority of the Bundestag. The first chancellor, Konrad Adenauer, was elected by a single vote (his own!), but most chancellors can depend on a solid majority from their party or a coalition of parties. Chancellors usually retain their seats as Bundestag deputies. In addition, the chancellor usually is the national leader of his or her party, directing party strategy and heading up the party at elections. Thus the chancellor has substantial authority as the chief executive and leader of a majority in the Bundestag. Instead of the separation of powers that is central to the American political system, control of the legislative and of the executive branches generally go together.

The West German parliamentary system is unique, however, in the limits it places on the degree of legislative and executive fusion. One set of factors increases the autonomy of the legislature vis-à-vis the executive branch. For example, the Bundestag and Bundesrat possess an unusual ability to criticize government actions and revise government legislative proposals. The Bundesrat's independent power base as a representative of the state governments further strengthens the autonomy of the legislature. The chancellor also lacks the discretionary authority to dissolve the legislature and call for new elections, something that is normally found in parliamentary systems.

More noticeable are the provisions of the Basic Law that limit the legislature's control over the chancellor and his cabinet. Most parliamentary legislatures possess the authority to remove a chief executive elected by it through a procedure known as a "no-confidence vote." During the Weimar Republic, however, extremist parties of the right and left used this device to destabilize the democratic system by opposing incumbent chancellors. The Basic Law sought to prevent such nihilist alliances by changing this procedure of legislative control to a *constructive no-confidence vote (konstruktives Misstrauensvotum)*: In order for the Bundestag to remove a chancellor, it simultaneously must agree on a successor. This ensures a continuity in political leadership and an initial majority in support of a new chancellor. The constructive no-confidence vote means that a chancellor does not have to maintain a majority on all legislative proposals. It also makes removing an incumbent more difficult: Opponents cannot simply disagree with the government—a consensus must exist on an alternative. The constructive no-confidence vote has undoubtedly contributed to the political stability of the Federal Republic.

Parliament has attempted to pass the constructive no-confidence vote only twice in the history of the Federal Republic—and has succeeded only once. In 1972, the Christian Democrats directed an intense opposition to the government's new policies toward Eastern Europe, and several Bundestag deputies changed their party affiliation. With the Bundestag deadlocked, the opposition parties attempted to replace Chancellor Willy Brandt with the CDU party leader. In a tension-packed scene, the government barely won the secret vote. This scenario was played out again ten years later. In the early 1980s, the governing parties (SPD and FDP) disagreed on how to deal with the Federal Republic's worsening economic problems. These policy differences eventually drove a wedge between the two coalition partners and moved the economically conservative FDP closer to the CDU/CSU. In late 1982, the Christian Democrats finally enticed the FDP to break with the Socialists and form a new government with the CDU/CSU. A successful constructive no-confidence vote replaced Chancellor Helmut Schmidt with the CDU party leader, Helmut Kohl.

The West German system also contains a second type of no-confidence vote, which is used by the chancellor to mobilize legislative support in the Bundestag. The chancellor may attach a simple no-confidence provision to a government legislative proposal. If the Bundestag defeats this proposal, the chancellor may ask the federal president to dissolve the Parliament and call for new Bundestag elections. This no-confidence procedure is used infrequently, but it enables the chancellor either to test the government's voting support or to increase the incentive for the Bundestag to pass legislation crucial to the government. For instance, Helmut Schmidt's government successfully used the simple no-confidence vote in early 1982 to demonstrate the strength of the governing coalition to its skeptics; nevertheless, within six months his critics were proven correct.

In addition, incumbent governments have used the simple no-confidence motion to arrange early Bundestag elections. After the unsuccessful, CDU-sponsored constructive no-confidence vote in 1972, Willy Brandt used the simple no-confidence procedure to call for new elections that could provide a popular referendum on the government's foreign policy and supply his government with a sizeable majority in Parliament. After Helmut Kohl won the chancellorship through a constructive no-confidence vote in August of 1982, his government intentionally lost a simple no-confidence provision in order to allow the voters to express their support for the new government at the polls. The framers of the Basic Law did not intend to give the government discretionary power to dissolve Parliament, but the Constitutional Court accepted the no-confidence motion as a method of circumventing this limitation.

The chancellor is the head of the executive branch, but the Basic Law defines the "federal government" (*Regierung*) as the chancellor and the chancellor's cabinet. There were 17 federal departments at the start of Kohl's second term in 1987, each headed by a federal minister. Cabinet ministers are formally appointed, or dismissed, by the federal president on the recommendation of the chancellor; Bundestag approval is not necessary. The Basic Law grants the chancellor the power to decide on the number of cabinet ministers and their duties.

The functioning of the federal government follows three principles laid out in Article 65 of the Basic Law. First, the *chancellor principle* holds that the chancellor alone is responsible for the policies of the federal government. The Basic Law states that the formal policy guidelines issued by the chancellor (*Richtlinienkompetenz*) must be followed by the cabinet ministers; these are legally binding directives. Ministers are expected to suggest and implement specific policies consistent with the chancellor's broad guidelines. The chancellor is aided in these activities by the large staff of the Chancellor's Office (*Bundeskanzleramt*), which supervises the actions of the ministries and formulates the government's broad policy goals. Thus, in contrast to the British system of shared cabinet responsibility, the West German cabinet is formally subordinate to the chancellor in policy making.

The second principle of *ministerial autonomy* (*Ressortprinzip*) grants each minister the autonomy to conduct the internal workings of the department without cabinet intervention as long as these policies conform to the government's broad guidelines. Ministers are responsible for supervising the activities of their departments. They guide the department's policy planning and the preparation of legislative initiatives and oversee the administration of policy within their jurisdiction. These duties involve managing the relevant activities of the federal government in addition to monitoring the implementation and administration of federal laws by the state bureaucracies.

The third provision of Article 65 is the *cabinet principle.* When conflicts arise between departments over jurisdictional or budgetary disputes, the Basic Law calls for them to be resolved by the cabinet.

The actual working of the federal government tends to be more fluid than the formal procedures spelled out by the Basic Law.[17] There are, of course, political limitations on the formal powers of the chancellor. In a coalition government, the number and choice of ministries to be held by each party is a major issue in building the coalition. Similarly, intraparty considerations may necessitate certain cabinet assignments. Cabinet members also may display considerable policy independence despite the formal restrictions of the Basic Law. Ministers are usually appointed because they possess expertise or interest in a policy area. In practice, they often identify more with their roles as department heads than with their roles as agents of the chancellor. Ministers become spokespersons and advocates for their departments; their political success is judged by their representation of department interests.

The cabinet thus serves as a clearing house for the business of the federal government. Specific ministers present policy proposals originating in their departments in the hope of gaining government endorsement. In practice, the chancellor seldom relies on formal policy instructions to guide the actions of the government. The chancellor defines a government program that reflects the consensus of the cabinet and relies on negotiations and compromise within the cabinet to maintain this consensus.

The personal style of the chancellor has a large influence on how this process actually functions. The first chancellor, Konrad Adenauer (Table II.2), virtually dominated the other institutions of government by the force of his personality and the magnitude of his popular support. He was the mayor of Cologne during the Weimar Republic and had retired from politics after Hitler came to power. He rapidly rose to a position of prominence in postwar Germany as head of the Christian Democratic Union, chair of the Parliamentary Council that drafted the Basic Law, and a sort of father-figure to the nation. As a simple example of his influence, the tale is often told that Bonn was chosen as the capital of the Federal Republic because it was within easy commuting distance of Adenauer's home! Adenauer liberally interpreted the formal powers of the chancellorship

TABLE II.2 *Governments of the Federal Republic, 1949-1987*

Date formed	Source of change	Coalition partners	Chancellor
September 1949	Election	CDU/CSU, FDP, DP	Adenauer (CDU)
October 1953	Election	CDU/CSU, FDP, DP, G	Adenauer (CDU)
October 1957	Election	CDU/CSU, DP	Adenauer (CDU)
November 1961	Election	CDU/CSU, FDP	Adenauer (CDU)
October 1963	Chancellor retirement	CDU/CSU, FDP	Erhard (CDU)
October 1965	Election	CDU/CSU, FDP	Erhard (CDU)
December 1966	Coalition change	CDU/CSU, SPD	Kiesinger (CDU)
October 1969	Election	SPD, FDP	Brandt (SPD)
December 1972	Election	SPD, FDP	Brandt (SPD)
May 1974	Chancellor retirement	SPD, FDP	Schmidt (SPD)
December 1976	Election	SPD, FDP	Schmidt (SPD)
November 1980	Election	SPD, FDP	Schmidt (SPD)
October 1982	Constructive no-confidence vote	CDU/CSU, FDP	Kohl (CDU)
March 1983	Election	CDU/CSU, FDP	Kohl (CDU)
January 1987	Election	CDU/CSU, FDP	Kohl (CDU)

DP is the German party; G is the All-German Bloc/Federation of Expellees and Displaced Persons.

in his favor, and was not hesitant to exercise this authority. Moreover, his leadership of the Federal Republic as it rebuilt its economy and recovered its sovereignty endowed on him a heroic image for many citizens. It is not far off to say that the Federal Republic was created according to his blueprints.

Subsequent chancellors (Table II.2) have never matched Adenauer's influence. Neither Ludwig Erhard nor Kurt Kiesinger was a strong leader. Erhard's stature as chancellor was dwarfed by Adenauer's larger-than-life image, and he never commanded the same authority or respect within his party. Kiesinger was chancellor during the Grand Coalition, when political authority was divided with the vice chancellor, Willy Brandt.

Brandt brought a new sense of vision to the chancellor's office in 1969, opening an era of far-reaching domestic and foreign policy reforms. Brandt's most dramatic innovations came in foreign policy. He personally directed a new foreign policy (*Ostpolitik*) of reconciliation with the nations of Eastern Europe and the establishment of formal ties with East Germany. In 1971, he received the Nobel Peace prize, an achievement with special significance for a German political leader. Helmut Schmidt was another strong chancellor. He entered the government with the reputation of a man of action, someone who could deal with difficult problems. During his tenure in office Schmidt was a forceful figure and seldom hesitated to speak his mind; he was fond of describing himself as "The Chairman of the Board of Germany, Inc." Yet, even he was forced from office by a constructive no-confidence vote. The present chancellor, Helmut Kohl, is a capable and experienced politician, but he is neither a forceful leader (like Adenauer or Schmidt), nor a visionary (like Brandt). Kohl is often criticized for his inability to direct the actions of the government and continue the tradition of chancellor democracy.

FEDERAL PRESIDENT

During the Weimar Republic, executive authority was divided between two offices—the chancellor and the president. The office of president was intended to provide a symbol of national identity, an *Ersatzkaiser*, with relatively modest political influence. One of the greatest structural weaknesses of the Weimar constitution was the provision, in the infamous Article 48, for the transfer of political authority to the president when Parliament became deadlocked.

The Basic Law retains the office of federal president (*Bundespräs-*

ident), but transferred most executive authority to the chancellor, leaving the presidency as a largely ceremonial post. The president's official duties include such task as greeting visiting heads of state, attending official government functions, and visiting foreign nations.

The federal president is removed from the competition of electoral politics. In the Weimar Republic, direct election of the president inevitably transformed the position into a partisan office as rival candidates competed for popular support. Furthermore, because both the president and parliament were popularly elected, both claimed to represent the national interest, even when they expressed differing views. The president of the Federal Republic is selected by a Federal Convention (*Bundesversammlung*), composed of all Bundestag deputies and an equal number of representatives chosen by the state legislatures. The term of office is five years, and the incumbent can only be reelected once. The ethos of the office also downplays the partisan aspects of the position. Even though the federal president usually comes from the senior leaders of the largest party in the Bundestag, the officeholder is expected to remain above partisan politics. The present officeholder, Richard von Weizsäcker, for example, is the former CDU mayor of Berlin. He stepped down from his party positions on assuming office in 1984.

This reduction in the president's formal political role does not mean that the incumbent is entirely uninvolved in the political process. The Basic Law assigns several ceremonial political functions to the president, who appoints government and military officials, signs treaties and laws, and possesses the power of pardon. In these instances, though, the president is merely carrying out the will of the government, and these actions must be countersigned by the chancellor. The president also nominates a chancellor to the Bundestag and dissolves Parliament if the government loses a simple no-confidence vote; in both instances, however, the Basic Law restricts the president's ability to act independently. The emergency law reforms of 1968 identified the president as a mediator, who in times of national crisis can declare a state of emergency. In contrast to Weimar, however, political authority would then pass to the Parliament and not the president.

A potentially more significant source of presidential power arises from the constitutional ambiguity over whether the president *must* honor requests from the government or can refuse these requests.

The president may possess the constitutional right to veto legislation by refusing to sign it. At least a half dozen pieces of legislation have been involved in such controversies since the founding of the Federal Republic. Similarly, the president may be able to refuse the chancellor's recommendation for cabinet appointments or even a request to dissolve the Bundestag. In 1982, for instance, there was great public speculation about whether Chancellor Kohl's request for a dissolution of the Bundestag would be granted (it was). These constitutional questions have not been tested by past presidents, and thus the extent of these powers has not been resolved by the courts. Most analysts see these ambiguities as another safety valve built into the Basic Law's elaborate system of checks and balances.

The political significance of the federal president also comes from factors that go beyond the articles of the Basic Law. The first incumbent, Theodor Heuss, envisioned the office as serving an integrative function for the nation. The president is someone who can stand above politics, someone who can speak frankly and morally about current issues. As a liberal who had suffered under the Third Reich, he used his office to nurture the development of democracy and humanitarianism in postwar Germany. His popular appeal and willingness to deal with the sensitive issue of Germany's past helped create a climate in which meaningful political change could occur.

Heuss's performance during two terms as president (1949-1959) set the standards by which the position is still judged. Most later presidents have tried to meet these standards.[18] Gustav Heinemann (1969-1974), for instance, saw himself as a people's president. He worked actively to bring public attention to the poor, the disadvantaged, and others who lived in the shadow of an affluent West German society. Walter Scheel (1974-1979) and Karl Carstens (1979-1984) were popular and highly respected presidents. Richard von Weizsäcker, who assumed office in 1984, also represents the best traditions of the office. Von Weizsäcker is a highly regarded political figure, much more than just a politician. His election to office was supported both by the governing parties and by the opposition Social Democrats. During his tenure in office, he has demonstrated his leadership ability and his broader view of the president's political role. For example, on the fortieth anniversary of the end of World War II in Europe, von Weizsäcker implored Germans to admit their complicity in the actions of the Third Reich as a necessary step in overcoming this legacy. This was a courageous act for someone from an aristocratic background whose father worked in Hitler's foreign service. Von Weizsäcker's statements were widely applauded inside and outside of the Federal Republic.

It is difficult to summarize the importance of the federal president in simple terms because of the ambiguity of the office. The formal powers of the presidency are limited, and the founders of the Federal Republic consciously sought to isolate the president from everyday political issues. At the same time, however, the potential application of the president's latent powers makes the office an important safety valve in case of extreme political crisis. Moreover, the informal role of the president is often underestimated. An active, dynamic president, such as Theodor Heuss, can exert a major influence in shaping the political climate of the nation and extending the nation's vision beyond the concerns of everyday politics.

THE JUDICIAL SYSTEM

A central concept in German legal theory is the *Rechtsstaat,* a government founded on law whereby government action could be restrained and the equality of the citizens guaranteed.[19] Past liberal reformers considered such a system of legal constraints on the Kaiser as the key to political modernization and reform. The rule of law was the individual's protector against the authoritarian state (*Obrigkeitsstaat*).

The events of the Third Reich shattered this confidence in the Rechtsstaat. The legal protections of the Weimar Republic did little to restrain Hitler's accession to office and his abuses of power. Moreover, the judiciary was a somewhat willing accomplice in many of these actions. The law was supreme and the courts could not overturn legal statutes passed by the government, even if that government was the illegal Nazi state; therefore, the court held even activities that violated basic human rights to be legal if they did not violate government statutes. This narrow view of law focused on procedures and ignored the content of government action.

Judicial reform was therefore a high priority for the authors of the Basic Law. The West German courts vary from the federal structure of the rest of government. The judiciary is a unitary system with six major branches (Figure II.3).[20] Federal law specifies the basic structure of the judicial system, but state law regulates the administration of most courts. States manage the lower levels of the court system, and only the highest appellate courts function at

FIGURE II.3 *Organization of the Courts*

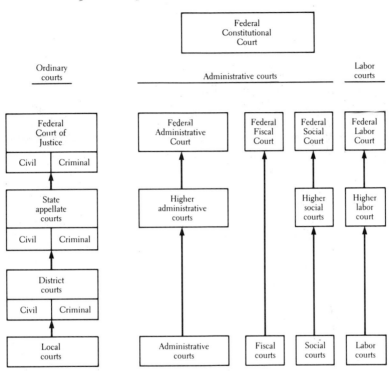

the federal level. The federal guidelines and the federal appeal courts ensure that the laws are applied uniformly throughout the nation, whereas the states' administration of the courts ensures their independence from the national government.

The largest branch of the judiciary is the system of ordinary courts, which are responsible for both civil and criminal cases. Over 500 local courts (*Amtsgerichte*) hear cases dealing with minor criminal offenses and small civil suits, as well as perform many routine legal functions, such as probating wills and land registry. At the next level of the judiciary are the nearly 100 district or state courts (*Landgerichte*), which are split into two sections, one dealing with major civil cases, the other with criminal cases. Each section is further divided into panels of judges who specialize in different types of cases. The district courts function both as courts of appeal for cases originally tried in the local courts and as a court of first instance for major civil or criminal cases. The twenty state appellate courts (*Oberlandesgerichte*) review points of law raised on appeal from the lower courts. The Federal Court of Justice (*Bundesgerichtshof*), can review the procedural and legal aspects of cases referred from the lower courts.

Other branches of the judicial system deal with cases in specialized areas. The administrative court hears complaints against government agencies, such as a citizen objecting to a planned highway or government licensing activities. For instance, much of the legal struggle over the location and safety standards for nuclear power stations has occurred in the administrative courts. The social courts handle matters of social insurance, unemployment compensation, medical insurance, and similar programs. Labor courts judge labor-management disputes and protect worker rights. The structure of labor-management relations in the Federal Republic is heavily dependent on the authoritative decisions handed down by the labor court (see Chapter VIII). The fiscal court decides on disputes over personal income taxes and other fiscal matters. Like the rest of the judicial system, these specialized courts are vertically integrated into separate systems of state courts, each topped by a federal appeals court.

The major structural innovation of the judicial system is the independent Constitutional Court.[21] The Western Allies insisted that the Basic Law provide for independent judicial review of legislation. This provision marked a break from German legal tradition in that it places one law, the Basic Law, above all others; it also implies limits on the decision making power of the Parliament and the power of judicial interpretation of lower court judges. The Constitutional Court has the authority to review the constitutionality of legislation, mediate disputes between levels of government, and protect the constitution and the democratic order. The court is divided into two senates; each has its own panel of eight judges, its own administrative staff, and its own chief justice. The first senate is responsible for the protection of civil liberties and judicial review of legislation. The second senate deals primarily with constitutional disputes between government agencies and the regulation of the political process.

In contrast to the U.S. Supreme Court, the West German Constitutional Court does not act as court of last appeals; this is the function of the Federal Court of Justice. The Basic Law limits the Constitutional Court's jurisdiction solely to constitutional issues; it can only hear cases involving questions of constitutional significance. By the mid-1980s, over half the articles in the Basic Law had been subjected to judicial review, and hundreds of cases had tested the constitutionality of federal and state legislation. Early court decisions, such as the 1951 Southwest case and the 1961 Federal Television case, defined the distribution of power between the Bund and state governments. Other cases have involved the court in major legislative debates over such issues as Ostpolitik, abortion, and anti-terrorist policies. The court has also displayed a willingness to involve itself in the "political" conflicts that the U.S. Supreme Court evades, such as reviewing party campaign financing legislation. The court is thus both a vital mechanism for conflict resolution within the West German system and an active protector of the system.

One of the most noticeable changes in the judicial system of the Federal Republic concerns the accepted uses of judicial action. Members of the court reject the neutral judicial role of German legal tradition.[22] In contrast to the judges of Weimar Republic, the justices view themselves as defenders of democracy and protectors of the basic human rights guaranteed by the Basic Law. Because of the importance of the Constitutional Court, the Bundestag and Bundesrat each selected half its members. Constitutional Court justices can be removed from office only for abuse of their position.

The West German judicial system is based on principles of Roman law that are fundamentally different from those of the Anglo-American system of justice.[23] Rather than relying on precedents from prior cases, the courts use an extensive system of legal codes. The codes define legal principles in the abstract, and the courts measure specific cases against these standards. Because the legal codes attempt to anticipate all the issues that might confront a court, they are quite complex and lengthy. In short, the system is based on a rationalist philosophy that justice can be served by following the letter of the law.

The legal system also emphasizes society's rights and the efficient administration of justice in comparison to the individual rights of a defendant. For example, the system gives equal weight to the evidence of the prosecution and the defense. Similarly, the rules of evidence are not as restrictive as in American courts. A unanimous decision is not even required in deciding some cases; a majority is sufficient for many types.

These basic legal principles affect the operation of the judicial process in several ways. Reliance on complex legal codes means that judges must have extensive legal training. They are not simply selected from the ranks of practicing lawyers; the two careers are distinct. Law students must pass a state examination at the end of their university training, which is followed by several years of applied training in various parts of the legal system. This apprenticeship period is followed by a second state examination to qualify the individual to practice law; successful candidates then decide whether they want to be lawyers or enter the judiciary. A candidate for the judiciary faces several more years of training and examination before entering the profession.

The emphasis on judicial expertise also means that less reliance is placed in decision making by lay jurors as is done in Britain and the United States. In the local courts, for example, most cases are decided by a single judge. The district courts are headed by a panel of three judges assisted by several "lay judges" chosen from among the local citizens. In the higher courts, lay judges are not even used. Furthermore, the judge (or panel of judges) normally votes along with the lay judges in deciding a case. Naturally, the judge's opinion can easily sway the votes of the lay judges. Justice is to be rational, fair, and expeditious; presumably this goal requires the expertise that only judges possess.

Because the West German judicial system aims to uncover the truth within a complex web of legal codes, the judge pursues an activist role in the court. Cross examining witnesses, determining what is acceptable as evidence, and generally directing the course of the trial are some of a judge's courtroom duties.

By Anglo-American standards, the inquisitorial system of West German justice might seem harsh, but it is a system shared by most other Western European democracies. Furthermore, the traditional definition of the Rechtsstaat is now tempered by a greater concern for the content of the law and an awareness of a higher standard of justice. The transformation of the judicial system has been one of the great successes of new political system of the Federal Republic.

A SYSTEM OF CHECKS AND BALANCES

The structure of the West German political system is undeniably complex, and simple comparisons to other parliamentary systems are difficult to make. There is, however, a logic to this complexity. Because of the Weimar experience, the Basic Law created a political system based on extensive checks and balances. These guidelines sought to distribute political power among the institutions of government and to create external limits on the power of each institution. The Basic Law grants each branch of government considerable authority to exercise its prescribed functions, but also provides checks on this authority and limits the ability of any one branch to dominate the entire government. This principle is the key to understanding the West German political system.

When one looks, for example, at the details of the federal system of government, the pattern of checks and balances is clearly evident. The Weimar system enabled Hitler to control the nation by controlling the national government. The Basic Law strengthens the power of the states as a check on the power of the federal government. The states' control of the police, the courts, and the administration of law enables the Länder to resist attempts at coercion by the federal government. The autonomy of the state governments and the legislative importance of the Bundesrat also create competing bases of political support. One single national election cannot yield total control of the political process to the victor.

The West German federal government deviates also from the normal pattern of parliamentary democracy. Both the legislative and executive branches possess extensive powers in their areas of primary responsibility. The *legislative* independence and oversight activities of the Bundestag and Bundesrat clearly exceed those of the British Parliament or French National Assembly. A similar concentration of *executive* authority is granted to the chancellor. What were presidential powers under the Weimar Republic were transferred to the chancellor. Moreover, the Basic Law makes the chancellor formally responsible for government policy. The chancellor is thus much more than the "first among equals" in the cabinet, as is normal in a parliamentary system. The West German chancellor is stronger than the prime minister in most other European parliamentary systems.

By creating two strong political institutions—Parliament and the chancellor—the Basic Law balances the political authority of the legislative and executive branches. At the same time, it limits the ability of one institution to dominate the other. The Bundestag lacks the normal parliamentary power to remove the executive from office through a simple no-confidence vote; the innovation of the constructive no-confidence vote partially insulates the executive from legislative dominance. Conversely, the chancellor lacks the authority to dissolve the Parliament at the government's discretion,

another power normally associated with parliamentary governments. Rather than a fusion of legislative and executive branches,
the political system of the Federal Republic emphasizes a greater
separation of powers (although the separation is not as thorough as
in the United States). The West German model of legislative and
executive relations lies somewhere between the British parliamentary system and the U.S. presidential system. The British prime
minister has less authority within the government than the West
German chancellor, but the British executive wields greater influence over the House of Commons. Alternatively, the West
German chancellor has less autonomy than a U.S. president, but the
chancellor generally can depend on a supportive majority within
the parliament.

The introduction of judicial review is another innovative feature
of the Basic Law. Traditionally the legislative supremacy of the
German parliament could not be challenged by the courts. The
judiciary became subservient to the leaders of the Third Reich. The
Basic Law created a higher standard of law by which the actions of
government should be judged. The Constitutional Court has powers of judicial review that are broader than those of the U.S. Supreme
Court, and this power is a strong check against government excess.

Other constitutional provisions seek to curb the partisan extremism that handicapped Weimar democracy (see Chapter IX). For
instance, parties must win at least 5 percent of the votes to share in
the proportional distribution of legislative seats; this makes it difficult for small extremist parties to win Bundestag representation. At
the same time, parties must also abide by the democratic principles
of the Basic Law. Under these provisions, the Constitutional Court
banned a neo-Nazi party in 1952 and the Communist party (KPD)
in 1956.

Finally, the Basic Law goes to unusual lengths to protect the
rights of individual citizens. The list of basic rights enumerated in
the first seventeen articles is even more extensive than the American
Bill of Rights. In addition, the Basic Law is one of the few constitu-
tions to state explicitly that all citizens have the right to resist any
person seeking to abolish the constitutional order. Moreover, these
protections of individual liberties are inviolable, that is, they cannot
be limited by constitutional amendment. The Federal Republic was
intended to be a Rechtsstaat, where citizens could depend on the
protection of law.

The Basic Law is thus an exceptional example of political

engineering—the construction of a political system to achieve specific goals. The authors of the Basic Law designed a parliamentary democracy that would involve the public, encourage responsibility among political elites, disperse political power, and limit the possibility that extremists might cripple the state or illegally grasp political power.

TEMPORARY BECOMES PERMANENT

The Basic Law was intended to create a political system that could temporarily serve the Federal Republic until both halves of Germany were reunited; this intention was stated in the preamble: "To give a new order to political life for a transitional period." The final article of the Basic Law looks forward to the eventual reunification of Germany under a new political system: "This Basic Law shall cease to be in force on the day on which a constitution adopted by a free decision of the German people comes into force." In spite of such expressions, this document today looks more permanent than temporary.

The Basic Law has, of course, been subject to major amendments. Two major controversies stand above the rest. In 1956, the Basic Law was revised to enable West Germany to rebuild its armed forces as part of the Western military alliance. Twelve years later, the "emergency powers" provisions provided a mechanism for the government to assume extraordinary powers during periods of national emergency.[24] Both constitutional changes caused intense public criticism and demonstrations against the government's action. Critics attacked the armed forces amendment for allowing German rearmament so soon after the war. Those who saw parallels to the infamous Article 48 of the Weimar constitution challenged the emergency powers amendments. A substantial number of other minor constitutional changes were implemented during the fifth Bundestag (1965–1969), when the Grand Coalition between the CDU/CSU and SPD provided the two-thirds parliamentary majority necessary for consitutional amendments.

In recent years, some members of the antiestablishment Green party have revived the topic of constitutional reform and advocated major changes in the political system, such as national referendums. On the whole, however, both the public and the political elites accept the Basic Law and the structure of parliamentary government it provides.

The more common source of constitutional change is judicial

review by the Constitutional Court. The entire question of federal-state relations is an ongoing controversy, requiring periodic clarifications by the Constitutional Court. The courts also periodically review and revise the roles of government institutions, political parties, and other political actors. Largely, however, the Court's decisions are not constitutional changes; rather, they represent the clarification and acceptance of the Basic Law as the measure of politics.

The Basic Law and the political system of the Federal Republic have now outgrown their temporary status. The political institutions that were meant to last a few years have functioned effectively for forty years. Although the framers of the Basic Law may have viewed their product as a transitional government, they also invested great care in the crafting of the political system. Although it was a system created to avoid the failures of the past, it has served the present with a record of stable and efficient government that few other nations can match.

NOTES

1. Alfred Grosser, *Germany in Our Time* (New York: Praeger, 1970), chaps. 1-2.

2. The government of the Third Reich required banks and insurance companies to invest all new monies in government bonds to finance the war. By 1945, the government debt amounted to 387 billion Reichmarks, or 95 percent of the total national wealth. Thus practically all savings were lost with the collapse of the Reich government. See Hajo Holborn, *A History of Modern Germany* (New York: Knopf, 1969), p. 757.

3. Karl Hardach, *The Political Economy of Germany in the Twentieth Century* (Berkeley: University of California Press, 1980); Eric Owen Smith, *The West German Economy* (London: Croom Helm, 1983); Werner Kaltefleiter, *Wirtschaft und Politik in Deutschland* (Cologne: Westdeutscher Verlag, 1968).

4. James Tent, *Mission on the Rhine: Reeducation and Denazification in American-Occupied Germany* (Princeton: Princeton University Press, 1983).

5. Grosser, *Germany in Our Time*, p. 66.

6. Kaltefleiter, *Wirtschaft und Politik in Deutschland,* p. 103.

7. See Peter Merkl's definitive account of these events, *The Origin of the West German Republic* (New York: Oxford University Press, 1963).

8. Merkl, *The Origins of the West Germaan Republic,* p. 178.

9. In 1952, three smaller states consolidated to form the land of Baden-Würtemberg, and the annexation of the Saarland in 1957 created the tenth Land.

10. Bavaria is the only Land with a bicameral legislature; one house is popularly elected and the second (the *Senat*) is composed of representatives of major social and economic groups.

11. Philip Blair, *Federalism and Judicial Review in West Germany* (Oxford: Oxford University Press, 1981), chap. 8.

12. Ursula Hoffmann, Lange, Helga Neumann, and Bärbel Steinkemper, *Konsens und Konflikt zwischen Führungsgruppen in der Bundesrepublik Deutschland* (Frankfurt: Peter Lang, 1980); Rudolf Wildenmann et al., *Führungsschicht in der Bundesrepublik Deutschland* (Mannheim: Lehrstuhl für politische Wissenschaft, 1982).

13. A minimum of 5 percent of the deputies, presently 26 members, is necessary to form a Fraktion. This requirement is especially important for small parties, which need to surpass the threshold in order to be represented in legislative committees and the formal structure of the Bundestag. In fact, very few deputies have been elected without the party ties that lead to Fraktion membership.

14. Winfried Steffani, "Parties, Parliamentary Groups and Committees in the German Bundestag," in *The Congress and the Bundestag*, ed. Robert Livingston and Uwe Thayson (Boulder: Westview Press, 1988).

15. Emil Huebner, *Die Beziehungen zwischen Bundestag und Bundesregierung im Selbstverständnis der Abgeordneten des V. Deutschen Bundestages* (Munich: Vogel, 1980).

16. E. Gene Frankland, "The Role of the Greens in West German Parliamentary Politics, 1980-1987," *Review of Politics* 50 (Winter 1988): 99-122.

17. Renate Mayntz and Fritz Scharpf, *Policy-Making in the German Federal Bureaucracy* (Amsterdam: Elsevier, 1975); also see chapter X.

18. When narrow partisan considerations have played a large role in the selection of president the results have lessened the significance of the office. The clearest example is Heinrich Lübke (1959-69), who combined a low regard for the status of the office with a clouded political past.

19. Donald Kommers, *Judicial Politics in West Germany* (Beverly Hills: Sage Publications, 1975), chapter 2.

20. The patent courts might be considered a seventh branch, although the Federal Court of Justice acts as the appellate court in these matters.

21. Kommers, *Judicial Politics in West Germany*, Chapter 3; Donald Kommers, *Constitutional Jurisprudence of the Federal Republic* (Durham: Duke University Press, 1989). Each of the states except Schleswig-Holstein, also has a state constitutional court.

22. Kommers, *Judicial Politics in West Germany*, chapter 5.

23. Henry Ehrmann, ed., *Comparative Legal Cultures* (Englewood Cliffs, N.J.: Prentice-Hall, 1976); Alan Katz, ed., *Legal Traditions and Systems* (New York: Greenwood Press, 1986).

24. The passage of the emergency powers legislation also removed the last Allied restriction on West German sovereignty. The Western Allies renounced their claimed right to take over the West German government in the event of a national or international emergency.

CHAPTER III

The Transformation of Society

WHEN THE NEW POLITICAL SYSTEM began to function in 1949, the leaders of the Federal Republic could not be content with the status quo. The economy was still critically weak, and unemployment remained high. The Federal Republic was a client state of the Western powers, not an independent member of the international community. Furthermore, the Basic Law only spelled out the structure of government; the development of an active democracy required much more than the formal institutions of government.

From this starting point, the Federal Republic achieved a remarkable record of success. The economy rebounded from the destruction of war and made tremendous advances. This spectacular growth came to be known as the Economic Miracle (*Wirtschaftswunder*). Along with extraordinary changes in individual economic conditions came parallel changes in the social structure, life styles, and social relations. The social context of politics was fundamentally altered as educational opportunities grew, access to information expanded, and individual horizons broadened. Virtually no one could have imagined at the end of World War II the social and political transformation that Germany would rapidly experience.

The first twenty years of the Federal Republic can be described as the *growth decades*. Social, economic, and political developments progressed rapidly. Not only was the rate of change exceptional, but socioeconomic trends reinforced one another, producing a cumulative pressure on the social and political systems. The Federal Republic developed characteristics that are generally identified with the concept of a *postindustrial* society.[1]

This chapter chronicles the accomplishments of the growth decades, looking at both the affluence created by the Economic Miracle and the broader social changes that transformed West German society. In addition, we consider how the economic slowdown of the past decade has moderated these trends and affected contemporary West German politics.

THE GROWTH DECADES

In 1949, the most immediate challenge for Adenauer's government was to resolve the pressing economic problems facing the nation. Despite the progress made up until 1949, the economy was still in dire straits. High unemployment and low wages meant severe economic hardships for many families; housing and general living conditions were barely sufficient for the nation's needs. Public opinion surveys documented the public's broad discontent with their condition. These sentiments created widespread concern among Allied and German political leaders that the Federal Republic might follow the path of the Weimar Republic—democracy collapsing under the weight of economic problems.

West Germany achieved phenomenal success in meeting this economic challenge.[2] Relying on Erhard's Social Market Economy, the country experienced a period of sustained and unprecedented economic growth. The Gross National Product (GNP) increased almost every year from 1947 until 1972 (Figure III.1). The GNP increased by 67 percent between 1947 and 1952; by 1950 its value reached the prewar level of 1936. In other words, the smaller West German state had recovered from the destruction of war within a few short years and matched the productivity of the larger German Reich at its prewar zenith. In the 1950s, the average annual growth rate for the GNP (6.2 percent) was considerably above those of most other Western industrial nations. In the 1960s the grow rate slowed, largely because of a slight recession in 1966 to 1968. This slowdown was only temporary, however, and the overall growth rate for the 1960s averaged about 4 percent—still high by Western standards.

Most other measures of economic performance showed similar improvement. By the early 1950s, personal incomes reached the prewar level, and growth had just begun. Over the next two decades, per capita wealth nearly tripled, average hourly industrial wages increased nearly fivefold, and average incomes grew nearly sevenfold. Goods that once had been luxuries for the upper classes became widely affordable. The most vivid example involves the Germans' love affair with the automobile. In 1950, very few average Germans could afford their own car; by the early 1970s, most fami-

FIGURE III.1 *The Growth of the Gross National Product, 1950–1985*

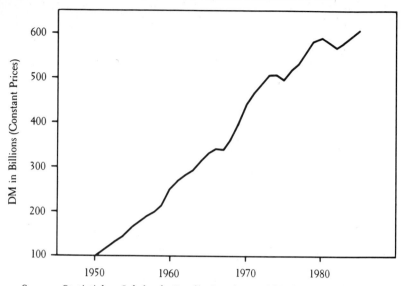

Source: *Statistiches Jahrbuch für die Bundesrepublik Deutschland,* various years.

lies had a car, and it was not unusual to see Mercedes sedans parked throughout working-class neighborhoods. By almost all economic measures, the West German public at the beginning of the 1970s was several times more affluent than at any time in prewar history. This economic success was labeled the Economic Miracle, and politicians were quick to strengthen the legitimacy of the Federal Republic by crediting this affluence to the working of the democratic political process.

A number of circumstances combined to create the Economic Miracle. To begin, the wartime damage to West German industry was not as extensive as is often assumed. Although transportation and housing damage was extensive, less than a quarter of Germany's industrial capacity was actually destroyed. Thus, there were significant resources to be developed under the social market program.[3] Many Germans favored greater government involvement in the economy, but the social market strategy decreased the government's role. The government removed price controls and limited the state's role in economic planning. Tax reductions, investment incentives, and the regulation of credit further encouraged economic growth. The economic incentives of the social market program stimulated competition, productivity, and capital investment. Just when a high production capacity developed within West German industry, the Korean war boom increased world demand for German exports and ensured economic recovery.

Several other factors contributed to the Economic Miracle. Foreign aid was a catalyst to economic recovery, first in the form of aid to occupied Germany and later through Marshall Plan aid (officially known as the European Recovery Program). Although the total direct aid to West Germany was relatively modest, it provided an important source of foreign revenue to finance reconstruction and purchase necessary imports. Moreover, the psychological impact of the Marshall Plan in eroding war-related animosity was as significant as its economic consequences. The contributions of the German populace were equally essential to the recovery. The traditional German work ethic was strengthened by the deprivations of war. Millions toiled for long hours under difficult conditions to rebuild the nation, and the productivity of West German workers exceeded most other Western economies. The influx of refugees from the east expanded the skills and size of the labor force. In addition, the work force accepted a growth in living standards slower than the expansion of industrial production. Moderate wage demands by the unions left industry with sufficient resources to invest in further economic growth. In the end, the Germans did not see the economic recovery as a miracle, but the result of a lot of hard work.

The social transformation of the growth decades was not, however, limited only to increasing affluence. Economic growth led to a massive migration from the countryside into the cities. In 1950, almost one-third of the population lived in rural areas; by 1985, this figure stood at 6 percent. West Germany is now a heavily urbanized society, with a population density ten times that of the United States. The continuing decline of rural populations and the growth of metropolitan centers stimulated further changes in life expectations and life styles. Urbanization means a growing separation of the home and the workplace, a greater diversity of occupations and interests, an expanded range of career opportunities, and more geographic and social mobility. Many farmers or their offspring moved to the cities and sought employment as industrial workers. In turn, many children from working-class families eventually entered middle-class occupations.

With these trends came changes in social organization and in-teraction. Communal forms of organization are replaced by voluntary associations, which are less institutionalized and more spontaneous in their organization. These changes reflect the fact that communities are less bounded, that individuals are involved in increasingly complex and competing social networks that divide their loyalties, and that interpersonal and institutional loyalties are becoming more fluid.

Advanced industrial societies also require a more educated and technically sophisticated public, and postwar affluence provided the funding for an expanded educational system (see Chapter V). The average educational level of the population steadily improved. In postwar Germany, citizens with only primary schooling outnum-bered those with a secondary school diploma (*Mittlere Reife*) by approximately five to one; today, the better-educated group is nearly two times larger than the lesser educated. These trends are even more pronounced at higher educational levels. Between 1950 and 1975, university enrollments increased by over 500 percent.

Other social trends reinforced this general developmental pattern. The growth of the electronic media, especially television, has been exceptional, providing the public with a volume and richness of political information unknown in prior German regimes. Affluence financed the expansion of social programs that provided a new-found sense of social security to the German people. The interna-tional scene changed substantially, too. European integration, for example, opened national borders and developed a more cosmopoli-tan view of the world.

The social transformation of the growth decades is thus more than just the politics of affluence. Affluence, life-style changes, alterations in the social structure, increases in educational levels, and new international conditions transformed the social bases of West German politics. Certainly, these trends are not restricted to the Federal Republic; similar changes are occurring in other West-ern industrial democracies. In Germany, however, these trends were more pronounced, because society began at a lower level of devel-opment due to postwar destruction and dislocation and the rates of change often exceeded those in other Western nations. In addition, the influence of these various factors tended to overlap, thereby magnifying their impact. The result has been a transformation in the social bases of West German politics.

CHANGING SOCIAL FORCES

German society traditionally has been marked by sharp social cleavages that structured political conflict. The nation often was torn by deep social divisions: urban interests against the landed estates, the working class against the industrialists, Protestants against Catholics. Policy makers in the Federal Republic have contended with the same cleavages. Yet the growth decades led to the restructuring, diversification, and decline of these social conflicts.

SOCIAL CLASS

The greatest social changes of the growth decades were in the class structure of German society. Social class is one of the major bases of cultural differentiation in German society. The German economy grew to a position of international prominence on the strength of its industrial sector. The steel industries and manufacturing plants lining the banks of the Ruhr were the heart of the German economy. The names of industrialists like Krupp and Thyssen were synonymous with the development of the economy and German nation. At the same time, the employees in these industries were the basis of a large working-class movement that competed against the conservative forces of business and the middle class. Ever since the Industrial Revolution spread to Germany, this division, between the proletariat and the bourgeoisie, was the line along which most political conflict flared up. This was certainly the area of conflict during the formative years of the West German republic. A dichotomous view of society was prevalent: "They're up there, we're down here." Social relations circulated within class strata and not across. The working class had mainly socialist economic beliefs, a conservative philosophy on social issues, and a limited world view. In contrast, the middle class milieu encouraged more conventional economic and social beliefs.

Class distinctions still exist between the traditional unionized working class and the old middle class (business owners and the self-employed), but the growth decades and the development of an advanced industrial economy attenuated these divisions. Spreading affluence narrowed the differences in life style among social classes. When workers spend Saturdays washing their Mercedes and Sundays driving in the countryside, it is difficult to think of politics in rigorous Marxian terms. Increased social mobility and a more diversified economy transformed the dichotomized image of social class into a more differentiated view.

The importance of class differences also lessened as a result of the changing composition of the labor force. The size of the traditional class strata generally decreased because of the pattern of postwar economic growth. The basis of the economy shifted from industry and agriculture to a rapidly expanding service sector. The proportion of workers in manual occupations, for example, dropped from 51 percent in 1950 to barely 40 percent in 1985. Over this same period, the percentage of the work force employed in the agricultural sector shrank from 22 to 6. Economic growth redirected employment to the service and technology sectors, and government employment nearly doubled over the past three decades. The largest occupational category now is composed of salaried white-collar workers (*Angestellte*) and civil servants (*Beamte*). This group is described as the new middle class, because it represents a new social stratum not tied to the traditional class interests of farmers, workers, or business owners.[4] By the mid-1980s the Federal Republic had neared Daniel Bell's threshold for a postindustrial economy, with the new middle class accounting for nearly half the labor force.[5]

The growth of the new middle class marks an important change in the social and political infrastructure of West Germany. This occupation group lacks a clear position in the traditional class conflicts between the working class and the old middle class of business owners and self-employed. The separation of management from capital ownership, the expansion of the service sector, and the growth of government (or nonprofit) employment creates a social stratum that does not conform to Marxian class analysis. Members of the new middle class do not share the political values of either the working class or the old middle class, adhering instead to a mix of economic centrism and social liberalism. The growth of the new middle class and its mixed political identity have thus worked to erode the importance of political issues based on traditional class divisions. The new middle class, for example, has provided a social base for the noneconomic political lobbies that have recently emerged on the German political stage; new middle class voters have also been a major source of change in West German electoral politics.

Significant differences remain in the socioeconomic condition of various class groups, especially in income inequality, access to higher education, and ownership of capital. On the whole, however, social status lines are blurring and traditional class-based politics is decreasing in importance in the Federal Republic.

RELIGION

Religion has served as another social dividing line in German politics ever since the Reformation. The *Kulturkampf* of the Second Empire and the existence of a separate political party for Catholics during the empire and Weimar Republic attested to the intensity of religious differences. Religious conflicts carried over to the Federal Republic, although the situation changed significantly. Catholics, who had been a minority in prewar Germany, found themselves at parity with Protestants. The postwar division of Germany included a balance of Catholic and Protestant regions within the Federal Republic, while East Germany became a predominately Protestant state. The Christian Democratic Union also changed the traditional religious alignment that pitted Catholics against Protestants by uniting both denominations in one religious party. The historical conflicts between Protestants and Catholics were largely replaced by differences between religious and nonreligious people.

The churches played a very large role in the postwar reconstruction of German society. In the social and moral vacuum at the end of the war, many individuals turned to the churches for guidance and inspiration. The churches were one of the few social institutions left intact, and church leaders rallied to the nation's needs. The Catholic archbishops of Cologne and Munich wielded almost as much influence as any elected leader, and the churches were major forces in determining the social and political norms of the new republic.

It is ironic, therefore, that the churches' contribution to the rebuilding of West German society also created the conditions that eroded some of their own influence. The modernizing forces of the growth decades produced a secularizing trend that reduced the public's participation in the churches. The number religious citizens, and therefore the social base of the churches, has steadily declined during the past thirty years. In 1953, about two-fifths of West German adults attended church on a weekly basis; by the 1980s, this proportion had decreased by nearly half. Other indicators of religious involvement, such as the number of church weddings and religious vocations, similarly slid downward; interfaith marriages increased. A significant number of people—about one-third of the public—still remain integrated into a religious network and are influenced by the strict moral and cultural norms of the churches. The general secularization of West German society, however, has steadily reduced the overall role of religion in politics.[6]

REGIONALISM

Regionalism has been another source of social and political division in German history. Cultural and historical differences separating the German regions coincided with economic and religious cleavages, creating distinct regional cultures. A substantial degree of regional government existed under the Second Empire and Weimar Republic, and even the "coordinating" efforts of the Third Reich were unable to homogenize the national character.

Several factors have worked to moderate regional differences within the Federal Republic, however. The boundaries of the ten West German Länder were arbitrary constructions of the occupation forces, designed to facilitate their administration of postwar Germany. Several small regions were combined into a fewer number of more manageable states, and the borders followed the lines of Allied military organization, rather than historical, cultural, or economic patterns. A few states maintain their historical identity as prewar regions, but in most instances the states have little historical continuity. In addition, the influx of millions of postwar expellees and refugees from the East attenuated regional differences within the population. Up to one-fifth of the Federal Republic's postwar population came from Eastern Europe, and their pattern of settlement often did not match the dominant social tendencies in a region. For example, Protestant farmers settled in heavily Catholic Bavaria, and many members of the Prussian middle class resettled in the Rhineland.

Despite their uncertain origins, the various states still display significant cultural and economic variation (Table III.1). Hamburg and Bremen, for example, maintain their historical continuity as former Hansa city-states. Their largely Protestant and urban composition produces sizable SPD pluralities in most elections. On the other hand, the two other northern states of Schleswig-Holstein and Lower Saxony are rural and heavily Protestant areas, sharing a common Prussian heritage. These Lander normally return Christian Democratic pluralities.

Northrhine-Westphalia constitutes the largest state, both in its population and economic importance. This Land was artificially constructed after the war and divides its cultural traditions between

TABLE III.1 *Characteristics of the West German States*

State	1987 Population (in thousands)	Area (square kilometers)	Population Density (per square kilometers)	Economic Conditions		Social Conditions			
				1986 GNP (million DM)	GNP per capita (DM)	Farm Employment (%)	Catholic (%)	Foreign Resident (%)	Governing Parties (June 1988)
Schleswig-Holstein	2,613	15,728	166	67.2	25,721	5.2	6.0	3.3	SPD
Hamburg	1,571	755	2,082	90.8	57,837	1.1	11.0	11.2	SPD-FDP
Lower Saxony	7,196	47,439	152	189.9	26,399	7.1	26.2	3.9	CDU-FDP
Bremen	654	404	1,618	27.2	41,677	0.0	10.1	7.5	SPD
Northrhine-Westphalia	16,677	34,067	490	514.0	30,821	2.5	52.4	8.1	SPD
Hesse	5,544	21,114	263	190.7	34,414	2.5	32.7	9.5	CDU-FDP
Rhineland-Palatinate	3,611	19,848	182	102.6	28,427	5.8	55.7	4.6	CDU-FDP
Baden-Württemberg	9,327	35,751	261	312.7	33,536	5.0	47.4	9.2	CDU
Bavaria	11,026	70,553	156	346.1	31,389	8.1	69.9	6.2	CSU
Saarland	1,042	2,569	406	28.9	27,806	1.9	73.3	4.5	SPD
West Berlin	1,879	480	3,914	73.3	39,026	.9	12.4	13.7	CDU-FDP
Federal Republic	61,140	248,709	246	1,943.9	31,795	4.7	44.6	7.4	CDU/CSU-FDP

Source: *Statistiches Jahrbuch für die Bundesrepublik Deutschland, 1987.*

the autonomous orientation of its Rhineland heritage and the Prussian orientation of Westphalia. The population is nearly evenly divided between Catholics and Protestants. Because of the strength of the labor union movement in the Ruhr and throughout the state, its has become a stronghold of the Social Democratic party.

Rhineland-Palatinate (Rhineland-Pfalz) and the Saarland represent the historical continuation of the prewar Rhine province. Their postwar division followed the administrative boundaries between the French and American occupation forces. Baden-Württemberg combines the two prewar provinces of Baden and Württemberg, and was unified only after formation of the Federal Republic. All three of these Länder have large Catholic populations and generally conservative political party orientations. Hesse, in contrast, traces its history back to the Grand Duchy of Hesse. It is located in central Germany, in the area from Frankfurt to Kassel, and its residents are predominately Protestant. Because of its traditional support for the SPD, in contrast to its more conservative neighbors, it earlier earned the nickname "Red Hesse."

The free state of Bavaria, of all Germany's Länder, has retained most of its regional identity. Bavaria is the modern successor to the Kingdom of Bavaria. The strong Bavarian regional identity enabled the state to maintain some degree of autonomy under the Third Reich. Even today, when one crosses the southern German border, billboards welcome the traveller first to *Der Freistaat Bayern*, then to the Federal Republic. The area is heavily Catholic and agrarian, and the residents are noted for their distinctive accent and dress. The existence of the CSU (Christian Social Union), which was organized as a separate political party representing the interests of Bavaria, underscores the state's political distinctiveness. The CSU has consistently polled the majority of the votes in Bavaria since 1953.

The decentralized structure of society and the economy reinforce these regional differences. Economic and cultural activities thrive throughout the nation, rather than being concentrated in a capital city, as in Britain and France. The Federal Republic's heavy urbanization has produced more than two dozen major metropolitan areas that function as regional economic centers. Economic activity is distributed among cities such as Frankfurt, Cologne, Munich, and Hamburg. The mass media are organized around regional markets, and there are even several competing "national" theaters around the country.

Although significant cultural and socioeconomic differences still separate the Länder, these differences have narrowed as the Federal Republic has become a modern cosmopolitan society. In addition to the social forces discussed above, the Basic Law calls for an equality of political rights and living standards across the states; as a result, the poorer states receive financial subsidies from the federal government and the richer states. The goal is to equalize government services and life conditions across the nation.

As well as class, religious, and regional cleavages, other social divisions have also decreased in size and importance. As society has become more urban, the rural-urban cleavage has lessened. Urbanization also decreases the importance and solidarity of community-based political organizations, as citizens move from small, closed villages to urban centers. People in cities are exposed to a greater variety of ideas, and their political beliefs become more pluralistic and individualistic. A changing labor force stimulates additional geographic and social mobility. The affluence of contemporary society further narrows the differences in life styles among all social classes.

GUESTWORKERS

Although most other social cleavages have lessened in size and effect, a potential new source of division within West German society is the nation's growing minority of "guestworkers" (*Gastarbeiter*).[7] When the economy expanded rapidly in the 1960s, a shortage of workers began to develop, threatening further economic growth. The government responded by recruiting foreign workers from southern Europe. The Federal Republic concluded a series of labor agreements with Greece, Spain, Turkey, Portugal, and Yugoslavia; these agreements regulated the number of workers coming to Germany and the terms of their employment. The West German government established labor offices in the originating nations that worked with local labor officials in finding people interested in working in the Federal Republic. After a screening process, the worker would leave for Germany with a short-term labor contract to work for Siemens, Ford, or another large firm. The number of guestworkers rapidly increased, from just under 330,000 in 1960 to about 2.5 million in 1973. During the early 1970s, a fleet of jumbo jets constantly ferried workers from southern Europe to their new jobs in West Germany.

The migration of guestworkers to Germany had benefits for both the originating country and the Federal Republic. Workers who might be unemployed or underemployed in their native country were able to find full-time employment in the West German economy. The migration of these unemployed workers lessened the economic burden of the originating nation. By living frugally, the guestworkers were able to remit several billion Deutschmarks a year to their families back home, further strengthening the economies of the originating countries. In addition, proponents hoped that this employment experience would develop job skills that would help the guestworkers and indirectly benefit the economy of their country when they returned home.

The economic advantages to the Federal Republic, however, were even greater. The influx of guestworkers was a necessary element in sustaining economic growth in the 1960s. Moreover, guestworkers aided the West German economy in several other, indirect ways. Foreign workers worked in Germany during their most productive years, after the originating country had already borne the substantial social costs of their childhood and education. Most guestworkers assumed jobs at the low end of the occupational ladder, jobs that Germans were reluctant to do, thereby enabling native Germans to move up the occupational ladder. The guestworkers also paid more in taxes and social insurance contributions than they received in benefits and thus subsidized the government benefits of the German population. By some calculations, these indirect benefits contributed nearly DM 10 billion a year to the West German economy throughout the late 1960s and early 1970s.[8]

Government policy originally assumed that guestworkers would be temporary visitors to the Federal Republic, staying between three and five years. Indeed, several million workers came, worked long enough to acquire skills and some personal savings, and then returned home. Many other foreign workers, however, chose to remain in West Germany and extended their stay indefinitely. When economic recession struck in the mid-1970s, the Federal Republic found itself with a population of over 4 million foreign residents. Critics of the government were quick to point out that the number of foreign workers exceeded the number of unemployed German workers.

Over the past decade, the government has taken the position that the Federal Republic will not become a nation of immigrants and has adopted policies aimed at reducing the number of guestworkers. A ban on further entry by non-European Community workers was implemented in November of 1973. Although this limited the number of new workers, it meant that workers already residing in the Federal Republic became more hesitant to leave. Foreign workers thus relocated their families in West Germany, which increased the number of foreign residents. The government then moved to restrict the immigration of family members. Other government programs used financial incentives to encourage guest-workers to return to their native country. In 1983, for example, the CDU-led government offered unemployed foreign workers a one-time payment of DM 10,000 and a refund of their pension contributions if they would return home along with their families. Government publicists proudly reported that the plan encouraged nearly half a million guestworkers, most of them Turkish, to leave the Federal Republic.

These policies to restrict the guestworker population have not substantially reduced the number of foreign residents in West Germany. The number of foreign residents has held fairly steady throughout the 1980s at about 4.5 million. Restrictive government policies were counterbalanced by the unification of families, a temporary influx of individuals seeking political asylum from Third World countries, and a high birth rate in the foreign worker community. This new social stratum now appears to be a permanent aspect of West German society. Over 7 percent of the population and about 11 percent of the work force are foreigners.

From the beginning, the guestworker situation has presented several potential political problems.[9] The foreign workers' place at the bottom of the occupational hierarchy makes them susceptible to discrimination on economic grounds; studies routinely find, for instance, that foreign workers pay substantially more than Germans for comparable housing—when they can find it. In addition, guest-workers are culturally, socially, and linguistically isolated from German society, especially in the case of Turkish guestworkers, because of the combination of ethnic, cultural, religious, and economic differences. Each major city has its own guestworker quarter, which resembles Ankara or Athens more than the Stuttgart or Berlin where it is actually located. The uncertain political status of guestworkers, since they lack the legal rights of citizenship, increases their vulnerability.

Most West Germans remain largely uninformed about the plight of the guestworkers, who face real problems of discrimination and social estrangement. A recent book, *Ganz Unten (At the Very Bot-*

tom), chronicled the experiences of a German who disguised himself as a guestworker; it became a best-seller, because it described a part of West German society unknown to most of its citizens. The lack of information leads to misunderstanding and intolerance. Social tensions often exist between Germans and the guestworker communities, because of their different social, cultural, and economic situations.[10] These social gaps are not easily bridged. The guestworkers themselves remain divided on whether they want to assimilate into mainstream German society or retain their cultural distinctiveness. Their children face an especially difficult future. Although raised in West Germany, they are not integrated into German society and do not possess the rights of German citizenship; their homeland, too, is a foreign country to them. Assimilating these second-generation guestworkers may pose even greater demands on West German society.

AN END TO GROWTH?

The years of seemingly inexorable economic growth abruptly came to an end in the early 1970s. A economic slowdown due to changing domestic conditions first became apparent in 1972. These economic concerns were soon overshadowed by more fundamental changes at the international level. The Organization of Petroleum Exporting Countries (OPEC) oil embargo in 1973 and subsequent price hikes precipitated a general economic crisis in virtually all industrialized nations. The oil price increases nearly tripled the Federal Republic's bill for energy imports. Moreover, the ensuing worldwide recession cut sharply into West Germany's export-oriented economy.

The economic indicators that had moved almost steadily upward for a quarter of a century turned in a new direction. As the worldwide recession worsened in 1975, the West German GNP actually shrank by 2.5 percent (see Figure III.1 above). Like other Western industrial economies, the Federal Republic was experiencing a new situation: "stagflation"—simultaneous stagnation and inflation. A sharp rise in unemployment was an even clearer result of the oil price increase. The jobless rate reached almost 5 percent in 1975, and, perhaps more important psychologically, the number of unemployed persons broke the 1 million barrier.

The incumbent SPD-FDP government attempted to moderate the effects of international economic conditions. There was a necessary retrenchment on domestic programs, and government deficits rose with the economic slowdown. The best assurance that Chancellor Helmut Schmidt could offer to voters in the 1976 election was that West Germany's substantial economic problems were still much less severe than those of its European neighbors.

Just as the economy was regaining some strength in the late 1970s, another OPEC price increase plunged the German and world economy into worse straits. The Federal Republic's GNP declined again in 1981 *and* 1982. The unemployment picture darkened, with more than 2 million individuals out of work; the number of jobless had been higher only during the Great Depression. These economic problems proved too great for the SPD-FDP government to manage, prompting a change to a more economically conservative CDU/ CSU-FDP government in 1982.

After an initial spurt, the West German economy is slowing again. Between 1980 and 1988, the nation's total economic output grew by about 1.5 percent a year, the slowest rate of the five largest advanced industrial democracies. Unemployment levels seem stuck at about the 2 million mark, about 9 percent of the labor force—far different from the years when severe labor shortages led to the importation of guestworkers. A strengthening of the Deutschmark on international currency exchanges and growing government budget deficits forecast uncertain economic times for the rest of the 1980s. Moreover, international conditions account for only part of these continuing economic uncertainties. More and more, financial analysts point to structural aspects of the German economy as a source of the continuing economic difficulties (see Chapter XI).

This leveling off of economic growth has inevitably affected other aspects of the social structure. Social mobility slackened as a stagnant economy and high unemployment restricted career opportunities. The growth in university enrollments leveled off as a result of a decline in the size of the university-aged cohort, a diminution of government educational benefits, and the decrease in the social value of a university degree. The new conservative government made modest cutbacks in virtually every social program. Probably the most significant consequence of the slowdown was the end to the optimism that characterized the growth decades; Germans no longer looked toward the future with a feeling of certainty that conditions would continue to improve.

The stabilization of West German society involved other factors besides economic conditions. Population increase is a basic source of social growth and also fuels economic growth; more people mean more families to buy furniture, more customers for the German automobile industry, and more consumers for the shopkeeper. After a steady increase in the population during the growth decades, demographic patterns began to change in the 1970s. The influx of refugees from the East ended with the building of the Berlin Wall in 1961, and the number of guestworkers stabilized in the mid-1970s. In addition, changing life styles and economic conditions led many younger Germans to develop new attitudes toward children and families. Birth rates in the 1970s were barely half the level of the 1950s and 1960s, and the overall population of the Federal Republic has held steady at about 61 million for over a decade. In fact, birth rates are at the point where the native German population is not raising enough children to maintain the present population level. In other words, the German public is voluntarily following a course of less-than-zero population growth.

The growth decades are over. The extraordinary economic and social changes that restructured West German society during the 1950s and 1960s will probably not be repeated. Yet the end of the growth decades does not mean an end to their consequences. The economy is still growing—but at a slower rate. Social conditions are still improving—but the pace is slower. The West German public is still characterized by a level of affluence, social and educational advancement, and modern life styles that typify an advanced industrial society. The Federal Republic has reached a new plateau, where the social transformation wrought by the growth decades will continue, but further change will be less explosive.

SOCIAL CHANGE AND POLITICS

For the foreseeable future, West German politics will be characterized by a mix of traditional and modern forces simultaneously at work. Traditional social divisions will remain a very important part of the social framework for West German politics and will continue to influence politics. Social cleavages structure the political values and beliefs of many citizens. Unionized industrial workers still give the majority of their votes to the Social Democratic party, and church-going Bavarian Catholics remain overwhelmingly CSU voters. Moreover, the social institutions underlying these cleavages—labor unions, business associations, and the churches—hold important positions within the West German political system (see Chapter VIII).

Yet the partial erosion of some of these social forces has laid the groundwork for the many political developments described in this book. Because an increasing proportion of the population is no longer integrated into these social networks, more individuals are susceptible to new cultural appeals. This openness to change led both to the Social Democratic reforms of the 1970s and to the alternative movement of the 1980s.[11] Traditional social institutions, such as the unions and the churches, are themselves becoming less monolithic and find themselves debating alternative social goals and alternative values. Moreover, these institutions are less able than they once were to enforce their political beliefs on their adherents. Thus, instead of being locked into an institutionalized set of political norms, many West Germans are now exposed to a diverse and changeable set of political influences, derived from friends, the media, and their own reading of political events.

These trends have continued on into the 1980s, even as traditional economic concerns have increased in salience. Several decades of prosperity have altered the social structure of West German society, protecting most citizens from the worst ravages of an uncertain economy and creating a pool of middle class voters potentially open to further political change. Uncertain economic conditions have neither revived the traditional class struggles of politics nor reversed the broader social trends of several decades. Indeed, we will see in subsequent chapters that the delayed effects of the growth decades are still transforming West German society and politics. In addition, the 1980s have witnessed the emergence of new social issues, such as sexual equality and relations with guestworkers. Thus, not only has past sociopolitical change been substantial, but the potential for further change remains.[12]

NOTES

1. Daniel Bell, *The Coming of Post-industrial Society* (New York: Basic Books, 1973); Alvin Toffler, *The Third Wave* (New York: Morrow, 1980).

2. Karl Hardach, *The Political Economy of Germany in the Twentieth Century* (Berkeley: University of California Press, 1980); Eric Owen Smith, *The West German Economy* (London: Croom Helm, 1983).

3. There were many critics of the social market system until its economic success became obvious. See Ludwig Erhard's account in *Prosperity through Competition* (New York: Praeger, 1958).

4. Kendall Baker et al., *Germany Transformed* (Cambridge: Harvard University Press, 1981), chap. 8.

5. Bell, *The Coming of Post-industrial Society.*

6. A great deal of the churches' remaining influence depends as much on their formal status as social institutions recognized by the state as on their direct influence on religiously-oriented individuals (see Chapter VIII).

7. Ray Rist, *Guestworkers in Germany* (New York: Praeger, 1978); Peter Katzenstein, *Policy and Politics in West Germany* (Philadelphia: Temple University Press, 1987), chap. 5.

8. Rudolf Blitz, "A Benefit-Cost Analysis of Foreign Workers in West Germany," *KYKLOS* 30 (1977): 479–502.

9. Rist, *Guestworkers in Germany*, chaps 5–10.

10. Marilyn Hoskin, "Public Opinion toward Guestworkers," *Guestworkers and other Immigrants in Industrial Societies*, ed. M. Rosch and D. Frey (New York: Academic Press, 1982); Marilyn Hoskin, "Public Opinion and the Foreign Worker," *Comparative Politics* (January 1985): 193–210.

11. Russell Dalton, "The German Party System between Two Ages," in *Electoral Change in Advanced Industrial Democracies*, ed. Russell Dalton et al. (Princeton: Princeton University Press, 1984); Wilhelm Bürklin, "Governing Left Parties Frustrating the Radical Non-established Left," *European Sociological Review* (1987): 109–126.

12. Elisabeth Noelle-Neumann and Renate Köcher conclude that "the Federal Republic is like no other nation in its openness to new values and influences," *Die verletze Nation* (Stuttgart: Deutsche Verlags-Anstalt, 1987); also see Richard Lowenthal, *Social Change and the Cultural Crisis* (New York: Columbia University Press, 1984).

CHAPTER IV

A Changing Political Culture

IMAGINE THAT YOU WERE a West German citizen in 1949. What political lessons would you draw from recent German history? Like most citizens, you probably would conclude that politics was something to avoid. Not only had three regimes failed during a brief thirty-year period, but supporters of the previous regime had often suffered after the establishment of each new political order. The treatment of the political opposition following the National Socialists' rise to power, as well as the denazification program after World War II, probably convinced many citizens that political participation was a questionable, if not risky, pursuit.

Most citizens were unfamiliar with, and possibly unreceptive to, the principles of democratic politics. German democracy lacked the historical tradition that was common to other West European nations. Under the Kaiser, citizens were expected to be subjects, not active participants in the political process. The turbulent interlude of the Weimar Republic did little to develop democratic values. The polarization, fragmentation, and outright violence of Weimar politics taught people about the weaknesses of democracy and not its strengths. The Third Reich then raised yet another generation of Germans under an authoritarian system.

Undoubtedly, many people also felt some suspicion toward the Federal Republic. The new political institutions were not solely the product of German efforts; they came from wartime defeat and were imposed by occupying powers. The new political system was seemingly dictated by forces beyond their control, rather than a natural result of German political development. In short, democracy was an unfamiliar, and somewhat alien, political system to many citizens.

These conditions led many political observers to ask whether

West Germany lacked a *political culture* congruent with a democratic political system. The political culture of a nation is what
people think and feel about politics; it encompasses everything
from beliefs about the legitimacy of the political system to opinions
about the adequacy and appropriateness of political input structures, governmental policies, and the citizen's role in politics.
Rather than the tolerant, supportive, and participatory political
culture that were identified with successful democratic political systems, observers of the West German culture saw it as detached, cyni-
cal, and unsupportive of democratic politics.[1] Many people feared
that West Germans lacked the political attitudes necessary for the
Federal Republic to endure and prosper politically. The various
aspects of this problem came to be known as the "German question": Could the Federal Republic overcome the negative aspects of
its cultural inheritance?

The experience of the Weimar Republic underscored the importance of the political culture. Weimar was seemingly never able to
develop a political culture supportive of the democratic political
process. From the outset, the Republic was stigmatized as a product
of treason; many of its citizens felt that the creation of the regime at
the end of World War I had contributed to Germany's wartime
defeat. Important sectors of the political establishment—the military, the civil service, and the judiciary—and large numbers of citizens questioned the legitimacy of the Weimar regime and retained
attachments to the political system of the former German Empire.
The fledgling democratic state then faced a series of major political
crises. The behavior of politicians and political parties during these
times of crisis did little to develop a sense of democratic values
within the political culture. In short, the political system was never
able to build up a pool of popular support or a commitment to
democratic politics. Consequently, the dissatisfaction created by the
Great Depression easily eroded support for the democratic regime.
What followed under the Third Reich then dramatically worsened
cultural traditions.

The remaking of the political culture thus was a primary goal of
Allied and West German elites. This task took on extra urgency
because the Federal Republic was born with many of the handicaps
that had plagued the Weimar Republic. Despite the early advances
of the Social Market Economy, the economic picture in 1949 was
still bleak. Like Weimar, the new political institutions came from
wartime defeat; even worse, they were imposed by the occupying

powers. The propaganda of the Third Reich undoubtedly poisoned many people's attitude toward democratic politics. Thus there were common fears that the Federal Republic would share the same fate as Weimar. For nearly a generation, the Federal Republic was haunted by the question, *"Ist Bonn doch Weimar?"* ("Is Bonn another Weimar?").

This chapter discusses the changing political culture through the postwar period. One objective of political elites was to develop a public commitment to the Federal Republic and democracy. The government undertook a massive program to reeducate the German public on these points; improving economic conditions cemented the public's attachment to the new regime. In a span of less than a generation, basic aspects of the political culture were remade. Cultural change is a continuing process, however. The nation's success in addressing these economic and political challenges transformed West German society, and this transformation also affected public values. The result is an ongoing process of cultural change.

THE CULTURAL INHERITANCE

The German political culture in 1949 reflected the historical legacy of the Second Empire and the Weimar Republic, but the influence of the Third Reich was most heavily felt. It is difficult to imagine the political climate of Nazi Germany solely from reading historical accounts, because the experience is so alien to life in contemporary Western democracies. Many historians draw a parallel to other German or European authoritarian regimes, but true comparisons are difficult to sustain. In an environment without pluralism or dissent, there were few controls on government behavior or opportunities to question the government. The Führer cult surrounding Hitler took on the trappings of a religion deifying a god. The film of the 1934 Nuremberg Nazi party rally, *The Triumph of the Will*, is an awesome testimonial to the power of Nazi propaganda. The intensity of support for the Nazi regime, or at least the public displays of support, indicated that a political fever had spread through Germany. The historian, Gordon Craig, recounts one not-atypical example.[2] In 1935 he was an exchange student in Munich; on the daily ride to school the occupants of the bus raised their right arms in unison as they passed the site of Hitler's 1923 putsch attempt and gave the straight-armed Hitler salute to the putsch memorial!

The Third Reich's control over the individual was nearly absolute. Individual will and responsibility were subordinated to the state. Those who questioned authority or held "alien" views soon disappeared—sent to concentration camps or worse. Outright resistance to the Nazi regime was virtually extinct by the start of World War II. The Nazi propaganda machine worked to remake the political culture in its own image. Most young people were members of some type of Nazi youth group, the media and education system became tools of the government, and Nazi organizations disseminated propaganda throughout the entire society. The average citizen was literally told by the government that "you are nothing, the nation is everything."

The National Socialists claimed to champion traditional German values, but the content of Nazi propaganda distorted these values into unrecognizable forms. The Nazis encouraged excessive nationalism to support Hitler's expansionist foreign policy; propagandists told the Germans they were the master race, destined to rule the world. The government's rabid anti-Semitic rhetoric helped to make acceptable its persecution of the Jews. The regime praised the family at the same time that the government destroyed the ethical and moral basis of German society. Only one political truth existed. The public learned that liberalism, democracy, and socialism were the enemies of Germany, and these enemies must not be tolerated.

What explains the breakdown of human values that occurred during the Third Reich? How could an entire nation ignore the oppression and eventual arrest of their Jewish neighbors, the imprisonment of socialists, communists, and liberals, and the destruction of individual rights? One explanation holds that this failure represented a specific flaw in the German political character, that intolerance was a prominent feature of the political culture under previous regimes and was encouraged by Nazi propaganda.

Intolerance alone is not a sufficient explanation, however. Many Germans disapproved of the Nazis' extremist policies but still did nothing. In an experiment designed to explore the psychology of the Third Reich, Stanley Milgram uncovered a pattern in human behavior that suggests a more ominous explanation.[3] Milgram asked volunteers in Connecticut to participate in his experiments to test "training" methods. Under the demands of the project director, these average Americans inflicted what they thought were painful, or even life-threatening, electric shocks to the trainee. Almost every volunteer submitted to the demands of the project director, even though they believed that this was just a college psychology experiment. The experiment, in short, showed that average people would perform inhuman acts under pressure from an authority figure. By comparison, for several generations German governments had conditioned the public to follow orders unquestioningly. The Nazi state exploited these authoritarian and intolerant aspects of the German political culture under a totalitarian system that severely punished dissent. Most Germans followed orders and did not openly challenge authority, until it was too late to act.

It is difficult to know how many Germans truly supported Hitler's actions and how many simply remained silent and followed orders.[4] Press accounts suggest that Hitler enjoyed broad popular support before the outbreak of World War II and during the early war years. The German people accepted policies aimed at strengthening the state, international expansionism, and discrimination against the Jews. As the war progressed, however, the Nazi state descended into a pit of horrors. Rumors of the atrocities committed by the German *Einsatzkommandos* in the Soviet Union were rampant, but discredited by the government. The public knew of the forced deportation of European Jews, but the regime claimed that they were destined for work camps. Certainly, thousands of government employees knew what was happening and participated in the atrocities, but the reality of the situation was always blurred for the general public. Forced to live in this environment riddled with fear and oppression, many people chose to believe what they wanted to believe. A common explanation of inaction after the war was that individuals withdrew into a self-created psychological shell ("inner migration"). It is certain, however, that the Third Reich left behind a political culture that provided a very poor foundation for the democratic process.

Within a few months of the end of the war, the U.S. military occupation forces surveyed public opinion to assess the legacy of the Third Reich.[5] These surveys indicated that concerns about the German political culture were well justified. Even after the collapse of the Third Reich, roughly one-sixth of the population were unrepentant Nazis. Sympathy for the Nazi ideology was even more widespread. For several years after the war, half the public felt national socialism was a good idea badly carried out, and nearly as many felt Nazism represented more good than evil. Anti-Semitic feelings were common, and a small core of extremists refused to believe the Nazi attempts to exterminate the Jewish race ever happened. After reviewing this evidence, Anna and Richard Merritt concluded that "even if the Nazi party and its leaders were discredited, it was by no means certain that their underlying principles were."[6]

Prospects for establishing a democratic political system were also suspect. Few individuals wanted to take the risk of becoming politically active. More than two-thirds of the residents in the U.S. occupation zone preferred to leave politics to others. In early 1946, a survey of community leaders found opinions nearly equally divided on whether democracy was possible in Germany.[7] This was the political culture inherited by postwar West Germany.

REMAKING THE POLITICAL CULTURE

Efforts to reshape the German political culture began nearly as soon as the war ended.[8] The Western powers immediately set up youth groups to counteract the earlier effects of the Hitler Youth organizations. Public addresses and the media were used in a concerted public education campaign. Only people with strong democratic beliefs could receive a license to publish newspapers, and the Allied forces strictly controlled the content of radio broadcasts. The denazification program (see Chapter II) was aimed at discrediting Nazi ideas as well as punishing individual crimes.

The Federal Republic continued these activities after 1949.[9] The efforts to reshape the political culture involved most social and political institutions. The government-controlled radio, and later television, contained a high proportion of public affairs programming that emphasized the value of democracy. The Basic Law explicitly directed political parties to participate in forming the political will of the public, and the government provided the parties with special funding to carry out these activities (see Chapter IX). The schools focused on developing a democratic consciousness among the next generation (see Chapter V). When the Economic Miracle took off, government officials were quick to portray affluence as the byproduct of the democratic system. Moreover, in contrast to the Weimar Republic, government leaders provided a generally positive example of competition in a democratic setting.

The effort to remake the political culture was very difficult, because it involved changing how people thought about themselves and society. For example, comparisons of democratic politics to the examples of previous regimes touched a sensitive nerve for many. How could schoolteachers lecture their pupils on the horrors of the

Third Reich when they themselves had been citizens of the Reich? How could parents who may have voted for Hitler explain Nazism to their children? How could the government publicly castigate National Socialism while some judges and civil servants of the Third Reich government still served under the Federal Republic?

The reeducation program, therefore, tended to place more emphasis on the positive advantages of democracy than on the negative lessons of the Third Reich. Political leaders talked of the success of democracy rather than the failures of Nazism. Attempts to avoid confronting the past occasionally went to extreme lengths. For instance, references to the Nazi military were cut from early German showings of Humphrey Bogart films, such as *Casablanca* or *The African Queen*. Imagine making sense of Rick's actions in Casablanca if there were no German officers in the movie! The emotional scene in *Cabaret*, in which a young boy leads beer garden patrons in singing a patriotic Nazi song was similarly deleted when the film was first shown in West Germany in the mid-1970s. These are extreme examples, but they illustrate the difficulties a nation faces when it tries to renounce a part of its own history.

In its political-education activities, the government had to maintain a fine balance between deficiency and excess. Too little action would leave the political culture unchanged, too much action would conjure up images of Nazi propagandizing. Similarly, if political leaders overreacted against threats to the state, the government would be criticized as undemocratic. If no action was taken, the government would be criticized for displaying Weimar's impotence. Not only must West German leaders create a democratic political culture, but their methods must be democratic.

Extensive public opinion polling identified the content of the German political culture and monitored the progress of the reeducation efforts. Scholarly perceptions of West German public opinion were heavily influenced by the findings from Gabriel Almond and Sidney Verba's *Civic Culture* study.[10] In comparing West Germany to the stable democracies of the United States and Great Britain, these researchers identified areas in which the German political culture was lacking. First, the public had not yet identified with the new political system of the Federal Republic. Second, belief in democratic values and support for democratic political procedures were weakly developed; political tolerance and acceptance of political competition was lacking. Third, the average citizen was quiescent and politically uninvolved, not an active participant in the democratic process. These were the priority areas where reeducation efforts needed to change the political culture.

STATE AND NATION

An essential element of the German political culture is a strong sense of community. A common history, culture, territory, and language developed a sense of national community long before Germany was politically united. Germany was the land of Schiller, Goethe, Beethoven, and Wagner, even if the Germans disagreed on political boundaries. The imagery of a single *Volk* bound Germans together, despite their social and political differences.

Previous regimes had failed, however, to develop a sense of political community as part of the German national identity. Succeeding political systems never fully developed a popular consensus on the nature and goals of German politics. The Kulturkampf and attacks on socialists during the Second Empire had alienated large sectors of the public from the political system. The failure of Weimar democracy led to further division. The Nazi state had forced a single political view on its subjects, but its brief life and eventual collapse left a void in this aspect of the political culture. Observers described Germany as a *Kulturnation* (cultural nation) but not a *Staatsnation* (state). The Federal Republic faced the challenge of developing a popular identification with the new West German state and the institutions of government.

The Germans make a distinction between *Macht und Geist* (power and spirit), and these two concepts are useful in discussing popular orientations toward state and nation. Despite the discontinuities of German political regimes, the public has always been conditioned to accept the power *(Macht)* of the state. German political theory is based on a Hegelian philosophy that views the state as a real entity, superior to individual citizens. In his memoirs, Konrad Adenauer acknowledged this inheritance:[11]

> For many decades the German people suffered from a wrong attitude to the state, to power, to the relationship between the individual and the state. They made an idol of the state and set it upon an altar; the individual's worth and dignity had been sacrificed to this idol. The belief in the omnipotence of the state, in the primacy of the state and in the power concentrated in the state above all else, even above eternal human values, was first enthroned in Germany after the victorious war of 1870-1 and the subsequent headlong economic development.

Hegelian theory sees the state as an independent force, which stands above individual needs as a protector of the moral and political interests of society. Hegel held that individual freedom could only be realized within the structure of the state; the absolute ethical order of the Prussian state, for example, created the social order Hegel thought was necessary for individuals to exercise "freedom."[12] Hegelian theory thus used the concept of liberty to justify the subordination of the individual and the independence of state authority. In extreme form, this philosophy furnished the groundwork for the authoritarian state (*Obrigkeitsstaat*) that typified the Second Empire and Third Reich.

These political norms were at least partially inherited by the Federal Republic. Indeed, these values helped stabilize the fledgling Republic and contributed to the initial legitimacy of Adenauer's government. The public obeyed the directives of the Bonn government just as they had obeyed prior regimes. Even today, the German concern for public order remains a distinct part of the political culture, though moderated by the sense of human and democratic values that Adenauer found initially lacking in his compatriots. The popular saying, *"Ruhe ist des Bürgers erste Pflict"* ("Public order is the citizen's first duty"), is still accepted at least implicitly by most Germans.

Although the *Macht* of the state was generally acknowledged, even though the form of government changed, much less consensus existed on the spirit (*Geist*) of German politics. Each political order was relatively short lived, and never fully developed a popular consensus on the nation's political goals. The Federal Republic faced a similar challenge: building a political community in a divided and defeated nation.

One major handicap was the uncertain status of the Federal Republic. Opinion was divided on whether the Federal Republic should even try to develop popular identifications with the new political system. Some public officials saw the Federal Republic as only an interim state, a "provisorium," until both Germanies could be reunited. Bonn was just a temporary capital until the government returned to Berlin, and a conscious effort was made to maintain this provisional status. The government resisted the need to build offices for the federal agencies in Bonn, because they would not be needed after the capital finally moved to Berlin. For over two decades, the Social Democrats maintained their national head-

quarters in "temporary" barracks on one of Bonn's main thorough-
fares.

In time, a sense of permanence gradually replaced the temporary
status of West Germany. The Federal Republic's strong ties to the
West—combined with the GDR's integration into the communist
bloc—obviated the possibility of German reunification. Gradually
the public and political leaders realized that the postwar division of
Germany would continue. Public support for reunification of the
two Germanies rapidly waned with the onset of Ostpolitik in the
1960s.[13] Citizens in West Germany see the Federal Republic as their
home, and the German Democratic Republic is perceived as a
separate country. Reflecting this change in the political loyalties of
the public, government buildings proliferated in Bonn and the SPD
finally moved into modern headquarters.

Another and equally important measure of the public's changing
political attitudes is the extent of popular attachment to the symbols
of past and present political systems.[14] In the early 1950s, most of
the public still looked favorably on the symbols and personalities of
prior authoritarian regimes, implying lingering public identification with these systems. Most people at that time felt that the
Empire or Hitler's prewar Reich had been the best times for
Germany.

These ties to previous regimes have gradually eroded since the
early 1950s. A sampling of several typical items from public opinion surveys is presented in Figure IV.1. Favorable ratings of Bismarck as the man who had "done the most for Germany" dropped
from 35 percent in 1951 to 18 percent in 1964; the already low evaluations of Hitler on this question also declined. The substantial
minorities who had once favored a return to the imperial flag and
restoration of the monarchy became a mere trace element in public
opinion surveys. Positive feelings toward National Socialism
showed an even more precipitous decline in the decade following
the formation of the Federal Republic.

As the bonds to earlier regimes weakened, the links to the new
institutions and leaders of the Federal Republic grew steadily
stronger (Figure IV.2). The number of citizens who believed that
Bundestag deputies represent the public interest doubled between
1951 and 1964. Public respect shifted away from the personalities of
prior regimes to the chancellors of the Federal Republic, especially
Konrad Adenauer. Other survey questions found that West Germans
overwhelmingly felt that the Federal Republic represented the best

FIGURE IV.1 *Decline in Support for Authoritarian Regimes, 1950–1978*

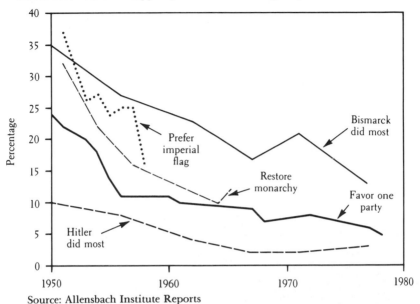

Source: Allensbach Institute Reports

time in German history. In fact, by the mid-1960s, political support was so widespread that annual monitoring of many of these basic indicators was discontinued. For perhaps the first time in modern German history, a consensus existed on the symbols and basic structure of the political system.

Despite these changes in the political loyalties of the West German public, something was still missing from the *Geist* of German political beliefs. Gabriel Almond and Sidney Verba stressed that a psychological commitment or emotional tie was necessary to cement public attachments to the political order, and they provided empirical evidence that the West German political culture was lacking in this quality. Comparing the sources of national pride in 1959, they found that West Germans were most proud of their character traits (such as honesty and industriousness), the success of the Economic Miracle, and Germany's past cultural and scientific achievements—but few individuals found pride in their new political system (Figure IV.3). This pattern was in marked contrast to the stable democracies of the United States and Britain. Only 7 percent of the West German public expressed pride in their political system, compared to 46 percent among the British and 85 percent among

FIGURE IV.2 *Increase in Support for the Democratic Regime, 1951–1986*

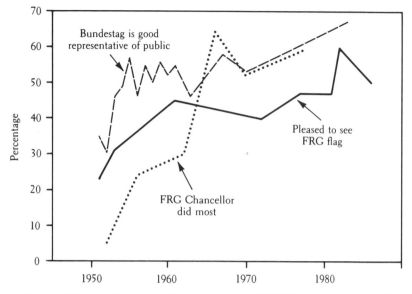

Source: The question on the Bundestag is from EMNID opinion surveys; the
other items are from Allensbach Institute Reports.

the Americans. In short, strong emotional ties to the political system had not developed, even if people accepted (and indeed preferred) the symbols of the new regime.

When this question was asked again in 1978, attitudes had
changed substantially. Almost one-third of the West German public
was openly proud of their political system and its democratic institutions, and another large group was proud of the domestic and
foreign policy accomplishments of the Federal Republic. Among
younger West Germans, the political system was the primary source
of national pride. Yet, it is also clear that German attachments to
the political system still lack the emotional basis found in other
Western democracies. A 1985 international study found that only 20
percent of the West German public was very proud to be German,
as compared to 42 percent among the French, 58 percent among the
British, and 87 percent among Americans![15] Furthermore, there is
little prospect that this situation will improve dramatically without
new forces coming into play, because national pride is even lower
among younger citizens, who are an increasing proportion of the
German electorate.

The tentativeness of the German political culture also manifests

FIGURE IV.3 *Changing Sources of National Pride, 1959–1978.*

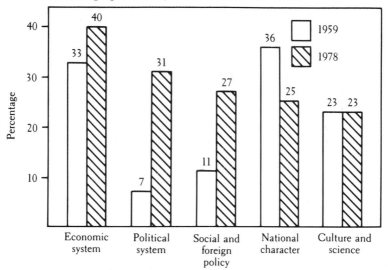

Source: David Conradt, "Changing German Political Culture," in Almond and Verba (eds.), *The Civic Culture Revisited* (Boston: Little, Brown, 1980), p. 230.

itself in the uncertain sense of national identity. The national identity is largely defined in negative terms: West Germans distinguish themselves from citizens of prior German Reichs; they are not East Germans, they are not Austrian or Swiss, and they are distinct from other West Europeans, although they share Western values. West Germans know what they are not, but they are less clear on what they are. The meaning attached to the label of nationality is less certain in the German case than for the British, French, or Italians. The fact that there is no widely used term for "citizen of the Federal Republic" is symptomatic of this unclear identity.

Attitudes toward the nation also represent the unique features of the German political experience. Although a sense of political community is part of the political culture of the Federal Republic, this feeling lacks the emotional attachment to state and nation that typifies political ties in many other nations. The trauma of the Third Reich burned a deep scar in the West German psyche. Excessive nationalism and unquestioning support of the state had been a source of weakness, not strength. The leaders of the Federal Republic believed that the nationalist excesses of the past should not be repeated. German feelings about politics might be best expressed by an exchange in Bertolt Brecht's play, *Galileo*: "Unhappy is the nation that has no heroes," said a character in the play. "No," Galileo replies, "unhappy is the nation that needs heroes."

Government reeducation efforts, therefore, aimed at developing popular attachments to the Federal Republic, without nurturing excessive nationalism. Such emotion-laden national symbols as are common in other industrialized democracies are rare in West Germany. There are few political holidays or memorials, the national anthem is seldom played, and the anniversary of the founding of the Federal Republic attracts little public attention. There is no real West German equivalent to Uncle Sam, Fourth of July celebrations, or the other symbols of U.S. patriotism. Compared to those of other nations, West German schools devote less time to such patriotic activities as singing national songs or pledging allegiance. West Germans seem more willing to boast about the accomplishments of Boris Becker, Steffi Graf, Bernhard Langer, and the national soccer team than to display pride in the political system.

Ambivalence toward the state reflects a continuing uncertainty about the nation's link to German history. Germans traditionally displayed intense conviction about their nation's "place" in history, and frequently used historical precedents to judge current political problems. Yet for most of the Federal Republic's existence, attempts to learn the lessons of history have gotten no further than 1933. The shadow cast by the Third Reich is so large that it obscures nearly all other aspects of German history. The lessons of the Third Reich are of critical importance, but there are other historical lessons—positive and negative—that also need to be remembered. The average citizen concludes that few positive lessons can be learned from other periods in German history, and is reinforced in this belief by the lack of political holidays that merit celebration or political figures that represent the better aspects of the German historical heritage. Thus the present German political culture lacks the sense of historical roots that adds continuity and strength to the political cultures of other nations. Several years ago, the former West German Federal President, Walter Scheel, warned that the Germans were in danger of becoming a people without a history.

Concern about the ambivalent national identity of West Germans has existed since the creation of the Federal Republic. Adenauer attempted to address this issue by developing a sense of European identity among the population, and as a consequence West Germans routinely display high levels of popular support for European integration. Supranational identity, however, is not a sufficient substitute for national identity. The Federal Republic's recent attempt to grapple with sociopolitical change and a changing international order thus revived debates on the national identity question.[16] This quest for the national identity is not a rejection of the social and political values of the Federal Republic, but an attempt to find a self-image that gives a broader meaning to West Germany's political existence. Moderate Leftists suggest placing greater stress on the democratic antecedents of the Federal Republic, such as the 1848 revolution. Some peace activists want to resurrect the concept of a nonaligned central European bloc, between East and West, united under the leadership of a neutralist Germany (FRG and GDR).[17] A small group of right-wing radicals reemphasize the traditional values of the German *Heimat*, with all that it implies.[18] Helmut Kohl and the conservatives attempt to define the national identity by stressing their conception of the positive aspects of German history and cultural traditions. The Kohl government has initiated an ambitious program of developing historical museums and expanding public education on German history. Recent events, such as Luther's 500th birthday and the 750th anniversary of the founding of Berlin, provide convenient settings for these activities. At the same time, Kohl has reintroduced words like *Vaterland* and *Patriotismus* into the German vocabulary, to assure people that it is now acceptable to express pride in the Federal Republic, its origins, and its accomplishments. Since 1985, the government-managed television networks have closed each broadcasting day with the playing of the national anthem.

This quest for a national identity is one aspect of the political culture that warrants attention in the years ahead. The Federal Republic can continue as a popular and effective political system without resolving the ambiguity in this aspect of its culture, but emotional feelings toward the political system and the resolution of the national identity question hold the potential for redirecting the goals of government. Moreover, the present divergence in national ideals may lead to increased political polarization if these views develop into political subcultures.

DEMOCRATIC NORMS AND PROCEDURES

For many West Germans in 1949, the rules of democratic politics—majority rule, minority rights, individual liberties, and pluralist debate—were new concepts that did not fit their past experiences. The state traditionally was viewed in an idealistic, almost mystical way. Progress, stability, order, and well-being were achieved by subordinating individual interests to the general interests represented by the state. Political power was absolute and flowed from the state, rather than the people. This model of the authoritarian state was basic to the political regimes of the Kaiser and the Third Reich.

The legitimacy of authoritarian governments was supported by German respect for the concept of a *Rechtsstaat,* that is, a state based on legal principles, clearly defined authority relationships, and comprehensive codes of political conflict. The Rechtsstaat is not the same as democracy or liberalism. In the Rechtsstaat, political actions, even those of elites, are governed by a code of law. German liberals saw the Rechtsstaat as a method of controlling the excesses of government, giving the people freedom *from* arbitrary government action. The concept of the Rechtsstaat is not, however, concerned with the content of law, and this is its weakness. Authoritarian governments utilized these legal formalities to legitimize their power.

To develop experience with democracy, the Federal Republic also drew upon this Rechtsstaat tradition. Government leaders constructed a Basic Law that formalized democratic procedures. Citizen participation in elections was encouraged and expected; policy making was legally defined to involve all legitimate interest groups.

The West German public learned democratic norms by working within the legal structures of the new political system. During the early years of the Federal Republic, political crises, such as debates over rearmament or government actions against *Der Spiegel* in 1962, were resolved without resort to undemocratic rhetoric and actions (either by elites or the public) and with little challenge to the basic principles of the republic. In domestic politics during the 1950s and 1960s, the republic exhibited political stability and an increasingly strong democratic political culture.

As a result of these experiences, a commitment to the democratic norms of the new political system gradually developed. For instance, whereas in the early 1950s a bare majority of the public expressed a preference for a democratic political system, by the mid-1960s there was nearly unanimous agreement that democracy was the best form of government. Equally important, David Conradt's work on the changing political culture finds a growing acceptance of democratic political procedures: a multiparty system, conflict management, minority rights, and representative government.[19] Other research indicates a substantial increase in political tolerance within the West German public.[20]

International surveys now rank West German public opinion as one of the most "democratic" in Western Europe (Table IV.1). In comparison to the British and French, West Germans are more likely to express satisfaction with the functioning of democracy. A larger proportion of the German public believes that their nation ensures freedom of expression and the legal rights of citizens. At the same time, the German political culture contains less support for undemocratic attitudes toward minority rights and political freedoms.

These changing perceptions of politics led to a dramatic increase in political involvement (see Chapter VI). General interest in politics and the frequency of political discussion displayed a remarkable upward climb. Participation in campaign activities and political organizations also increased. In sum, the traditionally uninvolved West German citizenry has changed into a public engaged in a wide range of political activities.

No democratic nation is immune to antidemocratic sentiments and the same applies to the Federal Republic. Indeed, because of Germany's history, concerns about the West German political cul-

TABLE IV.1 *National Support for Democratic Principles*

	Federal Republic	Great Britain	France
Satisfied with functioning of democracy	73	51	36
Democratic values			
Everyone is free to criticize	91	85	77
Everyone is free to do as they wish	72	67	66
Everyone is equal before the law	51	43	24
Undemocratic values			
Too much freedom could produce dictator	37	56	58
Small minorities are unpopular	36	59	60

Source: Eurobarometer 17 (October 1982). These data are available from the Interuniversity Consortium for Political and Social Research in Ann Arbor.

ture and the viability of democracy are difficult to dispel. Even today, it is not unusual to hear political commentators speculate about the ability of West German democracy to withstand economic downturns or other political crises.[21] Government leaders must feel that this is the political version of the German fairytale, *The Never-Ending Story*. Yet, despite these continuing doubts, a new political culture has taken root.

A good illustration of the strains on the culture and how it responds, is the Federal Republic's experience with radical terrorists.[22] The terrorist activities of the Baader-Meinhoff gang and the *Rote Armee Faktion* (Red Army Faction) during the 1970s appeared to some as new proof of the vulnerability of German democracy. These terrorists pursued a guerilla-warfare campaign designed to topple the economic and political systems.[23] In 1975, terrorists seized the West German embassy in Sweden and kidnapped the CDU mayoral candidate in Berlin; in 1977 they hijacked a Lufthansa airliner to Somalia and kidnapped and murdered a well-known industrialist. Attacks on military installations and personnel continued on into the 1980s; in late 1986 a senior official in the foreign office was assassinated. Despite the horror of these actions, too much emphasis should not be given to a very small group of extremists, never numbering more than a few hundred in a population of more than 60 million. The more important lesson to be drawn from this experience is how citizens and the political system responded to the terrorists.

The period of student revolt and terrorist violence was an important test for the West German political culture. On the negative side, the government's actions betrayed a still-uncertain commitment to individual liberties when the public order was threatened. An example of this excess is the Radicals Decree (*Radikalenerlass*) issued by the federal and state governments in 1972 in reaction to student radicalism. The Decree barred individuals with "anticonstitutional" attitudes from public employment. The government required loyalty checks for all new applicants for civil service positions, and many private employers informally adopted similar procedures. The decree was vague and difficult to apply fairly without violating civil liberties. Cases of abuse grew as the terrorist problem heightened security concerns, and it became obvious that the Decree could be used against legitimate opposition groups and innocent citizens as well as criminal radicals. Reflecting this changing political climate, public opinion surveys from the late 1970s showed a temporary downturn in several democratic values that had grown steadily over the preceding thirty years.[24] West Germans became slightly less tolerant of political opposition, less supportive of the political system, and more hesitant to express their political views. The federal government abandoned the Decree in 1979, but the terrorists had successfully eroded some of the optimistic climate of democratic reform that had characterized the early 1970s.

At the same time, several positive signs came from this experience. Most basic, the democratic system faced the onslaughts of urban guerrillas and survived with its basic institutions and procedures intact. Although some democratic values did decline slightly, a widespread public consensus still supported the principles and tenets of the Federal Republic. The terrorists had not attracted substantial popular support, even after economic problems arose in the late 1970s. The democratic political culture had passed a severe test.

Only time and events can completely prove the depth of the public's commitment to democracy. After nearly forty years of change, however, it is more appropriate to ask if West Germany is any longer an exceptional case. In other words, all political systems are vulnerable, but is the Federal Republic still exceptionally weak? The evidence from public opinion and political events suggests that the Federal Republic now appears at least as well prepared as many of its European neighbors to face any antidemocratic challenges. This aspect of the political culture has been remade.

EXPLAINING CHANGE

Perhaps even more amazing than the Economic Miracle has been West Germany's success in remaking its political culture. A public that was once politically quiescent, uncertain about democracy, and unsupportive of the political system became active and committed to the democratic political process—all within the span of a single generation.

Ironically, the success of the Federal Republic in remaking the political culture is partially due to the social destruction wrought by the Third Reich.[25] The traditional rule of aristocratic elites was first undermined by the Nazi purges and then ended with the fall of Hitler's Reich. The power of the great economic dynasties was similarly crippled. Thus the autocratic traditions of German politics practically disappeared from the political culture. In contrast to the experience of the Weimar Republic, the Federal Republic did not face significant opposition from political and economic elites committed to the prior regime. The scorched-earth policy of the Third Reich left society fertile for new developments. In short, Germany had a chance to start over, mindful of history but freed from its grip.

From the beginning, there was widespread support for a democratic political system among the leaders of the major political parties and other political elites in West Germany. Political extremism on the right had been discredited by the Third Reich, and the actions of the communist governments in the Soviet Union and East Germany undercut any remaining popular support for communism in the West. Small extremist parties on the right and the left challenged the democratic consensus, but they garnered few votes and were not a significant political force. Democracy was the only viable option.

Elite consensus in support of democratic ideals led to official efforts to reeducate the public to adopt a democratic political culture, but more important than formal reeducation programs were the positive experiences generated by the new political system. As A. J. P. Taylor argues in his history of modern Germany:[26]

> There was a great pother after the war about how we should educate the Germans in democracy. I never understood how this should be done. Democracy is learnt by practice, and not by sitting on forms at a political finishing-school.

Actual experience as democratic citizens increased the people's support for democratic and participatory norms. Furthermore, political leadership provided a generally positive example of political competition in a democratic setting. Despite initial fears to the contrary, West German democracy functioned fairly smoothly when crises arose.

A key factor in the success of these efforts to remake the culture was the economic and social performance of the political system. The accomplishments of the Economic Miracle and growth decades stood in marked contrast to the crises that had undermined the Weimar Republic. Instead of inflation and economic collapse, democracy in the Federal Republic was associated with affluence and full employment. The new regime's political and economic success was a very important source of popular support during the early 1950s, but became less important by the end of the decade as the public developed a more generalized commitment to democracy.[27]

Generational change constituted another important factor in the remaking of the political culture.[28] The positive political experiences of the Federal Republic influenced the attitudes of almost all citizens, particularly the young. Free of the negative political experiences of their elders, younger Germans proved more receptive to democracy. Public opinion surveys routinely show higher acceptance levels of democratic principles and more political involvement among the young. In other words, the political culture may have been remade less through the reeducation of the old than by the education of new citizens into the values and principles of democracy.

THE COMING OF A SECOND CULTURE

West German society made incredible progress in meeting the challenges it faced as a new political system in 1949. Chancellor Adenauer successfully charted a new course for German politics. The institutions of government quickly took charge of the political process and led the nation forward. The Economic Miracle resolved the economic problems of the immediate postwar period and eventually produced unprecedented affluence and economic security. The new German state regained its sovereignty within a single decade and became a full member of the Western Alliance. Furthermore, a popular consensus gradually developed in support of the new political system and its norms.

The Federal Republic's accomplishments in all of these areas made it the political success story of postwar Europe. This success led some political observers to proclaim that an age of affluence and consensus had arrived. Some analysts heralded an end to traditional ideological conflict as political differences among the established parties noticeably decreased.[29] It was as if having scaled an almost unconquerable mountain range, the Federal Republic had no more peaks on the horizon.

As is often the case, however, success in dealing with one set of objectives creates new challenges. Once West Germany made substantial progress in developing system support and addressing traditional socioeconomic needs, public interests broadened to include a new set of political goals. Beginning in the mid-1960s, the government faced new demands for reform in education and social programs. Issues like pollution, women's liberation, and co-determination increased in salience. Rather than consensus and moderation, new bases of political polarization and competition emerged.

VALUES IN CHANGE

The development of these new political orientations is generally explained by the broad theory of value change proposed by Ronald Inglehart.[30] Inglehart maintains that a person's value priorities are heavily influenced by the family and societal conditions of one's early formative years. In a time of depression or civil unrest, for example, economic well-being and security undoubtedly receive primary attention. If a society can make significant progress in addressing these goals, then some people may shift their attention to higher-order values, such as individual freedom, participation, and the quality of life. Or, aptly put in the German vernacular, *Erst kommt das Fressen, dann kommt die Moral.*[31]

The value change theory posits a process of sociopolitical development occurring within most Western societies. Affluence, the growth of the welfare state, expanding communication and transportation networks, domestic order, and international stability create the conditions in many nations that allow new political interests to come to the fore. Because individuals acquire their basic value priorities relatively early in life, these changing social conditions exert the greatest impact on the values of younger generations socialized in the postwar era.

The value change theory is a general description of political development in all advanced industrial democracies, but the theory is especially relevant in West Germany. The social, economic, and political changes within German society have probably been greater than those of any other country within Western Europe, and have produced vastly different life experiences for succeeding generations. Members of earlier generations, socialized before World War II, lived at least partially under an authoritarian government, experienced long periods of economic hardship, and felt the destructive consequences of world war. Given these experiences, it would not be surprising if many older Germans retain a relatively high priority for what Inglehart labels *material* values—economic security, law and order, strict moral values, and physical security—even after thirty years of the material well-being and political stability.

Younger Germans, in contrast, are growing up in a fundamentally different environment. Present-day living standards are several times higher than Germans ever experienced before World War II. The welfare state now protects most citizens from major economic problems. Members of the postwar generations also have a broader world view, reflecting their higher educational levels, greater exposure to political information, and more diverse cultural experiences. The past four decades have been one of the longest periods of international peace in modern European history. Under these conditions, the security concerns that preoccupied prewar generations may diminish in urgency. As a result, some members of the postwar generation are broadening their interests to include new, non-economic or *postmaterial* goals.

Because more than just economic values are involved, this process of value change is also described as a transition from *Old Politics* to *New Politics*.[32] The Old Politics comprise the traditional goals of industrial societies, such as economic well-being, social stability, and security. New Politics goals arise from two different sources. Some New Politics goals—freedom of expression, political participation, and personal freedom—represent an expansion of traditional European liberalism to a wider popular base. Other New Politics concerns—social relations, lifestyles, and environmental quality—represent the emerging political issues of advanced industrial societies. The overall nature of the New Politics might best be understood in comparison to Old Politics goals:

Old Politics (Material) Goals	*New Politics (Postmaterial)* Goals
Economic growth	Economic policy that ensures environmental quality
Marketplace economy based on mass consumption	Social-needs economy and subdued consumption
Representative government	Grassroots democracy
Strong military defense	Nuclear disarmament
Social order	Personal freedom
Traditional family	Equality of sexes

Instead of unlimited economic growth, postmaterialists believe that development must occur in harmony with nature. Instead of a highly structured and elite-dominated political system, postmaterialists want people to have more say in the decisions affecting their lives. Whereas materialists believe in national security through nuclear deterrence, postmaterialists generally feel that the best security comes from nuclear disarmament. Postmaterialists also argue that the social aspects of the Social Market Economy deserve much more attention than they have received. Postmaterialists do not necessarily reject materialist goals; rather, past progress in addressing material goals produces the situation where New Politics goals are added to the priorities of the past.

Many of the values promoted by postmaterialists have earlier roots in the political culture. Germans have always held nature in high regard, and the forests possess almost mystical qualities in literature and folklore. Some of these same values are seen in the appeals of the modern environmental movement. The unconventional, nonmaterialist, and romantic tendencies of many contemporary youth also evoke images of the *Wandervogel* movement of the early 1900s. Despite these historical precedents, postmaterialism represents a qualitatively new development for West German politics.[33] Whereas the Wandervogel never numbered more than a few thousand participants, the alternative Green party has nearly 50,000 members and received almost 4 million votes in the 1987 federal elections. Popular support for many New Politics issues is even more extensive. Earlier alternative movements held antidemocratic and *völkisch* views; the supporters of the contemporary alternative movement come from the opposite end of the political spectrum.[34] Finally, earlier movements were a reaction to a social and political context that bears little relevance to contemporary West German politics.

The breadth of value change can be seen most clearly in public opinion trends over the period of the postwar socioeconomic recovery. One question measures the priority given to four basic human freedoms: freedom of worship, freedom of speech, freedom from fear, and freedom from want (Table IV.2). In the harsh economic environment of postwar Europe, a plurality felt that freedom from

TABLE IV.2 *The Shifting Priorities of the Public, 1949–1975*

	1949	1954	1958	1963	1965	1970	1975
Which is the most important freedom:							
Freedom of worship	12%	16	16	14	14	10	8
Freedom of speech	26	32	44	56	54	58	54
Freedom from fear	17	17	10	10	8	11	16
Freedom from want	35	35	28	15	19	18	23
No answer	10	—	2	5	5	5	1
Total	100%	100%	100%	100%	100%	102%	102%

Source: EMNID Opinion Polls. The 1970 and 1975 totals exceed 100 percent because of rounding.

TABLE IV.3 *The Distribution of Values Across Generations*

Generation	1970		1986	
	Material	*Postmaterial*	*Material*	*Postmaterial*
Wilhelmine	62%	2%	—	—
Weimar	57	5	39%	9
Third Reich	48	8	20	12
Postwar FRG	44	11	22	13
Affluence FRG	32	18	13	20
Protest FRG	15	29	17	26
Total population	46	11	18	21

Source: 1970 European Community Study and Eurobarometer 25. The percentage of respondents giving mixed value priorities is not included in the table. These data are available from the Interuniversity Consortium for Political and Social Research in Ann Arbor.

want was most important. As the success of the Economic Miracle met these basic needs, there was a long term shift away from this materialist goal and a growing emphasis on freedom of speech.

Inglehart devised another measure of value priorities that asks individuals to rank the priority of material and postmaterial goals.[35] Data based on this set of questions show that the problems of economic well-being and security are still a major concern for many individuals (Table IV.3). At the same time, however, answers to these survey questions provide important evidence of value change. Most citizens are now concerned with a mix of material and postmaterial concerns. The number of postmaterialists has increased from 11 percent in 1970 to 21 percent in 1986—despite the difficult economic conditions of the intervening period. Furthermore, the generations differ markedly in their value priorities. Materialists predominate in the older generations, reared during the Second Empire and Weimar Republic; among the youngest age groups, the number of postmaterialists actually outnumbers materialists.

THE YOUTH MOVEMENT AND BEYOND

Because New Politics values are more common among the young and better-educated, it was no surprise that the first evidence of these changing values came from among university students.[36] German universities shared in the student unrest common in Western Europe in the late 1960s. Various left-wing student groups attacked the bureaucratic structure of universities, specific government programs, and the U.S. war in Vietnam. These criticisms soon broadened to question the social and political foundations of a society oriented primarily toward material goals.

The political impact of the student movement increased in 1966, when the two large parties, the CDU/CSU and SPD, joined forces to form the government of the Grand Coalition. Only the small Free Democratic party remained in opposition. Many leftist students saw the Grand Coalition as an unholy alliance that coopted the reformist goals of the SPD. Students mobilized outside of the parliamentary process to express their political views. The APO (*Ausserparlamentarische Opposition*) spearheaded resistance to the Emergency Powers legislation of 1968 as a threat to individual rights; it also consistently opposed the Federal Republic's support of the U.S. war in Vietnam. Student sit-ins and protests on university campuses frequently spilled over into the surrounding communities, leading to clashes with the police. The battles between students and the government were often violent.

Even though the APO faded from existence after a reform-oriented SPD-FDP coalition entered the government in 1969, the student movement marked a significant milestone in the development of West German politics. Amid the often radical rhetoric and tactics of the movement was evidence of a growing public concern with a new set of issues, which established political leaders were not addressing. The battles over university reform, for example, were symptomatic of a broader public interest in the further democratization of society. Student criticisms of the materialism of West German society reflected a view shared by a growing proportion of the general public.

Several different political currents eventually emerged from the student movement. One outlet is a counterculture movement based on postmaterial values. Distinct counterculture districts developed in several large cities. Natural food stores, biobakeries, cooperative businesses, leftist bookstores, vegetarian restaurants, and youth-oriented cafes offer a life style attuned to the new values. Small firms emphasize employee management of the company (*Büro ohne Chef*) and a more humane working environment, rather than just making a profit. Day-care centers and job-sharing explore ways of allowing women to participate more fully in the labor force. An extensive social network provides an environment in which an *Alternativkultur* could develop.

The student movement also laid the groundwork for organized efforts to pursue New Politics interests. One strategy called for young people to work for change within the existing political institutions. The reformist goals of the Brandt government attracted many young people into the Social Democratic party. The Young Socialists (*Jusos*) recruited a new constituency of young, middle-class activists to the SPD's traditionally working-class ranks. The social composition and political orientation of the SPD (and for a time the FDP) underwent gradual change from within.

Another byproduct of the student movement is the development of political action groups explicitly committed to New Politics goals (see Chapter VIII). These new social movements are important, because they provide an institutional base for new political orientations, harnessing the energies of political activists and representing their viewpoint within the political process. Newly formed environmental groups constitute a major new public interest lobby. Contemporary peace groups mobilize public opposition to government defense policy and indirectly influence policy options on defense. The women's movement works to change traditional sex roles. The creation of the Green party (*Die Grünen*) in 1980 further developed the political base of the New Politics movement. The partial institutionalization of the youth movement gives these new political values permanent representation in the West German political process.

The evolution of the New Politics movement is also evident in its political philosophy. Many early student activists were avowed Marxists or communists, and tried to interpret the problems of West German society in terms of Marxist principles. The Jusos of the early 1970s, for example, called for a renewal of socialist ideology in the SPD. Eventually, the shortfalls of Marxist ideology became apparent to most activists, and the movement searched for an alternative political philosophy. An eclectic humanist philosophy is developing, borrowing more from Marcuse than from Marx, more from E. F. Schumacher than from Adam Smith.

Public interest in the New Politics has gradually spread beyond its roots among the young and developed a wider base of popular support. Environmental protection, including opposition to nuclear energy, now attracts widespread public attention. There is renewed interest in extending the democratization of society and citizen participation in the political process. In foreign policy, more citizens actively advocate foreign aid for less-developed countries, disarmament, and increased international cooperation, including that between Western-bloc and Eastern-bloc nations.

The new style of direct political action pursued by the student movement also diffused into the society at large. The 1970s witnessed the flowering of a new form of political participation—citizen action groups (*Bürgerinitiativen*). Interested citizens form ad hoc groups to assert their interests more forcefully, whether in local education, the placement of a highway, or broader social reform issues. These groups resort to petitions, protests, and other direct actions to dramatize their cause and influence decision makers. This expansion of the public's direct involvement in the political process is a primary goal of the New Politics, and a natural extension of the growth of participatory democracy in postwar West Germany.

The New Politics is still a minority viewpoint in West German society, a "second culture" embedded within the dominant culture. At the same time, however, the evidence of substantial political change is already clear. Moreover, participation in party youth branches and the new political action groups is producing a cadre of future political leaders with new political values. The young people of the 1960s represents the next generation of economic and political leadership for the Federal Republic.[37]

A CLASH OF CULTURES

With the development of the New Politics, the West German political culture has moved closer to those of other Western democracies. Discussion of the "German question" is replaced by a New Politics debate similar to those in other European democracies. In addition, the social forces driving West German society no longer are focused on the cultural legacy of the past, but on the emerging problems of advanced industrial societies.

As has been the case in other European nations, the New Politics movement has not won open acceptance from the political establishment. These New Politics interests often generate division and tension within the political system. To some critics, the New Politics represents a rejection of the values that brought economic and political security to the Federal Republic. Having reached a significant level of economic progress, materialists fear that the proenvironment and nonmaterial aspects of the New Politics could undermine the nation's economic achievements. The protests and radical appeals of New Politics groups also conjure up images of political instability that worry many Germans.

The tension between Old and New is a very visible aspect of contemporary politics. Many confrontations between the alternative movement and political authorities have occurred over the past decade. The environmental movement organized massive protests against new nuclear power facilities at Whyl, Grohnde, Brokdorf, Wackersdorf, and Gorleben. Occasionally these confrontations led to clashes with police, as some protestors used violence in their attempts to occupy the construction sites or police overreacted to large unruly crowds. Violence by radicals at a 1987 environmental protest resulted in the death of a law enforcement officer. In another incident, opponents of *Startbahn West,* an expansion of the Frankfurt airport that would destroy a large forested area, were forcibly removed from the site by police after months of confrontation. This scenario is being played out over and over as new political controversies arise. Thus the West German public sees a continuing conflict between old and new that often exceeds the conventional boundaries of political discourse.

The clash of values also is visible in interpersonal relations. It is evident in everyday life as elderly Germans look askance at young people who dress and act in unconventional ways; in disagreements between parents who want their children to share their concerns for financial and personal security, and children who want more personal fulfillment. Older people who remember the economic and social instability of Germany's past cannot understand why the young do not share these concerns. The rhetoric of protesting youth often puts their elders on the defensive. The street graffiti of the alternative movement voices their alienation from Germany's past: "Better a demonstration by democrats than a nation of Nazis," "Better to occupy empty houses than foreign lands," "You are everything, the *Volk* means nothing!"

The alternative movement's attempts to work within the political system sometimes yield unsettling results. In Parliament, the political establishment is confronted by Green party deputies who challenge conventional political practices in both their appearance and their dramatic political style. Developers and community planners now face an active and well-organized environmental constituency. This clash of cultures is a common theme in contemporary German politics.

This cultural conflict represents a new stage in the development of the German political culture. On the one hand, conflicts between cultures reintroduces some instability and uncertainty into West German politics. Although the West German political system will likely remain one of the most stable in Europe, it will no longer be as tranquil or as predictable as in the past. A series of running battles between New Politics adherents and the political establishment can be expected to continue in the years ahead. These conflicts may even take an occasional violent turn, as with the post-Chernobyl clashes over nuclear power or earlier protests against the 1983 deployment of NATO missiles.

At the same time, however, the New Politics represents positive developments for the political culture. New Politics values emphasize democratic principles, and New Politics groups press for the Federal Republic to live up to its democratic rhetoric and expand the citizen's role in the political process. The New Politics movement also represents an openness to change and recognition of unmet social needs that many established political figures acknowledge were lacking in the political system. As one SPD leader has said, "The alternative Green movement is a sign of creativity in the Federal Republic which is not present to the same extent in France or the United Kingdom. German politicians should welcome the challenge they present." The New Politics represents a challenge to the political status quo, but it is a challenge that evolves from the past accomplishments of West German society.

NOTES

1. Gabriel Almond and Sidney Verba, *The Civic Culture* (Princeton: Princeton University Press, 1963); Sidney Verba, "The Remaking of the German Political Culture," in *Political Culture and Political Development,* ed. Lucian Pye and Sidney Verba (Princeton: Princeton University Press, 1965).

2. Gordon Craig, *The Germans* (New York: Putnam, 1982), p. 9.

3. Stanley Milgram, *Obedience to Authority* (New York: Harper and Row, 1974).

4. The issue of the German knowledge of the Third Reich's actions against the Jews is intensely debated. See: Sarah Gordon, *Hitler, Germans, and the "Jewish Question"* (Princeton: Princeton University Press, 1984), chap. 6; Walter Laqueur, *The Terrible Secret: Suppression of the Truth about Hitler's 'Final Solution'* (London: Weidenfeld and Nicholson, 1980).

5. Anna Merritt and Richard Merritt, *Public Opinion in Occupied Germany* (Urbana: University of Illinois Press, 1970); Anna Merritt and Richard Merritt, *Public Opinion in Semisovereign Germany* (Urbana: University of Illinois Press, 1980).

6. Merritt and Merritt, *Public Opinion in Occupied Germany,* p. 38.

7. Merritt and Merritt, *Public Opinion in Occupied Germany,* p. 74.

8. James Tent, *Mission on the Rhine: Reeducation and Denazification in American-Occupied Germany* (Princeton: Princeton University Press, 1983).

9. Walter Stahl, ed. *Education for Democracy in West Germany* (New York: Praeger, 1961); John Montgomery, *Forced to be Free* (Chicago: University of Chicago Press, 1957).

10. Almond and Verba, *The Civic Culture.*

11. Konrad Adenauer, *Memoirs* (Chicago: Henry Regnery, 1965), p. 39.

12. Leonard Krieger, *The German Idea of Freedom* (Chicago: University of Chicago Press, 1957); David Calleo, *The German Problem Reconsidered* (Cambridge: Cambridge University Press, 1978), chap. 6.

13. Gebhard Schweigler, "Whatever Happened to Germany," in *The Foreign Policy of West Germany*, ed. Ekkehart Krippendorff and Volker Rittberger (Beverly Hills: Sage Publications, 1980).

14. G. R. Boynton and Gerhard Loewenberg, "The Development of Public Support for Parliament in Germany, 1951–1959," *British Journal of Political Science* 3 (April 1973): 169–189; G. R. Boynton and Gerhard Loewenberg, "The Decay of Support for the Monarchy and the Hitler Regime in the Federal Republic of Germany," *British Journal of Political Science* 4 (July 1974):453–488; David Conradt, "The Changing Political Culture."

15. Russell Dalton, *Citizen Politics in Western Democracies* (Chatham, N.J.: Chatham House Publishers, 1988), chap. 11.

16. Werner Weidenfeld, ed. *Die Identität der Deutschen*, 2nd ed. (Munich: Hanser, 1983); Werner Weidenfeld, ed. *Nachdenken über Deutschland* (Cologne: Verlag Wissenschaft und Politik, 1985); Elisabeth Noelle-Neumann and Renate Köcher, *Die verletzte Nation* (Stuttgart: Deutsche Verlags-Anstalt, 1987).

17. Dan Diner, "The 'National Question' in the Peace Movement," *New German Critique* 32 (1984): 86–107.

18. Walter Laqueur, *Germany Today* (Boston: Little Brown, 1985), chap. 21.

19. David Conradt, "The Changing German Political Culture," pp. 221–225, 231–235; also see the Allensbach report, *Demokratie-Verankerung in der Bundesrepublik Deutschland* (Allensbach: Institut für Demoskopie, 1979).

20. Gerda Lederer, "Trends in Authoritarianism," *Journal of Cross- Cultural Psychology* 13 (September 1982): 299–314; Frederick Weil, "Tolerance of Free Speech in the United States and West Germany," *Social Forces* 60 (June 1982): 973–992.

21. For instance, the influential news magazine *Der Spiegel*, dramatically overstated the violent clashes between police and anti-nuclear demonstrations after the Chernobyl crisis in 1986 as the beginnings of a civil war.

22. Another case study involves the emergence of a radical right-wing party (the NPD) during the recession of the late 1960s; see Steven Warnecke, "The Future of Rightist Extremism in West Germany," *Comparative Politics* 2 (July 1970): 629–652.

23. Jillian Becker, *Hitler's Children: The Story of the Baader-Meinhoff Terrorists Gang* (New York: Lippincott, 1977).

24. David Conradt, "Political Culture, Legitimacy, and Participation," *West European Politics* 4 (1981): 18–34.

25. Ralf Dahrendorf, *Society and Democracy in Germany* (New York: Doubleday, 1967).

26. A. J. P. Taylor, *The Course of German History* (New York: Capricorn, 1962), p. 10.

27. Boynton and Loewenberg, "Decay of Support for the Monarchy;" Conradt, "The Changing German Political Culture."

28. Kendall Baker, Russell Dalton, and Kai Hildebrandt, *Germany Transformed* (Cambridge: Harvard University Press, 1981), chaps. 1–2.

29. Otto Kirchheimer, "Germany: The Vanishing Opposition," in *Political Opposition in Western Democracies*, ed. Robert Dahl (New Haven: Yale University Press, 1966).

30. Ronald Inglehart, *The Silent Revolution* (Princeton: Princeton University Press, 1977), chaps. 1–3; Baker, Dalton, and Hildebrandt, *Germany Transformed*, chap. 6.

31. This quote is from Bertolt Brecht's work, *Threepenny Opera:* "First comes the food, then comes morality."

32. Dalton, *Citizen Politics in Western Democracies,* chap. 5.

33. Joyce Mushaben, "Youth Protest and the Democratic State," *Research in Political Sociology* 2 (1986): 171–197; also see Walter Laqueur, *Young Germany: A History of the German Youth Movement* (New York: Basic Books, 1962).

34. Wilhelm Bürklin, *Grüne Politik: Ideologische Zyklen, Wähler und Parteiensystem* (Opladen: Westdeutscher Verlag, 1984).

35. Inglehart, *The Silent Revolution;* Ronald Inglehart, "Postmaterial Values in an Environment of Insecurity," *American Political Science Review,* 75 (September 1981); Ronald Inglehart, *Culture Shift in Advanced Industrial Society* (Princeton: Princeton University Press, 1989).

36. Richard Merritt, "The Student Protest Movement in West Berlin," *Comparative Politics* 1 (July 1969): 516–533.

37. Steven Szabo, *The Successor Generation* (London: Butterworths, 1983); Hermann Schmitt, *Neue Politik in alten Parteien* (Opladen: Westdeutscher Verlag, 1987).

CHAPTER V

Political Learning and Political Communication

JUST AS THE STRUCTURE OF government is an essential part of the political process, so too are the citizenry's beliefs about the government and politics. If political systems require congruent political cultures, as many political experts maintain, then one of the basic functions of a political system is the creation and perpetuation of these citizen attitudes. This process of developing the beliefs and values of the public is known as *political socialization.*

Political socialization is a lifelong process. Learning begins at an early age, long before children are old enough to participate formally in the political process. Most children acquire a sense of class, religious, and national identity before their teens. Early youth is also a time when basic political orientations develop, when the beliefs anchoring the political culture take root, and when partisan and ideological tendencies first emerge. This process continues on to adulthood. Citizens develop specific policy beliefs at least partially based on previously learned values. Elections regularly present slates of candidates and issues that must be evaluated by the voter. New attitudes are formed and old attitudes are influenced by new experiences. Some elements of the socialization process, such as the media, also perform a crucial communication function between citizens and political leaders.

The process of political socialization is viewed primarily as a source of continuity, with one generation transmitting the prevailing political norms to the next.[1] In West Germany, of course, socialization has also been an agent of political change. The shift from an authoritarian to a democratic system produced a break in past socialization patterns and a dramatic shift in the content of socialization. What steps did the government and political leaders take to remake the political culture and make it compatible with the new social and political structures of the Federal Republic? The transformation of the political culture described in Chapter IV could only be accomplished by an equally large change in the socialization process.

The study of political socialization patterns in West Germany, therefore, involves both change and continuity. During the 1950s, the government used the schools and the mass media in a large-scale reeducation program aimed at remaking the political culture. As the new system took root, new patterns of political learning developed to maintain these political norms. Thus, over this period, both the content of political socialization and the role of various agents of socialization changed substantially.

FAMILY INFLUENCES

In most societies, political learning begins in the family. Parents are usually the major influence in forming the basic values and attitudes of their children. Children have few, if any, sources of learning comparable to their parents. Family discussions can furnish a rich source of political information, and parents are political role models for their children. Through either imitation or explicit reinforcement, children often internalize their parents' attitudes and beliefs. Moreover, the child, almost completely dependent on the parents for basic needs, can do little to resist parental pressures to conform. Most parents and children share the same cultural, social, and class milieu, all of which provide additional, indirect political cues. For all these reasons, the family has a pervasive effect on the future adult's thoughts and actions.

During the early years of the Federal Republic, many observers were concerned about the role of family socialization in the political learning process. Researchers linked the pattern of social relations within the German family to the authoritarian aspects of the political culture. Scholars such as Theodor Adorno, Erich Fromm, and Erik Erikson maintained that the internal structure of the German family legitimized an authoritarian style of conflict resolution that political leaders adopted. As Ralf Dahrendorf noted, the father furnished a model for the Kaiser or the Führer:[2]

The German father is, or at least used to be, a combination of judge and state attorney: presiding over his family, relentlessly prosecuting every sign of deviance, and settling all disputes by his supreme authority.

According to Dahrendorf, the authoritarian values taught by the family were one of the reasons for the pathology of liberal democracy in Germany. This characterization is more true of the family earlier in the century, although this pattern of family relations partially carried over to the Federal Republic. Gabriel Almond and Sidney Verba, for example, found that Germans in the late 1950s were less likely than either U.S. citizens or Britons to say that they participated in family decision making during their youth. Furthermore, these nondemocratic family environments affected adult feelings about the democratic process.[3]

The family's role as a source of democratic political education was also limited by the political environment of postwar Germany. Many adults did not discuss politics openly with friends, co-workers, or family, because of the depoliticized environment of the early postwar years. The stigma of the Third Reich further limited the frequency of political discussion. Parents were understandably hesitant to discuss politics with their children for fear that this topic would arise. "What did you do in the war, father?" was not a pleasant source of conversation for the parents or their offspring. This compunction created a void in family discussions. A 1957 survey found that most parents had never spoken with their children about the end of World War II, and barely one-fifth had discussed Hitler's rise to power or the Third Reich's persecution of the Jews.[4] Because there was so little of the normal political commentary that children use to identify and adopt parental values, explicit political learning within the family was limited.

Even if parents had wanted to educate their children into the democratic norms of the Federal Republic, they were ill-prepared to do so. The political values and experiences of most parents were minimally relevant to democratic politics. Most parents in the 1950s had spent the majority of their adult lives under the authoritarian regimes of the Wilhelmine Empire or the Third Reich. These experiences served as examples of what politics should not be, rather than fostering political values that should be transmitted to their offspring. In other words, adults were learning the new political norms at almost the same time as their children.

Consequently, children were not exposed to a steady stream of information from parents that could socialize new political norms. Historical discontinuities made it difficult for parents to convey a traditional commitment to parties, democratic political institutions, or the political system as a whole. West German party attachments typify the frailty of the family socialization process. In the United States, partisanship is often treated as a family tradition—loyalties to the Democratic or Republican party extend across several generations. In Britain, too, ties to the Labour or Conservative parties are routinely passed from parents to children. In contrast, the disruption of the German party system meant that few German families could claim such long-term traditions, and even existing partisan attachments were not always communicated to the children. Many German youths remained unaware of their parents' party identification, although this was common knowledge for British and U.S. youths. Even as late as 1972, a public opinion survey showed that less than half of the adult public knew of their parents' general partisan leanings.[5]

Without much explicit political education, what little political socialization the family provided came primarily through indirect learning, such as through the authority relationships existing within the family. Indirect parental influence also came from the social cues of the family. In most families, parents and children share class, religious, and other social characteristics. This shared sociocultural environment transmits political values, even if there is no explicit parental socialization. That is, a manual worker and his son may both prefer the Social Democratic party, even if no discussion occurs between them, because they both experience the political values and partisan cues of the working-class milieu. Several socialization studies found that such indirect political learning had an important influence on value formation.[6]

From these uncertain beginnings, the content and importance of parental socialization has changed over the past few decades. As democratic principles and values came to be accepted, the frequency of political discussion increased; family conversations about politics are now commonplace. Moreover, since the late 1960s, most new parents are young, raised under the political system of the Federal Republic and without personal experience of the horrors of the Third Reich; Helmut Kohl describes them as "the generation blessed by the grace of late birth." These parents thus can pass on democratic norms and party attachments that they have held for a lifetime.

Recent research shows that parents now exert a stronger formative influence on the political values of their offspring. In one study, parents and their teenage children were both interviewed, and their opinions were compared directly.[7] Family agreement is far from perfect, but the correspondence between parent and adolescent values is often substantial. For instance, the young now are more likely to know their parents' partisan attachments and agree with them. A majority of parents who identify with the Social Democratic party have children who are also SPD partisans; the same applies for CDU parents and their offspring. Less than one-sixth of the teenagers express a loyalty to a party in opposition to their parents' partisanship. The impact of parental values is also detectable in basic attitudes toward political groups, the political system, and political participation.

As the explicitly political aspects of family socialization have changed, so too have social relations within the family. The dominating-father role has largely yielded to a more flexible authority relationship within the household, especially in middle-class families. West German parents now place more emphasis on teaching their children to be independent and self-sufficient.[8] One recent public opinion survey found two-thirds of young adults in their twenties would stress such values in educating their children, in contrast to only a quarter of the prewar generation of parents. To the extent that the traditional authoritarian family structure actually contributed to authoritarian politics, the new structure of the family may be equally conducive to a more participatory political culture.

Despite this strengthening of the family socialization process, sharp differences in the political beliefs of parents and children are often apparent. Today's young adults grew up in an environment fundamentally different both from the Germany of their parents and the Germany of their own children. In other words, whereas parents might engage in more frequent political discussion with their children, changing social conditions and the impact of other influences are still producing substantial generational differences in social and political beliefs. The *Political Action* study, for example, shows that the gap between parent and adolescent beliefs on specific political issues and policy goals is often larger in the Federal

Republic than in the other four democracies studied. German youth are more leftist than their parents, more positive about their political efficacy, more postmaterialist, and more likely to engage in protests and other forms of unconventional political action. Another recent comparison of young adults in West Germany and the United States uncovers striking differences in perceived family agreement (Table V.1). Whereas 77 percent of the Americans say they agree with their parents' moral values, only 38 percent of the Germans express agreement; 47 percent of the U.S. youths say they share their parents' political views, compared to only 33 percent of the Germans.[9] German parents and their children do not, however, disagree on fundamental issues, such as the structure of society or the political system; other surveys document basic consensus on these points. Instead, family differences are probably another sign of a shift in young people's values and the adoption of goals that conflict with those of their elders (see Chapter IV).

This continuing generation gap creates tensions in the German family and further erodes the authority of the parents. It is fairly common today to hear parents complain about the erosion of traditional authority and the lack of respect for authority. Some evidence supports this view. For instance, most (71 percent) young American adults believe that parents should be loved and respected regardless of their faults; only a minority of German youth (28 percent) share this view. More frequent political discussion and a more open family structure have not created a continuity of social and political values within the family. Such tensions are probably inevitable in a society that has changed so much, so quickly. Nevertheless, this

TABLE V.1 *Perceptions of Family Agreement by U.S. and West German Adolescents*

	West Germany	United States
Moral standards	38%	77%
Religious attitudes	39	69
Social attitudes	47	66
Political views	33	47
Attitudes about sex	14	43
None of these areas	13	1

Source: 1981 International Values Study; table entries are the percentage of 18–24-year-olds who say they share values with their parents. These data are available from Dr. L. Halman, University of Tilburg, Holland.

situation cannot be considered a positive feature of West German society. The family should play an important role in transmitting social norms and stabilizing social change in an established democratic society. The ambiguous role of the German family makes the process of political socialization uncertain.

THE EDUCATIONAL SYSTEM

Another key institution in political socialization is the educational system. Allied and German political leaders saw the educational system as an important source of political socialization in the new West German state. In contrast to the family, the schools were controlled by the government and could be used to develop new political values. Thus the school system was one of the institutions enlisted in the government's program of reeducating the public to accept democratic norms.[10]

The government had two methods for transforming the school system into an agent for democratizing postwar West Germany. First, the regime expanded the curriculum to include new courses in civics and more offerings in history. Instruction aimed at developing a formal commitment to the institutions and procedures of the Federal Republic. History courses worked to counteract the nationalistic views promulgated under Weimar and the Third Reich. Social studies classes stressed the benefits of the democratic system, drawing sharp contrast to the communist model.

The second method was to reform the mode of teaching. Modern teaching methods supplanted the authoritarian educational structures and classroom practices of the past. Social studies courses made greater use of informal classroom discussions, instead of fixed lesson plans. The secondary schools introduced rudimentary student government, and by the early 1960s nearly every school had, at least on paper, a student "co-administration" program. The expansion of student participation in educational decision making was even more extensive in the university reforms of the 1960s. These innovations marked a sharp change from the traditional, authoritarian ways of the German educational system.

These reforms restructured the educational system, but their success was not always complete. In West Germany, education is controlled by the individual state governments, and some Länder adopted the new educational style less enthusiastically than others. Some reformers criticized the curriculum because it emphasized a Rechtsstaat mentality, stressing the formal institutions and procedures of the democratic state rather than the principles of popular control of political process. Social studies texts in the 1950s defined the citizen's role in somewhat passive terms, such as keeping informed, maintaining social harmony, and having responsibilities to the state. The role of the citizen as subject was not rejected entirely.

Over time, the content of civics instruction underwent further change. Beginning in the mid-1960s, textbooks began to place more emphasis on the dynamics of the democratic system: interest representation, conflict resolution, minority rights, and the methods of citizen influence. The passive citizen model yielded to a more activist orientation. Education adopted a more critical perspective on society and politics. The new texts substituted a more pragmatic view of the strengths and weaknesses of democracy for the idealistic textbook images of the 1950s. The intent of the present system is to better prepare students for their adult roles as political participants.

Socialization research finds that the impact of formal schooling on political norms is greatest when there is little prior family learning, as was the case in postwar Germany. The reeducation program was at least partially responsible for developing a stronger sense of political interest and democratic beliefs among German youth. By the early 1970s, for example, West German students ranked highest in support for democratic values in a ten-nation study of youth.[11] Nevertheless, the broader social and political trends in West German society gradually made this program of formalized political education redundant. Social studies courses now reinforce the democratic political beliefs learned from parents and peers, rather than attempting to create them in the first place. Thus the political content of the German education system is now more similar to civics courses in the United States, Britain, and other established democracies.

Another important socializing effect of the educational system is its role in defining the social structure. Public education in most European societies has traditionally functioned with two contrasting goals. One goal is to emphasize personal growth and the development of intellectual creativity (*Bildung*) among the top strata of students who comprise the future leaders of society. Another goal is to provide more specifically job-oriented education (*Ausbildung*) for the masses. Adherence to these two differing educational models leads to a highly structured and stratified educational system.

Figure V.1 shows the general structure of the educational system, which varies slightly from state to state. The social stratification of the educational system is most evident at the secondary school level. All students attend primary school for the first four years, and then are divided into one of three distinct secondary-school tracks. Students attend separate schools with different facilities, teachers, and

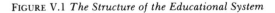

FIGURE V.1 *The Structure of the Educational System*

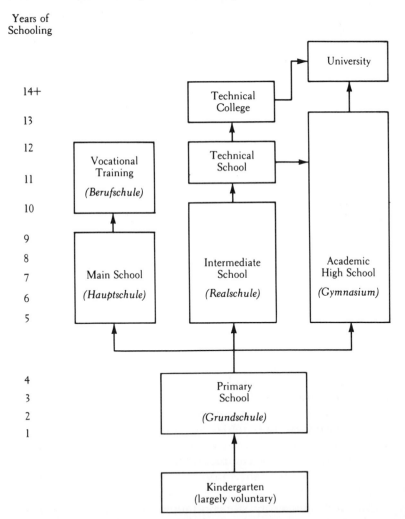

curriculums. One track, the main school or *Hauptschule,* provides a general education that usually leads to vocational training and a working-class occupation. The Hauptschule has a practical curriculum, focusing on German, arithmetic, a foreign language (generally English), and other necessary educational skills. This limited formal schooling lasts until age 15 in most Länder, and students then begin a program of vocational training. The first year consists of career orientation, followed by two or more years of apprenticeship, with only one day a week at the vocational school. Most students (about 40 percent) now follow this educational track.

The second track is the intermediate school, or *Realschule.* Enrollments in the Realschule have increased several fold over the past two decades; about 25 percent of secondary students presently attend a Realschule. The Realschule mixes vocational and academic training. For example, students study a second foreign language and must take higher-level mathematics courses; at the same time they take practical courses, such as typing and business mathematics. Students graduate from the Realschule at age 16 and receive a completion certificate (*Mittlere Reife*). At this point, graduates choose between an apprenticeship, leading directly to a career, or more technical training, perhaps even including study at a technical college. The Realschule certificate qualifies graduates for professions in technical, commercial or administrative fields. Most graduates work in lower middle-class occupations or the skilled trades.

A third track consists of purely academic training at a *Gymnasium,* an academic high school. The Gymnasium is the traditional route to social and economic success in German society. About 25 percent of secondary school students now attend a Gymnasium, enrollments having nearly doubled in the last two decades. Different Gymnasiums specialize in science and mathematics, foreign languages, or classical training. The curriculum stresses advanced academic topics as preparation for a university education. Foreign language instruction includes nine years of English, six of Latin or a modern language, and an optional third language. Mathematics, physics, chemistry, and biology are at or above the level of a U.S. high school. Humanities courses cover material normally learned in a U.S. university. After completing final year exams, the Gymnasium student receives an *Abitur,* which confers a legal right to attend a university.

Once at the university, students follow the German model of academic freedom. For the student this means the freedom to develop one's intellectual potential largely unfettered by regulations and formal course requirements. In many social science fields, students are free to develop their own program of studies; they can even mix courses from different universities. The courses themselves are often equally unstructured: no quizzes, no finals, no homework, no required attendance, and no grades. Sciences programs are usually more structured, but still relatively open by U.S. standards. Degrees are awarded after passage of field exams taken at the completion of one's studies. Moreover, universities do not charge tuition, and until very recently most students received a modest stipend from the government. The university system was designed for a small number of strongly self-motivated students, allowing great freedom to the individual.

As university enrollments exploded in the 1960s, the negative aspects of this system became more evident. Without a fixed program of studies or academic advisors, one was unsure how best to prepare for field exams. It was easier to learn about university social life than academic subject matter, and students made slow progress through the university. As class sizes increased, the educational value of an unstructured curriculum decreased. This led to a series of reforms in university education over the past decade. Enrollments in specialized programs (medicine, law, etc.) are now limited by a quota system; no longer is the Abitur a blank check. Most universities introduced more structure into their programs, with a fixed course of studies and more required courses. The government replaced the stipend with student loans. Still, by U.S. or British standards, the German university student lives a privileged existence.

This highly stratified system of public education in the Federal Republic has prompted criticism on several fronts.[12] One persisting criticism is that the money spent on educating students in the different tracks is unequal. The resources of the educational system are concentrated on the academic track rather than the vocational tracks. The Gymnasiums receive more generous financing and have lower student/teacher ratios than the Hauptschulen and Realschulen. Teacher qualifications for the Gymnasium are more rigorous than for the other tracks. University education is well-supported by the state. In short, an obvious distinction exists between education for the masses and education for elites.

This limited investment in mass education is further illustrated by the final years of "schooling." Students are required to stay in school until eighteen, but for most students the last few years consist of vocational training, in which only one day a week is spent in school and the rest is spent working. About four-fifths of the enrolled students at age seventeen are in vocational programs, and only one-fifth, primarily Gymnasium students, receive regular educational training.

The educational system did not create social inequality in West Germany, but the operation of the system tends to perpetuate this inequality. After only four to six years of primary schooling, students are directed into one of the three tracks, based on their school record, teacher evaluations, and parental preferences. At this early age, family influences are still a major factor in the child's development. Most children assigned to the academic track come from middle-class families, and most students in the vocational track are from working-class families. For instance, if the value 100 represents the average student's chance of attending a Gymnasium, then the chances for different social classes in 1980 were:

> Civil servant's child: 396
> Self-employed worker's child: 212
> Salaried employee's child: 140
> Manual worker's child: 21

In other words, the child of a tenured government official has nearly twenty times the chance of attending a Gymnasium as the child of a manual worker. These social differences are replicated in university enrollments, and have not greatly lessened over the years. Furthermore, because of the social and educational gap between secondary school tracks, few students take advantage of the option to transfer to a higher-level school. The educational system thus inevitably reinforces class distinctions within society.

Beginning in the 1970s, reformers have made repeated attempts to lessen the elitist bias of the educational system. One proposal, similar to the educational reform implemented in Britain during the 1960s, suggested, as an alternative to the separate-track system, a system of comprehensive secondary schools, with a varied curriculum, which all students would attend. Parents of Gymnasium students predictably opposed what they felt was an attempt to dilute the quality of their children's education, and broad social support for this reform was lacking. Without a uniform national policy, few state governments were willing to initiate such a radical restructuring of the educational system. Only a few SPD-led state governments supported comprehensive schools as an optional fourth track, and often their attempts at reform were thwarted.[13] Less than 5 percent of secondary school students are presently enrolled in comprehensive schools.

Reformers were more successful in other areas. In lieu of comprehensive schools, the state governments agreed on a curriculum reform that narrowed the gap between secondary schools. The curriculum of most Hauptschulen has shifted from the basic, practically oriented subject matter of the past toward a more specialized set of course offerings aimed at a higher conceptual level. The curriculum and resources of the Realschule underwent similar upgrading, contributing to its growing popularity and enrollments.

Another significant reform expanded access to the universities. In the early 1950s, only 6 percent of college-aged youth attended a university; today this proportion is almost 20 percent. The increase results, in part, from the growth of Gymnasium enrollments, giving a larger percentage of youth the Abitur necessary to enter the university. University programs also broadened to include technical fields and teaching preparation, previously handled in separate institutions. In addition, educators made a concerted effort to provide a second educational path (*zweite Bildungsweg*) into the universities for those who did not attend the traditional Gymnasium. For instance, holders of a Realschule certificate can obtain a Abitur by attending an Evening Gymnasium or special preparatory *Kolleg*; students can also transfer from a technical college into a university. Still, few students take advantage of these alternative pathways. The West German university system remains elitist in emphasis, but its upper-class accent is a little less distinct.

INFORMAL SOURCES OF POLITICAL LEARNING

In any nation, the network of informal personal relations among citizens is another important source of political learning. As soon as children begin to explore the world outside their parents' home, they develop friendships and peer-group ties that teach them about social (and implicitly political) relations. Co-workers in the factory are often a valuable source of information about political matters. Friends discuss politics, compare ideas, and debate current political issues. Although difficult to measure in a systematic fashion, these informal contacts constitute a crucial part of the socialization process.

The role of the peer group in the socialization of the young is very interesting, and controversial.[14] A distinct youth culture developed in most postwar European societies, but it may be especially pronounced in West Germany because of the uncertain nature of family socialization. It might be more accurate to speak of youth cultures, because young people have many choices: school groups, punkers, counter-culture groups, sports clubs, church groups, party activists, and dropouts. One of the most striking findings of Klaus Allerbeck and Wendy Hoag's comparison of youth attitudes in 1962 and 1983 is the emergence of distinct youth cultures structured around peer-group networks: In 1962, only 19 percent of young people said that they had belonged to a clique of some type; by 1983, this proportion had increased to 67 percent.[15]

Such peer groups can easily influence the values of their members. There is much interaction and exposure in the group, which persists even when the influence of family and schools begins to wane. Receptivity to the norms of the group is also high, because it is composed of individuals with strong personal ties and common interests.

Explicit political learning is a minor part of most youth groups, but under some circumstances the peer group may exert a substantial impact on political beliefs. For instance, a variety of biographical studies and impressionistic evidence suggests that the student movement of the 1960s created a youth subculture that socialized a new political perspective among many university students.[16] The friendships, networks, and subculture formed during this period have endured into adulthood for many activists of the 1960s. The environmental and peace groups of the 1980s created a similar subculture for many politically oriented young people.

Rather than politics, however, peer groups among the young are more notable for the "social learning" that they foster.[17] Personal interactions within a peer group develop social norms that influence general patterns of social behavior. Most peer groups engender a sense of commonality and a sharing of decision making, experiences that are often underdeveloped in adult-directed environments, such as schools and the family. Peer groups also provide a buffer from the pressures and criticisms of adults. Many young Germans feel that adults are harshly critical of youth, and the supportive environment of the peer group provides a more positive self-image among the young. By fostering a sense of community among the young, peer groups might actually contribute to the widening gap between West German youth and their parents. Indeed, the weakening of family ties over the past generation is mirrored by a strengthening of peer-group bonds.

As individuals age, the peer groups of youth become the friends and co-workers of adult life. In contrast to the open, casual, and outgoing style of U.S. social relations, Germans are more reserved and inward in their interactions.[18] Social interaction with strangers is kept to a minimum. Instead, most individuals develop very close relationships with a few friends or relatives. Most older taverns, for example, reserve a special table (*Stammtisch*), where small groups of friends meet on a regular basis for years, or decades. When these special relationships develop, they are recognized and reinforced by the distinction between formal (*Sie*) and informal (*Du*) terms of address in the German language. For the few allowed within this circle, personal ties are quite strong.

Rather than providing a source for learning new political values, most adult friendship networks act to reinforce previously formed beliefs. By adulthood most individuals have developed their basic political values, and any new learning must first overcome previous learning. In addition, people generally select friends with similar social and political values. Public opinion surveys find, for example, that most German voters believe their friends support the same political party as themselves. This lessens exposure to conflicting viewpoints that might alter long-standing opinions.

The interaction among friends and co-workers, however, is still very important for learning about and interpreting new political stimuli. A steelworker in the Ruhr, for example, hears about politics from his co-workers and other working-class neighbors and friends. This social milieu provides repeated cues on which issues are most important to people like oneself, which policies will provide the most benefit, and which party represents these interests. Similarly, a Bavarian Catholic learns about political issues at weekly church services, from Catholic social groups, and from his or her predominately conservative Catholic friends. The cues provided by such social networks are an important source of political information for many people.

Personal discussions with friends, family, and political activists have grown as a source of political information as changing political norms encouraged greater involvement in politics.[19] Equally important, personal interactions provide an information source qualitatively different from newspapers, television, and other mass media. Face-to-face communication is interactive. Information can be discussed until its meaning is understood; the transfer of information can be tailored to the recipient. Friendship ties often make personal communication a more persuasive source of information than impersonal newspaper accounts of the same events. Many communications researchers maintain that the information value of the mass media is strengthened when its message is reinforced by personal communication networks.

POLITICAL COMMUNICATIONS AND THE MASS MEDIA

Throughout their adult lives, citizens need information about current events and new political issues. The mass media are prime sources of such information. Citizens often have little direct experience with government and its policy results; in many instances, the media provide the only link between citizens and political affairs. Still, the role of the media as a socialization agent is usually limited. Contemporary research suggests that the media are less likely to socialize new political beliefs than are family, peers, and school. Rather, the information provided by the mass media reinforces existing opinions or helps in evaluating new events in the context of these opinions.

The information role of the media was especially important during the immediate postwar years, as a new political and social system was taking root. The communications role of the media during this period contributed to the remaking of the political culture. Studies found that the public was well informed about politics, even when few people wanted to participate openly.[20] The public relied heavily on the media to provide this information, a trait that persists to the present.

THE PRESS[21]

The significance of the print media is evidenced by government attempts, throughout German history, to control the press. The norm for government behavior was established under the Wilhelmine Empire. The government routinely suppressed stories that might embarrass the Kaiser or his government. Conversely, most newspapers had a distinct partisan or ideological viewpoint; often proclaiming these loyalties as part of the newspaper's title banner. The politicization of the news occasionally went further. Several different social and political groups developed their own network of newspapers. By the early 1930s, Catholic groups owned 448 newspapers with a combined circulation of about 20 million; about one-fourth of all newspapers had official or unofficial ties to a political party. Despite these circumstances, several newspapers during the Wilhelmine Empire and Weimar Republic developed international reputations for their reporting and news analysis, but these were the exceptional cases.

The exploitation of the press reached its worst level under the National Socialists. Alfred Hugenberg used his extensive communications empire to support Hitler's rise to power. Hugenberg's newspapers, news information service, and advertising agency made virulent attacks on the Weimar Republic and preached antidemocratic, anti-Semitic, and nationalist views. Hugenberg was rewarded with a cabinet seat in Hitler's first government, but was quickly swept from office as the government's "coordination" program gave it direct control of the press. The *Volkischer Beobachter* became the official organ of the National Socialist movement, substituting nationalism, racism, and antiliberal propaganda for factual news. The regime suppressed non-Nazi publications and eventually forced most to close; opposition to the government was not tolerated.

Those charged with overseeing the redevelopment of the press in the Federal Republic kept this historical legacy in mind. Immediately after the war, the Allied military forces licensed newspaper publishers within their respective occupation zones. Only newspapers and journalists who were free of Nazi ties could obtain a license. The Allies also tried to encourage political diversity in the media. The American occupation forces, for example, required a balanced mix of political views on the boards of the newspapers they licensed; apolitical or nonpartisan newspapers were preferred over the partisan and political organs of the past. The British created press diversity by licensing publishers with competing political philosophies. The Basic Law (Article 5) ensured that the press would be independent and free of censorship, and the authorities removed licensing restrictions in late 1949. By then, the overall structure of the postwar press was established.

Two consequences followed from this pattern of press development. First, journalists, publishers, and the government worked to create a new journalistic tradition, committed to democracy, objectivity, and political neutrality. During the early postwar years, the press played an important part in the political education of the public. Along with radio, newspapers shaped public images of the new political system and developed public understanding of the democratic political process. Today, the press is not only responsible for the dissemination of information, but monitors the actions of government and educates public opinion. Newspapers are expected to be social and political critics. The press laws passed by the individual states grant the press and the media specific legal rights for this task: the right of access to government information, the legal confidentiality of sources, restrictions on libel suits, and limits on government regulation. At the same time, most newspapers avoid the political propagandizing of the past by maintaining political neutrality and clearly separating factual news from editorial evaluation. This new media style marks a clear departure from past journalistic practices.

A second consequence of this developmental pattern is the regionalization of newspaper circulation. The licensing of independent newspapers within each occupation zone created a network of local and regional daily papers that continues today. Each region or large city has one or more newspapers that circulate primarily within that locale. In the early 1980s there were over 400 daily newspapers in the Federal Republic, with a combined circulation of about 25 million. A citizen of Hamburg reads the *Hamburger Abendblatt*, a Cologne resident subscribes to the *Kölner Stadt-Anzeiger*, the *Westdeutsche Allgemeine* is popular in the Ruhr area, and so forth. In smaller towns the citizens might subscribe to a small local paper, which devotes relatively more attention on local news and public interest stories. This pattern is common in the United States, but differs from the systems of nationwide newspapers found in Britain, France, and other Western European nations. The decentralization of the press makes for diversity and pluralism in political commentary, but it also means that West Germany lacks the common national media environment found in most other European states. In both content and circulation patterns, the regional West German press bears a closer resemblance to U.S. newspapers than to its German antecedents.

Although most people read a newspaper published in their town or a nearby city, some elements of a national press do exist (Table V.2). Five "quality" daily newspapers—*Frankfurter Allgemeine Zeitung, Die Welt, Süddeutsche Zeitung, Handelsblatt*, and *Frankfurter Rundschau*—have national reputations because of their sophisticated and detailed news coverage. Their quality is comparable to the *New York Times, Le Monde*, or the *London Times*. These papers are widely read by the political and business elite, and they are

TABLE V.2 *The Print Media*

Publication	1986 Circulation (in 1000s)	Political Orientation
Major Daily Newspapers		
Bild-Zeitung	5,032	Conservative
Süddeutsche Zeitung	371	Moderate
Frankfurter Allgemeine	341	Conservative
Die Welt	210	Conservative
Frankfurter Rundschau	195	Liberal
Handelsblatt	108	Conservative
Tageszeitung (TAZ)	35	Alternative Movement
Weekly Publications		
Bild am Sonntag	2,397	Conservative
Der Spiegel	975	Liberal
Die Zeit	452	Moderate
Welt am Sonntag	340	Conservative
Bayernkurier	157	CSU-sponsored
Rheinischer Merkur	122	Conservative
Vorwärts	55	SPD-sponsored

Source: Circulation figures are partially drawn from *Die Zeit* (Sept. 5, 1986), p. 24.

available by subscription or from newsstands throughout the country. Because of their elitist orientation, the circulation figures for the quality press are quite modest.

At the other extreme are the "boulevard" newspapers, sold on street corners and focused on sex, violence, and other sensational topics. The most notorious of these is the *Bild Zeitung* and its Sunday edition, *Bild am Sonntag*. The *Bild* is the only truly national paper in the Federal Republic; it is sold at every kiosk and newspaper stand and has a daily circulation of over 5 million. The contents of the *Bild* and the other boulevard newspapers are roughly on par with the British yellow press. A daily diet of such information can hardly develop a well-informed and sophisticated public.

Another important form of the print media are the weekly newspapers and news magazines. *Die Zeit* and the *Welt am Sonntag* are national papers that review the news of the past week and provide an analysis of recent events. Probably the most influential single publication in the Federal Republic is the weekly news magazine, *Der Spiegel*. The *Spiegel* was originally modeled after *Time* magazine in the United States, but has since developed its own unique style. The weekly issues combine coverage of ongoing news events with investigative journalism. *Der Spiegel*'s often biting critique of political figures frequently involves the magazine in political controversy.

Another component of the media is the partisan press. The *Bayernkurier* is the official representative of the CSU; *Vorwärts* is published by the Social Democrats; and the *Rheinischer Merkur* has informal ties to the CDU. The *Tageszeitung* (TAZ), published in Berlin, is the unofficial voice of the alternative movement.

The West German public places a high premium on being informed about political matters, and most citizens rely on newspapers and other printed media as a source of information on current events. Almost 85 percent of the adult public claim to read a newspaper every day; the per capita circulation of newspapers in the Federal Republic ranks among the highest in Western Europe.

The political independence of the press is reflected in the political content of most newspapers. Rather than acting as an agent of political socialization, newspapers serve as a vehicle for political communication. The media are probably more influential in determining what people think about, through their choice of news stories, than in actually influencing what people think. Still, newspaper readership is related to certain aspects of a participatory political culture. Studies regularly find that regular newspaper readers are more involved in politics, more informed about political matters, and more certain of their political judgments.[22] Reading a newspaper might not create these orientations, but access to a ready supply of political information is necessary to sustain this behavior.

The role of the media as a communication link between politics and the citizenry makes people sensitive to any threat to this connection. Observers frequently decry the declining diversity of the print media over the past quarter century.[23] Through mergers and consolidation, the number of papers with an independent editorial staff has steadily declined. In 1954, there were 225 independent editorial units; today, there are less than 125. Most editorial staffs publish several papers, each with the same core materials plus a few pages of local news. The largest of these publishing organizations is the Springer group, which publishes the *Bild Zeitung*, the two largest Sunday newspapers (*Bild am Sonntag* and *Welt am Sonntag*), one of the four quality dailies (*Die Welt*), two Berlin daily newspapers, and many popular magazines. At its high point, the

Springer consortium accounted for almost 40 percent of the daily newspaper market and 20 percent of magazine sales. Because of its size and the extreme conservative views of its late owner, Axel Springer, the Springer group evokes images of earlier German publishing empires. Springer used the pages of the *Bild Zeitung* to preach a form of German conservatism that caters to a reactionary undercurrent within society. The newspaper printed attacks on liberal West German political figures, and more recently the Green party, next to stories of murder and communist oppression in Eastern Europe, as if liberals and communist dictatorships pose equivalent threats to national security and domestic order. Springer's influence decreased in the years leading up to his death, as court decisions limited the size of his holdings and public stock offerings diluted his personal control of the corporation. Still, the general problem of press concentration remains a concern to politicians and the public.

Questions also arise over the political orientation of the press. On the one hand, liberals note that whereas most major newspapers profess impartiality by including such terms as *überparteilich* or *unabhängig* ("nonpartisan" or "independent") under the title banner, their editorials generally reflect a conservative tendency. The *Frankfurter Rundschau* and *Der Spiegel* are two notable liberal exceptions among a generally conservative press. On the other hand, conservatives point to evidence that most newspaper journalists lean toward the SPD or FDP. Periodic political criticism of press coverage is probably an inevitable feature of a free press, and West Germany is certainly not exceptional in this regard. Nevertheless, most of the major national newspapers are known for their attempt to separate editorial judgment and news reporting, giving the German public access to a diverse and high-quality press.

RADIO AND TELEVISION

Germany entered the age of the electronic media—radio and television—during the Weimar Republic. The radio became a regular part of everyday life in the 1920s; at the beginning of the decade, only a few hundred receivers existed in all of Germany, but by 1930 radios were common in the home. The radio quickly became an important source of news and entertainment for the average citizen. The world's first regular television service began in Berlin in 1935; television use grew very slowly, however.

The development of the electronic media differed in important ways from that of the printed press. Newspapers were privately owned; radio and television were considered public services. Consequently, the Weimar government owned a majority of the shares in the public broadcasting stations, and a government ministry regulated what went out over the airwaves. Radio also united the country into a single radio audience that made political communication an immediate and unmediated process.

The Third Reich fully exploited the power of this new medium. Hitler communicated directly with the population via the radio, which magnified his considerable oratorical skills. The Third Reich's propaganda ministry relied on radio broadcasts to generate public support for the regime and to develop a national consciousness. The Nazis considered radio's influence so powerful that receivers built during the war were constructed to receive only German stations, and listening to foreign radio broadcasts could warrant the death penalty.

The Allies determined the structure of the postwar media. The occupiers quickly reestablished radio service on a pattern of regional decentralization within each occupation zone. Radio broadcasting was still considered a public resource to be controlled by the government; private commercial radio and television stations were not allowed. To avoid the exploitation of the media by a strong national government, as happened during the Third Reich, the Basic Law made the states responsible for radio and television broadcasting. Control of the first broadcasting stations passed to the individual Länder governments; not every state has its own broadcasting corporation, however, because the stations were distributed according to the lines of the Allied occupation zones rather than state boundaries. Nine public broadcasting corporations are located in the Federal Republic and West Berlin.

At first, the public broadcasting corporations were responsible for all television programming, with everything done by the separate stations. In 1952, the individual state corporations agreed to cooperate in the production of a national television network, known as the first channel (or ARD). After extended political controversy, a second nationwide television service was introduced in 1964. The second channel, ZDF, is a single corporation, instead of a consortium, like ARD. All state corporations also broadcast their own regional programming on a third channel. The public thus has at least three channels of programs to choose from, or more if they can receive signals from nearby states.

Most of the state broadcasting corporations follow the same organizational principles. A broadcasting council (*Rundfunkrat*) sets the general policy for the corporation and watches over the public interest. In most Länder the broadcasting council is made up of representatives of the Land government, the churches, unions and business organizations, educational institutions, and other "socially relevant" groups. The broadcasting council selects the members of a smaller administrative council, which supervises the actual operation of the corporation. The corporations are financed primarily through a license fee on television and radio owners. The combined television license now costs 16.50 DM a month (about $9). Commercial advertisements on television are restricted to less than thirty minutes per day, with no advertisements after 8 P.M. on week-days and none at all on Sunday. Only about one-third of television revenue and one-fourth of radio revenue come from advertising.

Public control over radio and television has both positive and negative consequences. On the one hand, stations can devote a higher proportion of their programming to public service activities and cultural events because they are freed from the profit motive of commercial television. It is not unusual for symphony concerts, plays, or operas to be shown on prime time. During election periods, the political parties receive a modest amount of free advertising as a public service (there is no paid political advertising), and extensive air time is made available for interviews with party representatives and debates among party leaders. On the other hand, the quality and variety of West German television reflects its limited funding base and the small number of channels. One might see a documentary on truck assembly plants, for example, featured during prime viewing hours, and the quality of many third-channel programs often falls below the standards of U.S. or British television. Critics also complain that broadcasters have a paternalistic attitude toward the public, showing what they think people should watch rather than what the public prefers. More problematic are questions about the possible bias of government-controlled media. Members of the political opposition invariably complain about the pro-government bias of the media. Government control inevitably impinges on the media's ability to criticize policy makers. For instance, during the 1983 controversy over the stationing of new

NATO nuclear missiles in the Federal Republic, the anchorman of one TV news program was temporarily suspended because of his strong identification with the peace movement. Such instances are rare, and extensive efforts are made to assure the freedom of the press, but the potential for abuse is real.

In West Germany, as elsewhere, the popularity of television has increased tremendously. In the early 1950s, fewer than 5 percent of all households owned a television set; television ownership is now nearly universal. Opinion surveys find that the vast majority of the public claims to watch television on a regular basis. Indeed, a few years ago bar owners organized a protest because too many people were staying home on Tuesday night to watch episodes of *Dallas*, complete with J. R. Ewing machinating in impeccable German. The average adult spends about two hours a day watching television. This figure is low by U.S. standards (about 7 hours a day), but German viewership is limited by the restricted television schedule. Television broadcasts normally begin at about 6 P.M. and end before midnight; morning news programs began broadcasting only in the early 1980s.

Television and radio, like the printed media, are important sources of information about political events. Because radio and television are treated as public resources, an unusually large share of the programs are devoted to news, political discussions, current affairs, and other information programs. In 1982, two-fifths of ARD programs and one-fourth of ZDF programs dealt with public information themes; these proportions have been constant over the past two decades. The public information content of West German television ranks among the highest in Western Europe. Thus it is not surprising that a 1983 survey indicates that most citizens (88 percent) watch television news at least several times a week, and 77 percent listen to radio news as often. Moreover, when the importance of various media sources are compared, opinion surveys place television as the most important source of political information: Television, 51 percent; newspapers and magazines, 22 percent; personal conversation, 16 percent; radio, 6 percent; and other sources only 5 percent.[24]

During the early postwar years, the government used its control of the mass media to mold public images of the new political system and develop popular support of the democratic process. For instance, one fascinating field experiment conducted during the 1960s found a marked increase in political interest among families who had purchased their first television set.[25] Other studies regularly show a strong relationship between using radio or television as a source of political information and actual involvement in politics.

The 1960s were an exceptional period, however, and experts are divided on whether television still exerts such a clear impact on political attitudes and behavior. One of the strongest believers in television's effect is Elisabeth Noelle-Neumann, the director of one of West Germany's largest public opinion firms.[26] She contends that television produces an image of society, "a climate of opinion," that encourages people to adopt opinions consistent with the social norm. Subsequent research has questioned many of the assumptions and evidence underlying the simple form of Noelle-Neumann's theory, but few researchers doubt that television can exert a strong impact on opinions under the right conditions. For example, the showing of the American television drama, *Holocaust*, had a profound impact on West German society. Each episode was accompanied by a talk show and a viewer phone-in program. For the first time, many Germans discussed openly what life was like during the Third Reich. The personal story of one Jewish family led to a more open discussion and awareness of the past, something that had not been produced by innumerable books, articles, and documentaries. Television's strong visual impact, its reinforcing messages, and its widespread acceptance give it potentially greater influence than other mass media. Even in these examples, however, it is clear that the media exerts more influence when its message is reinforced by personal discussion.

THE NEW MEDIA

In recent years, technological advances have begun to erode the government's control over television broadcasting. The first inroads came in the entertainment area. In order to augment the limited offerings on the three government channels, many German families turned to video cassette recorders (VCRs). By the early 1980s, 5 million households owned a VCR, and movie rentals had become a booming business—even more so than in the United States.

More significant are the potential changes represented by satellite and cable television. The advent of satellite broadcasting may eventually end the government's television monopoly. Technological progress means that soon anyone can eavesdrop on the national television of nearby states or the newly created European commercial channels by using a relatively small satellite dish. When these possibilities first emerged in the late 1970s, the SPD-led government strongly opposed the development of these technologies. Chancellor Helmut Schmidt claimed that unrestricted television access could endanger "the structure of our democratic society." Under Schmidt's direction, the government used legal means in an attempt to block television satellite broadcasting into the Federal Republic.

The Christian Democratic government elected in 1982 is more receptive to these new communications technologies. It maintains that expanded television offerings will foster more freedom of opinion, more diversity, and more choice for the individual. Government officials also hope that the new technologies will create jobs, strengthen the nation's high-tech industry, and provide the skeleton for a national electronic information grid. The first private, satellite-delivered television station (SAT-1) was introduced in 1985. SAT-1 is owned by a consortium of publishing firms, including the Springer press, and provides a mix of popular entertainment and news. It has since been joined by 3-SAT (a combined production of German, Swiss and Austrian national television), a broadcast from Luxembourg (RTL-Plus), and several pan-European satellite stations.

The advent of private television does not mean that the government is willing to relinquish all control over what its citizens can watch. Access to nongovernment television channels is through the government-owned cable system being developed by the Federal Post Office. In 1983, the Post Office began an ambitious program of wiring the nation for cable television service, but progress has been slow. Excessively high cable fees also discourage usage. Of the 25 million homes that have a television, barely 5 percent now have access to cable service.

It is too early to judge the impact of the new technologies on West German politics. The new media are still opposed by many leftist politicians. An SPD Mayor of Hamburg labeled expanded television offerings a threat to family togetherness; the Green party opposes commercial television on several grounds. It is unlikely that the new media will transform the political process, as has happened in the United States, but some change is inevitable. The diversity of political information available to the average citizen will undoubtedly increase, especially exposure to non-German points of view. Similarly, it will be more difficult for the government to influence the political agenda through its management of the electronic media. The nature of electoral politics also might change, giving more emphasis to individual candidates and personal style, if news programs on private television networks play a role in election coverage. The government-owned stations may need to redefine their role in order to compete with the programming of the private stations. The next decade thus may produce important changes in how the German public learns about politics and how political leaders communicate with the citizens.

NOTES

1. Gabriel Almond and G. Bingham Powell, *Comparative Politics* (Boston: Little, Brown, 1978), chap. 4; David Easton and Jack Dennis, *The Development of Political Attitudes in Children* (New York: McGraw Hill, 1969).
2. Ralf Dahrendorf, *Society and Democracy in Germany* (New York: Doubleday, 1967), p. 139; also see Dahrendorf's chap. 23.
3. Gabriel Almond and Sidney Verba, *The Civic Culture* (Princeton: Princeton University Press, 1963), chap. 12.
4. Elisabeth Noelle and Erich Peter Neumann, *The Germans: Public Opinion Polls 1947-1966* (Allensbach: Institut für Demoskopie, 1967).
5. Kendall Baker et al., *Germany Transformed* (Cambridge: Harvard University Press, 1981), p. 228.
6. Kendall Baker, "Political Participation, Political Efficacy, and Socialization in Germany," *Comparative Politics* 6 (1973), pp. 73-98; M. Kent Jennings and Rolf Jansen, "Der Hang der Jugendlichen zu Veränderungen von Sozialstrukturfaktoren und der Familie," *Politische Vierteljahresschrift* (September 1976).
7. M. Kent Jennings, Leopold Rosenmayer, and Klaus Allerbeck, "Generations and Families," in Samuel Barnes, Max Kaase, et al., *Political Action* (Beverly Hills: Sage Publications, 1979), pp. 449-486; also see Jennings and Jansen, "Der Hang der Jugendlichen."
8. David Conradt, "Changing German Political Culture," in Gabriel Almond and Sidney Verba, eds. *The Civic Culture Revisited* (Boston: Little, Brown, 1980), pp. 251-252; Elisabeth Noelle Neumann and Edgar Piel, *Jahrbuch der öffentlichen Meinung*, vol 8. (Munich: Saur, 1983), p. 93.
9. Elisabeth Noelle-Neumann and Renate Köcher, *Die verletzte Nation* (Stuttgart: Deutsche Verlags-Anstalt, 1987). For additional evidence on family differences see Klaus Allerbeck and Wendy Hoag, *Jugend ohne Zukunft?* (Munich: Piper, 1985); *Youth of the World and Japan* (Tokyo: Youth Bureau of the Prime Minister's Office, 1978).
10. Walter Stahl, ed. *Education for Democracy in West Germany* (New York: Praeger, 1961); Richard Merritt, Ellen Flerlage, and Anna Merritt, "Democratizing West German Education," *Comparative Education* 7 (1981): 121-136.
11. Judith Torney, A. Oppenheim, and R. Farnen, *Civic Education in Ten Countries*, International Studies in Evaluation, vol. 6. (Stockholm: Almqvist and Wiksell, 1975).
12. Max Planck Institute, *Between Elite and Mass Education* (Albany, N.Y.: State University of New York Press, 1982); Wolfgang Mitter, "Education in the Federal Republic of Germany," *Comparative Education* 16 (1980): 257-66.
13. Arnold Heidenheimer, "The Politics of Educational Reform," *Comparative Education Review* 18 (1974): 388-410; Annegret Körner, "Comprehensive Schooling," *Comparative Education* 17 (1981): 15-22.

14. Jürgen Habermas et al. *Student und Politik* (Neuwied: Luchterhand Verlag, 1969); Walter Jaide, *Jugend und Demokratie* (Munich: Juventa, 1970).

15. Allerbeck and Hoag, *Jugend ohne Zukunft?*, pp. 38–46.

16. Der Spiegel, *Der Wilder 68er* (Hamburg: Spiegel Verlag, 1988).

17. Allerbeck and Hoag, *Jugend ohne Zukunft?*, chap. 2; Martin Greiffenhagen and Sylvia Greiffenhagen, *Ein schwieriges Vaterland* (Munich: List, 1979), pp. 262ff.

18. Dahrendorf, *Society and Democracy in Germany*, chap. 19.

19. Baker et al., *Germany Transformed*, chap. 3.

20. Almond and Verba, *The Civic Culture*, pp. 88–89.

21. John Sandford, *The Media of the German-speaking Countries* (Ames, Iowa: Iowa State University Press, 1976).

22. Baker et al., *Germany Transformed*, chap. 3; Helmut Norpoth and Kendall Baker, "Mass Media and Electoral Choice in West Germany," *Comparative Politics* 13 (October 1980): 1–14.

23. Arthur Williams, "Pluralism in the West German Media," *West European Politics* 8 (April 1985): 84–103.

24. Elisabeth Noelle-Neumann, ed. *The Germans: Public Opinion Polls, 1967–1980* (Westport, Conn.: Greenwood Press, 1981), p. 151.

25. The families with televisions also were compared to a control group of families without televisions; see, Elisabeth Noelle-Neumann, *Wahlentscheidung in der Fernsehdemokratie* (Würzburg: Verlag Ploetz, 1980), pp. 54–55.

26. Noelle-Neumann, *Wahlentscheidung in der Fernsehdemokratie;* Elisabeth Noelle-Neumann, *The Spiral of Silence* (Chicago: University of Chicago Press, 1984).

CHAPTER VI

Citizen Action

WHAT SETS DEMOCRACIES APART from most other political systems
is the existence of institutionalized methods for ordinary citizens to
participate in the policy-making process. When a Bavarian dairy
farmer is dissatisfied with the government's agricultural program,
he can make his views known to those in charge of the program.
When parents want reform in the school curriculum, the political
system furnishes them with an opportunity to become involved in
the policy process.

The primary function of political participation is, of course, to
provide citizens with a direct influence on government decision
making. The method used to exert this influence may take many
forms. Citizen participation is often equated with the selection of
government officials through competitive elections. The power to
select political leaders, or turn them out at the next election, is central to the democratic process. Other forms of action, such as lobbying, demonstrations, or protests, are attempts to exert more direct
pressure on policy makers beyond the confines of the electoral setting. These political activities have a persuasive influence on policy
makers, focusing attention on more specific policy concerns.

Political action can also serve as a communication link between
the public and decision makers. Political leaders need to know what
people want before they can act in the public's interest. If the Bavarian farmer contacts his party representative or meets with a local
government official, he provides information to decision makers
about the effect of policy on dairy farmers like himself. The simple
articulation of public interests is an important part of political
participation.

Political participation also functions as a source of national authority. Democracy is not a spectator sport; it requires the active involvement of its citizens in the political process. Citizen involvement integrates the public into the political process, if citizens accept the basic legitimacy of the system. Politically active individuals are better able to understand the principles of the system, and, in most cases, this makes for better citizens. The belief that one can influence the political process is an important source of popular support for the political system.

There is, of course, no simple, one-to-one relationship between the amount of citizen involvement and the extent of democracy in a nation. The hyperparticipation of the Weimar Republic illustrates a case when participation challenged the political order rather than serving as a source of political legitimacy. Still, meaningful citizen participation is a crucial part of the democratic political process. Citizens must be free to choose between these various ways of influencing the political process, and the political system must respond to these popular pressures. The test of any democracy, including the Federal Republic, is how it encourages and responds to citizen demands.

PARTICIPATORY NORMS

Developing public understanding and acceptance of democratic rules was an important accomplishment for the Federal Republic (see Chapter IV). Nevertheless, this still left many citizens as political spectators, as if they were following a soccer match from the grandstand. As late as the end of the 1950s, Gabriel Almond and Sidney Verba found that public attitudes toward the political system were relatively passive; people thought of themselves as subjects rather than participants.[1] Observers frequently wondered whether West Germans were merely *Fragebogendemokraten* (that is, democrats only when it came to answering a public opinion survey) or whether the new democratic norms were real enough to produce changes in behavior and political participation.

The final step in remaking the political culture was to involve citizens in the process—to have them come onto the field and become participants. From the first, the procedures of the Federal Republic induced many people to become at least minimally involved in the process. Turnout in national elections was uniformly high. West Germans developed an interest in political matters and became well informed about the democratic system relative to other electorates. Still, one had the feeling that most people were spectators, keeping political involvement to a minimum. Opinion polls showed that many people were hesitant to discuss politics openly. Citizens voted out of a sense of civic duty, rather than from a belief in the process and a sense of involvement. Participation beyond voting was fairly limited.

Slowly, attitudes toward political participation and the citizen's role in politics changed. After continued experience with the democratic system, citizens began to internalize their role as participants. Public opinion polls found that feelings of political effectiveness and civic competence had increased substantially since the *Civic Culture* study (Table VI.1). In 1959, only 38 percent of the public felt they could do something to change an unjust or unfair law from being passed by the Bundestag, and 62 percent thought they could do something at the local level. These perceptions of political competence were significantly below those displayed by Britons or Americans. By the mid-1970s, feelings of competency had risen significantly, especially at the national level, while British and American sentiments had declined slightly.[2] In other words, the majority of the electorate think that their participation can influence the political process—people believe that democracy works.

TABLE VI.1 *Feelings of Political Competence, 1959-1974*

	National Level		Local Level	
	1959	*1974*	*1959*	*1974*
Can do something to change unjust or unfair law	38%	56%	62%	67%
Organize informal group	7	19	13	36
Work through political party	6	6	3	3
Work through formal group	7	2	5	1
Contact elected official, media	12	24	15	25
Contact nonelected official	4	2	31	15
Contact lawyer	1	1	3	2
Vote	4	14	1	3
Protest, violent action	2	9	1	8
Other action	—	2	1	6
Can't do anything	62	44	38	33
Total	106%	123%	111%	136%

Source: Civic Culture Study, Political Action Study. Total exceeds 100 percent because multiple responses were possible. These data are available from the Interuniversity Consortium for Political and Social Research in Ann Arbor.

These changing perceptions of politics led to a dramatic increase in political involvement. In 1953, almost two-thirds of the public said they never discussed politics; by the 1980 election, almost two-thirds claimed they discussed politics daily during the campaign. Figure VI.1 displays this expansion of citizen involvement in graphic terms. In 1952, only 27 percent of the public expressed an interest in politics. The percentage of interested citizens grew steadily over the next three decades, reaching a peak of 57 percent during the 1983 election.

It is unlikely that the trend in political interest will continue the same upward trajectory in the future, because past increases were due to changes in the political culture and social conditions that have largely run their course. The public's involvement in politics has probably reached a plateau in the past decade, at a level substantially higher than many other West European democracies.[3] This expansion in citizen interest created a "participatory revolution" in the 1970s, as an increasing number of individuals became politically active.

FIGURE VI.1 *The Growth of Political Interest, 1952–1983*

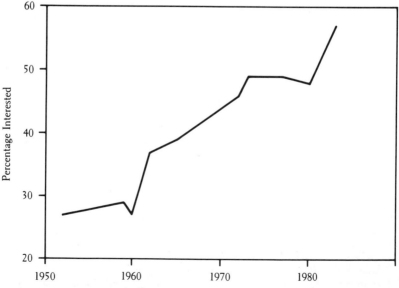

Source: Allensbach Opinion Reports.

Evidence from opinion surveys suggests that the participatory revolution has broadened the definition of the citizen's role to encompass a wider array of political activities. In 1959, citizens defined their role in fairly narrow terms (Table VI.1). Most people were hesitant to engage in group activities; the public tended to adopt an administrative view of politics. Especially at the local level, people were more likely to contact the bureaucracy about a political problem than work with other citizens or contact a politician. By the mid-1970s, participatory norms emphasized a more activist role. Group-based activities or direct contact with an elected official were the preferred means of participation. The repertoire of potential political action expanded to include protests, demonstrations, and other direct action methods. This chapter explores the public's ability to convert these changing norms into actual involvement in the political process.

WORKING WITHIN THE SYSTEM

Most discussions of citizen action equate political participation with involvement in the electoral process. This is because the electoral arena is the focal point for representative democracy, even though citizens can participate in a range of other activities. Democracy requires that citizens be able to exert control over decision makers; a key to this control is the public's ability to select political elites through periodic, competitive elections. Election campaigns are also important in providing a forum for the discussion and debate of political issues. Elections encourage the public and political elites to evaluate the government's recent performance and the political problems that lie ahead and to consider the options for addressing these problems. In other words, elections create a four-year cycle of civic education. Finally, voting is the most visible and widespread form of citizen action, the closest that many people come to the political process, and the broadest measure of citizen action.

By almost any standard, the West German public seems to relish the opportunity to cast their ballots (Figure VI.2). Participation in federal elections averages over 85 percent of the eligible electorate. In the 1970s, turnout topped 90 percent; a marked contrast to U.S. participation rates, which barely exceed 50 percent. Turnout in the state elections is somewhat lower, but still averages over 75 percent of those eligible.

FIGURE VI.2 *Turnout in Federal and State Elections, 1949–1987*

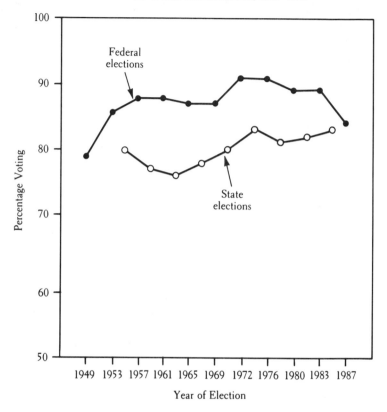

Several factors account for the high turnout levels in the Federal Republic.[4] For one thing, the political stakes are higher than in U.S. elections because the ideological differences between the West German parties are greater than between parties in the United States. The West German public has the choice of voting for a conservative Christian party, a Social Democratic party with a strong socialist heritage, a traditional European liberal party, an antiestablishment Green party, and many other parties, including communists and other radicals. Another major difference from the United States is the system of voter registration. West Germans are automatically included in the roster of eligible voters, and these electoral registers are updated by the government to ensure that nearly everyone is able to vote. Turnout is also encouraged by the scheduling of elections on Sundays, when more voters can find the time to visit the polls. Given the normal range of Sunday leisure-time activities in West Germany, some people might even consider voting an enjoyable pursuit. The West German electoral system of proportional representation (PR) also stimulates turnout because any party—large or small—can increase its representation as a direct function of its share of the popular vote.

Although participation in national and state elections is quite high, these statistics give a somewhat distorted view of public's total electoral influence. The actual number of electoral decisions made by the German voter is quite small by U.S. standards. Federal, state, and local elections usually allow the voter to make only one or two electoral decisions (see Chapter IX). The many elective offices normally found on a U.S. ballot (judges, sheriffs, schools boards, etc.) are nonelective positions in the Federal Republic. Such direct democracy techniques as the referendum and initiative are not used in West Germany at the national level and appear only infrequently at the state and local levels. The chief executives at the federal and Land levels are not directly elected, but chosen by the parliamentary majority. Between 1980 and 1985, for example, a resident of Mannheim could have cast a vote on only ten separate items in all of the local, state, federal, and European elections held during this period.[5] Thus, the actual electing done by the average West German citizen is far short of electoral decision making in the United States.

Participation in campaign activities is one way for citizens to extend their electoral participation beyond formal voting opportunities. Working for a party, attending campaign meetings, persuading others how to vote, membership in a party or political organization, and other forms of party activity expand citizen participation. These types of activities are more demanding of the individual than merely casting a vote. Campaign work requires more initiative from the participant and greater cooperation with other activists. Moreover, publicly displaying one's partisan support removes the anonymity of the voting booth.

Campaign activity can be an effective method of citizen influence.[6] Compared to the simple act of voting, campaign work exerts more intense and more direct pressure on political elites. Campaign activists are necessary for a party to be electorally successful, and party leaders are therefore more sensitive to, and more aware of, the policy interests of activists. In addition, the individual worker can influence the votes of other electors, magnifying the political impact of each campaign worker. Campaign activity can include a more focused policy content than simply choosing between pre-packaged party programs.

Although voting turnout has always been widespread, open participation in election campaigns was at first quite rare. Public displays of partisan support were not encouraged by a political culture that was still very tentative about participatory politics. Instead of a fluid group of occasional activists, the parties depended on a stable pool of party members for the bulk of campaign work. For many years, partisan campaign activity actually held a negative connotation for the average citizen.

Campaign involvement gradually expanded beyond the activist core of card-carrying party members. The greatest change came when author Günther Grass and other public figures began to drum up support for the Social Democratic party. In the 1969 election, for the first time, several voter initiatives (*Wählerinitiativen*) appeared. Composed mostly of nonparty members, these groups campaigned actively for the party of their choice. A very visible and dramatic change in the style of election campaigns occurred when ordinary voters began to show their support for a party by wearing tiny orange (SPD) or blue (CDU) lapel pins. In subsequent years U.S.-style campaign paraphernalia (buttons, bumper stickers, etc.) became a common feature of German elections. Attendance at campaign rallies shot up from only 11 percent of the public during the 1961 election to 20 percent by the 1976 contest. Moreover, 36 percent of the public claimed that they openly displayed their party support in some manner during the 1976 election.

After a rapid surge in campaign activity in the 1970s, participation in campaigns has leveled off in recent elections (Table VI.2).

TABLE VI.2 *Conventional Political Participation, 1974–1985*

Activity	1974	1980	1985
Tried to convince friends how to vote	22%	20%	25%
Attended political meeting or rally	22	15	18
Contacted public official	11	7	11
Worked for a political party	8	7	9
(Sample size)	(2307)	(2095)	(1843)

Source: 1974 and 1980 Political Action studies; 1985 Citizen Expectations of Government Study, directed by Max Kaase. Table entries are the percentage who have sometimes engaged in each activity.

Only the Green party emphasizes grassroots activities that involve a large number of their supporters, such as distributing literature or attending rock concerts with a political theme. For the established parties, the expanding electoral role of the mass media is lessening the importance of campaign activities designed to inform the public, such as campaign rallies, canvassing, and formal party meetings. The campaign is now fought on television rather than in meeting halls and auditoriums. The parties' television spots, nightly news reports, and the pre-election debate between the party leaders are the new battlegrounds of the campaign.

PROTEST POLITICS

In most cases, political participation occurs within the institutionalized structure of politics: voting, campaign activity, writing political officials, and the lobbying activities of citizen–action groups. In the late 1960s, however, citizen participation burst beyond the bounds of conventional politics to include demonstrations, protests, and other forms of unconventional political action.

The new wave of protests came from the university campuses in the late 1960s. Student demonstrators rallied for a restructuring of the educational system and broader reforms in West German society. Student sit-ins and protests frequently spilled over into the surrounding communities. For a time, West Berlin again resembled a war zone, as students and the authorities met in regular confrontations. Freiberg, Heidelberg, Tübingen and other university towns lost their quiet academic demeanor.

Protest is certainly not a new component of German politics, but the student demonstrations of the 1960s gradually evolved into a new style of protest activity.[7] Historically, it was the disadvantaged and politically frustrated who felt they had no other recourse and resorted to protest. Student demonstrations shifted the locus of protest from the ghettos and working-class districts to the privileged university campus. Partially because of its student origins, moderate protest became an accepted method of political action among the middle class and the better-educated. Moreover, as many different political groups began to use direct-action methods, these activities began to seem less revolutionary. Rather than just a method of political coercion, protest politics became a tool of political persuasion and a means of mobilizing popular support outside the narrow bounds of electoral politics. Protest now represents a continuation of conventional political participation by other means.

Contemporary protest politics takes many forms. The most visible activities are those designed to capture national media attention. Large demonstrations are now a routine method of involving the public and focusing political attention on an issue. Anti-nuclear power groups, for example, have staged massive demonstrations at nuclear plant sites to show local opposition to the facilities. In the years leading up to the 1983 decision to deploy new NATO missiles in the Federal Republic, the peace movement organized the largest demonstrations in West German history. Other protest actions attempt to capture public interest through novelty or drama. The peace movement protested the planned deployment of the NATO missiles with a 130-mile-long human chain between NATO headquarters in Stuttgart and the missile base at Neu Ulm; other groups organized a series of "die-ins" around the country to remind the public of the costs of war. In order to draw attention to pollution problems along the Rhine, members of Greenpeace suspended themselves by rope from a highway bridge and formed a human chain across the river. Such protests and demonstrations are not an effective way to persuade the government to change policy, but they are effective in getting people to think and talk about a political issue.

Dramatic actions are the most noticeable examples of protest politics, but they are only the tip of the iceberg. Even the large national organizations use a variety of unconventional political activities, from circulating petitions to organizing local protests to staging spectacular actions. Many local groups also embrace various forms of unconventional political participation. A neighborhood group opposed to a new highway might block access to the construction site, parents concerned about the schools might stage a demonstration, or dissatisfied tenants might organize a rent boycott. Most participants in unconventional political activities are actually concerned with local problems rather than broad national issues and large-scale national movements.[8]

Public opinion surveys provide a way to assess the public's overall involvement in various forms of protest politics (Table VI.3). On the whole, about half the public takes part in some form of unconventional political action. About one person of every three has signed a petition, and one in seven has participated in a lawful demonstration. A smaller, though still significant, number of citizens have participated in more intense forms of protest, such as boycotts or illegal strikes.

TABLE VI.3 *Unconventional Political Participation, 1974-1985*

Activity	1974	1980	1985
Signed petitions	30%	18%	30%
Participated in a lawful demonstration	9	5	11
Joined in boycott	4	1	5
Participated in unofficial strike	1	1	—
Occupied building	<1	1	—
Damaged property	<1	1	—
Committed personal violence	<1	1	—
(Sample size)	(2037)	(1305)	(1843)

Source: 1974 and 1980 Political Action study; 1985 Citizen Expectations of Government Study, directed by Max Kaase. The last four political activities were not included in the 1985 study. Table entries are the percentage who have engaged in each activity.

The dark side of unconventional politics is violence. Even with the student movement, there was a potential for extremism. Early student protests frequently led to violent clashes with the police; unruly mobs sometimes resorted to violence, such as smashing store windows. The fringe element of the student movement was a breeding ground for the political radicalism that eventually spawned the Baader-Meinhoff terrorists and Red Army Faction (RAF). In recent years political violence has appeared again, especially among opponents of nuclear power. Frustration after the Chernobyl disaster resulted in escalating violence between protesters and police during anti-nuclear demonstrations at Brokdorf and Wackersdorf. The most radical opponents of nuclear power also sabotaged the transmission lines that distribute the electricity from nuclear power plants in several attacks during 1986 and 1987. More ominous than the actual violence is the acceptance shown by leading activists in the New Politics movement, including some Green deputies in the Bundestag. Their public statements seem to condone violence if it is directed against property and not people. Such views are incompatible with democratic politics in an open political system such as the Federal Republic.

Violent actions go beyond the tolerable bounds of democratic politics and are fundamentally different from the protest behavior of most citizens. As Table VI.3 indicates, less than 1 percent of the population participates in such activities. Most citizens who protest want to change the actions of the democratic political process, not destroy it.

Many people claim that the period of protest is passing, but the evidence does not substantiate this claim. Public opinion surveys indicate that protest activities expanded rapidly in the late 1960s and early 1970s, dipped slightly in the late 1970s, and increased again thereafter. Beginning in 1981, the peace movement organized a series of massive protests that continued for several years. By some accounts, 10 percent of the West German public participated in demonstrations during a single week in 1983. As the peace movement began to fade, the anti-nuclear movement was revived by the Chernobyl disaster. More significant, however, is the diffusion of protest activities beyond these New Left groups. The present levels of protest are now more likely to reflect the sum of small actions concerning highways, schools, neighborhood issues, and other specific concerns. Protest now constitutes a common aspect of contemporary West German politics.

CITIZEN ACTION GROUPS

The Federal Republic's "participatory revolution" created new demands for citizen involvement that were not easily met within existing input channels. On the one hand, political participation traditionally is equated with election activity. Voting turnout, however, already is high, and more campaign activity cannot satisfy these new demands. Moreover, today's political activists are often skeptical or even critical of the political parties as representatives of their interests. Political parties are large, impersonal, and highly bureaucratic. Because parties seek to aggregate interests into broad social programs, it is difficult to use partisan channels to address specific issue interests.

On the other hand, there are limits to the effectiveness of protest as a method of political influence. Demonstrations can draw attention to a problem, but protest alone is not enough to generate policy change. Political activism must include working within the system, with politicians and government officials, to ensure that public demands are considered and implemented into public policy.

The public's new participatory demands have led to a new form of citizen involvement in the political process, with roots in both conventional and unconventional politics. Beginning in the 1970s, *citizen-action groups (Bürgerinitiativen)* proliferated in West German society.[9] A citizen-action group is an ad hoc group of interested citizens that lobbies decision makers on a specific policy issue. While sharing a common populist orientation with the voter-initiative groups, citizen-action groups work mainly outside the electoral setting and lack a partisan focus. Although they use protest tactics, citizen-action groups possess the personnel and organizational resources to pursue their policy demands after the protest is over. These groups are similar to civic action and single-issue groups in the United States, but they represent a novel development in a political system that structures and restricts the methods of citizen participation.

Citizen-action groups usually form in spontaneous reaction to specific issue problems and are informally organized. Most include fewer than thirty members, who share in making decisions. The numbers and concerns of citizen groups are quite fluid, because these groups rapidly emerge in response to a problem and often disband after accomplishing their objective. The motto of many of these groups is *"Noch ein Sieg, und wir sind verloren!"* ("Another victory and we are gone!").

At any one time several thousand citizen groups are working throughout the country. By most accounts, membership in the various citizen-action groups now exceeds formal membership in political parties. Public opinion surveys indicate that participation in these groups has increased throughout the first half of the 1980s.[10]

Citizen groups are most active at the local level, dealing with the specific problems of a city or neighborhood. Parents organize for school reform in their city, renters become involved in urban redevelopment projects, or taxpayers complain about the delivery of government services. Citizen groups also exist at the national level, often dealing with New Politics issues. The most visible example is the Federal Association of Citizen-Action Groups for Environmental Protection (BBU). In the early 1980s, the BBU was affiliated with about 1000 local citizen groups representing nearly 300,000 members. This coalition of national and local environmental groups has successfully organized opposition to the government's nuclear energy program and mobilized popular support for environmental protection.

Citizen-action groups are not limited to the New Left; these groups now cover the political spectrum and almost all possible issues. A study of over 1400 local citizen groups in small cities throughout the Federal Republic found that housing and urban development are the most common issue foci, followed by environmental concerns (Table VI.4).[11] Many groups are interested in problems related to the schools. Other groups deal with the problems of the socially deprived (convicts, the poor, and foreign workers), youth, tenants' rights, and a variety of other issues. Indeed, the strength of citizen groups is that they allow the public to control the framework of political participation. Citizen groups can define their own issue agenda and choose their own methods of influencing policy makers.

Despite lip service to the ideal of citizen participation in the West German political system, many political leaders were initially unreceptive toward citizen-action groups. This in part was in reaction to the unconventional political style of some groups: Citizen groups often resort to petitions, protests, and other direct actions to dramatize their cause and mobilize public support. An additional factor in the response of conventional political authorities was the challenge that citizen groups posed to them. Many party leaders saw the emergence of these groups as a criticism of partisan politics.[12] Citizen-action groups provide an alternative, and sometimes a political opponent, to parties in the policy process. Some party leaders even believed that citizen groups posed a threat to the social order,

TABLE VI.4 *Primary Issue Interests of Citizen Action Groups*

Issue	Percentage of Groups Interested
Housing, urban development	20.6%
Environmental protection	16.9
Nursery schools, playgrounds	16.9
Traffic	11.8
Youth issues	5.0
School issues	8.0
Socially deprived persons	7.0
Tennant issues	5.5
Cultural affairs	3.3
Historic monuments	2.5
Other	2.5
Total	100%
(Number of Groups)	(1403)

Source: Paul von Kodolitsch, "Gemeindeverwaltungen und Bürgerinitiativen," *Archiv für Kommunalwissenschaften* (1975): 264. Used by permission.

that they were aiming at revolutionary change and only using ecology or housing problems as a cover. The very visible excesses of a few citizen groups were generalized to the citizen movement overall. Government officials also had mixed reactions, especially those at the local level. The aim of many citizen groups, after all, was to criticize and change the policies of the government. Members of the bureaucracy saw citizen groups as an unnecessary disruption of the government's orderly planning and administration process. In short, the political elite welcomed participation in the abstract, but were not as eager to encourage citizen action when it meant frustrated voters challenging the parties, angry parents attacking school policy, or dissatisfied citizens drawing attention to the government's unsolved problems.

Citizen-action groups are an important new force in West German politics, and the policy process is gradually responding to their presence.[13] Several states and many local governments have instituted new procedures that enable, or even encourage, citizen groups to participate in forming and administration of public policy. Local governments are realizing that it is better to work with citizen groups rather than resist their input. At the same time, however, channels for citizen input at the federal level have not developed as extensively. Federal regulations have institutionalized but also restricted the timing and form of citizen involvement in federal policy making. On the whole, however, the proliferation of citizen-action groups represents a significant step in the development of participatory politics in West Germany.

A NEW STYLE OF CITIZEN POLITICS

Democratic societies aim to expand citizen participation in the political process and thereby increase popular control of the political elite. Therefore, increases in campaign activity, citizen-action groups, protests, and other forms of citizen action are a generally welcomed trend in West German politics. The traditional characterization of the average West German citizen as quiescent and uninvolved is no longer appropriate. Compared to other Western publics, West Germans are engaged in a wide range of political activities; the spectators have become participants.

As the public's political interest and sophistication have grown, the nature of participation has shifted toward more emphasis on citizen-initiated activities and unconventional forms of political action. Increases in citizen-action groups and direct action methods are especially significant, because they place greater control over the locus and focus of participation in the hands of the citizenry. Political input is not limited to the issues and institutionalized channels determined by the political elite. An individual or group of citizens can concentrate on a specific issue and select the timing and method of influencing policy makers. Citizen-action groups can use petitions, protests, lobbying, party work, or whatever technique is most appropriate to their goals. These direct action methods are high-information and high-pressure activities. They therefore meet some of the participation demands of an increasingly educated and politically sophisticated public—far more so than voting and campaign work.

At the same time, however, these changing participation patterns highlight a contradiction in the West German political culture. Whereas the political elite originally encouraged the public to become involved in politics, many of these same leaders harbored doubts about the political judgment of the average citizen. Memories of Wiemar created a lingering concern about the possible excesses of citizen participation. Thus the Basic Law emphasizes institutionalized channels of citizen input, which could restrain the popular will. The Basic Law narrows the public's electoral role by ending the direct election of the president and restricting the use of referendums. When the West German public was encouraged to participate in politics, it was assumed that this would be through elections and party activity. Unconventional styles of participation were not expected, and not always welcomed.

The skepticism of political elites is perhaps heightened by the types of people who use unconventional forms of political action. These participation methods are popular among young people and advocates of New Left causes. Thus the combination of radical rhetoric and tactics makes the threat appear even larger. Moreover, attention naturally focuses on the most dramatic examples of these new participation forms. The student protest that turns violent always receives more media attention than a peaceful protest for senior citizen benefits by the Gray Panthers. It is difficult for some officials to distinguish between people pursuing legitimate social protest and the political terrorists who threatened West German society throughout the 1970s. Even after citizen-action groups and direct action methods have moved into the mainstream of German society, many people continue to disapprove of unconventional political activities.[14]

West German politics is still trying to adjust to the "participatory revolution." By their very nature, direct action techniques disrupt the status quo and challenge the established institutions and procedures of the political system. An additional problem is that large protests are difficult for authorities to control. Even well-intentioned protests can turn violent because of the actions of a few radical provocateurs. Some critics contend that efficient and effective policy making must be based on a deliberative process, where the political elite have latitude in their decisions. A politicized public with minorities lobbying intensely for their special interests can strain the democratic consensus.

Still, it is probably more accurate to say that the West German political system provides too few opportunities for citizen participation, rather than too many. An electoral system that allows the average voter to make only a handful of political decisions during a four-year electoral cycle is hardly a national accomplishment. And despite the increases in political involvement documented here, only a minority of the population participates beyond casting a ballot. Reformists claim that more methods of citizen influence are needed; methods that balance the goals of social order and citizen control, methods that lie between the extremes of infrequent votes for a fixed party list and protest activities. Citizen-action groups are one good example, but the political process can be opened up in other ways. Several states allow some version of a referendum (*Volksentscheid*), often with the opportunity for citizen groups to place initiatives on the ballot (*Volksbegehren*).[15] Referendum campaigns in recent years have dealt with issues of school reform, environmental regulations, and policies toward guestworkers; the referendum, however, is still a form of political action that is infrequently used and only tolerated by the political elite. Another possible reform is the wider adoption of the electoral system used in Baden-Württemberg and Bavaria, which allows voters to alter the order of candidates on the party lists or even select candidates from different parties; this gives citizens more control over the selection of political elites. Bureaucratic reforms that foster citizen involvement, rather than restrict it, also broaden access to government.

The debate over how to balance the demands for participatory politics against the needs for rational policy planning and social order is likely to be a continuing theme of West German politics. How the nation resolves the debate will determine the Federal Republic's future progress toward its democratic ideals.

NOTES

1. Gabriel Almond and Sidney Verba, *The Civic Culture* (Princeton: Princeton University Press, 1963).

2. Samuel Barnes, Max Kaase, et al. *Political Action* (Beverly Hills: Sage Publications, 1979), chap. 5.

3. Russell J. Dalton, *Citizen Politics in Western Democracies* (Chatham, N.J.: Chatham Publishers, 1988), chaps. 3, 4.

4. G. Bingham Powell, "Voting Turnout in Thirty Democracies," in *Electoral Participation*, ed. Richard Rose (Beverly Hills: Sage Publications, 1980).

5. The total includes two votes in each of the 1980 and 1983 Bundestag elections, one vote in the 1984 European parliament election, one vote in the 1980 state parliament election, one vote in the 1984 state election, one vote in the city council election, and two votes in the mayoral election. By comparison, a citizen of Tallahassee, Florida could have cast a total of 145 votes during this same period.

6. Sidney Verba, Norman Nie, and Jae-on Kim, *Participation and Political Equality* (New York: Cambridge University Press, 1978).

7. Charles Tilly, "European Violence and Collective Violence Since 1700," *Social Research* 53 (1985): 159–184; Dalton, *Citizen Politics in Western Democracies*, chap. 4.

8. Max Kaase, "Political Action Revisited," in *Continuities in Political Action*, ed. M. Kent Jennings and Jan van Deth (forthcoming).

9. Jutta Helm, "Citizen Lobbies in West Germany," in *West European Party System*, ed. Peter Merkl (New York: Free Press, 1980); Bernd Guggenberger and Udo Kempf, eds., *Bürgerinitiativen und Repräsentatives System*, 2nd ed. (Opladen: Westdeutscher Verlag, 1984).

10. The 1980 Political Action study found that 6 percent of the public had participated in a citizen-action group, by 1985 membership had increased to 13 percent. Also see Hans-Dieter Klingemann, *Formen, Bestimmungsgründe und Konsequenzen politischer Beteiligung* (Freie Universität Berlin: Informationen aus Lehre und Forschung, 1985).

11. Also see Udo Kempf, "Bürgerinitiativen: Der empirische Befund," in *Bürgerinitiativen und Repräsentatives System*, ed. Guggenberger and Kempf, p. 301.

12. Joachim Rashke, ed. *Bürger und Parteien* (Opladen: Westdeutscher Verlag, 1982); Hermann Scheer, ed. *Parteien kontra Bürger* (Munich-Piper, 1979).

13. Charles Foster, ed., *Comparative Public Policy and Citizen Participation* (New York: Pergamon, 1980); Helm, "Citizen Lobbies in West Germany," pp. 589–592.

14. See the low levels of approval for various protest activities cited in Barnes, Kaase, et al., *Political Action*, p. 545.

15. Klaus Troitzsch, *Volksbegehren und Volksentscheid* (Meisenheim-am-Glan: Hain, 1979).

CHAPTER VII

Politics at the Elite Level

DEMOCRACIES ARE GOVERNMENTS *of* and *for* the people, but they are seldom governments *by* the people. Above the mass of West German citizens is a group of a few thousand elites who manage the actual workings of the political system. Public participation in politics is intermittent and limited in scope; elites are involved full-time in making political decisions. The public has limited knowledge and sophistication about policy matters; elites generally are experts on the costs and benefits of various public policies. The public expresses its policy preferences, elites make policy decisions.

The stratification of political influence is inevitable in any political system, including the Federal Republic. No one expects that the views of the average Herr or Frau Müller will carry the same weight as those of Chancellor Kohl. The question is how to ensure that political leaders remain responsive to public wants and to balance the relationship between the public and political elites. Effective and efficient decision making depends on the expertise and judgment of political experts who are in a position to make authoritative political decisions. At the same time, the goal of democracy is to assure that the political system responds to the public's needs and interests, even if this does not always maximize the efficiency of decision making. The public should ultimately control the politicians, and not the other way around.

The power and authority of political elites is a sensitive issue in German political history. Debates about the causes of Weimar's collapse and the Nazi's atrocities often revolve around the question of the relative role of the public and political elites. Indeed, even the choice of wording carries political overtones. The German word for a political leader, *"Führer,"* evokes negative images of Hitler's *Füh-*

rerkult, and so the term "elite" has been added to the German vocabulary as a politically neutral term for describing individuals in leadership positions.

The questions of who are the elites, how they are selected, and what views they represent are crucial to understanding the political system of the Federal Republic or any other democracy.[1] Elites are central actors in the policy process, and the nature of that role can have a significant impact on policy outputs. The principles, values, and expectations of elites are key elements in defining the political culture, as when the democratic consensus among postwar political elites facilitated the creation of a democratic political order. Moreover, if public wants and needs are to be represented within the policy process, that representation must come principally from the elites. The relationship between the public and political elites is the key to effective and representative government.

WHO GOVERNS?

Although nearly everyone agrees that elites govern, there is less consensus on what is meant when we use the term "elite." One approach stresses the concentration of political power in the hands of a few very influential individuals. This *power elite model* sees elites as a tightly interconnected network of top-level political, economic, and social leaders sharing distinct and common interests. Rather than representing the public interest, this model pictures elites as working to protect their wealth, status, or position. The power elite view of politics sees the people and political elites as antagonists—elites striving to protect their privileged position and the citizens challenging this oligarchy.

There have been several different variations of the power elite interpretation applied to the Federal Republic during its brief history. Throughout the early postwar years, many critics, especially the East Germans, claimed that the Nazi state had perpetuated itself under the guise of West German democracy. True, the break with the past was incomplete. Too many prominent political figures, from Adenauer's chief of staff, Hans Globke, to Chancellor Kiesinger, had links to the Nazi regime; the number of ex-Nazis in the administrative elite was particularly high. In overall terms, however, the Federal Republic marked the ascendence to power of a new group of political elites.[2]

A more persisting version of the power elite theory maintains that an alliance of economic and political elites holds a virtual monopoly of power within the West German political process.[3] The corporatist style of interest group politics in the Federal Republic reinforces this belief (see Chapter VIII). In some instances, political decisions are made by a small group of elites behind closed doors, and then legitimated by the political system. Radical leftists claim that these examples support Marx and Engels' predictions that democratic governments would become representatives of the bourgeoisie.

Most specialists on West German politics reject these simple power elite theories in favor of a more complex model of *competitive elites*.[4] The competitive elite model maintains that the diversity and complexity of contemporary society leads to a proliferation of politically relevant organizations, each represented by its own leaders. The political process incorporates a large number of these organizations, and not just the representatives of a few key social or economic groups. The potential range of relevant policy actors includes party leaders, government officials, administrative elites, major media figures, religious leaders, business and labor representatives, cultural and intellectual leaders, and other public figures.

A recent study of West German elites yields several illustrations of the diversity of elite politics.[5] The project first defined the most influential political figures in terms of formal positions inside and outside government, producing a list of over 3000 individuals. A sample of this group was then asked who they themselves turn to for policy advice; when these names are added, the pool of "elites" nearly quadruples in size and greatly increases in diversity. These informal reference networks make up a "core elite" of individuals who are regularly consulted by other elites on national policy issues. This core group includes many different elites (Figure VII.1). Politicians comprise the largest group in the core (37.4 percent). Business representatives (19.1 percent) and labor leaders (7.9 percent) make up two other large groups of core elites, but certainly do not hold a monopoly of influence. Media figures, academics, and civil servants are important players in the policy process, which includes representatives of the military, various cultural institutions, and even non-Germans.

A proliferation in the number of elites also corresponds to increased diversity in the political views of elites. Although the group of politically influential elites may be readily identifiable, they do not constitute an elite class per se; that is, they do not share a common political interest, as elites in traditional or authoritarian

FIGURE VII.1 *The Central Core of Political Decision Makers*

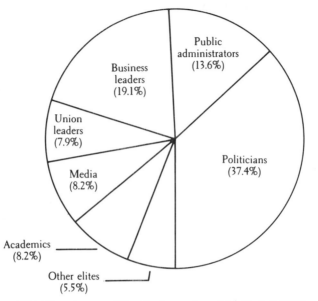

Source: 1981 West German Elite Study conducted by Rudolf Wildenmann, Max Kaase, and Ursula Hoffmann-Lange. This study is available from the Zentralarchiv für empirische Sozialforschung in Cologne.

societies often do. As a later section of this chapter will show, elites in the Federal Republic represent the diverse interests within West German society. Often there is as much or more diversity in policy preferences among elites as there is among the general public.

Even this picture of a differentiated core oversimplifies the distribution of political influence among West German elites. The number and type of competing groups change with the nature of the issue. Decision making on a foreign policy matter might involve representatives of defense contractors, corporations with large exports, and the military and political leaders who concentrate on foreign policy. Social policy involves representatives of employers' organizations, labor unions, the churches, and charitable organizations and relevant party and government officials. Even influential politicians and government administrators tend to specialize on a few issues or policy areas.

Another, more subtle implication of the competitive elite model is that the boundary between elites and nonelites is not clearly defined. Political influence has spread, both across the spectrum of political interest groups and over levels of political power. It is difficult, in fact nearly impossible, to draw a clear line between elites and the nonelite. Job title alone is not a sufficient measure of political influence; there are effective and ineffective cabinet ministers, influential and noninfluential Bundestag deputies. Beyond these primary policy actors is another layer of middle-level functionaries, such as party activists, local political officials and administrators, and the management level of interest group associations. Middle-level party officials and the cadre of active party members can exert substantial influence on overall party policy. State and local political leaders affect national policy, too, although their direct influence may be more difficult to trace than the actions of policy makers in Bonn. The expansion of citizen action groups and other forms of direct citizen involvement further blurs the dividing line between the public and elites.

Figure VII.2 illustrates a more realistic, but still oversimplified,

FIGURE VII.2 *Overlapping Circles of Political Influence*

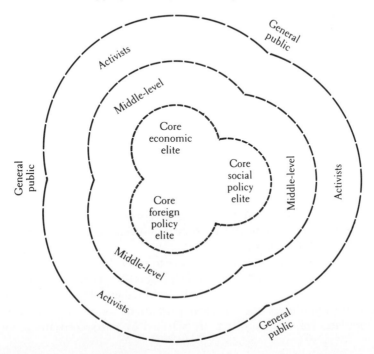

conception of elite politics. The core elites who are most influential in national policy making are pictured as a set of partially overlapping groups, whose compositions vary according to type of issue. In this illustration, only three broad policy areas are represented: economics, social policy, and foreign policy. These core elites are influenced by a larger group of middle-level elites. The boundary between core and middle-level elites is neither rigidly defined nor maintained, depending instead on the nature of the issues and the personal characteristics of the individuals. The middle-level elites are, in turn, surrounded by part-time political activists and the attentive public. This dividing line is even more permeable, with greater interchange between both groups. Finally, the general public provides the overall context for these political relations.

Political elites do indeed exist in the Federal Republic, and they wield disproportionate influence in the policy-making process. At the same time, one should avoid an overly simplistic view of elites as a small group of decision makers who rule over the public. Policy making in advanced industrial democracies, such as West Germany, has changed from being dominated by elites toward greater interdependence among the various participants in the policy process. The increasing diversity of competing elites should encourage elites to be more responsive to their constituencies, and thus enhance representation within the democratic process.

PATHS TO THE TOP

It has been claimed, arguably, that elite recruitment constitutes the most important function of government. The selection of elites determines who holds the formal positions of political power and who wields the political influence that accompanies these offices. The selection of players in the game of politics can often decide the outcome. The attitudes of elites determine the distribution of political orientations at the top levels of the policy process and the receptiveness of the political leadership to specific points of view. A political system may be better than its citizens, but it seldom can rise above poor leadership.

There are several different pathways to enter the ranks of the elite, and these pathways differ between elite groups.[6] Top-level political elites—elected government officials, cabinet members, and senior political appointees—are selected principally by political parties. Candidates for elective office are selected by party conventions or party selection committees, rather than by the general party membership or voters-at-large. A record of work for the party and partisan support are virtual prerequisites for nomination to national elective office or a top-level political appointment. Most political leaders can trace their career backward through a series of upward moves within the party's political or administrative hierarchy.

The political parties weigh several factors in screening potential candidates for office. Besides party loyalty, the personal political beliefs of the aspiring candidate are important. Candidates run for office as representatives of the party rather than as individuals; therefore, their views must be consistent with the party's program. Personal qualities are an important element in candidate selection. A candidate might excel on any of several different criteria: The forte of some political elites is technical or administrative expertise; others are noted for leadership or their effectiveness in representing the party in the policy-making process.

The parties attempt to ensure an appropriate balance in group affiliations among party candidates and appointed officials. In the case of the Christian Democratic Union, this balancing process has led to a formal *Proporz* system, which guarantees appropriate representation for the various social groups comprising its electoral coalition. For instance, Catholics and Protestants are allocated a specific number of positions on the CDU's candidate lists to ensure religious parity within the party. Similarly, the SPD works to balance the social composition of its candidate list, so that candidates represent the various social and ideological blocs within the party; although this balancing is deliberate, there is no formal quota.

Partisan activity and elective office often begin at the local and state levels, which provide a starting point for political recruitment. Local office provides a testing ground for further political ambitions. A local notable or aspiring political activist can get a feel of political life through serving in local government or party offices. At the same time, others can measure the aspiring leader's abilities, based on actual performance in office. Because of the federal structure of the political system, success at the state level often is a stepping-stone to national office. For instance, both chancellor candidates in 1987 and about one-third of Kohl's cabinet previously held political positions at the state level. Many Bundestag deputies first entered politics through state and local government, and they continue to maintain strong local ties.[7] The importance of local and state office as a recruitment pathway is probably greater in the Federal Republic than in most other Western parliamentary systems, because of West Germany's decentralized political structure.

The recruitment to political office begins as a fairly open process. The existence of several different ways to enter and succeed in politics ensures a broad representation of political and social interests among political activists. Some labor union officials become active in SPD politics to ensure that working-class views are heard within the party; research and administrative specialists are drawn into politics; business executives occasionally develop an interest in running for local government or working with the conservative parties.

Most top-level political elites began their careers outside of politics (Figure VII.3); about one-third started their careers in the economic sector, either as businesspersons or employees. The law profession provides another route to a political career, but not to the same extent as in other parliamentary democracies.[8] Instead, the civil service is an unusually important source in the recruitment of political elites. The prominence of this career path partially reflects the value Germans place upon administrative expertise. The political involvement of public employees is further encouraged by the fact that civil servants can count legislative service toward the calculation of their retirement pensions and retain the right to reinstatement upon their return to the bureaucracy. The percentage of top-level elites who began their careers in politics is fairly low, especially given the large number of local party and political officials. This underscores the fact that politics is not usually chosen as a career, but as a route to influence by the politically concerned.

The political recruitment process is a wide-mouthed funnel at the entry level, but the requirements for advancement steadily become more demanding and more restrictive. A long apprenticeship is required before entering the top stratum. Aspirants for the top-level political offices must develop their credentials with a record of party and political work. A political avocation gradually becomes a profession. A long apprenticeship means that political elites have considerable experience before attaining a position of substantial power. At the same time, this recruitment pattern limits the interchange among party, administrative, and economic elites. At the topmost level of the political process, the circulation of political elites is almost exclusively internal. For instance, members of a chancellor's cabinet nearly always come from a group of expe-

FIGURE VII.3 *Initial Careers of Top-Level Political Elites*

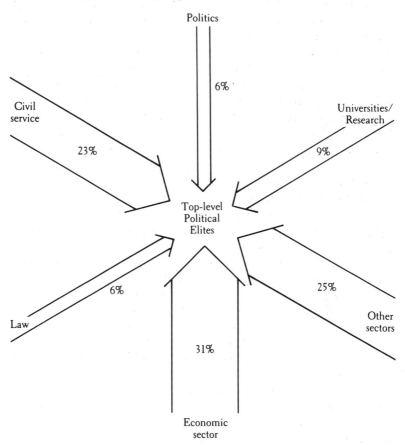

Source: 1981 West German Elite Study conducted by Rudolf Wildenmann, Max Kaase, and Ursula Hoffmann-Lange.

rienced politicians with extensive experience in state or federal government and strong party credentials. There have been only a handful of exceptions in the history of the Federal Republic, such as Karl Schiller, economics minister under Brandt, or Rita Süssmuth, who is Kohl's family and youth minister. Very seldom can business leaders or popular personalities use their outside success to attain a top-level position of political influence quickly.

The biography of the present chancellor, Helmut Kohl, provides a textbook example of the political recruitment process at work.

Kohl became a CDU party member while still in high school. He augmented his university studies with increasing involvement in the party. In 1953, he became a member of the executive committee of a CDU district association; the next year, he was elected deputy chairman of the CDU youth association in Rhineland-Palatinate. The year after receiving his doctorate he began working in the chemical industry and was also elected to the state parliament. Kohl was elected minister president of the state in 1969; four years later he was named national chairman of the CDU. After an unsuccessful try as the CDU/CSU chancellor candidate in 1976, he became chancellor of the CDU/CSU-FDP coalition in 1982. Not all political careers rise so rapidly or are as illustrious as Kohl's, but they often are as long.

Public administrators form another important elite in the public policy process. The highest level administrative elite consists of the career civil servants, the *Beamte*.[9] Beamte positions range from low-level positions in the postal or railway systems to the West German equivalents of the "super-grade" administrators in the American federal government. Higher-level Beamte hold most of the major administrative positions within the bureaucracy, which grants them a significant role in the formation and application of public policy.

The recruitment pattern for Beamte differs markedly from the selection process for political elites. One prerequisite for an administrative career is university training. Virtually all top-level state and federal administrators have a university degree, most often with a specialization in law or economics. Administrators are recruited for their technical and managerial expertise, and a university education is considered evidence of these skills.

The formal selection of Beamte is done through competitive exams after basic educational or occupational qualifications have been met. Bureaucratic norms are deeply ingrained in the West German administrative system, so that merit criteria are strenuously enforced as a requirement for entrance and advancement through the civil service.[10] The title "Beamter" is a highly regarded professional achievement. Moreover, the title and its status are invested in the individual and not the position. Once gained, a Beamter can hold the title for life.

Many members of the administrative elites chose their profession as an initial career (see Figure VII.4). Almost one-half of top-level administrators began their careers in the civil service. Another tenth

FIGURE VII.4 *Initial Careers of Top-Level Administrative Elites*

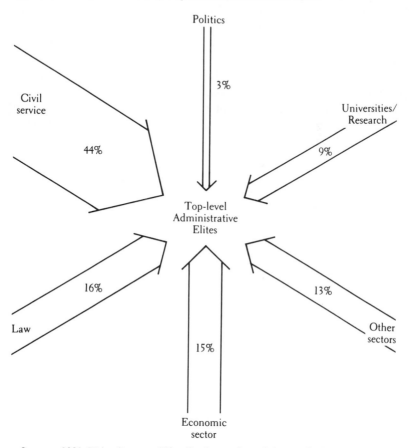

Source: 1981 West German Elite Study conducted by Rudolf Wildenmann, Max Kaase, and Ursula Hoffmann-Lange.

came from the universities, which are a branch of government (university professors are members of the civil service). There is a traditional closeness between the civil service and the legal profession, because German public administration emphasizes a legalistic approach; many civil servants studied law as university students. These career patterns suggest that the civil service is a more clearly defined profession than is elective politics; on average, members of the administrative elite spend about 90 percent of their careers in public service.[11]

Whereas entry to Beamte status and progression through an administrative career follows a clearly proscribed route, there is considerable crossover between administration and other elite sectors. The 1981 West German elite study found that most top administrators in the federal government had held an occupation outside the bureaucracy at some point in their career. A substantial number of middle-range civil servants take advantage of their life tenure to pursue outside opportunities or transfer to the state bureaucracy, at least temporarily. For instance, the Bundestag is commonly known as the parliament of civil servants because of the high proportion of Beamte among its members; during the tenth Bundestag (1983–1986) over one-third of the parliamentary deputies were Beamte or other government employees. A counterbalancing source of circulation into the administrative elite is the political appointment of individuals to fill top-level administrative positions. These appointments are normally limited to the offices with direct political responsibilities, such as *Staatssekretäre* or *Abteilungsleiter*. For example, the change to an SPD-led government in 1969 was marked by extensive turnover in top-level administrative posts, as was the CDU accession to power in 1982. These circulation patterns led Werner Kaltefleiter to describe public administrators as fulfilling a distribution function within West German society, supplying and using personnel from across elite sectors.[12]

Within the economic sector, the politically influential elites are usually the official representatives of business or labor union organizations (see Chapter VIII). The recruitment criteria for both these elite groups are similar to those required for advancement in a political career. Success in business, or a history of union activity, is an informal prerequisite for appointment as an interest group representative. The actual selection process for business leaders is probably less structured and more open than for most other elites. There is no formal test to become a member of the economic elite, accession to elite status does not follow a clearly proscribed route, and the reputations of business leaders are more important than their formal positions. Union representatives, in contrast, are chosen for office through a more formal process of nomination and approval at union congresses. Their success is largely based on leadership skills and organizational loyalty.

Business and labor leaders also differ in their circulation across elite groups. Although about one-half of the business leadership spend their entire career in the business sector, many of them do become active in other areas. The management skills, organizational abilities, and economic resources of businesspersons are highly regarded in administration and politics. Union leaders, in contrast, constitute a largely self-contained elite, recruited from within the working class, with limited circulation into other sociopolitical sectors. Only a handful of the elite in most other sectors have career experience in the union movement.

THE SOCIAL PROFILE OF ELITES

The recruitment process selects people for elite positions in politics, administration, business, or other social sectors. Despite the diverse recruitment standards of the various elites, critics continue to question the social diversity of elites. Is there an inner club or old boys network that provides a recruitment pool for future elites? Do the members of the various elites share a common social and/or cultural background? Such a common bond might provide the basis, or at least the appearance, of an elite establishment as suggested by power elite theorists.

Ralf Dahrendorf was one of the first to draw attention to the relative lack of social integration among West German elites.[13] The Federal Republic lacks a clear establishment class, in which future leaders share values, beliefs and attitudes, as well as sharing informal social relations. There is no real West German equivalent to the *Grandes Ecoles* of France, the elite Oxbridge campuses of Britain, or the Ivy League of the United States. The location and type of educational training vary greatly for West German elites. Consequently, the common socializing experiences and informal social networks that exist among elites in other Western democracies are less developed in the Federal Republic. Dahrendorf saw this situation as a potential handicap for West German politics; he felt that informal social ties among elites moderate social conflict across elite strata. Other people argue, however, that the absence of an elite establishment actually benefited the Federal Republic's democratic develoment by creating a new group of elites who were more open to political change.

Although the West German elite may not come from an exclusive class or travel in narrow social circles, clear social biases still exist among those individuals recruited to elite positions. The 1981 West German elite study compared the social background of high-level elites in several social sectors to the general population of actively employed persons aged 40 and over (Figure VII.5). Sixty percent of

FIGURE VII.5 *The Social Composition of Elites*

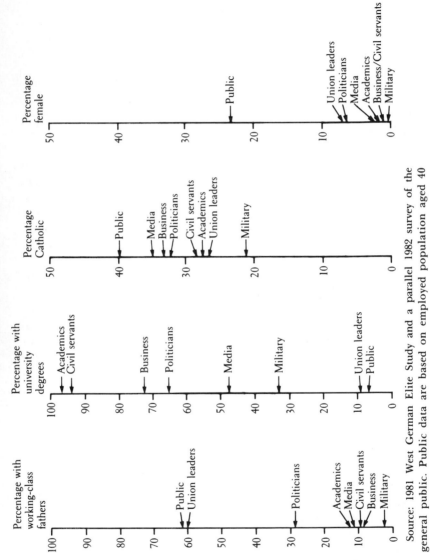

Source: 1981 West German Elite Study and a parallel 1982 survey of the general public. Public data are based on employed population aged 40 and over.

186

the general population were raised in working-class families, compared to only 15 percent among all elites. The family background of union leaders (61 percent working class) is fairly similar to the general public, but the middle-class bias of other elite groups is striking. The educational background of elites underscores this same theme. Only 6 percent of employed adults hold a university degree, versus 69 percent of the elites. The vast majority of political, business, administrative, and academic elites have earned a university diploma.

The upper-class backgrounds of elites is a uniform finding in most political systems, not just in the Federal Republic. In broad international terms, however, the upper-class bias among West German elites appears almost egalitarian. For instance, an international study of politicians and civil servants in six nations finds that the biases in education and parental social class among West German politicians is the lowest among the nations surveyed; West German civil servants also come from relatively diverse family backgrounds.[14] Ursula Hoffmann-Lange concludes that German elites are less likely to come from upper-class backgrounds than are their Australian or U.S. counterparts.[15] The Federal Republic's sociopolitical elite are disproportionately drawn from the upper class, but to a lesser extent than in most other Western democracies.

Religion constitutes another potentially important social division among West German elites. In the larger territory of prewar Germany, Protestants outnumbered Catholics, and Protestants predominated in most positions of social and political influence. The redefinition of West Germany's borders brought the number of Catholics and Protestants into rough balance and diminished the Prussian hegemony within German society. Catholics remain slightly underrepresented among contemporary elites, but the extent of underrepresentation varies widely (Figure VII.5). The proportion of Catholics is smallest in those elite sectors with more restrictive recruitment processes: the military, civil servants, and academics. At the same time, the more open elite groups—politicians and business leaders—display a religious composition that is relatively close to that of employed adults. Deliberate attempts to integrate Catholics into West German society have lessened the importance of religion in elite recruitment.

There is one way in which West German elites constitute a separate class. The Federal Republic is largely an *andrachy,* a society ruled by males. Women constitute slightly more than half of the adult population and about one-fourth of the active adult labor force. Yet there are practically no women among social and political decision makers. The representation of women among the elites surveyed in 1981 ranges from 6.9 percent among union leaders to 0.7 percent among administrative elites. Even the political parties, which must compete for the votes of women, are largely male preserves. About 7 percent of the Bundestag deputies since 1949 have been women, and only two of Kohl's seventeen cabinet members are women. Furthermore, a woman who does rise to a high political office is often restricted to policy roles on family or social issues. Although recruitment into elite positions may be opening for younger women, considerable bias still exists against women assuming elite positions in all sociopolitical sectors.

THE POLITICAL ELITE

One group of elites deserves our special attention: elites in the political sector. Various social interests attempt to influence the policy process, but only political elites actually make political decisions. Political elites hold prime responsibility for the policy outputs of government; they staff the policy making and administrative institutions of government. The process of policy making converges on political elites.

A focus on political elites also illustrates the gradations of "eliteness" that exist within each sociopolitical sector. The broadest definition of elites includes the approximately two million card-carrying political party members and a few million participants in citizen–action groups. Low-level political elites, such as local party officers and city officials, number in the tens of thousands. A few thousand persons hold middle-level positions in the government and political parties, such as delegates to the district, state, and national party conventions or important local offices. There are 1283 deputies in the ten Länder parliaments and roughly an equal number of other important political elites at the state level. Bonn contains several hundred more elites who reside at the top of this political pyramid. All of these people are part of the network of political elites because of the potential influence they can wield, either individually or collectively.

Party activists are the day laborers of the political process. They deal with the mundane aspects of electoral politics: attending party meetings, doing volunteer work for the party's election campaign, and proselytizing the unconverted. At this level of activity, party activists are in the upper 5 percent of the politically involved. Still, the social backgrounds of party activists are not far different from the public at large.[16] For instance, the middle class accounted for about 60 percent of party members in the mid-1970s, only about 5 to 10 percentage points more than for the general public. In fact, despite a process of social convergence in partisan support over the past two decades, the class differences among party activists (between SPD and CDU partisans) generally outweigh the differences between party activists as a whole and the public.

The next level of the political hierarchy consists of the middle-level elites. Party officials and local and state government office-holders have important political responsibilities. In addition, because of their intermediate position in the political system, middle-level elites provide the necessary link between top-level decision makers and the general public. Middle-level elites are in a better position to know the public's views on political issues and articulate these views to higher-level political authorities. At the same time, middle-level elites serve as a transmission belt from the government to the public. They explain the actions of government to the citizenry and attempt to mobilize popular support for government policies.

As one moves up through the various layers of political activists, the social bias of elite membership increases. A study of the Social Democratic party in Northrhine-Westphalia found that blue-collar representation within the party decreased from 44 percent among the rank-and-file membership to 30 percent among the precinct officials, 23 percent among precinct chairmen, and only 8 percent among district committee members.[17] Other studies of middle-level party elites and elected officials show that the class, religious, and gender biases of membership at this level are greater than among lower-ranking political officials. Robert Putnam describes this general pattern as the *rule of increasing disproportion:* The higher the office the greater the bias in the social characteristics of elites.[18]

Bundestag deputies probably are as close as we can come to defining a pool of top-level national political elites based on formal position alone. The Bundestag makes national policy; its committee chairpersons, policy experts, and legislative specialists play central roles in the policy process. Moreover, parliamentary government fuses several different aspects of political authority together in the legislature. The chancellor and most of his cabinet ministers are Bundestag deputies, as are most top party officials. The initials

"MdB" (member of the German Bundestag) after one's name are a sign of political influence.

Bundestag deputies also constitute a group of high-level political elites for whom a long series of social background information is available (Table VII.1).[19] The large number of Bundestag deputies with university education is several times greater than among the general public, and these percentages have risen steadily since the first parliament. At the same time, an exceptionally large number of legislators also maintain a union membership. Nearly all the SPD deputies are union members (an illustration of the party's traditional ties to the unions); about 20 percent of CDU/CSU and 10 percent of FDP deputies are members of a union or a professional association.

One significant change in the composition of Bundestag deputies concerns their generational background. The early parliaments consisted of deputies, such as Adenauer and Schumacher, who had gone through their formative years during the Second Empire, became politically active under the Weimar Republic, and then went into hiatus during the Third Reich. Gradually, new individuals were recruited into politics; the Weimar generation began to enter positions of political authority in the 1960s, and during the 1970s a large proportion of new deputies had been raised during the Third Reich. It has taken until the early 1980s for the Federal Republic to see its own children form the majority of Parliament.

The most recent Parliaments also display a marked increase in the proportion of women at the top of the political hierarchy. After the 1987 election, the percentage of women in the Bundestag nearly doubled to over 15 percent. This increase can be traced primarily to the efforts of the small Green party. Women occupy 24 of the Greens' 42 seats in the Bundestag; Petra Kelly, Jutta Ditfurth, and other women have risen to positions of national prominence within the Green party. The Greens follow their statements on behalf of women's rights with action; for instance, the party put up an all-female slate in the 1986 Hamburg state elections (and increased its vote share from 6.8 to 10.4 percent). While the established parties lament the lack of qualified female candidates, the Greens actively recruit women for political office.

The social profile of West German political elites clearly is not representative of the general public. The social class, education, religion, and gender of elites display the distinct social biases of the recruitment process. Biases in recruitment, however, are not the

TABLE VII.1 *Social Background of Bundestag Deputies*

	1949–1953	1953–1957	1957–1961	1961–1965	1965–1969	1969–1972	1972–1976	1976–1980	1980–1983	1983–1986
University education (%)	45.3	44.0	51.8	57.6	56.0	63.9	67.6	70.3	70.3	82.5
Civil servant (%)	—	—	—	—	—	36.7	34.9	35.5	35.9	33.4
Union members (%)	28.0	38.1	38.9	42.8	46.7	51.2	54.2	53.7	52.6	51.2
Catholic (%)	—	32.2	36.6	33.2	37.7	36.3	32.8	37.3	36.4	36.7
Generation										
Second Empire	73.7	61.5	50.4	37.3	18.7	5.3	1.2	1.2	0.0	0.0
Weimar Republic	25.1	36.1	40.8	47.2	48.6	40.6	23.3	12.0	6.1	2.7
Third Reich	1.2	2.4	8.5	14.6	27.6	39.8	44.2	41.9	32.7	28.8
Federal Republic	0.0	0.0	.2	1.0	5.0	14.5	31.3	45.5	63.3	68.5
Total	100%	100%	100%	100%	100%	100%	100%	100%	100%	100%
Average age (years)	50.0	50.9	51.8	52.3	50.9	49.0	46.6	47.3	47.0	48.1
Average years as deputy	—	1.9	4.0	5.7	6.6	6.4	5.7	6.7	6.8	7.2
First-term deputies (%)	100.0	48.1	30.6	25.1	25.5	30.1	28.0	22.6	24.9	17.8
Women deputies (%)	6.8	8.8	9.2	8.3	6.9	6.6	5.8	7.3	8.5	9.8

Source: Press-und Informationszentrum des Deutschen Bundestages, *Datenhandbuch zur Geschichte des Deutschen Bundestages 1949 bis 1982* (Bonn: Deutscher Bundestag, 1983); Wissenschaftlichen Dienste des Deutschen Bundestages, *Datenhandbuch zur Geschichte des Deutschen Bundestages 1980 bis 1984* (Baden-Baden: Nomos, 1986).

same as exclusivity. The recruitment of political elites is a fairly open process, with many alternative routes to political office. This process draws participants from differing social and political backgrounds. The SPD provides a recruitment pathway for individuals from working-class backgrounds, just as the CDU/CSU opens the recruitment process to Catholics. The affirmative-action program of the Green party is working to broaden the pool of potential candidates still further. The correct social background might facilitate advancement within West German society, but recruitment to elite positions is not based on an exclusive class background or social inheritance.

ELITE ATTITUDES

The question of possible bias in the recruitment of elites goes beyond that of their social representativeness; a more central issue concerns the political beliefs of individuals recruited into elite positions. What do elites think about the policy process and the desired outcomes of that process? Do elites enter the decision-making process with the same political orientations and policy preferences as the people whom they presumably represent?

One important question in this regard is that of the basic political loyalties of elites. From the Second Empire to the end of the Third Reich, many members of the top stratum of German political elites were antidemocratic. A critical failure of the Weimar Republic was its inability to generate elite support for the democratic system. Although some political and administrative elites struggled to make democratic politics work, others conspired to overthrow the political system.

The political leadership of the Federal Republic marks a sharp break from this pattern of elite orientations. A political consensus exists among members of the West German political elite. Authoritarian politics were discredited by the Third Reich, and the option of a Communist system was discredited by developments in East Germany. The Federal Republic's democratic institutions and procedures have commanded the allegiance of nearly all political elites. Moreover, the virtually unanimous elite support of a democratic political order led to systematic attempts to remake the political culture in this image. During the early years of the Federal Republic, and later, elites were the guardians of democracy.

Beyond this consensus on the general structure of the political and economic system, the various elites often differ in their political beliefs and policy orientations. The most basic political attitude is partisan preference (Table VII.2). Political elites are not included in this table, because, by definition they form homogeneous partisan blocs, but sharp partisan differences still exist among other elites. Labor union officials are unambiguous in their support of the Social Democrats, just as business and military leaders lean heavily toward the Union parties. Members of the media and academic elites display a distribution of partisan preferences fairly close to those of the German electorate. It is also noteworthy that the senior civil servants are politically diverse, splitting their partisan preferences about equally between the CDU/CSU and SPD.

The distinct political identities of the various elites shows more clearly on their attitudes toward the major policy problems facing the Federal Republic (Figure VII.6). On such economic issues as protection of the social services programs and extension of co-determination, differences among elites follow the traditional lines of political cleavage. SPD politicians and labor union leaders hold distinctly liberal views about these programs, whereas business leaders and their partisan allies in the CDU/CSU and FDP are conservative. Average citizen attitudes on these issues are more central, that is, between both partisan camps. Similar patterns of elite polarization appear on other socioeconomic issues, such as support for private television stations, stricter regulation of the banking industry, and expansion of comprehensive schools.[20] On most of these socioeconomic issues, the policy views of the leaders of competing interest groups—labor and business—are more divergent than the differences between their partisan representatives. These are the types of political controversies that have historically structured political conflict in West Germany and that yield a familiar Left/Right alignment of elite groups.[21]

Elites show quite different opinion patterns on noneconomic policies. For instance, differences of opinion among elites on the question of strict environmental standards were quite modest in 1981 (Figure VII.6). Elites tend to share a centrist viewpoint on the trade-off between the economy and the environment. The public is thus poorly represented, because the electorate's support for strict environmental regulations is stronger than for any of the established elites. The pattern on environmental issues is a common one for many New Politics issues. The established parties were hesitant to take clear stands on these issues, and other elites often found themselves internally divided on these policies; this limited the potential

TABLE VII.2 *Partisan Preferences of Elites and the General Public*

			Elite Groups				
Party	Union Leaders	Civil Servants	Media	Academics	Business	Military	General Public
CDU/CSU	13	37	43	38	66	65	38
FDP	1	18	19	17	13	9	7
SPD	80	31	17	15	6	2	23
Greens	1	—	3	1	1	2	7
No preference	5	14	18	29	14	20	25
Total	100%	100%	100%	100%	100%	100%	100%

Source: 1981 West German Elite Study and a parallel 1982 study of the general public conducted by Rudolf Wildenmann, Max Kaase and Ursula Hoffmann-Lange.

for these issues to provide a basis of political conflict, and opened the door for the development of a new Green party.

Foreign policy is another instance where differences of opinion among elites are often fairly small. The 1981 West German elite study included three foreign policy issues: strengthening the powers of the European Community (EC), reforming the Community's agricultural program, and expanding foreign aid to Third World countries. On each policy proposal, elites had only modest policy differences (the EC issue is presented in Figure VII.6). Party elites generally support European integration more than do other elites; the FDP is the more "European" party. The alignment of party and socioeconomic elites varies, however, according to the specific context of the policy proposal. The clear Left/Right alignment so apparent on economic issues is more difficult to detect on most foreign policy issues; there is more elite consensus on these issues.

One cannot make a simple assessment of whether elites or the political system faithfully represent the public's policy preferences, because the congruence in policy preferences between elites and the public varies across issues, and probably across time. On issues of long-standing controversy, such as economic and religious conflicts, the evidence suggests that political decision makers enter the policy process with policy preferences that reflect the views of the voter blocs and major interest groups they represent. On issues of more recent vintage, the evidence is less clear. Still, more detailed analyses of voters and party elites suggest that parties generally provide their supporters with institutionalized representation within the policy process.[22]

STYLES OF POLITICAL ACTION

A final decision to consider is how the people of power and influence think and act about politics. Each elite sector possesses its own political norms, which define what is appropriate and expected. These norms affect how each elite group exercises its role within the policy-making process.

Professional norms are perhaps most clearly seen in the case of the Beamte. The Beamte display their German heritage through traces of a Weberian style of administrative behavior. Max Weber maintained that the genuine civil servant does not engage in politics, but is an impartial administrator whose actions are based on facts and legal guidelines.[23] West German public administrators still

196

FIGURE VII.6 *Political Values of Elites and the Public*

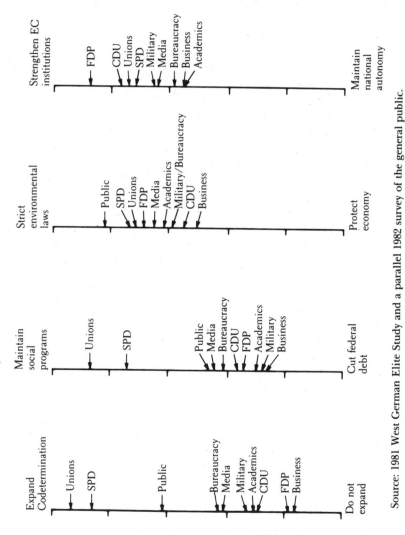

Source: 1981 West German Elite Study and a parallel 1982 survey of the general public.

believe in remaining above politics (*überparteilich*) and emphasize technical details and legal considerations as the bases of decision making. At the same time, the democratic climate of the Federal Republic, and the negative image of a bureaucracy blindly subservient to the Nazi state, has encouraged civil servants to become more sensitive to political factors. As one senior official said in describing his role: "We are not here to receive orders, mentally to click our heels, and to say Jawohl!"

Contemporary civil servants thus are more politicized and more pluralist than the traditional image of the German Beamte would suggest. The Weberian model of efficient German administration still exists, but is now tempered by a sensitivity to the political aspects of policy making and an acceptance of political considerations. An international study of bureaucrats showed that German civil servants scored above most other nationalities on measures of pluralism, populism and democratic values.[24] On measures of democratic norms, the Beamte are actually closer to the liberal SPD than to the conservative view of Christian Democrats.[25]

Weber also described the nature of political elites: rather than the rationalism of bureaucrats, the politicians base their actions on partisanship, narrow special interests, and ideology. Whereas the bureaucrat has a *Rechtsstaat* mentality, the politician seeks personal political power. Weber lumped politicians together with demagogues, lawyers, and saloonkeepers—occupations that he felt relied on charisma, argumentative skills, and low morals.

Weber based his critique of the political profession on the politicians of the Second Empire (he wrote his famous comparison of administrative and political styles in 1918). The petty partisanship of the Weimar Republic, and, even more, the behavior of the Third Reich's leaders, seemed horrible confirmations of Weber's claims. As has been stated repeatedly, however, most political elites in the Federal Republic rose above this heritage.

Political elites have two contrasting orientations. Politicians are, first of all, partisan animals. This is inevitable in a parliamentary system such as the Federal Republic. Parties provide virtually the only route to a political career, and candidates realize that their success is closely tied to their party's fortunes. Once elected to office, politicians structure their agenda around the party Fraktion, and their behavior closely follows partisan lines. The partisan differences in policy views discussed above (Figure VII.6) are more distinct than would be typically found between the major U.S. parties.

The potentially conflictual influence of partisan ties is counterbalanced by political norms that express a broader view of the policy process. In an attempt to avoid the fragmented politics of Weimar, the Basic Law states that deputies "shall be representatives of the whole people, not bound by orders and instructions, and shall be subject only to their conscience" (Article 38). A survey of Bundestag deputies and the general public found that both groups subscribe to this position.[26] Most voters say that deputies should follow their own consciences, even if their consciences are in conflict with the public's preferences. Most Bundestag deputies report, however, that although they *should* vote their conscience, in actual practice they are almost as likely to follow either party guidelines or voter preferences. International comparisons indicate that the autonomy of elites is valued higher in the West German political system than in several other Western European democracies.[27]

This broader view of policy making produces a more cooperative style of relations among contending parties and political figures (see Chapter X). The rhetorical excess that characterized exchanges between the SPD and CDU/CSU in the early terms of the Bundestag gradually gave way to a more cooperative tone between the major parties. West German politicians see policy making as a consensus building process among the relevant political forces rather than as a competition between hostile political camps. The unconventional tactics of the Greens have disturbed this consensual style, but the Greens are the first to acknowledge that these norms still influence the behavior of most German politicians.

The style of contemporary political elites also places greater stress on rational policy making and technical expertise. As the Beamte have become more political, politicians have become better public administrators. Perhaps this is inevitable because of the overlap in careers among Bundestag deputies and the administrative elite. In any case, many leading government and party officials hold positions of influence because of their specialized knowledge. Former Chancellor Helmut Schmidt probably best epitomized this more technocratic style of political decision making, basing policy on facts and "hard" evidence rather than ideology. Similarly, Gerhard Loewenberg's study of the Bundestag found that few deputies participated in debates on a wide range of issues; most focused their interest on a few areas of specialization.[28] Politicians have learned the truth of the old German saying *"Wissen ist Macht"* ("Knowledge is power").

The political behavior of economic elites reflects a different set of professional norms. Business and labor leaders are less accustomed to the public accountability of elected officials or the formal administrative guidelines of bureaucratic elites. Economic elites have a competitive, action-oriented style that sometimes seems ill-suited to politics. Although they support democratic principles, they are not used to decision making in an open forum. Their professions encourage them to advance the interests of the group as far as possible, not to emphasize societal interests. These tendencies are only partially suppressed when members of the economic elite engage in politics. Business and labor union leaders play a visible role within the democratic political process, but they are seldom noted for an open and pluralistic decision-making style.

Although the political norms of the Federal Republic generally place value on a consensual style of policy making, some tension and conflict at the elite level is inevitable. Konrad Adenauer and Kurt Schumacher had contrasting philosophies and styles, which symbolized the political differences between their parties throughout the 1950s. During the era of good feelings that characterized the Grand Coalition, intense political competition existed beneath the surface of partisan harmony. Contemporary elections still feature occasional political outbursts and personal attacks, with chancellor candidates calling each other names such as *"Lügner," "pissender Bulle,"* and *"Rentenbetruger."* There are still demagogues and saloonkeepers among the Federal Republic's political elite—even a few of the lawyers that Weber worried about.

One way to keep tensions among political elites in check is through a network of informal social ties that counterbalance political differences. Dahrendorf believed such ties were crucial for the effective operation of a democratic political system; he also believed such connections were underdeveloped in the Federal Republic.[29] As noted above, the exclusive social class and school ties that might have provided the basis for social integration are generally lacking among West German elites. Even among individuals who attain sociopolitical influence, the elite culture does not encourage purely social interaction across political and sectoral boundaries. In the words of one journalist, elites are the "The Unsociable Cream" of West German society.[30] The social and political diversity of the elite encourages this tendency toward aloofness, as does the regional decentralization in West Germany. The headquarters of major businesses, the media, union organizations and other sociopolitical groups are dispersed throughout the country, which lessens communication between elites. Bonn does not provide a focus for elite interaction; even many Bundestag deputies regard it as a city to be endured and left behind as soon as business is over.

Instead of extensive *informal* methods of social integration, the Federal Republic has developed numerous *formal* channels of communication among elites. Civil servants are officially encouraged to stay in close touch with relevant interest groups and monitor their policy preferences. Elites from several sectors interact through committee hearings in the Bundestag and government committees at the federal and Länder levels. Official and unofficial "planning groups" also provide forums for competing groups to discuss their interests in anticipation of future policy proposals. International surveys thus find that formal interaction among elites in their policy-making roles is more frequent and more open in West Germany than in most other Western democracies.[31]

THE NEXT GENERATION

In recent years there has been growing evidence that the political goals and consensual style described in this chapter are being challenged by a new generation of political leaders, the so-called "successor generation."[32] The origins of this change can be found in the student movement of the late 1960s. The student movement was a breeding ground for a new generation of Leftist activists and future political leaders, and this environment differed sharply from that in which members of the established elites grew. The views of the established elites were shaped by a series of powerful experiences: World War II and the reconstruction period, the Economic Miracle, and the political tensions of the Cold War era. The successor generation has no direct personal experience with most of these events. Instead of identifying with the Economic Miracle, many younger elites have nonmaterialist goals, the kind that were overlooked in the pursuit of economic advancement. The young do not remember the Berlin Airlift and intense Cold War rivalry of the 1950s; instead they learned of America through protests against the Vietnam war. In short, the generation of university students from the late 1960s and early 1970s, the same individuals who will rise to positions of political and social prominence in the 1990s, were socialized into a political *Weltanschauung* markedly different from their elders.

Student activism initially turned to unconventional channels of political action: demonstrations, student protests, and the unpredictable behavior of the *Spontis*. The APO provided a temporary organizational base, but it faded with Willy Brandt's arrival in the chancellery. The strategy of the counterelite movement then changed. Student leader Rudi Dutschke called for young activists to change the political process from within. In his words, the young should begin "the long march through the institutions" to positions of social influence.

The progress of this march is most evident on the Left, since the student movement was basically a Leftist phenomenon. Many student activists first became involved in the young Socialist organization of the SPD (*Jusos*) and then moved into the ranks of SPD activists. The creation of the Green party in 1980 provided an even clearer rallying point for young activists, extending both the style and political goals of the student movement. Thus the up-and-coming political figures in both the SPD and the Green party frequently are alumni of the student movement, like Josef Leinen, Joschka Fischer, Wolfgang Roth, and Christian Züpel.

Two factors distinguish this rising generation of political elites from its predecessors. First, the successor generation cares more about New Politics issues facing the Federal Republic and sees these issues in the context of a contemporary West Germany greatly changed. Younger elites both inside and outside the established parties have more interest in issues such as environmental quality, women's rights, consumer protection, and the further democratization of society. In short, political elites are not immune to the same process of value change that is affecting the West German public (see Chapter IV).

Second, young elites often have a different political style. Instead of the pragmatism fashionable among established elites, younger elites are again turning to ideological principles to interpret and explain political problems. Members of the successor generation are more likely than their elders to approach politics in ideological terms. Along with this more ideological rhetoric, younger elites are adopting a political style based on competition and confrontation. Whereas older elites value political cooperation and compromise in reaction to the excessive political polarization of the Weimar Republic, younger activists decry the lack of political competition and reform in West German politics. The successor generation is more prone to protests and other forms of direct citizen action. This confrontational style also carries over to the behavior of elected officials. As the successor generation enters political office at the state and local level, they stimulate political debate and inject a new intensity into the political process. At the federal level, the Green Bundestag deputies aggressively question and challenge the government, far more than the larger SPD delegation.[33] Similar developments are taking place at the state and local level.

While the successor generation is primarily restructuring the West German Left, there is a contagion effect on the Right. The *Junge Union* has experienced a revival in interest among young CDU supporters. Young conservatives also express concern with issues such as environmental protection and human liberties, but offer different solutions to these problems. While the New Left might question the need for the NATO alliance, young conservatives criticize the social programs of the West German welfare state. Moreover, young conservatives are adopting the competitive and ideological political style advocated on the Left.

In other words, younger political elites on both the Left and Right approach politics with a more competitive and ideological style than their elders. The political activism among younger Leftists that Dutschke proposed is often matched by stronger efforts among young conservatives. As a result, elite studies generally find greater political polarization on both traditional socioeconomic issues and New Politics goals among younger elites. A recent study of party activists, for example, finds a wide gap between the ideological self-images of younger SPD and CDU party members, but much less difference in the self-images of older party members.[34] The successor generation thus reverses the trend toward consensual politics and represents a more politically active and polarized group of elites.

Given historical precedents, there is reason to be concerned that such a stylistic change might strain the democratic process as the successor generation moves into positions of political and social leadership in the decades ahead. Indeed, the negative consequences of earlier periods of polarization undoubtedly weakened Weimar democracy. Many political commentators see parallels in the fundamental opposition advocated by some members of the successor generation. This stylistic change is likely to be compounded by an attempt by some members of the successor generation to reassess some of West Germany's basic policy goals, such as the Federal Republic's position within the Western Alliance or the role of the state in directing German society and economic development. Yet there are some indications that the contemporary situation differs in important ways from other historical examples of polarized elite politics. Younger elites are politically more sensitive and more sympathetic to ideological concerns, but some evidence suggests that partisan hostility is declining among the young. Support for democratic politics and political tolerance is also greater among the successor generation than among older, established elites. If this is the case, the future style of West German elite politics might be marked by a greater ideological distinctiveness between political blocs, but also a more "open" and compromising kind of political competition. The willingness of younger elites to embrace party competition and political tolerance may thus determine how well the Federal Republic can adopt to the changing political style of the successor generation.

NOTES

1. See, for example, the analysis of citizen and elite interactions in the United States described in V. O. Key, *Public Opinion and American Democracy* (New York: Knopf, 1951).

2. Lewis Edinger, "Post-totalitarian Leadership: Elites in the German Federal Republic," *American Political Science Review* 54 (1960); Alfred Grosser, *Germany: The Colossus Again* (New York: Praeger, 1955).

3. For example see Stanislaw Ehrlich, *Der Macht der Minderheit: Die Einflussgruppen in der politischen Struktur des Kapitalismus* (Wien: Europa, 1966).

4. Ralf Dahrendorf, *Society and Democracy in Germany* (New York: Doubleday, 1967); Wolfgang Zapf, *Wandlungen der deutschen Elite, 1919–1961* (Munich: Piper, 1965); Klaus von Beyme, *Die Politische Elite in der Bundesrepublik* (Munich: Piper, 1974); Karl Deutsch and Lewis Edinger, *Germany Rejoins the Powers* (Stanford: Stanford University Press, 1959).

5. Ursula Hoffmann-Lange, "Positional Power and Political Influence in the Federal Republic of Germany," Paper presented at the World Congress of the International Political Science Association, 1985; Ursula Hoffmann-Lange, "Surveying National Elites in the Federal Republic of Germany," in *Research Methods for Elite Studies*, ed. George Moyser and Margaret Wagstaffe (London: Allen and Unwin, 1987).

6. Werner Kaltefleiter, "The Recruitment Market of the German Political Elite," in *Elite Recruitment in Democratic Polities*, ed. Heinz Eulau and Moshe Czudnowski (New York: Wiley, 1976); Joel Aberbach, Robert Putnam, and Bert Rockman, *Bureaucrats and Politicians in Western Democracies* (Cambridge: Harvard University Press, 1981), chap. 3.

7. Half the members of the Bundestag are selected in single-member district elections; this encourages these deputies to retain their local ties. See Gerhard Loewenberg, *Parliament in the German Political System* (Ithaca: Cornell University Press, 1967), pp. 70–85.

8. Gerhard Loewenberg and Samuel Patterson, *Comparing Legislatures* (Boston: Little Brown, 1979), p. 71; also see the discussion of the law profession in Dahrendorf, *Society and Democracy in Germany*, chap. 15.

9. Nevil Johnson, *State and Government in the Federal Republic of Germany*, 2nd ed. (New York, Pergamon Press, 1983), chap. 6; Renate Mayntz and

204 Politics at the Elite Level

Fritz Scharpf, *Policy-Making in the German Federal Bureaucracy* (Amsterdam: Elsevier, 1975), chap. 4.

10. Wolfgang Pippke, *Karrieredeterminaten in der öffentlichen Verwaltung* (Baden-Baden: Nomos, 1975).

11. Ursula Hoffmann-Lange, "Structural Prerequisites of Elite Integration in the Federal Republic of Germany," in *Studies of the Structure of National Elite Groups*, ed. Gwen Moore (Greenwich: JAI Press, 1985); also see Aberbach, Putnam, and Rockman, *Bureaucrats and Politicians in Western Democracies*, chap. 3.

12. Kaltefleiter, "The Recruitment Market of the German Political Elite," p. 254; also see Ursula Hoffmann-Lange, Helga Neumann, and Bärbel Steinkemper, *Konsens und Konflikt zwischen Führungsgruppen in der Bundesrepublik Deutschland* (Frankfurt: Peter Lang, 1980), pp. 38–46.

13. Dahrendorf, *Society and Democracy in West Germany*, chaps. 14–18.

14. Aberbach, Putnam, and Rockman, *Bureaucrats and Politicians in Western Democracies*, chap. 3.

15. Hoffmann-Lange, "Structural Prerequisites of Elite Integration in the Federal Republic of Germany."

16. Ursula Feist, Manfred Güllner, and Klaus Liepelt, "Structural Assimilation versus Ideological Polarization," in *Elections and Parties*, ed. Max Kaase and Klaus von Beyme (Beverly Hills: Sage Publications, 1978); Samuel Eldersveld, "Changes in Elite Composition and the Survival of Party Systems: The German Case," in *Does Who Governs Matter?*, ed. Moshe Czudnowski (Dekalb: Northern Illinois University Press, 1982).

17. Feist, Güllner, and Liepelt, "Structural Assimilation versus Ideological Polarization," p. 182.

18. Robert Putnam, *The Comparative Study of Political Elites* (Englewood Cliffs, N.J.: Prentice Hall, 1976), p. 33.

19. Heino Kaack, "Social Composition of the German Bundestag," in *The Congress and the Bundestag*, ed. Robert Livingston et al. (Boulder: Westview Press, 1988).

20. Ursula Hoffmann-Lange, "Eliten zwischen Alter und Neuer Politik," in *Wahlen und politischer Prozess*, ed. Hans-Dieter Klingemann and Max Kaase (Opladen: Westdeutscher Verlag, 1986).

21. Also see Russell Dalton, *Citizen Politics in Western Democracies* (Chatham, N.J.: Chatham House, 1988), chap. 7; Hermann Schmitt, *Neue Politik in alten Parteien* (Opladen: Westdeutscher Verlag, 1987).

22. Ursula Hoffmann-Lange, "Congruence of Political Beliefs among Elites and Voters as an Indicator of Representation," Paper presented at the Future of Party Government Conference, Florence, 1984; Dalton, *Citizen Politics in Western Democracies*, chap. 10.

23. Max Weber, "Politics as a Vocation," in *From Max Weber: Essay in Sociology*, ed. H. Gerth and C. Wright Mills (New York: Oxford University Press, 1946).

24. Robert Putnam, "The Political Attitudes of Senior Civil Servants in Britain, West Germany, and Italy," in *The Mandarins of Western Europe*, ed. Mattei Dogan (New York: Wiley, 1975); Aberbach, Putnam, and Rockman, *Bureaucrats and Politicians in Western Democracies*, chap. 6.

25. Wildenmann et al., *Führungsschicht in der Bundesrepublik Deutschland 1981*, p. 51–54; Ursula Hoffmann-Lange, "Eliten als Hüter der Demokratie? *Politische Vierteljahresschrift*, Sonderheft "Politische Kultur" (1987).

26. Barbara Farah, *Political Representation in West Germany*. Unpublished PhD dissertation (Ann Arbor: University of Michigan, 1980), chap. 6.

27. Farah, *Political Representation in West Germany*, chap. 6.

28. Loewenberg, *Parliament in the German Political System*, p. 105.

29. Dahrendorf, *Society and Democracy in West Germany;* also see Hoffmann-Lange, "Structural Prerequisites of Elite Integration in the Federal Republic of Germany."

30. Hans Otto Eglau, "Die ungessellige Creme," *Zeit-Magazin* 18 (1983): 30-35.

31. Aberbach, Putnam, and Rockman, *Bureaucrats and Politicians in Western Democracies,* chap. 7.

32. Steven Szabo, ed. *The Successor Generation* (London: Butterworth, 1983); Russell Dalton, "Generational Change in Elite Political Beliefs," *Journal of Politics* 49 (November 1987): 976-997.

33. E. Gene Frankland, "The Role of the Greens in West German Parliamentary Politics," *Review of Politics* 50 (Winter 1988): 99-122.

34. Eldersveld, "Changes in Elite Composition and the Survival of Party Systems," pp. 80-81; also see Ursula Hoffmann-Lange, *Politische Einstellungsmuster in der westdeutschen Führungsschicht.* Unpublished PhD dissertation (Mannheim: University of Mannheim, 1977).

CHAPTER VIII

The Representation of Interests

POLITICS ARISES FROM CITIZEN needs and demands for government action. The political process thus begins with the expression of public interests. When a business owner struggles against unfair foreign competition and concludes that government help is needed, these views must be made known to policy makers in Bonn. When university students are dissatisfied with the financial aid furnished by governmental programs, they have to communicate these feelings to the government. When citizens see the need for new programs to protect the environment, they seek a government response.

The process of bringing public wants to the attention of policy makers is known as *interest articulation*. Government must become aware of what the populace wants before any action can possibly be taken. Interest articulation occurs in part through individual political participation (Chapter VI), for example, when citizens write to their Bundestag deputies or work in a political campaign. Individual effort at communicating interests, however, is not always an effective method of determining broad social needs. The process is complicated from the standpoint of both the public and political elites. The individual citizen can easily become overwhelmed by the magnitude and complexity of government: where does one turn for a sympathetic hearing from someone who can influence policy? Dealing with government agencies often requires technical or administrative expertise. A single individual, or even a group of individuals, cannot be certain that their petitions will receive a fair hearing even after identifying the appropriate government agency. Conversely, it is equally difficult for policy makers to know what is in the public interest. No one can really speak for the public as a whole, but every petitioner of government claims to do so. Is a single letter from a constituent symbolic of a broader social need, or merely the unique views of one individual? Should a petition by a business owner receive serious consideration, or be treated as a self-serving statement contrary to the public interest? When so many people are trying to express their views, it is difficult to know which voices to listen to.

Given the potential communication problems between individual citizens and the government, the articulation of public interests frequently depends on the efforts of an intermediary institution: the interest group. An interest group speaks for a distinct clientele with a common viewpoint, so that the members' views are expressed with more clarity and force than if they petition the government individually. Many interest groups are organized to provide the political and administrative expertise necessary to monitor government activities and lobby policy makers successfully. Because they keep a foot in both camps, interest group officials can present the views of their members in terms that political elites understand. Direct forms of citizen participation may integrate the public into the political process and communicate broad social preferences, but interest group activities are more focused ways of interest articulation.

This chapter describes how interest groups act as intermediaries in the West German political process. Even more than in the United States, interest groups are an integral part of the policy-making process. Many groups are widespread, tightly structured, and command a favored political position. Other groups are struggling to gain this same degree of legitimacy and influence. The interplay between contending interest groups partially structures the policy performance of the political system.

THE ORGANIZATION OF INTERESTS

There are many different social groups in contemporary West German society. Citizens can choose between professional groups, cultural associations, religious groups, social clubs, and many other voluntary groups. Most citizens belong to at least one voluntary organization, and many individuals belong to several. Not all social groups are equally relevant, however, for our study of politics.[1]

Groups that function as interest intermediaries in the political process usually display several traits. First, the organization must concern itself and its members with political matters. For instance, sports clubs and rifle clubs (*Schützenverein*) have very large national memberships that might be mobilized for political action, but unlike the National Rifle Association in the United States, these German groups are largely apolitical organizations that shun politics. Groups with more direct political interests are obviously more relevant to our study.

Another common trait of politically effective interest groups is an organizational structure that enables the group to maintain a presence as public policy is being made. Without such an organizational base, a group would find it difficult to monitor the actions of government and articulate the interests of its members through the entire policy process. *Anomic groups,* for example, consist of individuals who spontaneously unite in a public expression of discontent, such as an unorganized demonstration or protest. Often these groups lack any common bond; they are simply individuals who briefly coalesce for their own reasons and disperse when the excitement is past. Students might spontaneously protest a new government policy, or residents might demonstrate against a new development project in their neighborhood. Political leaders may react to such popular outbursts, but the group itself is not directly involved in the decision-making process, because it lacks an organizational structure to ensure its existence after the protest stops.

West German society also contains a variety of *latent* or *nonassociational groups,* composed of individuals with a common interest but without formal representation within the political system. The 4 million guestworkers are the most prominent example; they are an important economic entity with distinct social and cultural needs, but lack sufficient formal representation in the political process. Other clearly identifiable groups, such as housewives, consumers, pensioners, and regional or ethnic groups, also fall into the nonassociational category. Nonassociational groups may capture the attention of policy makers through brief bursts of activity, such as the wildcat strike by Turkish workers at a Cologne automobile plant in 1973, but they lack the institutional infrastructure to participate in the policy-making process.

Their capability of successful political action makes *associational groups* the most visible interest groups in the West German political system. Associational groups maintain a specialized organization designed to represent specific social interests. Some of these groups are fairly small, representing distinct subgroups of the population such as farmers or refugees. Other associations encompass a broad membership, such as trade unions, professional associations, and religious groups. Over a thousand such groups are formally registered as lobbyists with the federal government in Bonn, and hundreds more are active in the state capitals.

NEO-CORPORATISM

One of the most distinguishing features of the major West German associational groups is an organizational structure markedly different from that of interest groups in the United States. In the United States, politics is predicated on a *pluralist* model of interest groups derived from Madison's *Federalist Papers*. Madison held that the division of interests into loosely structured, competing factions was a prerequisite for democracy. Open political competition is the key to the pluralist system. Many groups compete to represent the same social interests, and struggle against each other within the policy process. The government's role is to provide a neutral arena for interest group activities. Competition among a large number of groups assures that no one group wields a dominant influence within the policy process and that the influence of a group depends on the support it can mobilize. Competition thus encourages group leaders to remain responsive to their members in order to maximize support for the organization.

Many of the leading West German interest associations follow a contrasting *neo-corporatist* model of interest group politics.[2] In the twentieth century, social and political forces have led to the consolidation and institutionalization of social interests into a highly structured system of interest representation. According to Philippe Schmitter, neo-corporatism[3]

> can be defined as a system of interest intermediation in which the constituent unions are organized into a limited number of singular, compulsory, noncompetitive, hierarchically ordered, and functionally differentiated categories, recognized or licensed (if not created) by the state and granted a deliberate representational monopoly within their respective categories in exchange for observing certain controls on their selection of leaders and articulation of demands and supports.

Neo-corporatism evolved from earlier corporatist tendencies in German and European society; the monarchy and then authoritarian politicians sought to contain social change with a strict organizational framework. The roots of this system, therefore, lie in antimodern and antidemocratic soil. Analysts added the qualifier "neo" to the corporatist label to denote a more moderate form of this interest group structure, in which highly stratified interests and a strong democratic state have developed new patterns of interest intermediation.

Whereas, in a pluralist system interest groups are fragmented, a neo-corporatist system organizes interests into a few unified organizations. Similar interests unite under the umbrella of one large, all-inclusive, national "peak-association" (*Spitzenverband*). Affiliation with a peak association is often compulsory for members of the relevant social sector. Moreover, most peak associations are hierarchical: Policy decisions flow from the leadership down, rather than up from the membership. The national office sets the goals and strategies of the entire association. In short, instead of a fluid, competitive system of interest representation, neo-corporatism is a highly structured and institutionalized system of interest group politics.

The style of interest group interaction also differs in a neo-corporatist system. Little competition for representation exists within each social sector, because each peak association exercises a monopoly of representation. This monopolistic organization often receives formal or informal sanction from the government; one group is officially acknowledged as the legitimate representative of an entire social interest. In addition, the organization of interests follows clearly defined functional lines, with fewer of the overlapping affiliations that can moderate interest group differences in a pluralist system. Thus, one organization speaks for labor, one association speaks for the employers, and so forth.

This style of neo-corporatist politics is not restricted to the Federal Republic; it is widespread in Scandinavia, for instance. It is a distinctive characteristic of West German politics, however, one that influences both the method of organizing interests and the pattern of policy formation.

THE ESTABLISHED INTEREST LOBBIES

Most discussions of West German interest groups focus on the large associational groups that represent the major socioeconomic forces in society, the so-called big four: business, labor, the churches, and the agricultural lobby. These are certainly not the only significant interest groups active in the political process, but these groups wield substantial influence on policy matters relevant to their interests and on policies broadly affecting West German society. A brief introduction to these four major interest groups is the first step in understanding the West German system of interest articulation.

BUSINESS AND INDUSTRY

Business and industry are two of the most powerful groups in society. Business leaders are an important element of the central core of policy elites, both on economic and noneconomic matters (see Chapter VII). The directors of the major interest groups for business are prominent public figures who influence citizen and government views on national policy questions. The political parties on both the left and right are necessarily sensitive to the opinions of the business community. The support of business leaders is crucial to the success of government economic policy, and the success of the economy provides a common measure of governmental performance. The Federal Republic is a capitalist nation, and when business talks, the government listens.

Any individual business, whether it be a large multinational or a small *Tante Emma* store, has needs that require some representation of the firm's interests. The owner of a machine shop, for example, is concerned about government policy that impacts on the business' interests, the labor agreements affecting the employees, and the business opportunities for the firm. In short, a businessperson wears many hats. In the first case, the business needs its views expressed in Bonn and the state capital as policies are being made. In the second instance, the firm must be represented in negotiations with the labor unions. In the third area, the owner may need assistance in developing new customers or identifying new suppliers. Separate organizational networks, each headed by a national peak association, address each of these three areas.

The single most important representative of business interests in the policy process is the Federation of Germany Industries (*Bundesverband der Deutschen Industrie* [BDI]). Following the neo-corporatist model of interest representation, the BDI is a peak association for thirty-nine national trade associations, ranging from the association of the automobile industry to the machine tool industry. The BDI is a centralized and inclusive business lobby, comparable to the Confederation of British Industry (CBI) and more important than the National Association of Manufacturers (NAM) in the United States. The trade associations in the BDI account for over 90 percent of all industrial firms; NAM's membership includes only a small minority of American industry. The centralized and hierarchic structure of the BDI enables the organization to present a united front in advocating the interests of business.

The BDI is the primary political spokesperson for the business community; it acts as a conduit between business and the government and consults with its member associations to establish the position of the business sector on matters of public policy. Once these positions are determined, the BDI articulates them by lobbying the national and state governments on pending policy matters. Conversely, when the government is interested in hearing the views of business on a policy matter, it consults the BDI. The Federation also provides its members with information on pending government proposals and newly enacted legislation. This helps the separate trade groups understand the implications of government legislation and perhaps initiate their own lobbying efforts.

The Confederation of German Employers' Associations (*Bundesvereinigung der Deutschen Arbeitgeberverbände* [BDA]) is the second major representative of the business sector. The BDA is a peak association of fifty-nine separate employers' associations: twelve regional organizations (including the employers' associations within each Land), and forty-seven national trade associations organized by economic sectors. Industrial associations account for the bulk of the BDA member groups, but the confederation spans the full spectrum of business activity—banking, insurance, trade, transport, crafts, and other fields. Virtually every large or medium-size employer in the nation is affiliated with one of the employer associations comprising the BDA.

The BDA serves employers primarily by coordinating and advising on social and labor policy. In this role, the BDA negotiates with the labor union association in setting general wage and salary guidelines for the specific contract agreements of their members. The Confederation acts at the state and national levels as a pressure group on legislation dealing with social security, wages and income policies, labor practices, and social services. The BDA also advises the government by nominating business representatives to government committees dealing with these policy areas. The BDI and BDA thus share a division of effort; while the BDI focuses its attention on the economic and broad political interests of business, the BDA represents management's interests on social policies.

The final member of the business triumvirate is the Association of German Chambers of Industry and Commerce (*Deutscher Industrie- und Handelstag* [DIHT]). The DIHT is comparable to the Chambers of Commerce in the United States, except that the German association is more inclusive in its membership. The law requires all firms that are liable to pay business taxes to join their local chamber and pay membership dues. Nearly 3 million German companies belong to the Association, organized into sixty-nine district and local associations.

The DIHT office in Bonn articulates the interests of business on economic issues affecting its members. But because the Association represents such a broad range of companies, its lobbying efforts focus on general and consensual issues in the business community. One of the more distinct policy functions of the DIHT is representing German business in foreign nations and on matters of international trade. Of more practical value to the members are the informational, advisory, and liaison services provided by the Association. For instance, the DIHT furnishes its members with comprehensive information on economic and market conditions, financial and training advice, and assistance in dealing with government agencies.

The tripartite division of the business lobby raises an inevitable question: Are three heads better than one? The three peak associations for business overlap in their membership and produce at least a partial duplication (triplication) of effort. Still, periodic efforts to consolidate business interests into a single organizational structure, known as a "marriage of the elephants," all ended in failure. Besides bureaucratic rigidity, the existence of three separate organizations reflects the belief by business people that different organizations are the best way to address their various needs. Specialization allows the BDI to focus its efforts on political matters, the BDA on social and labor policy, and the DIHT on commercial concerns. Seldom do the three organizations work at cross-purposes. In those instances where the three organizations do function as a united front, their lobbying impact is difficult for policy makers to resist.

LABOR UNIONS

The labor unions were among of the first organizations to emerge from the rubble of postwar Germany. Trade unionists who had survived Hitler's purges began organizing in anticipation of the Allied military advance, and by late 1945 the first unions appeared in the British occupation zone. There were sharp disagreements, however, on what form the labor movement should follow. Under the Weimar Republic, a number of highly politicized unions—Marxist,

Christian, nationalist, Communist—competed for political influence and the support of the working class. Many trade unionists rejected this model of ideological trade unions with formal ties to a preferred political party.

The union movement in the Federal Republic follows a different pattern than its historical predecessors. One basic principle is that the labor movement is organized into a unitary, autonomous organization, independent of religious or partisan ties (*Einheitsgewerkschaft*). In sharp contrast to the Weimar Republic, contemporary unions are formally separated from the political parties, although unions obviously lobby the parties on issues affecting the interests of the working class. Second, unions are now organized along industrial lines; all employees at one plant belong to the same union regardless of their occupation. An electrician at an auto assembly plant belongs to the metalworkers union, and an electrician at a plastics company joins the chemical industry union. This structure gives unions more bargaining power in negotiations with employer organizations, because one union represents all the workers in an industry. Decentralization is a third distinguishing feature of the West German labor movement. Individual unions generally follow a federal structure, with local, district, Land, and national offices.

A fourth, and final, principle of the modern union movement is a reliance on the legal process for the protection of workers' rights. The unions worked to ensure the status of the movement primarily through the passage of legislation by the government, rather than through direct negotiations with business representatives. For instance, the structure of industrial relations, the conditions for strikes and industrial lockouts, the requirements of union membership, and basic social welfare benefits are all determined by labor law legislation. This strategy allows the unions to rely on state guarantees for their basic political status, and thereby focus their contract negotiations on improving the economic conditions of the workers. At the same time, however, this strategy makes the union movement dependent on the government and on the way that state agencies interpret labor legislation. Unions are deeply involved in adjudication, and the decisions of the Federal Labor Court (*Bundesarbeitsgericht*) are a major determining factor for industrial relations in West Germany.[4]

The economic influence of the labor movement extends beyond the simple number of union members. Around 40 percent of the labor force belongs to a union, about average for Western industrial democracies.[5] The voluntary nature of union membership partially accounts for the modest level of union membership. The law requires an open shop; workers are free not to join the union representing their plant, and workers cannot be treated differently whether they are union members or not. However, although less than half the work force belongs to a union, over 90 percent of all jobs are covered by collective bargaining agreements negotiated by the unions. Union actions thus directly affect nearly all working people.

The labor movement is an example of a neo-corporatist interest group. Most of the labor movement is incorporated into a single peak association, the German Federation of Trade Unions (*Deutscher Gewerkschaftsbund* [DGB]), which embraces seventeen separate unions accounting for over 80 percent of all unionized members of the labor force, or nearly 8 million members (Table VIII.1). The

TABLE VIII.1 *The Membership of the German Federation of Trade Unions*

Union	1986 Members (in 000s)	Percentage of Total Members
Metalworkers (IG Metall)	2,598	33.5
Public service and transport (ÖTV)	1,199	15.4
Chemical, paper, and ceramics (IG CPF)	654	8.4
Construction workers (IG BSE)	485	6.2
Postal workers	463	6.0
Commerce, banking, and insurance (HBV)	376	4.8
Mineworkers (IG Bergbau)	355	4.6
Railroad workers (GdED)	351	4.5
Food processing (NGG)	266	3.4
Textile workers (GTB)	256	3.3
Education and science (GEW)	193	2.5
Police (GdP)	163	2.1
Wood and plastics (GHK)	143	1.8
Printing and paper workers (IG DRUPA)	143	1.8
Leather workers	48	.6
Horticulture and forestry (GLF)	43	.6
Artists and musicians (Kunst)	28	.4
Total	7,765	100%

Source: *Statistisches Jahrbuch für die Bundesrepublik Deutschland, 1987,* p. 600.

DGB's broad-based membership includes almost all organized industrial workers, the vast majority of white-collar employees, and large numbers of government employees. IG Metall alone accounts for one-third of the unionized labor force and is the largest union in the noncommunist world.

Two other smaller unions exist in the shadow of the DGB. The German White-Collar Employees' Union (*Deutsche Angestellten-gewerkschaft* [DAG]) consists solely of salaried employees. Despite its emphasis on the interests of the white-collar employee, the DAG only represents about 20 percent of the unionized white-collar workers, with a total membership of under half a million. Government civil servants are represented by the German Civil Servants' Federation (*Deutscher Beamten Bund* [DBB]). The DBB is sometimes described as a union, but it comes closer to being a lobbying organization, because as public employees the Beamte cannot strike or engage in collective bargaining.

Even though the DGB serves as the peak association for the labor movement, it is not monolithic.[6] A division of effort prescribes separate roles to the Federation and its member unions. On one side, the DGB articulates the interests of labor in social discourse and in the policy-making process. The government regards the Federation as the official spokesperson for the labor movement and the official representative of labor in discussions of policies affecting the working class. DGB officials are very active in the policy making process at national and local levels, advising cabinet members, informing party leaders, and testifying before parliamentary committees. On the other side, each union's task is to advance the welfare of the employees that it represents through the collective bargaining process. Most unions focus their attention on contractual issues that directly affect their members. While the DGB prowls the halls of government, the unions negotiate at the bargaining table.

The individual unions within the Federation also retain considerable autonomy. The DGB may suggest broad guidelines for its member unions to follow in contract negotiations, but each union acts independently in setting its own contract terms. During the economic recession of the mid-1970s, for example, the DGB and the BDA agreed to wage and price control guidelines for their member organizations, but the radical unions pressed for more extensive worker benefits when their contracts expired.

The independence of individual unions arises from the diversity of interests and political philosophies within the labor movement.

The DGB membership divides into "radical" and "moderate" factions. The radicals, led by IG Metall, advocate a more assertive style in challenging business interests and advancing the cause of the working class. Thus IG Metall took the lead in pressing for co-determination in the early 1950s, for dramatic wage gains in the next decade, and for the 35-hour work week today. The radical unions are more willing to strike when collective bargaining fails to reach an accord and more willing to involve the labor movement in broader issues of social reform. In contrast, the moderate unions (such as IG CPK, IG BSE, IG Bergbau, GTB, and NGG) prefer a strategy of working together with employers for steady, moderate economic growth that benefits both labor and capital. The moderates accept the economic philosophy of cooperation between labor and management in search of mutual benefit. They are, therefore, less demanding in their contractual negotiations and less willing to resort to industrial strikes. Neither faction dominates the actions of the DGB, but with the persisting economic problems of the past decade the radical unions are gaining in strength.

In overall terms, the DGB lacks the broad control that characterizes the peak associations of other interest groups, especially the business lobby. This lack of control sometimes makes it difficult for the DGB to speak with authority on collective bargaining issues, whereas the BDA usually does speak for its members. Contract negotiations are not the primary domain of the DGB's authority, however. In policy matters affecting the fate of the average employee, the DGB is an authoritative representative of the unions and the working class.

INDUSTRIAL RELATIONS

There is inevitably some conflict between business and labor. Union attempts to improve the conditions of the work force are sometimes seen as interference in the prerogatives of management, just as unions view some corporate decisions as callously indifferent to the situation of workers. When both sides meet at the bargaining table, an adversarial relationship frequently exists; the higher wages sought by the unions mean lower profits to the employers. Labor leaders and business leaders also hold differing personal values and political loyalties (Chapter VII). Most union officials lean toward the Social Democratic party, and most business leaders prefer either the CDU/CSU or the FDP. Labor favors extensive social programs, and business endorses a conservative social agenda.

These economic and political differences are not unusual; they are a normal part of industrial relations in most Western economies. What makes the Federal Republic exceptional is the degree to which business and labor subjugate these differences and work together within the economic system. During the early postwar years, intense differences in philosophy separated labor and business. The Munich program, which guided the activities of the DGB, had a decidedly Marxist tone, and the business sector reacted with inevitable opposition. Within a few short years, however, management and labor began to reconcile their differences. Both sides informally agreed that their first priority was to develop the national economy, from which both sides would prosper. By the late 1950s, the mainstream of the labor movement had shifted from radical Marxist rhetoric to pragmatic social reform.[7] This *social partnership* reshaped industrial relations from an adversarial relationship to one primarily based on mutual benefit.

The social partnership of West German industrial relations is perhaps best illustrated by the pattern of strike activity. The Federal Republic protects the rights of unions to strike against employers, but this right is exercised with caution. In West German industrial relations, one important goal is the reconciliation of contract differences through voluntary arbitration. The breakdown of arbitration is implicitly an admission that both the unions and employers failed to reach a mutually beneficial agreement. These norms are underscored by labor legislation that discourages the use of both strikes and lockouts as part of the contract negotiation process. In order for a union to call a strike, 75 percent of the membership must vote in favor of the walkout. Furthermore, labor laws prohibit "wildcat" strikes when a contract is in force, or the use of strikes for noncontractual political goals. These strike limitations are matched by equally strict limitations on the use of lockouts by employers. As a result of these conditions, work time lost through strikes and work stoppages is consistently lower than in most other Western European nations. West Germany has roughly the same size labor force as in Britain, France, and Italy; but in the five-year period from 1978 to 1982, Italian strikes averaged 968 lost workdays for every thousand workers, 531 days in Britain, 130 in France, and only 29 in the Federal Republic. Most West German unions and employers clearly prefer arbitration to conflict over strike barricades.

Another example of social partnership in industrial relations is the participation of workers in corporate decision making. Employees participate in their company's managerial decisions at two levels: on the shop floor through works councils (*Betriebsrat*) and at the company level through a process of co-determination (*Mitbestimmung*).

In every firm with five or more employees (about two-thirds of the active labor force) the workers are entitled to establish a works council. The council is separate from the union hierarchy, and its members are directly elected by the permanent employees. The council grants workers more say in matters affecting their employment and work conditions. The company management must gain the approval of the works council for decisions involving working conditions, personnel policy, vocational training, and pay structures. The issues might be as mundane as the length of coffee breaks, or as major as disputes over compensation arising from a reduction in the work force. For fundamental plant changes, such as personnel planning, restructuring of the plant, or other significant changes in work or production techniques, management must seek the advice of the works council. To a real extent, the works council represents a partnership between workers and management on decisions made at the plant level.

The West German system of co-determination provides even more extensive opportunities for worker self-management at the corporate level.[8] Co-determination originated in the coal and steel industries (*Montanmitbestimmung*) in a form that gives equal parity to management and labor. Under 1951 legislation, the management of corporations in these industries falls under the control of a supervisory board (Figure VIII.1). The board consists of equal numbers of worker and shareholder representatives, along with one neutral member acceptable to both sides. The board's authority is similar to the board of directors of a U.S. corporation. It meets periodically throughout the year to set corporate policy and provide direction for the management board that handles day-to-day affairs. Co-determination offered two immediate benefits: It gave the unions a share of the economic democracy they desired, and it provided another check on the actions of two industries that had been a vital part in Germany's past war-making activities.

Upon its introduction, there were dire forecasts about co-determination's negative effect on German industry. Business leaders feared that employees would destroy their companies, either through ignorance or by pursuing policies of narrow self-interest. The system has functioned fairly effectively, however, fostering bet-

Coal and Steel Industry

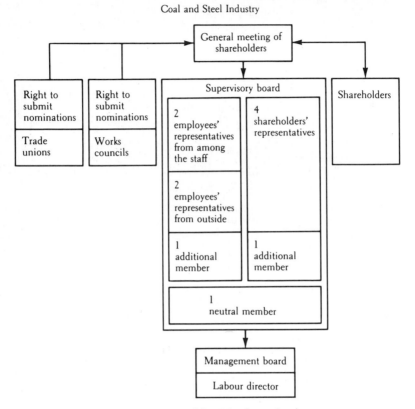

FIGURE VIII.1 *Models of Co-determination*

ter labor-management relations and providing sound economic management. Indeed, the coal and steel industries led the economic recovery of the early 1950s. A more modest form of co-determination was extended in 1952 to all corporations with over five hundred employees, and worker participation became a cornerstone of the West German economic system.

Under continuing pressure from the labor movement to extend parity co-determination to industries other than coal and steel, the SPD-FDP government passed a new co-determination law in 1976. This legislation applies to all private firms with over two thousand employees not covered by Montanmitbestimmung—roughly 500 companies. The size of the supervisory board varies from twelve to twenty members, depending on the number of employees in the

1976 Co-determination Legislation

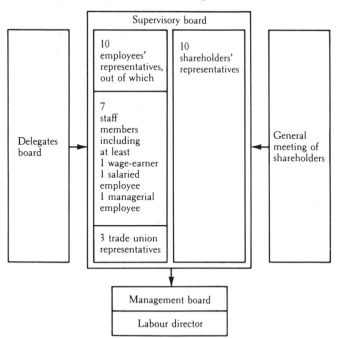

FIGURE VIII.1 (*Continued*).

firm. Among large firms (20,000 and more employees) the board consists of ten employee representatives, including at least three union officials and at least one each from among the blue-collar workers, salaried white-collar employees, and managerial employees (Figure VIII.1).

The unions expressed disappointment with the provisions of the 1976 law, because it deviates from Montanmitbestimmung by restricting the unions' formal participation to less than one-third of employee seats. In addition, this newer form of co-determination does not grant full parity to the employees; if labor and management cannot agree on a neutral committee chairperson, the shareholders' representatives can unilaterally select the chairperson whose vote decides split ballots.

Many employer groups vehemently opposed the expansion of co-determination to their firms. Despite the generally positive record of co-determination in the coal and steel industries, business interests maintained that worker participation in management would undermine the efficiency and competitiveness of German businesses. When their appeals to parliament failed, and the legislation was passed, the employers' association challenged the constitutionality of the act in the Federal Constitutional Court. The BDA argued that the 1976 co-determination law excessively favored the workers, gave virtual majority status to the workers on the supervisory board, infringed upon the entrepreneurial freedom of business, and violated other freedoms guaranteed by the Basic Law. The courts rejected the employers' appeals, but this controversy severely strained labor–management relations. Despite the reservations expressed by both labor and management, the 1976 co-determination reform marks a significant advance in worker participation in the firm without fundamentally changing the nature of corporate decision making.

Labor and business have both praised and panned the unique West German system of social partnership. Some labor activists, for example, criticize the social partnership as a turning away from fundamental socialist goals in favor of short-term, limited economic benefits. The labor movement has made a strategic decision to pursue incremental reform rather than fundamental social change; the evolutionary nature of change should not lessen appreciation for the overall accomplishments of this approach. Most labor leaders stress the extensive social benefits the unions have won for their members: a growing share of the national income, subsidized savings plans for employees, an extensive social security system, and liberal fringe benefits, including an average six weeks of paid vacation and holiday leaves (also see Chapter XI). Jutta Helm's evaluation of co-determination concludes that this program has benefited workers financially, increased employee satisfaction, and provided better training programs and other company benefits.[9] The advances of co-determination are even more striking in international perspective. For most other industrial democracies, the concept of worker participation in management is a fanciful dream. When the Chrysler corporation appointed the head of the United Auto Workers union to the board of directors in the early 1980s, it was a newsworthy event because of its uniqueness, and it remains a novel event in American industry. French socialists have long discussed *autogestion,* and British Leftists tirelessly debate proposals aimed at worker self-management, but few nations outside Scandinavia rival the progress won by the West German unions.

Sentiments within the business community are also mixed. Some business leaders look at the gains posted by the labor movement and conclude that business must be disadvantaged by the social partnership. They claim that the workers' extensive social welfare provisions make West Germany less competitive in international markets. Even after the courts upheld the 1976 co-determination law, the publications of the BDI still encouraged their members to adhere only to the minimal requirements of the law. Yet these criticisms overlook the substantial gains that businesses have also enjoyed. The success of the Economic Miracle was built upon the cooperative style of West German labor relations. Industrial harmony and limited strike activity facilitated the economic growth of the 1950s and 1960s. The increases in business profits over the postwar period have generally exceeded the rise in wages. Routine foreign trading surpluses attest to the relative vitality of the West German economy.

In sum, the social partnership has yielded mutual benefit to both business and labor. Neither side has maximized it own immediate benefits, but society as a whole has prospered because of the partnership.

THE CHURCHES

Religious associations constitute the third major set of organized interests in West German politics. In contrast to the U.S. tradition of the separation of church and state, the two institutions are intertwined in Germany. During the Empire and the Weimar Republic, the churches pursued their earthly and spiritual goals through the political process. The Catholic church was affiliated with the Catholic Zentrum party and was deeply involved in attempts to affect public policy. The Protestant presence was less visible, but its subtle influence was pervasive in the conservative political establishment. The state legitimized the political role of the churches, granting them a special legal status as public law corporations.

The churches are one of the few institutions to survive the Third Reich relatively intact, but they were not untouched by the experience.[10] The Catholic church was an unwitting accomplice in the Nazi consolidation of power in 1933.[11] When the Vatican and Hitler's government signed a treaty (*Reichskonkordat*) guaranteeing the church's rights under the new state, the church withdrew from politics and allowed the Zentrum party to disband. The Protestant church suffered years of internal division during the Third Reich.

An extreme, "nationalist" denomination openly embraced the Nazis, the church establishment meekly accepted the authority of the state, and only a small "confessional" movement questioned Nazi policies.

Their experiences with the Third Reich profoundly affected the postwar churches' view of the political process and their role within it. The Protestant church broke with the traditional Erastian principle of passive subordination to the authority of the state. Instead, Protestantism took the view that "the church's moral responsibility to the nation entailed a political responsibility and . . . that this political responsibility lies not in passive obedience, but in independent judgment of the acts of the state."[12] The Catholic church similarly established a renewed political commitment, but in a manner different from past Catholic action. The church no longer directly involves itself in partisan politics; a new Zentrum party failed to gain church support, the church's direct participation in election campaigns decreased, and priests are discouraged from pursuing elective office. Rather than resume direct partisan involvement, the Catholic church became a lobbying organization.

An equally profound change is the creation of an ecumenical union between Protestants and Catholics. The formation of the Christian Democratic Union in place of the Zentrum party marked an attempt to bridge the historic gap between denominations by uniting both Catholics and Protestants within a party broadly committed to religious values. The traditional political conflicts between Catholics and Protestants over church–state relations no longer divide the two religious communities. Each church still retains its own distinct spiritual and political identity, but interdenominational differences are now overshadowed by the split between religious (Catholic and Protestant) and nonreligious interests.

The Protestant church in West Germany maintains a loose organizational framework. The Evangelical Church in Germany (*Evangelische Kirche in Deutschland* [EKD]) is the peak association for 17 autonomous provincial churches. Instead of directing the activity of its member churches, the EKD functions mainly as a coordinating body. The EKD maintains a sense of community among the various Protestant congregations and promotes intercongregational exchange.

Politically, the EKD is the formal representative of the West German Protestant churches and the national voice of the Protestant community, articulating the church's interests in contacts with the government, presenting the church's viewpoint in matters of public debate, and representing its member congregations in formal agreements with the government over church–state issues. The EKD maintains a branch of the church chancellery in Bonn with all the trappings of a lobbying organization. Its staff keeps informed on pending legislation and lobbies the ministries on upcoming policy proposals.

The Catholic church in West Germany is tied to the Vatican and therefore does not have the autonomy of the Protestant denominations. Decisions about theology and the overall political role of the church are made in Rome. The major organizational body within the German Catholic church is the Bishops' Conference, which brings together the approximately seventy West German bishops for semiannual meetings. At these meetings, the bishops deal with the pastoral and religious matters facing the church. In addition, the conference attendees discuss contemporary social issues and establish a common church policy on political matters of relevance to the church. The Bishops' Conference also provides a focal point for a very active network of Catholic lay associations.

The Catholic church is more assertive than the EKD in its style of political involvement. The Bishops' Conference has a permanent secretariat in Bonn, which monitors the Parliament and the ministries. Church leaders and church organizations are not hesitant to lobby the government on legislation dealing with social or moral issues. It is not uncommon to see a bishop meeting with national political leaders, or a pastor conferring with local officials. Catholic leaders even host a social/political club for Catholic legislative and ministerial figures, which meets every Tuesday in Bonn during the Bundestag session. The Catholic church, with its considerable resources and extensive organizational network, is often a visible participant in policy making.

The churches believe they have a legitimate and extensive role to play in the political process. More than a right, political participation is seen as a duty and responsibility of the religious communities. For several decades, a focal point of this participation was government support for church-run schools. Up until the mid-1960s, most primary school students attended either a Catholic or Protestant school, where religious education was buttressed by a Christian perspective on substantive topics. Catholic parents gradually abandoned the church schools; the percentage of students attending a religious school decreased from 57 percent in 1967 (40 percent Catholic and 17 percent Protestant) to around 10 percent in the 1980s. Religious education is now generally a moot issue, since even Catholic parents prefer sending their children to nonconfessional schools.

The churches still remain very active on matters of social policy (*Sozialpolitik*). The churches are prime providers of social services in many areas: homes for the blind, orphanages, kindergartens, daycare centers, hospitals, old age homes, youth hostels, and training programs. Separate Catholic and Protestant social service organizations manage these activities and work with government agencies on social issues. Church representatives are also deeply involved in influencing government policies dealing with youth, education, and family affairs.

Although both denominations participate in a broad range of political matters, the Protestant hierarchy has taken the lead in involving the church in controversial political topics when they feel an issue involves spiritual values. In the 1950s, church officials voiced open opposition to the remilitarization of the Federal Republic. In the midst of the student revolt, the 1968 annual report of the EKD discussed the church's concern with the Vietnam War, emergency powers legislation, student unrest, and nuclear nonproliferation—not the type of issues normally identified with religious groups. More recently, the issues of peace, aid for less developed countries, and nuclear war have stimulated a new activism within both churches, especially among the young. For instance, the controversy over the recent deployment of a new generation of NATO nuclear weapons found Protestant and Catholic groups supporting the peace movement.[13] The EKD was a sponsor of the Krefeld Appeal, which collected the signatures of 2.5 million Germans on a petition for peace; the biennial church day (*Evangelische Kirchentag*) intermixes bible reading groups with organizations discussing homosexual rights, the Nicaraguan Sandinistas, and spouse abuse—with most young participants wearing the purple scarf symbolizing support for the peace movement. These examples highlight the broader sense of political responsibility that characterizes the churches in postwar Germany.

THE AGRICULTURAL LOBBY

The conservative alliance between agriculture, industry, and the state was a major force in German political development throughout most of the Empire and Weimar Republic. With the formation of the Federal Republic, the economic importance of agriculture decreased. First, the large agricultural estates in the east became part of East Germany or Poland, which meant that the Federal Republic became a predominantly industrial economy. Second, the size of the agricultural sector in the West steadily eroded, so that today barely 5 percent of the populace makes a living through farming.

Despite the decreasing role of agriculture in the national economy, the agricultural lobby continues to exert a surprisingly strong influence within the political process.[14] The political impact of agriculture is due in part to the social and political homogeneity of the agricultural community. The farm lobby presents a united front when dealing with policy makers—unity and the intensity of their views gives them a qualitative strength in excess of their numbers. Agriculture also occupies a key economic and political position within society. People cannot live without food, and conservative parties cannot win without rural voters. The peak association of the agricultural lobby, the German Farmers Association (*Deutscher Bauernverband* [DBV]), exploits these strengths to their fullest.[15]

The agricultural lobby focuses its efforts very narrowly on farm issues. It has been remarkably successful in convincing the state to protect the financial status of farmers through generous programs of price supports, subsidies, and agricultural grants. Even though these programs make West German food costs among the highest in Western Europe, the programs are relatively immune to reform. Under both CDU- and SPD-led governments, the Ministry of Agriculture aggressively works on the farmers' behalf. Agricultural budgets have been virtually untouchable under both the Schmidt and Kohl administrations. Furthermore, the guidelines for many agricultural policies are determined by the Common Agricultural Program (CAP) of the European Community. International efforts to reform CAP are notoriously unsuccessful.

Judging by size alone, the agricultural lobby should provide little competition to the business and labor lobbies, but its record of achievements earns the agricultural lobby the title of the mighty midget of West German interest group politics.

THE NEW POLITICS MOVEMENT

In recent years, a new set of political interests have arisen to challenge business, labor, religion, and agriculture. These new political contenders trace their roots to the student movement of the 1960s and the citizen–action groups of the 1970s. Instead of the predominantly socioeconomic concerns of the major established interests, these new groups focus their efforts on the life-style and quality-of-life issues facing West German society. Three political movements—environmentalists, the women's movement, and the peace lobby—constitute the core of this New Politics movement.

Political movements are certainly not a new aspect of German politics. The political organizations spawned by the labor and agrarian movements (and groups that organized to represent opposing interests) are central actors in contemporary policy making. Still, research on the New Politics movement argues that these groups differ from traditional interest groups in several fundamental ways.[16]

The New Politics movement is attempting to develop a new social model for dealing with the conditions of advanced industrial societies like the Federal Republic.[17] Instead of stressing wealth and economic growth, these movements advocate an economy in harmony with nature and the personal needs of its citizens. New Politics supporters are skeptical of technology as a solution to modernization's side effects. Individuals must control society, rather than society controlling the individual; personal fulfillment and self-expression should be maximized. For instance, nuclear energy is opposed not just because of its environmental consequences, but also because it signifies the domination of industry and technology over the individual. The quest for a new *Weltanschauung* is admittedly unfinished; New Politics groups are often more articulate in criticizing the norms of established German society than in producing an alternative model. Still, these groups espouse a new set of goals and a new way of thinking about politics.

It is difficult to characterize the viewpoints of New Politics groups in terms of the established interest groups. New Politics groups sometimes appear to oppose everyone and everything in established West German society, but the reality is more complex. Movement supporters at times confront an opposing alliance of business interests and labor unions on issues such as nuclear power. In other cases, the unions are an ally, or the environmental movement finds supporters among agricultural interests opposing industrial development projects that might threaten the environment. The peace lobby has surprisingly strong links to various religious organizations and some ties to the DGB. New Politics groups represent a new force in West German politics, not easily located in terms of established political alignments.

The political style of New Politics groups also contrasts with the neo-corporatist pattern of the major established interest associations. Rather than having a single, all-encompassing, and hierarchic organization, New Politics groups are characterized by diversity. Most of these groups seemingly prefer a decentralized, open, and pluralist structure that reflects the participatory tendencies of their members. Much of their activity occurs below the national level in local citizen–action groups and informal personal networks, which are ever-changing in their membership and organizational framework. In contrast to the collaboration between state organs and interest groups in the neo-corporatist system, many New Politics groups consciously remain outside of the institutional framework of government, displaying an antiestablishment bias in their rhetoric and actions. For instance, a major national environmental lobby refused to open an office in Bonn, despite the advantages of proximity to government policy-making agencies, because such a move was seen as a symbolic acceptance of the political establishment. New Politics groups seem to typify a pluralist style of interest group politics more than the neo-corporatist tendencies seen among the established interest groups.

The environmental lobby is the most visible part of the New Politics movement.[18] In the 1970s, a group of ecologists drew public attention to the contemporary problems of environmental protection (industrial pollution, nuclear power, chemical wastes, etc.) and linked these matters to failures of the economic and political systems. Environmentalists reminded the public that the water in the Rhine once was pure, and blue skies once shone above the Ruhr— and insisted that this degradation of the environment threatened the public's health and quality of life. Hundreds, even thousands, of local citizen-action groups formed to deal with environmental problems in their region.

Following this flowering of the environmental movement, many different organizations now compete to represent the public's new interest in environmental matters. The New Politics core of the movement is a set of national organizations formed in the 1970s and 1980s: BBU (*Bundesverband Bürgerinitiativen Umweltschutz*), Greenpeace, Robin Wood, and a number of environmental centers and research institutes. Antinuclear groups popped up like mushrooms around nuclear power facilities, and local environmental action groups proliferated. These different groups provide a network of political activists that determine the political identity and strategy of the movement. The leftist orientation of many of these activists developed environmentalism into a source of social and political criticism, not just a political lobby. This environmental network also channels the energies of the movement into political action. For instance, at the high point of its influence in the late 1970s the BBU coordinated the activities of over one thousand local citizen action groups, and nearly one million people have participated in some type of environmental organization. The older and more well-established nature conservation groups (BUND, *Deutscher Naturschutzring*, the Federation for Bird Protection, etc.) are more conservative and less assertive. Still, the public education and lobbying activities of this part of the environmental rainbow sensitize citizens and elites to environmental issues. In short, the emergence of an organizational structure to mobilize popular concern about the environment has thrust the issue onto the political agenda.

Another part of the New Politics network is the women's movement.[19] In the late 1960s and early 1970s, women organized to change the traditional male bias within West German society. Despite guarantees of sexual equality in the Basic Law, women still face discrimination at home and at the workplace. Traditionally, society defined the women's family role in terms of the three K's— *Kinder* (children), *Kirche* (church), and *Küche* (kitchen). Activists in the women's movement developed a dualistic strategy to improve the status of women: changing the consciousness of women and reforming the laws. Activities at the local level nurture the personal development of women; most large cities now host a women's center, self-help groups, women's bookstores, and a network of women's organizations. The political action arm of the movement remains underdeveloped, however. While there are some interest associations at the national level, most activists are skeptical of an institutionalized women's lobby, which they fear might come to dominate the movement. This attitude undoubtedly handicaps the efforts of the women's movement to lobby policy makers in Bonn, but the handicap is a cost the movement accepts. Instead of structured national associations, the movement coordinates its work through informal networks, conferences, ad hoc policy groups, and work with other interest associations. The women's movement wants to remain a force for personal change as well as political change, and not become a highly institutionalized political lobby.

The early 1980s saw a large and assertive peace movement join the New Politics lineup.[20] The peace movement grew in reaction to the proposed stationing of a new generation of NATO nuclear missiles in the Federal Republic. Peace groups pressured the government to move toward arms control and try to avoid deployment. The peace movement displayed an open disdain for the neocorporatist style of interest group politics; instead of a centralized leadership, a loosely structured coordinating committee (*Koordinierungsausschuss* [KA]) provided a communications network between over two dozen diverse groups involved in peace activities (feminists, environmentalists, party representatives, youth groups, radical Leftists, and church groups). The KA coordinated large national protests and political campaigns that required collaboration between the member groups, but KA itself was not the official representative of the movement. There was no official representative; a common saying held that "no one spoke for the movement, but everyone spoke within the movement." The peace lobby remained a fluid coalition of individuals and groups united by a common opposition to nuclear weapons. With strong ties to other New Politics groups, many peace activists linked the NATO decision to what they believed were the broader structural problems of West German politics. When the Bundestag finally voted in favor of deployment in October 1983, the focal point of the movement was lost. Public involvement in the peace movement declined as dramatically as it had grown, although public interest in the nuclear weapons and security issues still remains.

These three political movements, and other New Politics groups, have distinct issue interests and their own organizations, but they also can be seen as elements of a single movement. Their concerns show a common interest in the quality of life for individual citizens, whether it is the quality of the natural environment, the protection of human rights, or peace in an insecure world. Ideological bridges also link the different groups; in their analyses, they trace the problems they address back to the excesses of the Federal Republic's economic and social systems. The leadership of these groups comes mostly from a single pool of political activists—young, highly educated, adherents of a New Left ideology—that comprise the successor generation (see Chapter VII). The creation of the Green party in 1980 finally brought these diverse elements together in a single political organization.

The New Politics movement certainly does not wield the influence of any of the major established interest groups in West German society. Still, in a few short years these groups have become important and contentious actors in the political process. Established interest groups and political parties are forced to respond to the criticisms raised by New Politics groups. Indeed, the movement seems to relish its role as social critic, raising issues that have been overlooked or denied by the established interests. The movement has had only limited success, however, in implementing policy reforms; policy remains dependent on decisions made by the political establishment. Thus the larger significance of the New Politics movement may lie in the future: Can it actually rival the influence of business or labor? How will society respond to the challenges posed by the movement?

PATTERNS OF INTEREST INTERMEDIATION

In exercising their role as intermediaries, interest groups choose among several different methods in attempting to influence policy makers. The federal structure of government means that important political decisions are made in Bonn and the state capitals, so interest groups lobby at either or both levels. The separation of powers between the executive and Parliament means that both branches of government are access points to policy making. Interest groups can reach government ministers and agency officials at the same time they lobby Bundestag deputies and appear before parliamentary committees. The political parties are openly receptive to appeals from their supporters. Finally, of course, a group can always call its members into the streets and attempt to influence the political process through public persuasion. The West German political system probably contains more points of access for interest groups than do most European parliamentary democracies, although fewer than in the wide-open U.S. system.

Many factors come in to play when a group chooses among these points of political access. Institutional opportunities heavily determine the choice of political tactics. If a policy decision will be made in the executive branch, then lobbying activities should focus on this target. More often than not, several political institutions are involved in the decision-making process, and interest groups must consider multiple points of access. The resources of the group are another prime consideration. Labor union officials oversee a mass membership; business owners command large financial resources; other groups possess unique technical expertise. Control of significant political resources might provide general access to the government decision-makers, but interest groups exploit the tactics that best utilize their capabilities—mobilizing voters, providing parties with financial support, or lobbying policy specialists. The self-identity of a group also predisposes its political behavior. Whereas business leaders might hesitate to stage a public protest even if it would be effective, this tactic seems to come naturally to student groups. Finally, groups often hold differing goals in dealing with the same issue; one group might favor passage of new legislation while another attempts to block passage. These contrasting objectives might lead to differing strategies of action, as groups calculate the best way to achieve their goals.

Knowing what opportunities for political influence are generally open to interest groups is crucial to understanding interest group politics in the West German system. What are the major points of access to the political process, how open are these channels, and what are the properties of each channel? In other words, what are the political options that face an interest group wanting to influence government?

Political parties furnish one of the major channels of interest intermediation, although relations between groups and parties sometimes resemble those in a soap opera. The political system grants special importance to the parties in determining electoral choices and organizing the structure of policy making (see Chapter IX), yet because of the partisan excesses of the Weimar Republic, many interest groups avoid the formal party ties that characterize interest group politics in other European democracies. The labor unions and business associations take pride in their formal status above partisan politics (*überparteilich*), and do not officially endorse a party at election time. The churches similarly shun the direct party ties that characterized their political behavior during Weimar. New Politics groups are probably the most vocal critics of partisan politics.

Despite public pronouncements of partisan innocence, many of these same interest groups carry on close affairs with the parties. Although the labor unions do not formally endorse the SPD at election time, strong informal ties bind the unions and the party. The unions' motto holds that they are politically nonpartisan but not politically neutral. Union members provide a large proportion of SPD party activists and the core of party volunteers during elections, and the partisan preferences of union leaders are unmistakable for anyone who listens. Even while proclaiming electoral neutrality, the Catholic church's political affinities are well known.

One typical story is of a Catholic pastor in the Christian Social Union's home state of Bavaria. On election Sunday, the pastor would stand in the pulpit and proclaim, "It is not for me to tell you how to vote. But I do say: Vote Christian! Vote Social!" Up until the 1969 election, the Catholic bishops issued pastoral letters encouraging their followers to vote for a "Christian" party. Church leaders made it appear to be a religious duty to vote for the CDU/CSU. Conversely, the Protestant church subtly displays its preference for the SPD. While business gives some support to all of the established parties, its affinity for the CDU/CSU is apparent, and the farmer's association has close ties to the Free Democratic party. So important is partisan politics that even the antipartisan New Politics groups felt compelled to create the Green party to represent their views.

Most citizens thus are aware of the partisan preferences of the major interest groups in West Germany (Table VIII.2). About three-fourths of the people polled saw big business and the Catholic church as leaning toward the CDU/CSU during the 1983 election. The Social Democratic tendencies of labor are equally pronounced. The group bases of party support constitute a long-standing feature of the West German party system, and public perceptions have changed only slightly during the history of the Federal Republic. This pattern of interest group alliances affects both the ideology and the policies of the parties. In addition, these group cues help electors determine which party is most likely to represent their social interests.

The Bundestag is another major arena of interest group activity.

TABLE VIII.2 *Public Perceptions of the Political Tendencies of Interest Groups*

Party Tendency	Catholic Church	Industry	Labor Unions
More toward CDU/CSU	78%	72%	2%
To neither party	12	6	6
More toward SPD	0	2	79
Both parties; no opinion	10	20	13
Total	100%	100%	100%

Source: Infas, *Politogramm: Infas Report Bundestagswahl 1983* (Bonn: Infas, 1983), p. 129.

Monitoring legislation is obviously a prime concern for most political lobbies, and Bundestag decisions can have a major impact on an interest group's fortunes. Most groups concentrate on the specialized committees: testifying before committee hearings, lobbying committee members, and interacting with committee staff. It is within the committees that many of the political decisions of the Bundestag are actually made. Moreover, the system of specialized parliamentary committees enables interest groups to direct their efforts to those committees primarily concerned with policies affecting the group. Unions and business groups confront each other in the Labor and Social Relations Committee; agriculture is concerned with the Nutrition, Farming and Forestry Committee; social welfare groups focus their attention on the Youth, Family, and Health Committee; and so forth. This kind of interest group politics is not much different from what transpires in the halls of the U.S. Congress.

The pattern of interest group politics in the Bundestag is distinguished by the formal affiliation between deputies and interest groups. Since the Bundestag first began keeping records in 1972, about half the deputies report that they are employed by an interest group or hold an executive position in a group. Despite the Basic Law's mandate, that deputies represent the public interest, these formal ties are accepted as a legitimate aspect of politics. In practical terms, many party candidates are selected as representatives of specific interests, and it is considered better to acknowledge that fact than to deny reality. Economic groups maintain the largest representation in the Bundestag, around one-quarter of the deputies are affiliated with a union, business lobby, or other class-based association (Table VIII.3). About one-sixth of the deputies have ties to religious or cultural associations, and a sizable number are linked to social groups.

As might be expected, the interest group affiliations of Bundestag deputies follow party lines (Table VIII.3). The registered trade union representatives in the Bundestag are heavily concentrated within the ranks of the SPD, and over 90 percent of SPD deputies are members of a DGB-affiliated union, at least in name. The CDU also contains a modest labor wing (*Sozialausschusse*), but its influence within the party Fraktion is limited. The CDU/CSU is the bastion of industrial and business interests. Most of the deputies affiliated with business groups and the employers' associations (88 percent) and middle class groups (87 percent) are in the Union par-

TABLE VIII.3 *Percentage of Bundestag Deputies with Formal Interest Group Ties*

Interest	All Deputies	Distribution Among Parties				
		Greens	SPD	FDP	CDU/CSU	Total
Unions, employees' organizations	11.9	0.0	69.4	0.0	30.6	100%
Industrial, employers' organizations	3.3	0.0	11.8	0.0	88.2	100%
Middle class organizations	10.6	0.0	5.5	7.3	87.3	100%
Culture, research, religious groups	16.7	6.9	26.4	5.7	60.9	100%
Social associations (welfare, women, youth, etc.)	11.5	3.3	40.0	0.0	56.7	100%
Leisure sector groups (sports, etc.)	3.3	0.0	41.2	5.9	52.9	100%
Public bodies	0.6	0.0	33.3	0.0	67.7	100%
Percentage of deputies formally representing an interest group	58.1	28.6	50.5	34.3	70.6	

Source: *Datenhandbuch zur Geschichte des Deutschen Bundestages 1980 bis 1984*, p. 246.

ties. Cultural, religious, and social groups are similarly concentrated in the CDU/CSU Fraktion. The interest group networks of the CDU/CSU are most extensive, with over two-thirds of these deputies representing some interest group. Green deputies, in contrast, are the least likely to possess formal group ties, except for the party's involvement with the women's movement.

Ferdinand Müller-Rommel has shown that these general partisan tendencies are often accentuated within the key Bundestag committees that deal with matters relevant to competing interest groups.[21] For instance, in 1983, deputies with farming ties occupied 17 of the 27 places on the agricultural committee; deputies with business or labor interests accounted for a majority of the labor committee; and cultural interests dominated the education committee.

The West German system of involving interest groups in the policy process reaches even further than the range of normal lobbying activities we have discussed. The neo-corporatist system encourages the state ministries and governmental agencies to develop formal ties to interest groups.[22] A prerequisite of this relationship is recognition of an interest group by the government. Recognition might come through legislation regulating the activities or internal structure of a group. The nonpartisan nature of the labor unions, for example, is defined by the Basic Law, and many procedural aspects of industrial relations are governed by labor law legislation. In some occupations (medicine, the law, and other self-employed professions) professional associations are established by law. The government grants these associations legal sanction to certify professional competence and establish professional standards, making them quasipublic bodies. This formal legal status strengthens a group's position as the representative of its members.

In other instances, interest groups receive financial support or other resources from the government. The churches, for instance, obtain the majority of their income from a "church tax" collected by the government. A surcharge (about 10 percent) is added to an employee's income tax and this amount is transferred to his or her church. Citizens can officially opt out of the tax by renouncing their religious affiliation, but social norms discourage this. Similarly, the church-run primary schools in several states receive government funding, and the churches are granted government subsidies to support their various social programs. This pattern of financial dependence applies to other groups as well. Many environmental organizations and women's groups depend on government grants for a substantial part of their income, as is the case with other citizen lobbies.

Official recognition by the government often results in the granting of formal consultative status by government ministries. Federal administrative regulations require that relevant national associations be consulted and asked to provide testimony on proposals under consideration by a ministry. To meet this requirement, Federal ministries maintain a set of standing advisory committees, in which membership is allocated to what the ministry believes are the relevant interest groups. Most ministries have a number of such committees (Table VIII.4); some deal with admittedly minor topics (such as the agricultural committee on potato research), but other committees have large staffs and wield substantial influence within the political process (such as research advisory groups in several ministries, and expert committees dealing with topics such as cartels, nuclear safety, and trade). Moreover, the number of such committees has grown over the years, from 264 in 1969 to 358 in 1977. Current estimates place the number of such committees at an even higher level.

TABLE VIII.4 *Government Advisory Committees by Ministry*

Ministry	Number of Committees	Total Budet (000 DM)
Foreign Ministry	12	43
Interior Ministry	60	5,313
Justice Ministry	12	367
Finance Ministry	9	185
Economics Ministry	9	162
Ministry for Agriculture	56	242
Ministry for Labor	75	1,435
Transportation Ministry	11	164
Ministry of Defense	5	80
Ministry for Youth, Family, and Health	84	1,280
Ministry for Planning	8	106
Ministry for Research and Technology	12	313
Ministry for Education and Research	2	62
Other ministries and agencies	3	245
Totals	358	9,997

Source: German Bundestag, *Drucksache 8/484* (May 26, 1977).

In addition to these formal advisory committees, government administrative regulations encourage direct contact between representatives of the recognized interest groups and ministry officials when new legislation is being considered. Ironically, the same opportunities for political discussion need not be granted to Bundestag deputies, nonrecognized groups, or the public at large.

Interest groups are also formally represented on committees that supervise the activities of some government agencies and policy programs. The law establishing the Second Television Network (ZDF), for example, allocates two seats on the supervisory board to representatives delegated by the Evangelical church, two seats to the Catholic church, three seats to the trade unions, two seats to the BDA, two seats to agriculture, two seats to the newspaper federation, four seats to specific charities, one seat to the Federation of Expellees, one seat to the German Sports' Federation, and so forth. Other administrative boards oversee the post office, railroads, social security system, and other important governmental activities.

These formal channels of interest group participation open policy formation and administration to the established interest groups. The German Federation of Labor, for instance, is a member of forty-six ministry committees and twelve administrative boards. The representation of business and religious interests is just as extensive. In short, official recognition by the state almost ensures that a group is formally represented within the policy process.

In other cases, the interaction between interest groups and government occurs informally or through unofficial channels. Most often, the interchange between policy makers and interest group officials takes the predictable forms of business meetings, social gatherings, and unofficial discussions. Such communication keeps the policy process working smoothly. In a few prominent instances, however, these informal networks have partially circumvented the public policy process.

The privatization of the public policy process is most clearly seen in the example of Concerted Action (*Konzertierte Aktion*).[23] In reaction to the economic crises of the early 1970s, the government instituted an on-going private conference with top representatives of business (BDI and BDA) and labor (DGB) to decide basic elements of national economic policy. These meetings sought a consensus between competing interests on wage and price increases and other aspects of government economic policy. Once a consensus was reached, the government implemented the policy and group representatives sought compliance by their members. Concerted Action was not an aberration in the West German policy process; a similar network was established to discuss reform in the steel industry, another was formed in 1977 to deal with public health issues, and calls for a reintroduction of Concerted Action were heard in the early 1980s. Rather, Concerted Action is an exaggerated form of a general style of policy making in which interests are incorporated into the policy process rather than held at a distance.

This pattern of formal and informal cooperation between government and the interest groups constitutes another characteristic of the neo-corporatist style of interest group politics. Neo-corporatism institutionalizes the role of interest groups in the policy process. Governments feel that they are responding to public demands when they consult with designated interest groups. Conversely, formal consultation and participation in government committees ensures group officials of access to the policy process. Moreover, this style of interest group politics encourages group members to depend on the organization for the representation of their views, making interest groups the prime intermediaries between the public and government decision makers.

Analysts sharply debate the advantages and disadvantages of neo-corporatist politics. A major advantage of neo-corporatism is that it increases the efficiency of the governing process. The relevant interest groups can negotiate on policy without the pressures of public debate and partisan posturing. In a period of crisis, when government may become overloaded by pressing problems, this is an important consideration.

The critics note, however, that efficient government is not necessarily the best government, especially in a democracy. Under the neo-corporatist system, decisions are reached in conference groups or advisory commissions, outside of the representative institutions of government decision making. The "relevant" interest groups are involved, but this assumes that all relevant interests are organized, and only organized interests are relevant. The views of latent groups, such as consumers, are seldom represented when business and labor combine within a neo-corporatist structure. Decisions affecting the entire populace often are made beyond the public's eye. At the same time, democratically elected representative institutions— state governments and the Bundestag—are sidestepped as interest groups deal directly with government agencies. Neo-corporatism intrinsically contains illiberal and antiparliamentary tendencies, which must constantly be monitored.

Although neo-corporatism is well entrenched in the West German policy process, some interest groups exceed the bounds of conventional politics and resort to protests and similar forms of political action. Protest is not new to contemporary politics, but the nature and goals of protest have changed: Rather than an act of desperation or coercion, protest is a form of political persuasion. This new form of protest politics is most closely identified with citizen groups and the New Politics movement. Lacking the resources of labor or business, citizen groups struggle for recognition. Learning from the 1960s protests, these groups find that a spectacular public event or a big protest often provides immediate public exposure. In addition, the media attention that accompanies dramatic events enables a group to mobilize the popular support that is the basis of the group's political influence. Political movements are like sharks: They have to keep moving to stay alive.

The forms of unconventional political action are only as limited as the imagination of the organizers. Local groups orchestrate school boycotts or street blockades to protest the policies of government. During the NATO missile debate in the early 1980s, many groups organized local nuclear-free zones, complete with little signs in front of each house in the neighborhood. National groups often resort to more dramatic events to capture national media attention or demonstrate the extent of their popular support. The peace movement organized massive demonstrations in the years leading up to the decision on deploying NATO missiles; by several accounts one-tenth of the population was involved in demonstrations during a single week in the fall of 1983. Environmental protests often encompass elements of street theatre: hanging banners from smokestacks, dying industrial discharges to demonstrate the reach of pollution, building a human chain across the Rhine, or depositing dead fish at the doors of the Rathaus. Not just pure theater, these events are attempts to educate the public to the problem and possible solutions.

The choice between the various forms of conventional lobbying and protest activities is open to all interest groups. Although few groups limit themselves exclusively to one form of political action, interest group politics tends toward extremes. The major established interests benefit from a closed system that grants them formal representation within the policy process while excluding other interests. Participants in this neo-corporatist system see it as a defensible method of policy making, one which benefits their supporters. Conversely, new political interests see a closed, neo-corporatist system, in which their attempts to participate are not equally accepted. Thus, their initial criticisms of policy frequently spread to general criticism of the policy process itself. While still relying on unconventional methods, many environmental and other New Politics groups find that they must pursue normal lobbying activities, such as meeting with policy makers and administrators, in order to affect policy outcomes. The West German political system needs to reconcile these contradictions—opening the neo-corporatist system to wider participation and developing new mechanisms of accommodating the interests of citizen groups—if it hopes to remain a dynamic system, representative of the changing social and political interests of its citizens.

NOTES

1. See the discussion of various types of interest groups in Gabriel Almond and G. Bingham Powell, *Comparative Politics: Systems, Process, Policy*, 2nd ed. (Boston: Little, Brown, 1978), chap. 7.

2. Philippe Schmitter and Gerhard Lehmbruch, eds. *Trends toward Corporatist Intermediation* (Beverly Hills: Sage Publications, 1979); Gerhard Lehmbruch and Philippe Schmitter, eds. *Patterns of Corporatist Policy Making* (Beverly Hills: Sage Publications, 1982).

3. Philippe Schmitter, "Modes of Interest Intermediation and Models of Societal Change in Western Europe," in *Trends toward Corporatist Intermediation*, ed. P. Schmitter and G. Lehmbruch, p. 65.

4. Peter Katzenstein, *Policy and Politics in West Germany* (Philadelphia: Temple University Press, 1987), pp. 65–66.

5. By comparison, about 50 percent of the British labor force and less than 20 percent of U.S. workers are unionized. See Klaus von Beyme, *Challenge to Power: Trade Unions and Industrial Relations in Capitalist Countries* (Beverly Hills: Sage Publications, 1980), pp. 75–76.

6. Andrei Markovits. *The Politics of the West German Trade Unions*. (Cambridge: Cambridge University Press, 1986), chap. 3.

7. The growing strength of reform elements within the labor movement paralleled similar trends within the Social Democratic party. The transformation from Marxism to reformism was finally formalized in the 1963 Dusseldorf Program of the DGB. See Markovits, *The Politics of the West German Trade Unions*, pp. 91–104.

8. Peter Katzenstein, *Policy and Politics in West Germany*, ch. 3; Federal Minister of Labor and Social Affairs, *Co-determination in the Federal Republic of Germany* (Bonn: Federal Ministry of Labor and Social Affairs, 1980).

9. Jutta Helm, "Codetermination in West Germany: What Difference Has it Made?," *West European Politics* 9 (October 1986): 32–53.

10. As one example of the historical continuity of the churches, the regional boundaries of both the Protestant and Catholic churches date back to the 1800s, rather than following administrative boundaries within the Federal Republic. In addition, both churches included dioceses in East Germany and Poland until these areas separated in the 1960s.

11. Several prominent postwar figures critized the church's activities under the Third Reich in their literary works; see Rolf Hochhuth's *The Deputy* and Heinrich Böll's *Billiards at Half-Ten*.

12. Frederic Spotts, *The Churches and Politics in Germany* (Middletown, Conn.: Wesleyan University Press, 1974).

13. Siegfried Scharrer, "War and Peace and the German Church," in *European Peace Movement*, eds. Walter Laqueur and Robert Hunter (New Brunswick: Transaction Books 1985); Alice Holmes Cooper, "The West German Peace Movement and the Christian Churches," *Review of Politics* 50 (Winter 1988).

14. Erich Andrlik, "The Farmers and the State: Agricultural Interests in West German Politics," *West European Politics* 4 (January 1983); Edmund Neville-Rolfe, *The Politics of Agriculture in the European Community* (London: Policy Studies Institution, 1984), ch. 3.

15. Although membership in the DBV is voluntary, all farmers are required by law to join the League of Agricultural Chambers (*Verband der Landwirtschaftskammern*), which acts as an equivalent to the DIHT in the business sector.

16. Karl-Werner Brand, Detlef Büsser, and Dieter Rucht, *Aufbruch in eine andere Gessellschaft* (Frankfurt: Campus Verlag, 1983); Herbert Kitschelt, "New Social Movements in West Germany and the United States," *Political Power and Social Theory*, vol. 5 (Greenwich, Conn.: JAI Press, 1984); Claus Offe, "New Social Movements: Challenging the Boundaries of Institutional Politics," *Social Research* 52 (Winter 1985): 817–68.

17. Rudolf Bahro, *Building the Green Movement* (Philadelphia: New Society Publishers, 1986); Fritjof Capra and Charlene Spretnak, *Green Politics* (New York: Dutton, 1984); Lester Milbrath, *Environmentalists: Vanguard for a New Society* (Buffalo: SUNY Press, 1984).

18. Dieter Rucht, "Environmental Movement Organizations in West Germany and France," in *Organizing for Change: Social Movement Organizations Across Cultures*, ed. Bert Klandermans and Sidney Tarrow (Greenwich, Conn.: JAI Press, 1988).

19. Myra Marx Ferree, "Feminist Politics in the United States and West Germany," in *The Women's Movements of the United States and Western Europe*, eds. Mary Katzenstein and Carol Mueller (Philadelphia: Temple University Press, 1987); Brand, Büsser, and Rucht, *Aufbruch in eine andere Gessellschaft*, ch. 3.

20. Thomas Rochon, *Mobilizing for Peace* (Princeton: Princeton University Press, 1988); David Gress, *Peace and Survival* (Stanford: Hoover Institutions, 1985); Joyce Mushaben, "The Struggle Within," in *Organizing for Change*, ed. Klandermans and Tarrow.

21. Ferdinand Müller-Rommel, "Interest Group Representatives in the German Bundestag," in *The US Congress and the German Bundestag*, ed. Robert Livingston et al. (Boulder: Westview Press, 1988).

22. Claus Offe, "The Attribution of Political Status to Interest Groups," in

Organizing Interests in Western Europe, ed. Suzanne Berger (New York: Cambridge University Press, 1981), pp. 123–158.

23. Rolf Seitenzahl, *Einkommenspolitik durch Konzertierte Aktion und Orientierungsdaten* (Cologne: Bund, 1974); Andrei Markovits, *The Politics of the West German Trade Unions,* pp. 108–111, 213–214.

CHAPTER IX

The Party System and Electoral Politics

THE POLITICAL PARTY IS PROBABLY the most important innovation of modern democratic politics. Parties are key institutions of governance; they link the public to the policy process, mold the political culture, and structure competition within the political system. So great is the role of parties that one American political scientist claimed that modern democracy is unthinkable without political parties!

Although political parties are central to the democratic process, the Federal Republic inherited a partisan tradition unconducive to the development of a strong democratic system. The Second Empire did not consider partisan opposition to government as legitimate; both the Social Democratic party and Zentrum party were suppressed for challenging government authority. Political parties during the Weimar Republic often exemplified the weaknesses of democratic politics rather than its strengths. The parties frequently failed to perform the normal functions of parties in a democratic system. Rather than uniting specific political interests into broad programs, the Weimar parties directed their appeals to narrow sectors of society; the parties were merely concealed interest associations. The party system was highly fragmented and polarized; more than forty parties competed in the 1928 election, and fifteen won seats in the Parliament. Instead of accepting the democratic values of tolerance and pluralism, many party leaders functioned on the basis of narrow partisan self-interest. Several parties—on the extreme left and extreme right—even opposed democratic politics and actively worked to overthrow the political system. Weimar's party system thus contributed to the instability of the political system and the eventual rise of National Socialism. The actions of the Nazi party further stigmatized the image of partisan politics.

Because of this negative inheritance, policy makers were very cautious in framing the party system of the Federal Republic. If the democratic process were to succeed, the pattern of partisan politics must be changed. The Allied occupation forces began the process by licensing only political parties that were free of Nazi ties and committed to democratic procedures. This concern with the party system carried over to the provisions of the Basic Law.

The Basic Law is unusual in that it makes specific reference to political parties (the United States Constitution, for instance, does not). Because parties were suppressed during the German Empire and the Third Reich, Article 21 of the Basic Law guarantees the legitimacy of parties and their right to exist—if they accept the principles of democratic government. The Basic Law also calls for public accountability within political parties. The law requires parties to follow democratic procedures in making decisions and to provide public statements of their financing and expenditures.

As a result of these provisions and other aspects of the political process, the evolution of the West German party system followed a course quite different from that of Weimar.[1] In 1949, a fragmented party system had fourteen parties competing in the first national elections, with eleven winning seats in the Bundestag. Time, though, brought a consolidation of the party system and a decline in the number of electorally successful parties. Since 1961, three parties—the Christian Democrats (CDU/CSU), the Social Democrats (SPD), and Free Democrats (FDP)—have accounted for about 90 percent of the popular vote. Only these three parties were represented in the Bundestag from 1961 until the Greens entered parliament in 1983.

Along with the consolidation of the party system came a growing legitimacy for parties as institutions of democratic government. The leadership of the major political parties were united in their support of the democratic system and displayed a pattern of democratic political competition that overcame the negative images of previous party systems.[2] Kenneth Dyson observes that "the parties were the special instruments of democracy; the grip of democratic ideals was secured by party penetration of other institutions."[3] The concept of a "party state" (*Parteienstaat*) was no longer antithetical to democratic government. Popular images of political parties reflected the changing realities of the West German party system. In the early postwar years, the public was skeptical of political parties; to be called a "partisan" carried largely negative connotations. With continued exposure to an effectively running party system, people slowly developed attachments to their preferred party and accepted the importance of parties in the political process.

This chapter describes the many functions that parties perform within the West German political process and tells how specific parties have evolved. The consolidation and stabilization of the party system was a major accomplishment, but in recent years the parties have faced new challenges that test the continuing vitality of West German democracy.

A PATTERN OF PARTY GOVERNMENT

Political observers often use the term "party government" to describe the working of the West German political process.[4] Party government is based on the principle that party competition provides a method of popular representation and political accountability for the actions of government. The political parties are central institutions in this governing process because they interconnect the various elements of the political process: voters, interest groups, decision makers, and even public administrators. Parties integrate these political actors into a coherent political process and thereby provide the public with some control over this process through the selection of parties at election time. The West German political scientist, Kurt Sontheimer, went so far as to claim that[5]

> all political decisions in the Federal Republic are made by the parties and their representatives. There are no political decisions of importance in the Germany democracy which have not been brought to the parties, prepared by them and finally taken by them. This does not mean that other social groups have no power but that they have to realize their power within the party state.

Sontheimer's enthusiasm for party government is overstated, but parties are an essential part of the political process.

The state formally recognizes the role of political parties as institutions of governance in several ways. In the same way that the state sanctions neo-corporatist interest groups, the parties often act as official organs of the state. The Basic Law and legislation such as the 1967 Party Law spell out the responsibilities of the parties in unusual detail. These legal guidelines provide the parties with official guarantees of their status in the political process and allocate them formal political responsibilities not performed by political parties in many other democracies. At the same time, the state furnishes the parties with legal and financial support for their activities. This institutionalization of the relationship between government and the political parties goes beyond the normal pattern of party activity in most other Western European democracies.

Primarily, political parties act as intermediaries between the public and the political system. This process first requires articulating the interests of their voters, much as an interest group speaks for its constituency. The party leader who warns of the impact of trade legislation on business or talks about the needs of farmers for agricultural subsidies is usually articulating the interests of the party's supporters. Parties also resemble interest groups in their attempts to mobilize their clientele in support of the party's program. Election campaigns, for instance, combine both the articulation of public interests by the candidates and the attempt to mobilize voters behind the party's position. The West German parties usually limit their mobilizing activities to the electoral arena, but they sometimes involve the public in rallies and other public pressure tactics.

Political parties are, however, more than just interest groups. Most interest groups speak for a single interest, whereas today's political parties are institutions of *interest aggregation*. This means that the specific concerns of single interests are combined into a coherent program for government action. This requires that a party reconcile the demands of one group with those of its other supporters. At election time, voters then make a choice between competing party programs that spell out how diverse, and sometimes contradictory, social needs are to be addressed.

In addition to serving as representative institutions, the parties have an educational function, spelled out by the Basic Law. Political parties are directed to "take part in forming the political will of the people." In other words, the parties should take the lead in developing public opinion and not merely respond to citizen preferences. Each of the major parties maintains a large and well-staffed foundation, supported with funds provided by the federal government, to carry out these activities. The CDU foundation once appropriately resided in a castle outside of Bonn, and the Green party headquarters are located in a renovated building that formerly housed mental patients. Party foundations pursue several different public education programs for young people and adults, conduct research on social and political issues, and foster international exchange. The foundations are the public education arms of the parties.

Political parties also differ from interest groups in that party leaders who articulate and aggregate social interests also hold political decision making positions. This enables parties to link interest representation to government decisions, because the parties control the selection of political elites. Party leaders and party organizations exercise nearly complete control over the recruitment of individuals for political office. There are no direct primaries that would allow the public to select party representatives in Bundestag elections. Instead, district candidates are nominated by the relatively small group of official party members, or a committee appointed by the membership. Independent or nonpartisan candidates are extremely rare in West German elections. Moreover, the hybrid nature of the electoral system (see below) means that one-half of the Bundestag deputies are directly elected from "party lists" compiled at state party conventions. The average voter is usually unaware of the composition of these party lists. Thus, the party leadership has considerable control over who is elected under the party's label, which ensures that party officeholders adhere to the basic tenets of the party's policy program.

The dominance of party displays itself throughout the electoral process. Most voters view the candidates merely as party representatives, rather than autonomous political figures. Even the district candidates are elected primarily because of their party ties. The government generously finances election campaigns. Free campaign advertising on the public radio and television stations are available to the political parties on a proportional basis. Again, however, government funding and access to the public media go to the parties, not to individual candidates, as in the United States. The government continues to fund the parties between elections, to assist them in their information and educational functions as prescribed by the Basic Law. In 1983, the parties together received 83 million DM for the activities of the party foundations.

After the elections, political parties are key institutions in structuring the governmental process. Bundestag deputies form strictly defined party groups (*Fraktionen*); each Fraktion must have at least 5 percent of the parliament (26 members). The Bundestag is organized around these Fraktionen, and they are central institutions in the formation of public policy. Especially for the opposition parties that lack the support of government agencies, the party Fraktion is essential in translating the party's broad policy goals into specific legislative proposals. Deputies on both sides of the aisle spend a large part of their time in party caucuses, formulating party programs and positions on the legislation pending before Parliament. Voting decisions made within the Fraktion are then carried out on the floor of the Bundestag. It would not be unfair to say that the real voting decisions of the Bundestag take place within the Fraktionen.

As a result of these partisan structures and the imperatives of a parliamentary form of government, the cohesion of parties within the Bundestag is exceptional. Most votes follow strict party lines. Party discipline is rigidly enforced, and few deputies deviate from the party line; more than 90 percent vote in agreement with their party's majority. The parties thus structure the political activities of the Bundestag and, once in government, have enough cohesion to carry out their policy programs. In short, parties, not individual deputies, are the policy makers that voters can award or punish at the next election.

This emphasis on party cohesion does not mean that the West German parties have no internal disagreements. Policy decisions are often the result of compromise and consensus building among the various political views represented within a party. The amount of disagreement, however, is usually smaller than that found within the two major parties in the United States. Once agreement is reached, moreover, the West German parties vote as a bloc. The type of individual entrepreneurship displayed by members of the U.S. Congress is not tolerated in the Bundestag. A party maverick in the Bundestag is unlikely to be renominated by the party and generally cannot circumvent the party hierarchy by directly appealing to the voters in a primary election. West German parties are more likely to act as single entities, compared to the loose and open structure of U.S. parties.

The last link in the chain of party government is control over the executive and administrative activities of government. The parliamentary system ensures that the ruling party coalition in the Bundestag selects the chancellor and most of the cabinet from within its ranks. Thus the parties link executive and legislative authority. Moreover, through patronage, the executive can maintain a party presence within the bureaucracy. About 800 high ranking government positions are filled by political appointments, as well as numerous positions on regulatory and advisory boards.

Parties are not the only actors at each step in this political process. There are several different ways for citizens to articulate interests beside through the parties; policy initiatives come from outside the parties; factors beside party enter into legislative decision making and the actions of the executive. In fact, in recent years there has been increasing criticism of how the parties perform these functions.[6] The countervailing influence of other institutions, such as the Bundesrat and federal system of government, means that the importance of party to policy making is less than in Britain and other pure parliamentary systems.

Still, the party government process in the Federal Republic creates a central framework for integrating the various elements of the political process—providing the public with indirect control over the policy outputs of government through the electoral choice of parties that possess the political resources to carry out their campaign promises. The linkage is not always perfect, but political parties are the primary institutions of representative democracy. West German democracy *is* virtually unthinkable without political parties.

THE PARTY SYSTEM

The West German party system has passed through several phases in its brief history as partisan politics responded to the larger political trends in West German society. The early postwar years were a time of partisan volatility and instability, as voters divided their choices between a large number of parties. Soon, however, the Christian Democrats consolidated the support of moderate and conservative voters, and the Social Democrats strengthened their position on the left. The Federal Republic developed a "two-and-a-half" party system, with the large CDU/CSU and SPD contending for government control and dependent on the support of the small Free Democratic party. This partisan framework persisted relatively unchanged for more than two decades, as political power alternated between the major parties. In recent years, however, this stable party system has experienced new turbulence, as new political issues altered these stable party alignments and a new political party, the Greens, entered the Bundestag to challenge established patterns of partisan politics.

CHRISTIAN DEMOCRATS (CDU/CSU)[7]

Conservatism in postwar West Germany was an orphan, stigmatized by the actions of nationalists, conservatives, and right-wing extremists during the Weimar Republic and Third Reich. Yet moderate, reputable conservative politicians from the Weimar era, who had not become involved in the Nazi regime, were recruited by the occupation forces to help in the rebuilding of the postwar German government. Although they had no ideology of their own, these conservative politicians began working for a nonsocialist alternative to the rapidly growing Social Democratic party. Gradually, a patchwork of nonleft groups developed at the local level, and then developed regional and national networks.

The central force in this loose conservative alliance was the Christian Democratic Union, CDU (*Christlich Demokratische Union*). The CDU represented a sharp break with the tradition of German conservative parties. The party was composed of a heterogeneous group of Catholics and Protestants, business people and trade unionists, conservatives and moderates. The party united behind the principle that West Germany should be reconstructed along Christian and humanitarian lines, without an exclusive Catholic or Protestant orientation. The CDU was anti-Nazi and anti-Communist, and extolled conservative values and the merits of the Social Market Economy. Konrad Adenauer, the party's first leader, sought to develop the CDU into a conservative-oriented "catch-all party" (*Volkspartei*) appealing to a wide spectrum of the electorate—a sharp contrast to the fragmented ideological parties of the Weimar Republic.[8]

The Union ran in the 1949 election as a loose association of state party organizations. The election results were greeted with surprise as the Union emerged as the largest single party and Adenauer proceeded to construct a coalition government to take control of the new state (Tables IX.1, IX.2). Adenauer rapidly emerged as the dominant figure in postwar German politics. In many senses the CDU as a national party was Adenauer, and Adenauer was the party. The new government generally followed Adenauer's own policy preferences and these were endorsed by the CDU-led majority in the Bundestag. The success of these programs enhanced Adenauer's stature and the electoral appeal of the CDU. The Christian Democrats made impressive electoral gains in 1953 as they absorbed the support of smaller centrist and conservative parties. In 1957, the Union (together with the CSU) became the first and only West German party to ever win an absolute majority in a national election.

The CDU is a national party, except in Bavaria, where it allies itself with the Christian Social Union, CSU (*Christlich-Soziale Union*). The CSU reflects the strong regional identity of Bavarians

TABLE IX.1 *Party Shares of the Bundestag Vote (Second Vote), 1949–1987*

Party	1949	1953	1957	1961	1965	1969	1972	1976	1980	1983	1987
CDU/CSU	31.0%	45.2%	50.2%	45.4%	47.6%	46.1%	44.8%	48.6%	44.5%	48.8%	44.3%
FDP	11.9	9.5	7.7	12.8	9.5	5.8	8.4	7.9	10.6	7.0	9.1
SPD	29.2	28.8	31.8	36.2	39.3	42.7	45.9	42.6	42.9	38.2	37.0
Greens	—	—	—	—	—	—	—	—	1.5	5.6	8.3
Communist parties	5.7	2.2	—	1.9	1.3	0.6	0.3	0.4	0.2	0.2	0.1
Neo-Nazi parties	1.8	1.1	1.0	0.8	2.0	4.3	0.6	0.3	0.2	0.2	0.6
Other parties	20.4	13.2	9.3	3.0	0.3	0.5	—	0.2	0.1	0.1	0.6
Total	100%	100%	100%	100%	100%	100%	100%	100%	100%	100%	100%

TABLE IX.2 *The Distribution of Party Seats in the Bundestag, 1949–1987*

Party	1949	1953	1957	1961	1965	1969	1972	1976	1980	1983	1987
CDU	139	243	270	242	245	242	225	243	226	244	223
FDP	52	48	41	67	49	30	41	39	53	34	46
SPD	131	151	169	190	202	224	230	214	218	193	186
Greens	–	–	–	–	–	–	–	–	–	27	42
Other parties	80	45	17	–	–	–	–	–	–	–	–
Total Deputies	402	487	497	499	496	496	496	496	497	498	497

as well as their more conservative political views. The two Union parties generally function as one in matters of national politics. In national elections, the CDU runs in every state except Bavaria, where only the CSU is present on the ballot. The Union parties campaign together under the CDU/CSU banner, from a single Fraktion in the Bundestag, and have always entered the government as a coalition.

During the 1950s, the CDU was a weakly knit collection of conservative politicians and state party organizations. It was a party comprised largely of local notables, and the most notable politician was its head, who held together its diverse elements through his personal contacts. When the "old man," as he was (ir)reverently known, began to fade, the party shared his struggle. Adenauer was 85 years old at the time of the 1961 election (more than a decade older than Reagan at his last election in 1984). The CDU lacked direction and goals, as displayed by Adenauer's seeming indifference to the building of the Berlin Wall two months before the election. The CDU/CSU was returned to government, but its voting lead over the opposition Social Democratic party was cut nearly in half. Replacing Adenauer was inevitable, but certainly not something the party looked forward to—both because Adenauer resisted what he considered to be a premature retirement and because his political stature was irreplaceable. After extended maneuverings, Ludwig Erhard became chancellor in 1963. Erhard was the architect of the Economic Miracle and a competent administrator, but he was unable to infuse the Christian Democrats with new vision once postwar recovery had been attained.

The era of CDU dominance was slowly coming to an end, and the precipitating factor was the economic recession that struck West Germany in 1966. Confronted by opposition to its proposed economic program from the FDP, the CDU/CSU joined with the Social Democrats to form the *Grand Coalition* in November 1966. This historic compromise between "Black" and "Red" parties had been unthinkable a short decade earlier. The two major parties shared governing responsibility. Kurt Georg Kiesinger (CDU/CSU) was the chancellor, Willy Brandt (SPD) was the vice chancellor, and the cabinet positions were distributed between the two parties (ten to the CDU/CSU and nine to the SPD). Only the small Free Democratic party was left on the opposition benches. The Grand Coalition's economic policies generally reaped success, and by 1968 the nation was well along the road to economic recovery.

In 1969, the voters had a difficult time distinguishing between the two major parties that had shared government control. Furthermore, until the election was over it was unclear whether the CDU/CSU and SPD would continue the Grand Coalition. When the votes were in, the SPD allied itself with the Free Democratic party and gained control of the government by a narrow margin of only 12 seats (Table IX.2). For the first time in the history of the Federal Republic, the CDU/CSU became the opposition party.

The Christian Democrats were very uncomfortable on the hard seats of the opposition benches. The CDU/CSU remained the largest party in the Bundestag, and having the most deputies had traditionally entitled a party to form the governing coalition. Many party leaders considered the loss of power an unfortunate mistake or an unfair manipulation of the electoral process by the SPD-FDP coalition. In their own minds, CDU officials believed that this mistake would soon be recognized and corrected. The Union parties thus emphasized their role as a shadow government, waiting for what they believed was their inevitable return to power. Yet during this time the CDU/CSU lacked a clear policy direction. The party maintained its emphasis on Christian values and conservative economic principles, but party members could not always agree on how these goals should be translated into specific policies. When the party finally did challenge the government on its attempt to regularize relations with East Europe, the party chose a policy on which the public did not support the CDU/CSU's position.

The CDU/CSU suffered a symbolically important electoral defeat in 1972. Even though the party's share of the popular vote decreased by less than 2 percent, the CDU/CSU no longer could lay claim to being the largest party in the Bundestag. This event forced the party to reevaluate its position and to begin the long process of rebuilding itself into a viable electoral alternative. The CDU expanded its membership base and developed the organizational resources of the national party organization. At the head of the national party was an aggressive young minister-president from Rhineland-Palatinate, Helmut Kohl.

Buoyed by a rejuvenated organization and new programs, Kohl ran as the CDU candidate for chancellor in 1976. The CDU/CSU made large gains by capitalizing upon the public's resurgent fears about economic and social conditions. The party's campaign evoked the CDU/CSU's past glory and the potential for reviving Christian and social values. The election results were even closer than the 1969 contest, but the CDU/CSU lost to the SPD-FDP coalition by the barest margin (1.9 percentage points). The CDU/CSU then struggled to learn the lesson of this near miss. Kohl realized the difficulty of winning an absolute majority for the CDU/CSU or any party, and so he advocated a centrist strategy that would attract moderate voters and possibly yield a new parliamentary coalition with the FDP. Others, especially the CSU leader, Franz Josef Strauss, claimed that the CDU/CSU could win the votes of a "silent majority," if only the party would present a clear conservative option to attract these voters.

Strauss was always a larger than life figure in West German politics. He assumed leadership of the CSU at a fairly young age, and quickly became a rallying point for German conservatives. His list of political accomplishments is impressive, but controversy always seemed to follow his actions. As Defense minister he authorized the government raid on the headquarters of *Der Spiegel* in 1962, because the magazine ran an exposé on the Federal Republic's defense preparedness; this led to his forced resignation from office. As minister president of Bavaria and occasional Bundestag deputy he retained a presence in national politics, constantly pressing the CDU/CSU to adopt more conservative policies. Following Kohl's 1976 loss, Strauss threatened dissolution of the CDU/CSU electoral alliance as one ploy to force a more conservative electoral strategy on the coalition. Some CDU moderates finally agreed to allow Strauss to test his conservative strategy as the CDU/CSU chancellor candidate in 1980. After all, the chance of a CDU/CSU victory seemed unlikely in the face of a strong SPD-FDP record and Helmut Schmidt's popularity as chancellor. For party moderates, this was one way to resolve Strauss's perennial demands for a greater role in the coalition once and for all, while preserving their own energy for the next election.

The results of the 1980 campaign were entirely predictable. Strauss vigorously attacked Helmut Schmidt and the SPD-FDP coalition and their governing record, which most voters admired. Strauss' excessive conservatism and acerbic political style alienated many traditional CDU/CSU voters. The silent majority would not speak, and Strauss' conservative strategy led the CDU/CSU to a decisive defeat. The CDU/CSU vote share dropped to its lowest level since 1949.

Perhaps the biggest winner of the 1980 election was Helmut Kohl. His position within the party benefited from his performance as leader of the CDU/CSU Fraktion in the Bundestag. As head of the CDU's national party organization, he had continued rebuilding the party structure and forging new programs. Kohl emerged from the 1980 election as the unchallenged leader of the opposition. Moreover, it was an opposition that was preparing itself for government. The CDU mapped out a new party program based on conservative economic policies derived from Thatcher and Reagan, along with a more moderate approach to social and foreign policy issues. These policies increased the political compatibility between the CDU/CSU and FDP, which Kohl also nurtured through personal contact with the FDP leadership.

When the SPD-FDP governing coalition stumbled in 1982, Kohl and the CDU/CSU were waiting in the wings. The liberal Social Democrats and the economically conservative FDP could not agree on a program to deal with the nation's worsening economic conditions. Voters' dissatisfaction with the SPD-FDP government increased support for the Christian Democrats in a series of important state elections. In mid-1982, the FDP leadership decided to break with the Socialists and form a conservative government with the CDU/CSU. Helmut Schmidt was removed from the chancellorship through the first successful use of the constructive no-confidence vote and replaced by Helmut Kohl and a new CDU/CSU-FDP team. The new government arranged for early elections in March 1983, which endorsed the change in government by providing the CDU/CSU with a major electoral victory.

The Kohl government faced a number of imposing problems. Government finances were in disarray, the economy was struggling, and foreign policy tensions ran high over the imminent decision on whether to accept new NATO nuclear missiles in the Federal Republic. In addition, a number of political scandals befell the government during its first years in office. For a time, it appeared that the CDU-led government might be overmatched by the problems it faced. Slowly, but steadily, the government made headway in dealing with these problems. The NATO issue was resolved by the end of 1983, government deficits were cut back, and the economy staged a substantial recovery. Kohl also displayed surprising skill in consolidating his position as leader of the Union parties.

The 1987 elections were a partial setback for the CDU, but probably strengthened Kohl still further. Although the CDU/CSU's vote share decreased slightly, these votes went to its coalition partner, the FDP. With a more even balance between conservative (CSU) and centrist (FDP) forces within the coalition, Kohl can probably exercise more discretion in initiating government programs that reflect his own philosophy and that of his party.

SOCIAL DEMOCRATS (SPD)[9]

The revival of the Social Democratic party (*Sozialdemokratische Partei Deutschland* [SPD]) started immediately after the war's end in 1945. Former SPD activists reappeared after spending the years of the Third Reich imprisoned, in exile, or in early political retirement. Local branches of the SPD began organizing even before being licensed by the occupation forces, and within a few months a new SPD was forming to claim the leadership of postwar Germany.

Kurt Schumacher emerged as the leader of the SPD and began to reconstruct the party along the lines of its Weimar predecessor. The party reestablished its earlier organizational structure, with a highly centralized party organization and numerous social organizations to provide a tight-knit social milieu for the working class. The new SPD defined itself as an ideological party, representing the interests of unions and the working class. In the early postwar years, the Social Democrats espoused a reformist program derived from Marxist doctrine, which included the nationalization of major industries and the implementation of state planning. Until his death in 1952, Schumacher consistently opposed Adenauer's Western-oriented foreign policy program, preferring reunification of the two Germanies even at the cost of accommodation with the Soviet Union. The SPD's image of West Germany's future was radically different from that of Adenauer and the Christian Democrats.

The SPD's hope for governing Germany were dashed by the 1949 election results and the creation of a CDU-led government. In subsequent elections, the party gained support, but it seemed to be locked in a 30-percent ghetto. The party's program appealed to the socialist core of the working class, but not to the wider spectrum of German society. In simple terms, the public preferred the economic and foreign policies of the Christian Democrats over those of the SPD. The SPD's poor electoral performance generated internal pressures for the party to broaden its political appeal beyond its working-class base. Reformers within the SPD, such as Herbert Wehner, Carlo Schmid, Fritz Erler, and Willy Brandt, called for the party to shed its radical image.

In 1959, the SPD undertook a historic change in course. At the Bad Godesberg conference, the party abandoned its traditional role as advocate for socialism. In a single act, the party renounced its policies of nationalization and state planning and embraced Keynesian economics and the principles of the social market economy. Karl Marx would have been surprised to read the Godesberg program and learn that free economic competition was one of the essential conditions of a social democratic economic policy. The SPD attempted to shed its anticlerical image and begin a rapprochement with the churches. The party replaced opposition to NATO and the Western Alliance by acknowledging the Federal Republic's Western leanings. The party continued to represent working-class interests, but by shedding its ideological banner and more extreme policies the SPD hoped to attract new support from liberal middle-class voters. The SPD began to transform itself into a liberal-oriented catch-all party that could compete with the Christian Democrats.

The Godesberg Program marked a dramatic step toward a new political style for the SPD. With a young, vibrant Willy Brandt leading the party as chancellor candidate, the SPD posted steady electoral gains. In fact, from its low point in 1953, the Social Democrats enjoyed a nearly constant 3-percent gain from election to election in what came to be known as the "comrade trend." Still, the SPD remained under a cloud of public doubts about its political reliability and capacity to govern. The SPD's reputation for virulent government opposition, dating back to the Second Empire, had been revived by Schumacher's confrontational style. The party's actions and policies led many people to conclude that the SPD opposed the basic goals of German society, a perception the CDU/CSU eagerly encouraged in early election campaigns.[10] To convince the public of the SPD's reliability and intentions, the party initiated a strategy of embracement (*Umarmung*) with the CDU/CSU. By responsibly sharing the reins of government with the Christian Democrats, the Social Democrats hoped to increase public confidence in the party and open the way for an SPD-led government.

The opportunity to complete this embracement strategy arose in November 1966, when the CDU/CSU joined the SPD to form the Grand Coalition. The SPD not only improved its image of reliability and trust by sharing national governing responsibility, but it also played an active role in resolving the nation's problems. Its minister of economics, Karl Schiller, was credited with Germany's recovery from the economic recession of 1966–1968. Willy Brandt was instrumental in laying the groundwork for Bonn's new foreign policy, and Gustav Heinemann assumed the office of federal president after a successful tenure as minister of justice.

The SPD share of the popular vote in the 1969 election nearly reached parity with that of the CDU/CSU. More important, the small FDP decided to align itself with the Social Democrats. A new government coalition was formed, with Willy Brandt as chancellor and Walter Scheel, the FDP leader, as minister of foreign affairs. The new center-left coalition entered the government with a program of political reform and modernization.

The most dramatic initiatives came in foreign policy. West Germany's relations with Eastern Europe had been marked by confrontation and hostility since the onset of the Cold War. Brandt proposed a fundamentally different policy toward the East (*Ostpolitik*), in which the Federal Republic accepted the postwar political divisions within Europe and sought reconciliation with the nations of Eastern Europe. Treaties were signed with the Soviet Union and Poland to resolve disagreements dating back to World War II and to establish new economic and diplomatic ties. In 1971 Brandt received the Nobel Peace prize for his actions. Finally, a "Basic Agreement" with East Germany formalized the relationship between the two Germanies.

The SPD-FDP coalition also instituted a series of domestic policy reforms. These reforms generally aimed at expanding social services and equalizing access to the fruits of the Economic Miracle. A series of government measures expanded and equalized access to higher education and generally improved the quality of the educational system. Social spending nearly doubled between 1969 and 1975; new benefits were enacted in old age security, health insurance, and social services (see Chapter XI). Proud of these accomplishments, the SPD boasted in the 1972 elections that they were creating the "*Modell Deutschland*" that other European democracies could emulate.

The pace of social reform slacked in the mid-1970s, mainly as a result of the worldwide economic problems arising from the increasing price of oil. The Federal Republic simultaneously suffered from economic stagnation and inflation. Willy Brandt left the chancellorship in 1974. Ostensibly the precipitating cause was a spy scandal involving a member of his staff, but both Brandt and the SPD seemed to look forward to his retirement from office. The new SPD chancellor, Helmut Schmidt, held a reputation as a crisis manager who could handle the nation's problems. Little money was available for new social programs, so there was a necessary retrenchment on domestic policy reforms. Still, Schmidt reassured the public and pointed out that West Germany's economic problems were much less severe than those of its European neighbors.

Although the SPD retained government control in the 1976 and 1980 elections, these were trying times for the party. The SPD and FDP frequently disagreed on how the government should respond to continuing economic problems. Policy divisions also developed within the SPD.[11] For example, the SPD's traditional union and working-class supporters favored nuclear energy and a renewed emphasis on economic growth as means of lessening unemployment. At the same time, many young, middle-class SPD members opposed nuclear energy and economic development projects that might threaten environmental quality. Other disagreements arose over defense policy and the Federal Republic's willingness to accept a new generation of NATO nuclear missiles.

These policy strains eventually caused the downfall of Schmidt's government. Unable to reconcile the conflicting policy goals of Old Left and New Left groups, the SPD was losing its capacity to govern. As the economic and political situation worsened in the months following the 1980 election, the governing parties were unable to agree on a common program to deal with these problems. When the Free Democrats decided to switch coalition partners and ally themselves with the CDU/CSU, the SPD was forced out of office. Schmidt chose not to run again as the SPD chancellor candidate, and Hans-Jochen Vogel struggled to bring the party together in the March 1983 elections.

Once again in opposition, the Social Democrats face an identity crisis. The party is challenged on the left by the new Green party, and on the right by the Christian-Liberal government. Should the party attempt to assimilate the Greens, or adopt a centrist program in competition with the government? The SPD has been unable to resolve this dilemma, in part because of its own internal divisions. The traditional core of the party—the labor unions and the working class—favors a centrist strategy that emphasizes the party's traditional commitment to economic growth and social programs. The New Left elements in the party advocate a policy agenda more closely aligned with the Greens.

In the 1983 elections, the SPD found that it could not ride both horses simultaneously; attempts to satisfy both camps left the public uncertain about the party, and its vote share dropped dramatically.

In subsequent Länder elections, state SPD organizations pursued different strategies. In the Saarland, Oskar Lafontaine became the New Left star of the party, coopting the Greens' program and winning an absolute majority for the SPD. The SPD leader in Northrhine-Westphalia, Johannes Rau, expressed open contempt for the Greens and also won an absolute majority. In other Länder, the SPD entered into governing coalitions with the Greens, although these proved to be unstable alliances. The larger lesson for party strategy was unclear, and the SPD's general voting strength was declining. Even with the highly popular Rau at the head of the SPD ticket in 1987, the party's fortunes slipped slightly below the 1983 election results (Table IX.1).

Until the SPD resolves this identity crisis, it probably will continue to struggle at the national level. Neither wing of the party offers an electoral strategy that will broaden its base of support. This indecision means that the party cannot present itself to the voters as a viable opposition to the CDU-led government. If the SPD cannot decide what it stands for, how can it expect to win the confidence of the electorate? The resolution of this dilemma will determine the SPD's future in the West German party system.

FREE DEMOCRATS (FDP)[12]

The Free Democratic party (*Freie Demokratische Partei* [FDP]), was created in 1948 to continue the liberal party tradition from prewar Germany. The party began as a loose coalition of local and regional liberal groups. There were competing views about what the term "liberal" stood for, but the party soon developed a distinct political philosophy. The FDP stressed the legal protection of individual liberties and the concept of the Rechtsstaat. On social and economic issues, the party positioned itself as an alternative to both the CDU/CSU and SPD. The party was a strong advocate of private enterprise and opposed the socialist orientation of the SPD; at the same time, the FDP's secular views contrasted with the Christian orientation of the Union parties. The FDP was for "people who found the CDU too close to the churches and the SPD too close to the trade unions."[13] The party drew much of its electoral support from business interests, the Protestant middle class, and farmers.

Its early start as one of the first four parties licensed by the occupation forces enabled the FDP to win representation in the preliminary round of state and local elections. This electoral base helped the Liberals to emerge from the 1949 elections as the third largest party in the Bundestag. Its economic policies made the FDP a natural ally of the CDU/CSU. From 1949 until 1957, and again from 1961 until 1966, the FDP was the junior coalition partner of the CDU/CSU. As part of the government, the FDP advocated policies aimed at stimulating West Germany's postwar development, represented the interests of agriculture, and endorsed Adenauer's Western-oriented foreign policy.

All political marriages experience some tensions, and this certainly applied to the FDP's alliance with the Christian Democrats. Anxious to maintain independence from their larger coalition partner, the FDP left the government in 1957 over a controversy involving modification of the electoral law. In 1961, the Liberals ran as a third force without prior coalition agreements and renewed its alliance with the CDU/CSU only after the election. During the later part of the 1960s, the Free Democrats were developing a new party image consonant with the liberal democratic values of its leader, Walter Scheel.

The FDP's exile to the opposition benches during the Grand Coalition stimulated this remaking of the party. The transformation was completed by the decision to form a new alliance with the Social Democrats following the 1969 Bundestag elections. The new F.D.P. (punctuated by the addition of periods to the party's official acronym) shed its conservative image and stressed the reformist elements of its liberal tradition. The party called for the democratization of society, social reforms, and more socially minded economic policies. The party moved from a nationalist foreign policy stance to advocacy of Brandt's Ostpolitik. The two governing parties worked closely together on the social modernization that characterized the early years of the Brandt-Scheel government. The F.D.P.'s public image and prestige steadily grew; Scheel became Federal President in 1974, and Hans-Dietrich Genscher took over the party helm. In the divisive 1980 election, Genscher projected the image of a statesman, leading the F.D.P. to a resounding electoral victory. The party was riding a crest of public popularity.

With the worsening of economic conditions in the early 1980s, the Free Democrats reasserted their conservative economic policies. Whereas the SPD was concerned with protecting workers from the economic downturn, the F.D.P. focused on the budget deficits generated by the government's liberal social programs. The F.D.P. Economics Minister, Count Otto von Lambsdorff, displayed little moderation in criticizing the SPD's policies. In addition to these tensions, the party's failure to win representation in a series of state elections convinced F.D.P. leaders that a change was necessary. The

Free Democrats surreptitiously planned to dissolve their marriage with the Social Democrats and renew their earlier bonds with the CDU/CSU. In September 1982, the coalition came to an end, and soon after the FDP and CDU/CSU formed a new government.

Each time the FDP had changed direction, in 1957 and 1969, the party had suffered at the polls, and this was the case in 1983. Genscher's popularity plummeted, and many FDP supporters deserted the party. Pre-election surveys raised serious doubts as to whether the party could survive the election. The party's vote share dropped from 10.6 percent in 1980 to 6.9 percent in 1983, barely enough to ensure the FDP's presence in the Bundestag and the continuation of its alliance with the CDU/CSU. This downward slide continued after the election; a series of state elections eliminated the party from five of ten state parliaments and the FDP failed to win representation in the 1984 European Parliament elections.

Just as political analysts were preparing eulogies for the FDP, however, the party made a dramatic recovery that even Lee Iacocca would admire. The Free Democrats began to exert their presence within the governing coalition, pressing for fiscal policies that would lessen the federal deficit and restore economic growth. Foreign Minister Genscher won public favor by continuing to advocate détente with the East. The Free Democrats generally acted as a moderating force on the CDU/CSU, tempering government policies. The FDP thus roared back from the grave in 1987, winning votes from both CDU and SPD supporters. The results of the election were widely interpreted as a sign that the public wanted to strengthen the FDP's position as a moderating influence on the Union parties.

The record of the Free Democrats underscores the potential importance of small parties in a multiparty system. Although the FDP is the smallest of the established parties, its influence in the party system greatly outweighs its share of the popular vote. Government control in the West German parliamentary system, at the federal and state levels, routinely requires a coalition of parties. The FDP normally controls enough votes and a strategic centrist ideological position to play a pivotal role in forming government coalitions and directing the course of West German politics. The FDP has the option to form coalitions with either of the major parties. On economic matters, its conservatism draws the party toward the CDU/CSU, while its social and foreign policies are often closer to those of the SPD. It might be fair to conclude that the German electorate does not determine the government, the FDP does.

The Free Democrats' position as a perennial coalition partner endows them with a unique political position. Its service in government for four-fifths of the Federal Republic's history means that the party acts as a source of continuity in the political process. FDP ministers possess detailed knowledge of the personnel and procedures of government that is carried forward from one administration to the next, even if the party's coalition partner changes. Politically, the Free Democrats generally moderate the policies of their coalition partner. The centrist tendencies of the FDP can work to temper the conservative policies of the CDU/CSU or the socialist leanings of the SPD. Such was the message of the 1987 election. Indeed, the longevity of the FDP might be directly traced to the electorate's conscious attempt to maintain the party as a check against the concentration of political power in the hands of any one party. In performing this balancing role, the FDP acts as a halfway house for dissatisfied voters, providing citizens with an alternative between the two large parties. As an FDP campaign banner proclaimed in 1983: Germany without the FDP would be like television without "Dallas."

THE GREENS[14]

Environmental issues first began attracting widespread public attention in the late 1960s and early 1970s. As the Federal Republic enjoyed the economic products of the Economic Miracle, some citizens drew attention to the degradation in the quality of the environment that was a by-product of unregulated growth. The catalyst for citizen concern was often a local problem, such as pollution by a local company or the siting of a nuclear power plant. The established parties generally were unresponsive to environmental issues, because all were committed to maintaining high rates of economic growth and saw environmental interests as a threat to this goal. Therefore, the environmentalists began by organizing citizen–action groups outside the party system to lobby on environmental issues. The largest environmental organization, the BBU, boasted a membership of more than one million members among its affiliated local groups.

In the late 1970s, the environmental movement entered a new phase. Frustrated by the lack of progress in working from outside the political system, a variety of local and regional ecological parties formed to work for change from inside the system. The first environmental party list appeared in the 1977 local elections in Schleswig-Holstein. Within a year, environmental parties were sprouting up like mushrooms across the Länder. These parties displayed surprising strength in several state elections, and in 1979 an environmental party won representation in the Bremen state parliament.

The environmental movement lacked a single political identity at this point, and there were several different environmental parties across the country. In Berlin and Hamburg, for instance, the movement had a distinct leftist cast, recruiting many former activists from radical student groups and Marxist organizations, the "K-groups," labeled for their communist sympathies. The parties in Bavaria and Baden-Württemberg, by comparison, were organized by more moderate environmental reformers. In some cases, competing environmental parties ran in the same election.

Efforts soon began to construct a national coalition of environmental parties. In 1979 a single environmental slate ran in the European parliament elections under the label "Other Political Associations: The Greens." The party surprised most poll watchers by winning 3.2 percent of the vote. This spurred efforts to develop a national party in time for the 1980 Bundestag elections.

In 1980, the nascent party held two founding congresses—the first to decide on the party structure and the second to establish a common party program. These congresses produced a new political party, the Greens (*Die Grünen*), that united the various environmental groups under a single banner. The Greens proclaimed themselves as a party of a new type, advocating a society in harmony with nature and a party free of bureaucratic structures. From the outset, the party was a multicolored rainbow. The "green" Greens were solely concerned with nature conservation and environmental protection. The "red" Greens came from Marxist and radical leftist groups and saw the party as a vehicle for fundamental social change. The "brown" Greens saw environmental problems as a security issue, that is, a threat to human and national survival. The party attracted a heterogeneous mixture of students, farmers, and middle-class supporters. Prominent party figures included a former CDU Bundestag deputy, former Maoists, a retired army general, and a convicted student terrorist.

The Greens fared poorly in 1980, capturing only 1.5 percent of the popular votes, but the party's strength then grew in a series of state elections. By the end of 1982, the Greens had won representation in six state legislatures, and more than a thousand Green officeholders served at local levels of government. During this period the party also developed a more extensive political program, which included stands such as opposition to the stationing of new nuclear weapons in the Federal Republic and support for women's liberation, minority rights, and the further democratization of society and the economy. This new ideological focus drove many conservative members out of the party, as the Greens became a representative of New Left and alternative political viewpoints. The party's 1983 election manifesto called for such predictable environmental policies as the immediate halt of all nuclear power activity, the dismantling of nuclear power plants, and the elimination of pesticides and herbicides from agriculture. But the Greens also called for more unconventional policies: prohibition on the sale of war toys; the immediate abolition of TV and radio advertisements as well as all advertisements for cigarettes, candy, liquor, and agricultural chemicals; mandatory home economics and child-rearing classes for both male and female students; an end to discrimination against homosexuals and lesbians; the elimination of assembly-line work and night shifts; and the conversion of the German arms industry to the production of energy and environmental systems. The Greens obviously represented a new political philosophy in West German partisan politics.

In the 1983 elections, the Greens were remarkably successful in moving the issues of environmental protection and nuclear weapons toward the top of the campaign agenda. Public concern about environmental problems reached a new peak, propelled by accounts of Germany's national forests dying under a cloud of acid rain. Debates over the stationing of NATO Pershing and cruise missiles intensified as the decision date drew near, and only the Greens unequivocally opposed deployment. Riding on these two issues, the Greens gained enough popular support to surmount the 5-percent hurdle (5.6 percent) and win 27 seats in the Bundestag.

Using their new political forum, the Greens vigorously campaigned for an alternative political view on matters of the environment, defense policy, citizen participation, and minority rights. At the same time, the Greens added a bit of color and spontaneity to the normally staid procedures of the political system. The Greens were a party of youthful exuberance.[15] They celebrated their entry into the Bundestag with a rag-tag parade of deputies and their supporters; the normal dress for Green deputies is jeans and a sweater, rather than the traditional business attire of the established parties. Many political analysts initially expressed dire concerns about the impact of the Greens on the governmental system, but most now agree that the party was instrumental in bringing necessary attention to previously overlooked political viewpoints. Based on this performance, the Greens increased their share of the popular vote to 8.3 percent (42 seats) in the 1987 Bundestag elections.

Despite their electoral success, the Greens also face an internal identity crisis. On many matters of tactics and political goals, the party splits along factional lines. The radical wing of the party is composed of the so-called *Fundis* (or fundamentalists), those who believe the party should maintain an uncompromising commitment to its principles. The Fundis attract the leftist ideologues who demand a radical restructuring of West German society and politics. The Fundis fear that participation in parliamentary politics, and the inevitable compromises that result, will sap the vitality of the movement. Purity of thought and action—and eventually radical social change—is more important than short-term results. The moderate wing of the party, the *Realos* (or realists), are more pragmatic about politics. They work within established channels for incremental social reform, even accepting positions in local and state governments. Ideological dogmatism and political tactics generally overlap in these two party factions. Whereas the Fundis are portrayed as uncompromising radicals, the Realos as pictured as sacrificing basic social reform for illusionary short-term gains. Whereas the Fundis abhor collaboration with the political establishment, the Realos are willing to consider political alliances with the Social Democrats. Whereas the Fundis are slow to criticize political violence, the Realos emphasize the nonviolent aspect of the movement.

The Fundi and Realo factions provide different views of what a Green future might look like. It is no wonder that the critics and admirers of the party have a difficult time agreeing on the social and political implications of the Greens. At present, the two factions are about evenly balanced among the party's leadership; Jutta Dittfurth, Rudolf Bahro, and Thomas Ebermann are prominent among the Fundi faction; Otto Schily, and Joschka Fischer are notable members of the Realo faction. Many party activists remain uncommitted to either persuasion. The resolution of these factional battles will determine the party's future.

THE INNER WORKINGS OF THE PARTIES

Political parties are complex organizations involving hundreds of top-level elected officials, thousands of party workers, and millions of voters; the organization of these resources are often critical to a party's success. Some parties are fairly successful in organizing these activities; disorganized parties often find they are unable to compete and become extinct. The organization of a party may also be a reflection of the party's goals and can influence what the party will accomplish. Organizational resources can determine how effectively the party links together the various elements of the party government model and how the party acts at each step in the process. Organization also determines how power is distributed within a party and the relative influence of the various elements of the party. In short, a party's organization, formal and informal, affects how the party makes decisions and the ability of the party to carry out these decisions.

It is possible to discuss the organizational structure of political parties in great detail, and such detail is sometimes necessary to understand party actions. Yet discussions of party structure and the distribution of political influence within parties normally focus on the interrelationship between three key components. One component is the elected party officials who act as the political leadership of the party. Another component is the formal party organization, the party's national headquarters, party secretary, and support staff. The third basic component is the party membership, organized into constituency associations or local party groups. Our examination of party structure concentrates on these three components to illustrate the basic organizational characteristics of the West German parties.[16]

THE SPD AS A MASS PARTY

The SPD developed the organizational form of the modern mass party. The SPD was originally founded to mobilize the working class in support of socialist goals, and the postwar SPD retained this structure. Formal party membership was encouraged by party and trade union leaders as a display of working-class solidarity, and many ancillary organizations (socialist youth groups, social clubs, women's groups, and sports associations) integrated members into an exclusive social milieu. This emphasis on rank-and-file support was evidenced by the size of the Social Democrats' membership base. During the 1950s, the number of card-carrying SPD members exceeded CDU membership by two or three times (Figure IX.1). This mass membership was the foundation of the party; it provided a core group of party workers for election campaigns and was a major source of party funds. Moreover, ultimate authority within the party is formally vested in the membership. According to SPD

FIGURE IX.1 *Trends in Party Membership, 1950–1985*

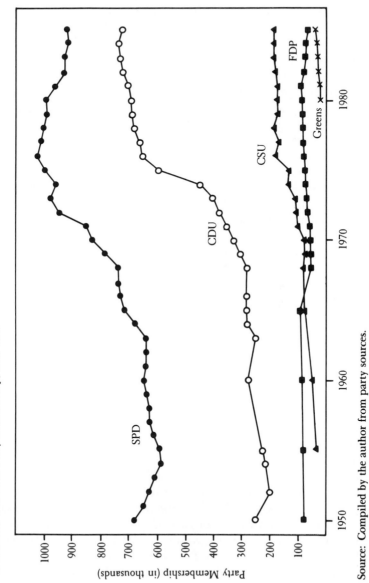

Source: Compiled by the author from party sources.

271

statutes and the Party Law of the Federal Republic, the biennial party convention (*Parteitag*) of representatives from the local SPD constituency associations is nominally the supreme party organ.

The irony of mass parties is that most members lack the time or political expertise to fully manage the party's affairs, and so party control gravitates to the party leadership. Party elites realized that the mass membership base can be used more effectively if the party's course is set by an authoritative leadership corps and enforced by a centralized party bureaucracy. A centralized power structure can marshal a party's resources more efficiently during an election campaign, giving the party an advantage over its less-organized competitors. Such a party is also better able to enforce party discipline in the legislature and maintain firm control over the governing apparatus once in power. Despite the strong principle of internal democracy within the party, historical studies of the SPD noted a persisting tendency toward the concentration of power in the hands of party elites. Robert Michels described this phenomenon in the pre-Weimar SPD as the "iron law of oligarchy."[17] Michels maintained that organizational incentives inevitably lead any political party to concentrate power in the hands of a small group of leaders at the top of the party hierarchy.

Many analysts believe that Michels' characterization still applies to the present-day SPD. The SPD has a highly centralized and bureaucratized party machine, with political power residing at the top of the party. In practical terms, the most important institution in the party is not the party congress. Instead, the party's dual executive organs, the Federal Executive (*Vorstand*) and the Praesidium, are where political decisions are made. The Federal Executive consists of about three dozen party leaders, elected by the party congress. The members of the Executive are generally representative of the political factions within the party. The Executive is responsible for controlling the activities of the party organization, but in recent years it has adopted a more passive role on policy matters, routinely endorsing decisions made by the Praesidium. The Praesidium represents the inner circle of party elites; it is elected by the Federal Executive and is generally synonymous with the party leadership. In its weekly meetings, the Praesidium carries out the business of the party, handling budgetary matters, addressing administrative questions, and dealing with campaign issues. On policy matters the Praesidium frequently finds itself endorsing policies and programs that originate with the chancellor and his cabinet when the SPD is in government or the leadership of the Bundestag Fraktion when the party sits in opposition. The Federal Executive and party congress nearly always ratify these decisions, and a well-staffed national party apparatus administers them. The SPD is a party where power flows from the top down.

The hierarchic tendencies of the SPD do not, however, mean that the party structure is monolithic. Over the last two decades, the party has displayed organizational tendencies counter to its previous oligarchic style. Left-wing SPD militants are more assertive in questioning the policies advocated by the party hierarchy. Many local party associations (*Ortsverein*) are now composed of middle-class members caught up in the participatory spirit of the times; these constituency groups are more active in expressing their views within the party. Recent party congresses have been significant focal points in debates between party factions. Divisions at the top of the party may have contributed to these trends. During its last years in government the formal positions of leadership within the party were divided among three people: Helmut Schmidt was the chancellor, Willy Brandt was the head of the national party, and Herbert Wehner was the Bundestag Fraktion leader. This division of power inevitably increased the potential that the party would not speak with a single voice—which it often did not. This division of offices has continued through the 1980s, reflecting the persisting factional diversity in the party. Still, power in the SPD resides at the top of the pyramid; although many may debate party policy, party leaders make the final decisions. The classic characterization of the SPD as an oligarchy still largely applies to the party today.

THE INSTITUTIONALIZATION OF THE CDU

Whereas the organizational structure of the SPD was purposively created with the goal of forming a mass-based party, the Christian Democratic Union is the product of evolution. Through its formative years, the CDU was a loose collection of local and regional conservative groups. The party then evolved a federal structure similar to U.S. parties; a weak national party combined with strong state party organizations (*Landesverbände*). The SPD's highly centralized and bureaucratized party organization was consciously rejected by CDU officials. The CDU was essentially a party of local notables who were not eager to have a national party organization restrict their prerogatives. During the 1950s, the national party was described as no more than an electoral association to support Chancellor Adenauer (*Kanzlerwahlverein*). The party organization coalesced for election campaigns and then faded away as soon as the last vote was counted. Formal party institutions existed, but Adenauer's personal leadership really provided the structure and continuity of the party at the national level.

With Adenauer's retirement in 1963, the structure of the CDU evolved further. The Fraktion leaders in the Bundestag directed the party for the rest of the 1960s; a collective leadership replaced the personal dominance of Adenauer. In the early 1970s, the party strengthened its national organization to provide the CDU with the political resources and management skills to match the better organized Social Democratic party. Membership drives greatly expanded the core of party workers (Figure IX.1). In 1969, the CDU claimed barely 300,000 members; this number doubled by the 1976 campaign and more than tripled by 1980. Party representatives aggressively solicited financial support from business interests and other conservative groups. Party income spurted from about 73 million DM in 1973 to 100 million in 1975 and over 200 million in the early 1980s. This renewal of the party was accompanied by a shift in the locus of party control. The head of the party organization, Helmut Kohl, was not a member of the Bundestag; renewal came from outside the parliamentary delegation.

The evolution of the CDU resulted in a complex party structure. The Federal Executive (*Bundesvorstand*) is the major executive body of the party. Its fifty to sixty members are drawn from the elected national leaders of the party (mostly from the cabinet when the party is in office or the Fraktion when in opposition), important CDU officeholders from the Länder, and officials of the party machine. The Executive is too large and meets too infrequently to actually guide the party. Instead, political leadership resides in a smaller subset of the Executive, known as the Praesidium. The Praesidium consists of an inner circle of the highest-level elected CDU officials. It meets on a regular basis to determine the party's position on pressing matters of policy and party administration. The party also holds minicongresses (*Bundesausschuss*) semiannually, at which the Federal Executive and Länder leaders meet with representatives of the party's auxiliary organizations and other leading party activists. These assemblies do not decide policy, but rather serve as a vehicle for party leaders to convey their views to the membership and build consensus for the party's stated program. Every two years, there is a full party congress of several hundred party activists. The party leaders stage manage these biennial congresses, at which members ratify leadership decisions.

The CDU's organization is a blend of several traits. First, the party retains a federal structure, but the influence of the state party organizations has moderated. State party organizations direct many essential party activities and are formally represented in the party's national executive, but the state organizations are now more accountable to the national party office. Second, despite the expansion of mass membership, the CDU is still a party of notables. The Federal Executive is not elected by the party membership, as is the case with the SPD. Most seats go to the holders of specific national and state offices, and the party congress elects only a minority of the Federal Executive. The Praesidium is comprised entirely of ex-officio members. Thus the role of the rank-and-file membership within the CDU is even more restricted than in the SPD. Third, although the CDU seeks to avoid the bureaucratic administrative style of the SPD, the Christian Democrats' own national party office has grown in importance with the renovation of the party organization in the mid-1970s. The national party apparatus has a bigger role in directing and coordinating the activities of party organs. Thus the organizational patterns of both major parties are converging; as decentralist trends have somewhat lessened the hierarchical structure of the SPD, organizational reform has increased the centralization within the CDU.

This complex structure of the CDU does not place absolute power in the hands of any one institution. The Praesidium normally acts in concert with the Bundestag Fraktion, state party organizations, and the central party apparatus. In recent years, however, political authority has been concentrated in the person of Helmut Kohl. Kohl has been the National Chairman of the party organization since 1973; he was head of the Bundestag Fraktion from 1976 until 1982; and he now directs the party from his position as chancellor. Like a heavyweight boxer, he has unified the various titles of party leadership. The overlap between these offices has raised Kohl to a position of political dominance within the party; only Adenauer exerted more control over the inner workings of the CDU.

THE STRUCTURE OF THE FDP

Rather than relying on a highly developed party infrastructure, the Free Democratic party exists as a loose association of like-minded politicians—who are often of different minds. The FDP is organized as a federation of state party organizations, each of which jealously guards its autonomy and maintains its own definition of "liberalism." The national party headquarters lacks the authority or resources to direct the activities of state parties or other party functionaries. The formal party institutions, Federal Executive, Praesidium, and party congress, similarly lack strength.

The intentional structural weakness of the FDP enables it to accommodate the political diversity in the party, especially between the economic conservatives and social liberals. No single party orthodoxy is enforced, so all liberal views can be tolerated. The lack of structure also allows the party leadership substantial autonomy and limits the political influence of mid-level party elites and the party membership. The FDP makes no pretense of being a mass party, and the membership plays only a minor role in party decision making. Party elites are often free to act as they choose, without the internal party controls implied in the party government model. The autonomy of party leaders was vividly apparent in the decision to end the coalition with the SPD in 1982. Only a handful of FDP leaders were involved in the decision, which was then presented to the rest of the party as a *fait accompli*. The FDP is what the FDP party elites do.

THE ANTI-PARTY PARTY

If the established West German parties in general adhere to Michels' iron law of oligarchy, then the Greens consciously set out to break the law.[18] On paper, the Greens' organizational chart looks much like those of the other parties, with a federal executive, national steering committee, and party congress, but the process of party decision making differs dramatically from the established parties. The organizational culture of the Greens places the highest priority on avoiding the elite domination, bureaucratization, and concentration of power that they see in the other parties. The ideal is "basic," or grassroots, democracy, instead of oligarchy and hierarchic party controls. The inner workings of the Greens differ so markedly from the established parties that Petra Kelly described them as the "anti-party party."

The goal of the Greens is to ensure that power flows up from the membership, rather than down from party elites. The party for the most part determines its ideological and policy directions at the party congress, through consensus. Like the rest of the party, the membership meetings have an unconventional air. The normal congress comes complete with children playing in the aisles, dogs running through the hall, and people yelling at the top of their lungs. Unrestricted, often chaotic, political debates are the hallmark of Green party politics. Party bylaws also ensure an open-door policy for the members, guaranteeing them access to all party functions and the deliberations of all party organizations.

The formal institutions of the party lack the hierarchical structure typical of established political parties. Party organizations at the local, district, and state levels retain the greatest possible autonomy. All state party organizations, and some local party units, maintain their distinct identity and control over their own activities. National party organs do not have authority. For instance, the Federal Executive cannot command lower levels of the party organization. The Executive instead performs a coordinating role, mediating between the competing interests in the party. Decentralization and the diffusion of power produce a "stratarchical" party structure.[19]

The Greens have taken extraordinary steps to guard against the oligarchic fate predicted by Michels by restricting the power and prerogatives of party elites. The Greens have three coequal party spokespersons, so that no one individual can dominate the party's public image. At all levels of the party, there are limitations on the number of offices an individual might hold and limits on reelection. The most well-known effort to avoid the concentration of elite power is the rotation principle (*Rotationsprinzip*).[20] Halfway through their first term in the Bundestag, Green deputies were required to resign from office and yield their seats to their alternates. The party's policy now encourages rotation after one term of office, and many state parties also maintain some form of rotation. Rotation means the loss of expertise and continuity, but it symbolizes the party's mistrust of elites. The Greens believe that the party's leadership does not have to be elitist, that ordinary people can make reasonable and informed political decisions just as well (or better) than career politicians. So far, rotation has apparently not damaged the electoral or political vitality of the party.

Although the Greens unique organization was created in the name of grassroots democracy, these institutional forms have had some unintended consequences. The lack of structure limits accountability and political continuity within the party; if no one is in charge then no one can be held responsible by the party members or the voters. The Greens' pervasive mistrust of elites, sometimes bordering on paranoia, makes it difficult to attract competent individuals to positions of party responsibility. To the Greens, party office is something to be endured, rather than the source of personal and political rewards that normally attract individuals to political office. The most telling criticism is the limited public involvement in the party. Despite the party's populist rhetoric, it has been relatively unsuccessful in attracting party members (Figure IX.1). The factional conflicts in the party and the lack of regularized participation opportunities mean that party involvement comes at a high cost to the individual. As a result, only a small core of highly motivated political activists participates in party affairs, and the turnover in party membership is extremely high. The number of party members per thousand voters is far smaller than for any of the established parties—a sharp indictment of the Green form of grassroots democracy.

STRUCTURAL PROBLEMS

Although each West German political party functions in its own unique way, they all share several structural problems that seem to lack easy solutions. At the top of the list is the question of internal party democracy. Article 21 of the Basic Law states that a party's "internal organization must conform to democratic principles." In actual practice, the oligarchic tendencies within most of the parties leave them far short of this ideal. The democratic process is based on nondemocratic institutions, in which decisions are routinely made at the top and then passively ratified by the democratic organs of the party. Surveys of party activists regularly show signs of alienation caused by the lack of true input opportunities for the average member, which encourages people to turn to more rewarding forms of participation, such as citizen-action groups. Those who are not formal party members—about 90 percent of the electorate—have even less impact on party behavior. The leaders of the established parties are aware of these problems; innumerable party commissions, research projects, and reports have been produced in recent years. Lingering elitist doubts, however, about the wisdom of the masses, and a hesitancy to share power, postpone the adoption of true internal party democracy. These doubts are reinforced by the experience of the Greens. What the Greens proclaim as grassroots democracy and participatory politics, the established party leaders see as anarchy. The parties need to find a middle route, where they can expand party democracy and still meet their organizational needs.

Another pressing problem for party elites is party finance. Although party revenues have steadily increased, expenditures have grown even more rapidly. In 1968, the three established parties had a total income of a little more than DM 100 million; by 1984, their revenues exceeded DM 500 million. In order to keep up electorally and politically with the competition, each party feels the pressure to spend more and do more than last year. To meet these increasing demands, the parties turned to several sources. The SPD traditionally draws a large part of its support from its mass membership (see Table IX.3). The party increased dues and regularized their collection, but the Social Democrats still went into debt trying to compete with the better-funded Union parties. The CDU/CSU and FDP aggressively pursue contributions from their regular supporters among industrialists and the middle class, but more could be done with additional funds. The parties also receive generous subsidies from the federal and Land governments; in fact, the antiestablishment Greens receive the largest proportion of their income from these government subsidies. Still, spending continues to exceed income.

Party financing became a political crisis when the Flick scandal broke in 1982. The large Flick corporation had sold its share in Daimler-Benz for a large profit, and sought a multimillion-mark tax exemption through a creative interpretation of foreign trade

TABLE IX.3 *Sources of Party Financial Support in 1983*

	SPD	CDU	CSU	FDP	Greens
Membership fees	33.9%	28.4%	19.5%	13.6%	9.6%
Donations	6.1	27.2	35.6	31.2	15.2
Reimbursed election expenses	23.9	21.5	17.1	32.9	69.5
Credits	24.6	9.6	17.4	.5	—
Contributions from deputies	7.7	8.5	7.8	5.6	1.0
Investment income	1.2	1.8	.9	1.9	1.5
Other income	2.2	1.0	.4	13.0	3.1
Total	100%	100%	100%	100%	100%
Total in million DM	207	176	45	35	20

Source: *Datenhandbuch zur Geschichte des Deutschen Bundestages 1949 bis 1982*, p. 94ff.

regulations. To make political leaders more receptive to their questionable application for a tax exemption, Flick representatives made generous financial contributions to all the established parties. The money trail led to the top party leadership and a series of criminal indictments, although no convictions were ever obtained.

The Flick scandal led to reforms in party financing in early 1984. The parties receive a subsidy for campaign expenses according the number of votes they receive; these subsidies were increased from 3.50 DM per vote to 5 DM. The government enacted stronger reporting requirements and restrictions on tax-deductible party donations; new laws also require more detailed financial record-keeping.[21] Such reforms may not end the pressure for parties to keep up financially with their competitors, but they may lessen the likelihood that this pressure will lead to abuse of the political process.

These structural problems of the parties and their perceived policy deficiencies have generated growing public skepticism of the parties and the party system in general.[22] Events such as the Flick scandal and a more recent scandal over election dirty tricks in Schleswig-Holstein portray the parties as self-interested and self-centered organizations. The Greens repeatedly noted that *all* the established parties accepted the Flick funds; the abuse of office was not limited to one party bloc. Critics also rap the parties for their failure to deal with the nation's problems. Neither the SPD- nor CDU-led coalitions have resolved the fundamental economic problems that generate high unemployment and limit economic growth. In part, the problems are international in origin and beyond the control of any one government; but the governing parties many times have avoided making hard policy decisions for fear that the decisions might alienate their potential voters. On the new political issues, such as environmental quality, nearly all observers agree that the established parties were negligent in their duty.

There are indications that these developments are eroding popular support for the parties. The decline of voting turnout in 1987 is explained in part as a protest against the government. Electoral volatility, the amplitude of vote swings between elections, is generally on the rise, as fewer voters feel committed to a single party. More fundamental problems are indicated by evidence of growing distrust or dislike of political parties in general. A 1983 survey of better-educated West Germans found that political parties evoked the least faith of any of the dozen social and political institutions included in the survey![23]

It is highly unlikely that parties will lose their unique position as intermediaries between citizens and the political process. But political parties cannot rest on their achievements. Changes in their internal structure and the larger political context suggest that parties no longer exert the internal control and external influence that they once possessed. This situation represents not so much the decline of parties as growing competition from other political actors, such as interest groups and citizen initiatives.

THE ELECTORAL CONNECTION

One of the essential functions of political parties in a democracy is the selection of political elites as a method of interest representation. Elections give individuals and social groups an opportunity to select officeholders who share their views. In turn, these choices lead to the representation of group interests in the policy process, because a party must be responsive to its voters if it wants to retain their support. Although Bundestag deputies are selected in free and open contests, the West German electoral system differs decidedly from the U.S. or British system.

ELECTORAL SYSTEM

The framers of the Basic Law had two goals in mind when they designed the electoral system. One was to reinstate the proportional representation (PR) system that was used in the Weimar Republic. A PR system allocates legislative seats on the basis of a party's percentage of the popular votes. If a party receives 10 percent of the popular vote, it should receive 10 percent of the Bundestag seats. Other individuals saw advantages in a system of single-member districts, like those in Britain and the United States. They thought that this system would avoid the fragmentation that shattered the Weimar party system and ensure greater accountability of each representative to his or her electoral district.

To satisfy both objectives, the lawmakers devised a hybrid system of "personalized proportional representation," with elements of both models.[24] When a German citizen votes in Bundestag elections, he or she casts two votes (Figure IX.2). The first vote (*Erststimme*) is for a candidate running to represent the district. The candidate with a plurality of votes is elected as the district representative. The Federal Republic is divided into 248 electoral districts of approximately 110,000 voters each. One-half of the Bundestag deputies are directly elected from these districts.

FIGURE IX.2 *Sample Ballot*

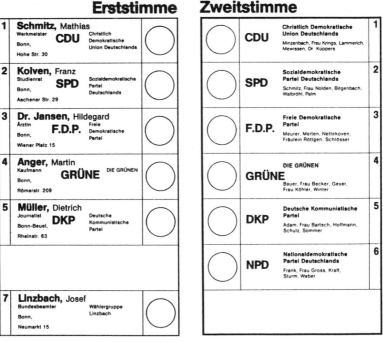

Stimmzettel

für die Wahl zum Deutschen Bundestag im Wahlkreis 63 Kreisfreie Stadt Bonn

am ⋯⋯⋯⋯⋯⋯⋯⋯

Sie haben 2 Stimmen

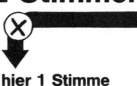

hier 1 Stimme	hier 1 Stimme
für die Wahl	für die Wahl
eines Wahlkreis-	einer Landesliste (Partei)
abgeordneten	- maßgebende Stimme für die Verteilung der Sitze insgesamt auf die einzelnen Parteien -
## Erststimme	## Zweitstimme

	Erststimme			Zweitstimme	
1	**Schmitz,** Mathias Werkmeister **CDU** Christlich Bonn, Demokratische Hohe Str. 30 Union Deutschlands	◯	◯	**CDU** Christlich Demokratische Union Deutschlands Minzenbach, Frau Krings, Lammerich, Mewissen, Dr Küppers	1
2	**Kolven,** Franz Studienrat **SPD** Sozialdemokratische Bonn, Partei Aachener Str. 29 Deutschlands	◯	◯	**SPD** Sozialdemokratische Partei Deutschlands Schmitz, Frau Nolden, Bilgenbach, Walbröhl, Palm	2
3	**Dr. Jansen,** Hildegard Ärztin **F.D.P.** Freie Bonn, Demokratische Wiener Platz 15 Partei	◯	◯	**F.D.P.** Freie Demokratische Partei Meurer, Merten, Nettekoven, Fräulein Röttgen, Schlösser	3
4	**Anger,** Martin Kaufmann **GRÜNE** DIE GRÜNEN Bonn, Römerstr. 209	◯	◯	**GRÜNE** DIE GRÜNEN Bauer, Frau Becker, Geyer, Frau Köhler, Winter	4
5	**Müller,** Dietrich Journalist **DKP** Deutsche Bonn-Beuel, Kommunistische Rheinstr. 63 Partei	◯	◯	**DKP** Deutsche Kommunistische Partei Adam, Frau Bartsch, Hoffmann, Schulz, Sommer	5
			◯	**NPD** Nationaldemokratische Partei Deutschlands Frank, Frau Gross, Kraft, Sturm, Weber	6
7	**Linzbach,** Josef Bundesbeamter Wählergruppe Bonn, Linzbach Neumarkt 15	◯			

Source: Courtesy of Generalkonsulat der Bundesrepublik Deutschland.

With their second vote (*Zweitstimme*), citizens select a party and thereby the overall distribution of the parties in Parliament. These second votes are added nationwide to determine each party's share of the popular vote. A party's proportion of the second vote determines its total representation in the Bundestag. Each party is then allocated additional seats, so that its percentage of the combined district and party seats equals its share of the second vote. The additional party seats are distributed according to lists prepared by the state parties before the election. One-half of the members of the Bundestag, 248 deputies, are elected as party representatives.

One major exception to this proportional representation system is the 5-percent clause. The electoral law stipulates that a party must win at least 5 percent of the national vote, or three constituency seats, to share in the distribution of party-list seats. The 5-percent clause was intended to avoid the proliferation of small extremist parties that plagued the Weimar Republic. In practice, however, this electoral hurdle has handicapped all minor parties and contributed to the consolidation of the party system. People are hesitant to risk their votes on a small party if they fear it will fall below the 5-percent mark.

A practical example can help illustrate the workings of this two-vote system. Table IX.4 displays the distribution of votes in the 1987 Bundestag election. The SPD received 37.0 percent of the second votes cast in the election; this sets the party's total seats in the par-

TABLE IX.4 *Allocation of Bundestag Seats in 1987*

Party	Second Vote	Allocation of Seats by Proportional Representation (PR)	District-elected Deputies	List-elected Deputies	Total Seats
CDU/CSU	44.3%	222	169	54	223[a]
FDP	9.1	46	0	46	46
SPD	37.0	186	79	107	186
Greens	8.3	42	0	42	42
Other	1.3	0	0	0	0
Total	100%	496	248	249	497[a]

[a] The CDU won more district seats in Baden-Württemberg than it was entitled to under proportional representation; the size of the Bundestag was thus increased by one to accommodate this additional deputy.

liament at 37.0 percent of the 496 seats, or 186 seats. Since the Social Democrats won 79 district seats through the first votes on the ballot, the party received an additional 107 party-list seats to yield their 186 seat total allotment. Occasionally, a party will win more district seats in a state than they are entitled to under strict proportional representation, as the CDU did in 1987. In this case, the party keeps any "extra" seats, and the size of the Bundestag is increased. Given this complexity, it is no wonder that public opinion surveys routinely uncover public confusion about the workings of the two-vote system.

This unique electoral system has several important political consequences. In general, the party-list system gives party leaders substantial influence over who will be elected to Parliament. The lists are headed by prominent and popular figures within the party. Because positions near the top of the list carry a high likelihood of election, these people are virtually assured of election; lower positions have only symbolic value. Each party attempts to represent the major political factions on the party list in proportion to their influence; the CDU takes this even a step further, enforcing a strict *Proporz* system to ensure that the number of Catholic and Protestant candidates is balanced. The various social interests within a party (such as business, labor, women's groups, agriculture, and youth groups) receive list positions in keeping with their party rank. The organization of the party lists thus provides unusual insights into the distribution of political power within a party.

The PR system also ensures fair representation for the smaller parties. The FDP has not won a direct candidate mandate since 1957, and yet it receives Bundestag seats based on its national share of the vote. In contrast, Great Britain's district-only system discriminates against small parties; in 1987 the Liberal-SDP Alliance won 23 percent of the national vote, but only 3 percent of the parliamentary seats. Without proportional representation, neither the FDP nor the Greens would presently be in the Bundestag.

The West German two-vote system also affects campaign strategies. Although most voters cast both their ballots for the same party, the FDP traditionally encourages supporters of its larger coalition partner to "lend" their second decisive votes to the Free Democrats. In the last two federal elections, these split ballots were instrumental in keeping the FDP and the Greens above the 5-percent cut-off point. Finally, research indicates that district and party representatives behave differently in the Bundestag. District candidates are somewhat more responsive to their constituents' needs and are slightly more likely to follow their district's views when voting.[25]

ELECTORAL COALITIONS

These last two chapters underscore the theme that West German politics, especially partisan politics, is built upon a social base. Political parties originally defined their identity in terms of the social groups they represented. The parties maintain formal or informal ties to their respective clientele groups and depend on them for financial and institutional backing. Electorally, the support of clientele groups provides the core of the parties' electoral coalitions.

Within the West German party system the major lines of political cleavage follow a Left/Right axis defined by social class and religion.[26] The CDU/CSU is still seen as the party of business, the middle class, and Catholics (see Table VIII.2). The word "Christian" in each party's name proclaims their religious orientation. Conversely, the Social Democrats are viewed as the party of the working class and the unions. The small FDP has its own social identity, tied to the Protestant members of the middle class and farmers.

During the early postwar years, the social and economic divisions between the major parties were sharply drawn. The traditional split between the middle class and working class had deep roots in German politics; after all, Marx and Engels had partially based their revolutionary theories on the German experience. Religious antagonisms were just as intense and just as closely linked to the political system. The major parties based their electoral appeals on these social divisions. The SPD proselytized for its socialist ideology and harshly criticized the capitalist and religious values of the Christian Democrats. In return, the CDU/CSU warned the public that all socialist roads lead to Moscow.

In such an environment, an individual could easily decide how to vote depending on his or her position in the social structure. Most members of the working class supported the SPD, whereas a majority of Catholics voted for the Christian parties. Social networks were closely drawn, and voters listened to the advice of the unions or church leaders in making their electoral decisions. Voting behavior studies found that social characteristics were potent predictors of voting patterns in the early Bundestag elections.[27] In the 1957 election, for example, only 24 percent of the middle class supported the SPD, but 61 percent of the working class cast SPD ballots. Religious voting differences were equally stark. One acted politically as one was defined socially.

The social transformation of West Germany and the deliberate actions of the parties lessened these social divisions over the next two decades. Affluence, social mobility, geographic mobility, and changing life styles eroded traditional group and institutional networks. Party actions also hastened the gradual filling in of these traditional cleavages. Early CDU/CSU governments followed economic policies partially intended to moderate the class cleavage, just as the ecumenical coalition of the Christian Democrats lessened the intensity of the religious cleavage. The Social Democrats took a dramatic step to lessen ideological tensions with the reforms of the Godesberg Program. As a result, political differences gradually narrowed as both the CDU/CSU and SPD became catch-all parties.

In broadening their electoral coalitions, the major parties blurred the social bases of party support. Class voting differences in recent elections merely hint at earlier class polarization, and most other social divisions have similarly narrowed.[28]

The image of earlier social alignments can still be seen in 1987 voting patterns, but in muted form (Table IX.5). The Christian Democrats' support arises from the conservative sectors of society, such as members of the middle class and religious voters. Of the CDU/CSU voters in 1987, 56 percent were Catholics, although Catholics constitute only about 45 percent of the population. Residents of Southern Germany (Bavaria and Baden-Württemberg) and rural areas constitute another substantial proportion of the party's electoral coalition.

The SPD's base is almost a mirror image of the CDU/CSU's. A disproportionate share of the Social Democratic voters come from the working class or households with a union member. The party's strength is concentrated in the central and northern states of Hesse, Northrhine-Westphalia, Bremen, and Hamburg, especially in the cities. Protestants and nonreligious voters are also disproportionately represented in the party.

The narrowing of policy differences between the CDU/CSU and SPD has produced a substantial overlap in the coalition each party represents. Although the CDU/CSU is perceived as the party of the middle class, 38 percent of its voters come from the working class, and 16 percent are union members. Similarly, one-half of the SPD's support now comes from middle-class voters—especially the salaried white-collar employees and civil servants who comprise the new

TABLE IX.5 *Socioeconomic Composition of the Parties in the 1987 Bundestag Elections*

	Greens	SPD	FDP	CDU/CSU	Total Public
Occupation					
Old middle class	13%	7%	14%	15%	12%
New middle class	59	43	55	47	46
Workers	28	50	27	38	42
Union member in house					
Yes	36	42	18	16	28
No	64	58	82	84	72
Education					
Primary	30	68	33	60	60
Secondary	48	26	35	32	31
Advanced	22	6	32	8	10
Religion					
Catholic	42	38	34	56	45
Protestant	43	55	63	41	49
Other, none	13	7	3	3	6
Church attendance					
Frequent	12	12	18	29	20
Occasionally	30	45	50	49	46
Seldom, never	58	43	32	22	34
Region					
North	22	25	6	18	21
Central	46	40	46	35	38
South	32	35	48	47	41
Size of town					
Less than 20,000	34	34	49	44	40
20-100,000	29	26	12	26	25
More than 100,000	37	40	39	30	35
Age					
Under 40	82	38	47	31	40
40-59	13	35	20	37	33
60 and over	5	27	33	32	27

Source: January 1987 West German Election Study. Mannheim: Forschungs-gruppe Wahlen (N = 1545). These data are available from the Zentralarchiv für empirische Sozialforschung in Cologne.

middle class. In recent Bundestag elections this social stratum has split its votes almost equally between the CDU/CSU and the SPD.

The one party with a distinct electoral base is the Greens. Party voters are predominantly from the groups identified with the New Politics movement.[29] The party is a representative of the better-educated, new middle class. Although only 10 percent of the population has advanced education, 22 percent of the Green voters do. Moreover, Greens also have ties to secular and urban interests. The most striking social differences in party support are based on age group; most Green voters (82 percent) are under forty.

The declining emphasis on traditional social cleavages has not totally dismantled the social bases of party support, but it has stimulated significant changes in the West German electorate. Even voters with a well-defined position in the social structure are now less likely to rely on social cues as a basis of their voting decisions, because these cues are less relevant to their political interests. Moreover, the transformation of West German society has freed a substantial number of voters from the traditional network of social alignments. The most noticeable example of this partisan change is the new middle class. This social stratum belongs neither to the unionized working class nor the old middle class of business owners and the self-employed. Consequently, the voting patterns of the new middle class are difficult to predict and subject to greater change between elections. The secularization of West German society similarly lessens the salience of religious cues. This independence from traditional cleavages is especially evident among the younger voters reared in a period when social divisions are waning.

West German electoral politics has gradually shifted the bases of party coalitions away from socioeconomic groups to issue-based groups, that is, individuals with similar ideological and issue positions. Most elections, after all, are not conflicts over historical social cleavages, but deal with more contemporary problems (which, of course, might reflect long-term conflicts). More and more, voters select the party that is politically compatible with their views, rather than the party that is socially compatible. The addition of new interests to the political agenda has further eroded the parties' traditional social bases of support; for instance, middle-class voters are drawn to the SPD on social policy issues and working class voters gravitate to the Union parties on security issues.

The growing electoral importance of policy positions has led the parties to alter their policy images. The public's placement of the parties along a general scale of Left/Right political orientations illustrates these changing images (Figure IX.3). The voters' own self-placement is virtually unchanged through the 1980s (the average was 6.3 in 1980, 6.2 in 1983, and 6.1 in 1987), but other significant aspects of the partisan landscape are shifting.

Public perceptions of the two minor parties changed substantially

FIGURE IX.3 *Party Positions along the Left/Right Scale*

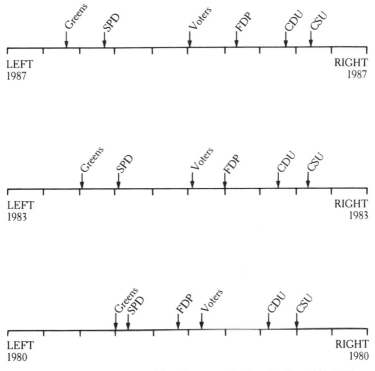

Source: Forschungsgruppe Wahlen, German Election Studies, 1980–1987.

Note: Figure entries are the average location that voters give to the parties on an 11-point Left/Right scale, and the voters' own self-placement.

during this decade. As they exchanged coalition partners, the Free Democrats jumped from left of center in 1980 to the conservative side in subsequent elections. This dramatic ideological shift was accompanied by a restructuring of the party's electoral coalition; middle-class conservatives replaced liberal defectors. The public's image of the Greens also changed. In 1980, the Greens were still a heterogeneous group of ecologists, and the party's overall image was very similar to that of the SPD. The Greens have moved steadily leftward since 1980, until they now occupy a position near the very end of the political spectrum.

The images of the major parties are also evolving, albeit at a slower pace. The SPD has attempted to consolidate the leftist opposition to the CDU government by strengthening its stance on Old Left and New Left issues. On one track, the party has rallied to the defense of unemployed workers and challenged CDU efforts to cut back on social programs enacted under earlier SPD-led governments. On the other track, recent SPD party congresses have passed liberal resolutions on NATO missiles and nuclear power in an attempt to attract voters from the Greens. This twin-track policy slowly shifts the SPD leftward in the public's eye. Conversely, the conservative economic and social program of the government produces a corresponding rightward drift in CDU and CSU party images.

The clarity of the policy options provided by the political parties

TABLE IX.6 *Public Issue Opinions and Issue Images of the Parties*

	Public Preferences	Perceived Party Agreement with Policy			
		Greens	SPD	FDP	CDU/CSU
Economic Issues					
Tax incentives for business	61%	8%	31%	75%	86%
Reduce national debt	54	10	25	66	85
Limit unemployment compensation	54	9	24	61	79
Relax rent controls	24	3	15	55	75
Do not increase taxes on wealthy	11	10	8	34	27
Increase medical copayments	9	2	21	55	75
Foreign Policy Issues					
Work closely with U.S.	44	4	31	67	82
Station NATO missiles	25	2	20	58	82
New Politics Issues					
Stronger environmental laws	80	83	62	55	58
Halt nuclear power construction	35	89	24	5	2
Initiate referendum	43	58	20	12	12
Other Issues					
Limit number of guestworkers	64	15	35	57	86
Stricter abortion limitations	35	5	12	32	72
Longer alternative service	30	3	16	48	76

Source: Forschungsgruppe Wahlen, *West German Election Study* (March 1983). Table entries for the public are the percentages considering each issue as good for the nation to pursue; party entries are public perceptions of whether the party favors the issue.

has apparently increased during this decade.[30] Some analysts consequently speak of the growing bipolarization of the West German party system—between the two governing parties and two opposition parties—but this oversimplifies the choices. Rather than competing along only one issue, parties compete across many political issues, and the relative positions of the parties is not always the same.

Public perceptions of the policy differences among the parties in the 1983 elections illustrate the policy diversity offered to the West German electorate (Table IX.6). The major economic issues facing society—taxes, unemployment, federal deficits, and the need to strengthen the economy—can be placed along the traditional lines of Left/Right conflict in the West German party system: economic competition between the haves and have-nots. On virtually all of these issues, the public perceives a fairly clear Left/Right ordering of the parties. For example, few voters (8 percent) think the Greens favor tax incentives for business; this percentage steadily increases as attention shifts to the SPD (31 percent), the FDP (75 percent), and the CDU/CSU (86 percent). The Greens have outflanked the SPD on all of these issues, to stand as the clearest advocate of an extreme Leftist viewpoint. The FDP maintains a centrist posture, and the CDU/CSU has a markedly conservative economic image. The impact of these issue images on voting patterns far exceeds the influence of social characteristics, even though these issues reflect class-based concerns.[31]

There is a similar polarization of party images or most other issues. The most pressing foreign policy issues in 1983—relations with the United States and the stationing of NATO missiles—exhibit sharp, step-like party differences in public perceptions from the Greens to the CDU/CSU. The same applies to domestic issues, such as limiting the number of guestworkers and restricting abortions. The West German public perceives great diversity in party policy positions.

A major exception to this basic Left/Right party alignment involves New Politics issues. On these issues, the political divide generally separates the Greens from the three established parties. The Greens are clearly seen as advocates for strict environmental regulation, limitations on nuclear power, and the further democratization of society through the use of referendums. The SPD, FDP and CDU/CSU are perceived as holding more conservative and generally similar views on these matters. This lack of responsiveness to

New Politics issues is what necessitated the formation of a new party, the Greens, to represent these issues within the policy process. Moreover, the Greens' positions are seen as closer to the public's on these issues than are the policies of the governing parties.

The contemporary West German party system is thus structured around three broad policy coalitions.[32] The CDU/CSU and FDP represent the conservative pole in partisan politics, offering voters some choice in advocating policies oriented toward conservative economic and social policies. The SPD is the voice of the Old Left constituency, advocating extensive social programs and policies to protect the average working person. The Greens represent the New Left, espousing environmental protection, participatory politics, and quality of life issues.

It is likely that all three of these political currents will continue to drive partisan politics in the years ahead, but it is still too early to determine how these pressures may reshape the party system. Outflanked on both sides, the SPD continues to explore new ways to broaden the base of the party's support. The Christian Democrats are likewise responding to the public's new interest in environmental issues with policy initiatives far beyond those of its Social Democratic predecessors. Given the unconventionality of the Greens, predicting their future is nearly impossible.

NOTES

1. Gerhard Loewenberg, "The Remaking of the German Party System," in *Germany at the Polls,* ed. Karl Cerny (Washington: American Enterprise Institute, 1979).

2. Small extremist parties on the right and left challenged this consensus but garnered few votes. Eventually the failure of these extremist parties to endorse the democratic consensus led to the courts banning the neo-Nazi Socialist Reich party as unconstitutional in 1952 and the Comunist party in 1956.

3. Kenneth Dyson, "Party Government and Party State," in *Party Government and Political Culture in Western Germany,* ed. Herbert Döring and Gordon Smith (New York: St. Martin's, 1982), p. 84.

4. Gordon Smith, *Democracy in Western Germany,* 3rd ed. (New York: Holmes and Meier, 1986); Döring and Smith, ed. *Party Government and Political Culture in Western Germany;* Francis Castles and Rudolf Wildenmann, eds., *Visions and Realities of Party Government* (Berlin: deGruyter, 1986); Richard Katz, ed. *The Future of Party Government* (Berlin: deGruyter, 1987), especially chapter by Rudolf Wildenmann.

5. Kurt Sontheimer, *The Government and Politics of West Germany* (New York: Praeger, 1973), p. 95.

6. Joachim Rashke, ed. *Bürger und Parteien* (Opladen: Westdeutscher Verlag, 1982). For a contrasting view see Klaus von Beyme, *Political Parties in Western Democracies* (New York: St. Martin's Press, 1985).

7. Geoffrey Pridham, *Christian Democracy in Western Germany* (New York: St. Martin's Press, 1977).

8. See Otto Kirchheimer, "Germany: The Vanishing Opposition," in *Political Oppositions in Western Democracies*, ed. Robert Dahl (New Haven: Yale University Press, 1966).

9. Gerard Braunthal, *The West German Social Democrats, 1969–1982* (Boulder: Westview Press, 1983; Douglas Chalmers, *The Social Democratic Party of Germany* (New Haven: Yale University Press, 1966); David Childs, *From Schumacher to Brandt: The Story of German Socialism, 1945–1965* (Oxford: Oxford University Press, 1966).

10. Although the SPD's opposition to the Third Reich may have partially rehabilitated its image, popular doubts about the party soon returned. See Kendall Baker, Russell Dalton, and Kai Hildebrandt, *Germany Transformed* (Cambridge: Harvard University Press, 1981), pp. 234–39.

11. Gerard Braunthal, "The West German Social Democrats: Factionalism at the Local Level," *West European Politics* 7 (1984); Ursula Feist and Klaus Liepelt, "Neue Eliten in alten Parteien," in *Wahlen und politisches System*, ed. Max Kaase and Hans-Dieter Klingemann (Opladen: Westdeutscher Verlag, 1983).

12. Christian Soe, "The Free Democratic Party," in *West German Politics in the Mid-Eighties*, ed. H. Peter Wallach and George Romoser (New York: Praeger, 1985); Emil Kirchner and David Broughton, "The FDP in the Federal Republic of Germany," in *Liberal Parties in Western Europe*, ed. Emil Kirchner (Cambridge: Cambridge University Press, forthcoming).

13. Soe, "The Free Democratic Party," p. 124.

14. Gerd Langguth, *The Green Factor in German Politics: From Protest Movement to Political Party* (Boulder: Westview Press, 1986); Donald Schoonmaker, "Greens—Between Party and Movement," in *Why Parties Fail*, ed. Peter Merkl and Kay Lawson (Princeton: Princeton University Press, 1988); Horst Mewes, "The Green Party Comes of Age," *Environment* (1985).

15. The average Green deputy in 1983 was nearly a decade younger than the typical Bundestag member, and six of the ten youngest deputies in Parliament were Greens.

16. See the extensive material on party structures in Stephen Padgett and Tony Burkett, *Political Parties and Elections in West Germany* (New York: St. Martin's Press, 1986).

17. Robert Michels, *Political Parties: A Sociological Study of the Oligarchical Tendencies of Modern Democracy* (New York: Collier Books, 1962).

18. Herbert Kitschelt, *The Logic of Party Formation* (Ithaca: Cornell University Press, 1989).

19. Kitschelt, *The Logic of Party Formation*.

20. Brigette Jäger and Claudia Pinl, *Zwischen Rotation und Routine: Die Grünen im Bundestag* (Kiepenheur und Witseh, 1985).

21. Because of the public accountability requirements for the West German parties, extensive information is available on the level and general sources of party finances. See *Datenhandbuch zur Geschichte des Deutschen Bundestages 1949 bis 1982*, p. 94ff; Arthur Gunlicks, "Campaign and Party Finance in the West German 'Party State'," *Review of Politics* 50 (Winter 1988): 30–48.

22. Rashke, ed. *Bürger und Parteien;* Merkl and Lawson, ed. *When Parties Fail.*

23. U.S. Information Agency, "West Germany's Successor Generation: Their Social Values," Research Memorandum (Washington, D.C.: U.S. Information Agency, 1984).

24. Max Kaase, "Personalized Proportional Representation," in *Choosing an Electoral System*, ed. Arend Lijphart and Bernard Grofman (New York: Praeger, 1984).

25. Barbara Farah, *Representation in West Germany*, PhD dissertation (Ann Arbor: University of Michigan, 1980).

26. Russell Dalton, "The German Party System Between two Ages," in *Electoral Change in Advanced Industrial Democracies*, ed. Russell Dalton et al. (Princeton: Princeton University Press, 1984).

27. Baker et al., *Germany Transformed*, ch. 8; Franz Pappi and Michael Terwey, "The German Electorate," in *Party Government and Political Culture in Western Germany*, eds. Herbert Döring and Gordon Smith.

28. Russell Dalton, *Citizen Politics in Western Democracies* (Chatham, N.J.: Chatham House Publishers, 1988), ch. 8; David Conradt and Russell Dalton, "The West German Electorate and the Party System," *Review of Politics* 50 (Winter 1988).

29. Wilhelm Bürklin, "The Greens: Ecology and the New Left," in *West German Politics in the Mid-eighties*, eds. H. Wallach and G. Romoser.

30. See the supporting evidence in Hans-Dieter Klingmann's analyses of public perceptions of the parties over time, "Der vorsichtig abwägende Wähler: Einstellungen zu den politischen Parteien und Wahlabsicht," in *Wahlen und politischer Prozess*, eds. Hans-Dieter Klingemann and Max Kaase (Opladen: Westdeutscher Verlag, 1986); also see Wilhelm Bürklin and Werner Kaltefleiter, "Die Bundestagswahl 1987: Streitfragen einer neuen Konfliktdimension," *Zeitschrift für Politik* 34 (1987): 400–425.

31. Manfred Küchler, "Maximizing Utility at the Polls," *European Journal for Political Research* 14 (1986): 81–95.

32. Claus Offe, "New Social Movements," *Social Research* 52 (Winter 1985): 856–868.

CHAPTER X

Policy as a Process

DEMANDS FOR ACTION converge on government from many different directions: citizens, interest groups, political leaders, and government officials. All of these demands often interact in making public policy; therefore it is difficult to trace the true genesis of any specific policy proposal. Once a new policy is proposed, moreover, other interests and political actors come into play in supporting, amending, or opposing the policy.

Still, at some point a new proposal must enter the stream of formal policy making in order to be considered as a public policy. The articulation of interests must lead to formal consideration by the institutions of government, because governmental institutions are responsible for the allocation of public resources. Depending on the nature and scope of the issue, its resolution might take place at the local, state, or federal level. Some cases involve only administrative decisions by a government agency; others can be resolved only by new legislation.

Although we may speak of policy making as a single process, no single model explains how all policies are made. Even at the national level, the pattern of interaction among policy actors varies with time and the nature of the issues. One set of groups focus their attention on issues of industrial relations, for example, using the methods of influence that will be most successful for their cause. In one instance, this would be an appeal to a federal ministry for new legislation; in other cases, interest groups approach sympathetic members of Parliament or seek to change policy through the courts. A very different set of interests may assert themselves on defense policy, and possibly use different methods of influence. Even within a policy domain, specific issues cause particular constellations of political forces and distinct patterns of decision making. In different cases, the executive branch, the legislature, or the courts are the authoritative decision-maker. Indeed, one of the most distinctive aspects of the West German policy process is the dispersion of power and the diversity of institutions involved in the process.[1]

Despite this variation in the policy process, the formal governmental framework for implementing public policy is relatively uniform in all policy areas. The Basic Law defines the structure for passing new legislation and judicial review of this legislation. The standing orders of Parliament determine how legislative proposals are evaluated and decided. Similarly, the rules of procedure guide federal ministries in initiating legislative proposals and consulting with relevant interests. Furthermore, the norms of policy behavior, or what might be called a West German policy style, guide the actions of policy makers within this process. This chapter examines this formal and informal framework of policy action in the Federal Republic, describing the various political arenas in which policy actors compete, and considers the balance of power between these institutions.

EXECUTIVE ACTION

As is the case in most representative democracies, policy initiatives generally come from the executive branch. One reason for the predominance of the executive is that the cabinet and the ministries manage the affairs of government. They are responsible for formulating the federal budget, proposing necessary administrative procedures, and the other basic activities of government. The government also holds specific constitutional responsibilities for formulating legislation dealing with foreign affairs and the budget. The political system of the Federal Republic follows the common pattern, in which the executive generally *proposes* legislation and the Parliament *disposes*.

The chancellor has more influence in policy making than any other single political actor. In contrast to the normal parliamentary system of shared cabinet responsibility, such as in Britain, in the system defined by the Basic Law, the chancellor is formally responsible for determining the broad outlines of government action. The organization of government agencies and the appointment of ministers are the responsibility of the chancellor. Ministers are legally subordinate to the authority of the chancellor. The Basic Law further provides that the chancellor can define the broad policy goals for ministerial action through policy directives (*Richtlinien-kompetenz*). These directives are legally binding guidelines on the policy activities of government agencies; the ministries' policies must follow these broad guidelines.

In actuality, the formal powers of the chancellor are restricted by practical political considerations; coalition partners must be satisfied, ministers often have their own clientele groups to represent, and some policies involve conflicting priorities that are not easily reconciled. In many cases, the chancellor, instead of an independent force, is the balance point between contending forces in the government. Even under Konrad Adenauer, a politically strong chancellor, the majority of cabinet positions were decided by negotiations within the governing coalition of parties. Official policy directives are also used sparingly, usually when a consensus on policy already exists within the governing coalition. The formal authority of the chancellor vis-à-vis the cabinet thus lies between the U.S. model of a presidential cabinet and the British system of shared cabinet responsibility.

The policy influence of the chancellor also stems from the informal political resources of the office. Standing at the head of the party list at election time, the chancellor candidate is the primary policy spokesperson for the party and the prospective government. The public's images of the chancellor candidates play a prominent role in federal election campaigns, even though people do not directly vote for the individual candidates. The 1980 election focused on the differences between Schmidt and Strauss, for example, just as the personalities of Kohl and Rau were an important part of the 1987 campaign. Once in government, the chancellor articulates the administration's policy agenda in speeches, interviews, and formal policy declarations. At the start of each parliamentary session, the chancellor provides a blueprint for government action through the rest of the term (*Regierungserklärung*). Because the chancellor can speak both as the head of government and leader of the majority of the Bundestag, the public generally equates the chancellor's views with those of the government.

The chancellor defines the broad course of government policy, but many policy proposals come from the ministries. Each of the seventeen cabinet ministries has its own distinct area of responsibility (Table X.1). The main function of each ministry is to develop and review policy proposals. Indeed, the staffs of most ministries are so small that they cannot hope to oversee the administration of policy, and they lack the legal right to supervise the implementation of

TABLE X.1 *Federal Government Ministries in 1987*

Ministry	Minister's Party
Foreign Affairs	FDP
Interior	CSU
Justice	FDP
Finance	CDU
Economics	FDP
Food, Agriculture, Forestry	CSU
Labor and Social Affairs	CDU
Defense	CDU
Youth, Family Affairs, and Health	CDU
Transport	CSU
Post and Telecommunications	CDU
Regional Planning, Building and Urban Development	CSU
Research and Technology	CDU
Intra-German Relations	CDU
Education and Science	FDP
Economic Cooperation	CSU
Environment	CDU

federal statutes in detail. For instance, the Ministry of Justice and the Ministry of Labor and Social Affairs each employs about a 1000 people in their central organizations; by contrast, the U.S. Justice Department employs over 60,000, and the U.S. Labor Department employs 25,000.[2] The bulk of activity in the West German Ministries is devoted to initiating legislation necessary to carry out the government's policy objectives.

Federal ministries are usually fairly hierarchical. Each ministry is divided into departments with specific functions; an average ministry has between five to ten departments. The departments are then further divided into smaller sections (*Referate*). These sections are small working groups of maybe a dozen people, each possessing a specialized policy responsibility. Department and section heads are formally responsible for the activities of their units, and every organizational unit protectively guards its area of authority.

Policy initiatives usually emerge from a dialogue between the political leadership of the ministry and the specialized experts of the ministry sections. The impetus for action on major new policy initiatives or on politically controversial proposals comes from the minister's or chancellor's office. The minister's office defines specific policy needs and determines how legislation should be formulated; the relevant sections then draft the necessary legislative proposals.

For most routine legislation, policy proposals are initiated at the section level. Using their expertise and prompted by the demands of relevant interest groups, the bureaucracy identifies a policy matter requiring new legislation. Most of these proposals involve changes in existing legislation designed to improve the administration of existing policy goals. Significant new policy proposals also originate within the bureaucracy, however. Most government legislative proposals are first formalized at the section level and then subjected to review and revision by higher administrative units in the government.

The ministries are also the focal points for the lobbying activities of many interest groups. Government administrative regulations *require* that a ministry formally consult with organized interests that are directly affected by a legislative proposal and give the group's representatives sufficient time to formulate a response. Furthermore, the department has the discretion to decide which are the relevant interests for a specific proposal; the tendency is to establish ongoing relationships with the major national interest associations dealing with the general policy responsibilities of the ministry. Interest groups realize the importance of the executive branch, and usually work with the federal ministries—rather than the Parliament—when they seek new legislation. For example, a study of the official policy memoranda of the Federation of German Industry (BDI) in the 1950s found that over 80 percent of the group's policy correspondence was directed toward the executive branch and less than 10 percent went to the legislature;[3] a more recent study would probably find a similar distribution of attention.

The large role of the ministry sections in initiating proposals yields both advantages and disadvantages for the overall policy process. On the one hand, the sections possess considerable technical and administrative expertise in their area of policy responsibility. This reliance on the bureaucracy presumably makes for more rational and efficient policy by treating problems in "objective" terms. The bureaucracy further provides a continuity in policy experience that transcends changes in administrations and political leadership.

On the other hand, this bureaucratic approach to policy making also contains distinct limitations.[4] In most government agencies the minister's own office has a very limited staff, which restricts his or her ability to provide political direction to the numerous sections under the minister's control. As a result, political control of section activities is based as much on the sections anticipating the reactions of their superiors as on formal control from the top. In private, most ministers admit that they sometimes feel the bureaucracy is running the ministry.

The hierarchical rigidity of the bureaucracy affects the policy process by limiting broad policy planning. Ministry sections are small organizational units with narrow policy responsibilities. The sections consequently are concerned with formulating specific proposals and in responding to policy demands from above. Inter-action over policy proposals occurs vertically, through the hierar-chy, seldom horizontally, across department or section boundaries. The sections define policy issues so that they fit the organizational structure, rather than developing intersection or interdepartment task forces that can deal with a policy area in its entirety. (A few interdepartment task forces do exist.) This procedure tends to com-partmentalize policy making. The major problems of contemporary societies seldom fit into small, well-defined policy boxes, however. The Federal Republic's increasing need for policy planning that anticipates future programs is ill-served by this bureaucratic style of policy making. Ministry sections think small and react to demands, rather than considering large issues and potential issues.

Efforts to develop a more active and planned style of policy mak-ing have not proven workable so far. Some ministries experimented with a central planning and coordination department under the min-ister's direction, but the other departments within the ministry often viewed this as a restriction on their authority and were uncoopera-tive. At present, most departments have their own planning and analysis effort. This helps coordinate the activities of sections in the department, but still leaves the minister with overall coordination and control problems. Ministers must depend on political appointees to coordinate the activities of the various departments and provide a broader, forward-looking view of agency priorities.

Before a ministry finalizes legislative proposal, they circulated it among other ministries with related policy interests. For example, a bill dealing with drug addiction might be referred to the Youth and Family Ministry, the Justice Ministry, and the Labor and Social Affairs Ministry. These ministerial exchanges are attempts to con-firm that a consensus exists before the proposal is submitted to the full cabinet. The chancellor exercises a crucial part in ensuring this consensus. The chancellor's office coordinates the legislative proposals drafted by the various ministries. If the chancellor believes that a bill conflicts with the government's stated objectives, he may ask that the bill be withdrawn or returned to the ministry for restudy and redrafting. If a conflict on policy arises between two ministries, the chancellor mediates the dispute, or the ministries negotiate to resolve their difference. Only in extreme cases are the ministries unable to reach an agreement; when this happens, policy conflicts can be referred to the full cabinet.

Legislative proposals are approved by the cabinet before being advanced to the Parliament. In addition to this hurdle, the ministers of Interior, Finance, and Justice can veto proposals that conflict with the authority of these ministries; for instance, the Finance minister can veto bills that exceed the government's budget.[5] The decision-making process in the cabinet emphasizes consensus, and there are few formal votes. Because of its large size and full agenda, the opportunity for extensive discussion and policy formation at the cabinet level is limited. In most cases cabinet members ratify policy proposals that already were worked out in interministerial negotiations or in the policy subcommittees of the cabinet. By one account, 75 percent of the cabinet proposals in the Brandt administration were passed without discussion. In a minority of cases—often the most politically important—the cabinet is called upon to resolve policy conflicts between contending ministries or the parties in the governing coalition.

The chancellor plays an important part in setting the pattern of cabinet activity and in directing the outcome. The chancellor balances the conflicting interests of the ministries in order to reach an agreement that the government as a whole can support. The chancellor is more than just a fulcrum, however; a strong chancellor can set the government's policy goals and shape the policy alternatives under consideration by the cabinet. The dual role of government and party leader gives the chancellor considerable influence with cabinet members. Seldom does a majority of the cabinet oppose the chancellor.

Each chancellor has exercised his own "cabinet style" in setting the pattern of cabinet activity. Konrad Adenauer's (1949–1963) forceful leadership style made the West German system the model of "chancellor democracy." Adenauer directed the government; ministers were subordinates, expected to follow the chancellor's policy directives. Even when confronted with opposition from within the government, Adenauer displayed an uncanny ability to adjust his political position and control the outcome. Helmut Schmidt (1974–1982) was another strong chancellor. Schmidt approached the office like the chairman of the board for a large corporation. His political influence was derived from the strength of his personality and knowledge accumulated through a series of governmental offices. Schmidt's strong management style developed his reputation of a *Macher* (doer), a man who could get things done.

Other chancellors used a more open cabinet style. The sharing of governing responsibility during the Grand Coalition, for instance, led to a style of shared cabinet responsibility under Kurt Georg Kiesinger (1966–1969). Willy Brandt's cabinet style (1969–1974) was more eclectic; he was not one for formal detail and strict management procedures. Especially during Brandt's second term in office, cabinet meetings often rambled, with little structure or direction from the chancellor. Brandt was a decisive leader on matters of foreign policy, but on domestic issues the cabinet followed a very collegial and unstructured style of decision making.

The present chancellor, Helmut Kohl (1982), follows a decision-making style markedly different from that of his predecessor. He emphasizes the consensus building function of his role, trying to find the middle ground rather than controlling the policy process.[6] Instead of relying on the formal deliberations of the cabinet, for policy advice, the chancellor draws upon an informal network of policy advisors developed over years as the head of the Christian Democratic Union. Kohl has also deemphasized the central planning activities of the chancellor's office, giving the ministries more latitude in their actions.

While executive action generally follows a predictable pattern, each legislative proposal has its own life history. Throughout this chapter we will illustrate some of the possible variations in this process with the life history of two policy initiatives.

One proposal was for legislation to ensure that new chemicals on the market are safe for consumers.[7] The initiative for the proposal was a call for chemical safety standards issued by the Commission of the European Community in 1976. Officials of the German Chemical Industry Federation (VCI) worked in close consultation with the section in the Economics Ministry responsible for chemical industry (*Chemie Referat*). Together they drafted a proposal that called for only modest testing and reporting procedures on new products. At the same time, a working group in the Interior Ministry, which was then responsible for environmental policy, began drafting stricter regulations of chemical products. The views of the Economics Ministry and the VCI eventually won out, and their proposal was presented to the European Community in the name of the West German government.

Less typical is the case of reform in the criminal law prohibiting abortion. The initiative for action came from outside the formal institutions of government; during the early 1970s, women's groups and liberal politicians pressed for reform of the law banning abortions as a criminal offense (§ 218). The cabinet was internally divided on the issue; most FDP leaders favored liberalizing abortion regulations, as did many SPD ministers. Other SPD ministers, however, some with strong ties to religious groups, opposed reform or were hesitant to deal with such a sensitive political issue. In addition, Brandt and other SPD leaders worried that enacting a liberal abortion law might jeopardize the party's improving relationship with the Catholic church. The task of drafting legislation fell to the Justice Ministry. Nearly a dozen draft proposals were circulated within the government during the first Brandt administration, but none was able to satisfy the widely divergent views of the cabinet. The lack of cabinet agreement forestalled government action, although public pressure for reform continued to mount. This case illustrates the convergence of several influences in the initiation of a policy proposal. Furthermore, once a policy comes under consideration, cabinet consensus is necessary before the government will undertake a major policy initiative, especially if the issue evokes intense political feelings.

LEGISLATING POLICY

Most laws begin as cabinet proposals to Parliament. Since the formation of the Bonn Republic, about two-thirds of the legislation considered by Parliament originated in the cabinet, and the proportion of government initiatives has gradually increased over the years (Figure X.1). The second source of legislative initiative is the Bundestag itself. Thirty members of the Bundestag may jointly introduce a bill. Bundestag proposals accounted for nearly 40 percent of all legislation in the first several parliaments, but the percentage has fallen to about 20 percent in recent parliaments. Besides being scarce, most proposals originating in the Bundestag are of limited political significance; they deal with minor matters and are some-

FIGURE X.1 *The Sources of Legislative Proposals, 1949–1986*

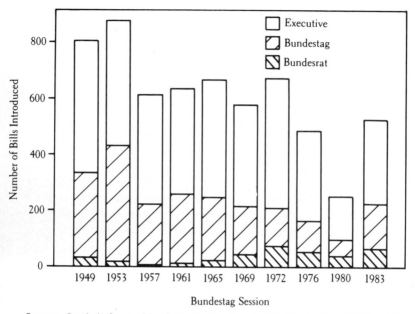

Bundestag Session

Source: *Statistisches Jarhbuch für die Bundesrepublik Deutschland 1987,* p. 92

what equivalent to the private member bills in the U.S. Congress. Opposition parties sometimes offer Bundestag proposals for their public relations value, but these have little chance of passage because the sponsoring party is in the minority. The Bundesrat is the third and final source of legislative proposals, but because it requires a majority of state governments in the Bundesrat to propose legislation, Bundesrat initiatives are infrequent. Even when the opposition CDU/CSU controlled the upper chamber during the late 1970s, barely one-tenth of all legislative proposals were introduced by the state governments.

Although the legislative process sometimes has the appearance of a maze, it is possible to track the normal course of policy proposals through it (Figure X.2). Government legislative proposals are first submitted to the Bundesrat for review. The Bundesrat has six weeks to respond to most government proposals; this review period may be cut to three weeks if the government requests urgent consideration. Because of this short time frame, most proposals are examined

FIGURE X.2 *The Legislative Process*

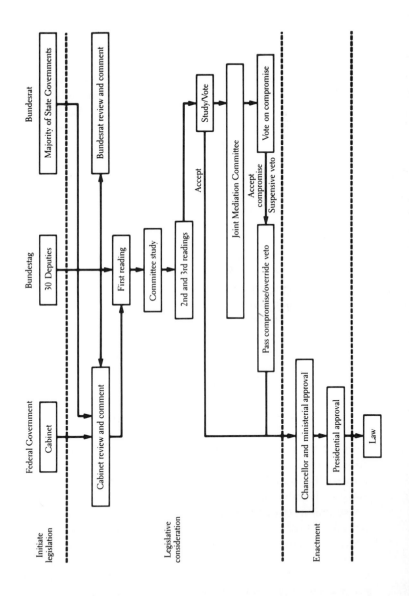

in committee. This brief review primarily serves to inform the Bundesrat of the government's intentions and to provide the states with an opportunity to react. The Bundesrat's comments are transmitted to the cabinet, which then forwards the proposal to the Bundestag along with these comments and the government's response.

Legislation that originates in the Bundesrat is sent to the cabinet for comment and transmission to the Bundestag. Proposals that originate in the Bundestag can bypass these initial reviews and receive immediate consideration by the chamber. In a few instances of pressing urgency, the government has had its own proposals submitted by a group of Bundestag deputies in order to avoid the delay of Bundesrat review.

Once submitted to the Bundestag, legislative proposals are referred to the Council of Elders. The relevant party working groups almost simultaneously begin to review the bill; throughout the legislative process party deliberations will parallel the formal actions of Parliament. The proposal is placed on the legislative calendar for a first reading before the Bundestag. The first reading has gradually become a formality, with most policy discussions and party debate reserved for later steps in the process. If a majority of the Bundestag supports a proposal, the Council of Elders refers it to the relevant committee or committees.

Much of the real work of the Bundestag takes place in these specialized committees.[8] The committee structure generally follows the divisions of the federal ministries, such as finance, transportation, budget, labor, or agriculture. In marked contrast to the United States, the committee chairperson positions are proportionally allocated to all parties in the Bundestag, giving the opposition parties the leadership of several major committees. Within each committee, however, the governing parties constitute a majority of the membership, so that party control of committee chairs is less significant than in the U.S. Congress. The committees have reasonably sized staffs and access to the policy research of the party Fraktionen. These committees provide the Bundestag with a basis of policy expertise to review and amend government proposals.

Most committees meet behind closed doors, but official published reports and informal accounts provide a detailed picture of what transpires in these smoke-filled rooms.[9] The executive and legislative branch work hand-in-hand in the committees. Indeed, the Basic Law (Article 43) ensures that government representatives have "access to all meetings of the Bundestag and its committees. They must be heard at any time." The ministries frequently send representatives to committee meetings. Usually there is an unfettered interchange between the ministry and committee members. The ministry representative is not a witness but a participant in the process, joining in on committee discussions, explaining the background of legislation, and providing policy expertise. These government–committee ties inevitably strengthen over time, and government officials can become virtual nonvoting committee members.

The committees also provide an opportunity for interest groups to influence the policy process. Usually, sympathetic deputies on the committee represent concerned interest groups.[10] Farming interests are understandably overrepresented among members of the Food and Agriculture Committee, just as union and business representatives are concentrated in the Labor and Social Policy Committee. Interest groups can also submit written statements or ask to testify before the committee. Public hearings enable some interest groups to continue lobbying activity that began during preparation of the bill, and broadens policy access to include other interests excluded at the ministerial level. The Bundestag uses its committees for policy input more than most legislatures, but there are very few open committee meetings. About 90 percent of the committee sessions in the U.S. Congress, for instance, are open to the public, compared to less than 10 percent in the Bundestag.

The dynamics of committee decision making are a mix of partisan considerations and the shared policy interests of committee members. Most legislative proposals involve simple administrative procedures or minor policy issues. On these matters, the committee acts as a group of experts, focusing on the legalities. The intent is to ensure that the legislation is formally correct and adequate for the purpose intended. Partisan and political considerations play a secondary role, and committee members usually can achieve a consensus on these proposals.

When policy conflicts appear within committees, they generally follow partisan lines. Committee members from each party usually act as a bloc in presenting viewpoints previously endorsed by the party Fraktion. Occasionally the conflict may transcend party lines, as when dissension in the cabinet carries over to parliamentary deliberations or when a parliamentary party delegation differs from its cabinet leadership. Even in these conflicts, however, the internal dynamics of most committees encourage cooperation and compromise between contending factions. Rather than following a strategy of fundamental opposition and losing all influence over committee decisions, the minority party frequently proposes amendments that might win majority support. This consensual style is facilitated by the closed-door setting of most committee meetings and the reliance on informal rules of procedure, which encourage consensus-building and unanimity. Both the SPD and CDU/CSU practiced this style of moderate opposition during their recent experiences on the minority side of the aisle. Only the Greens regularly shun this cooperative style and strive to maintain their ideological purity. Yet even the Green deputies come to committee sessions well-prepared to represent their party's viewpoint. Most committees are therefore instruments for party action, although some of the prestigious committees—such as Judiciary, Defense, Foreign Affairs, and Interior—have enough political stature to maintain somewhat more independence from the party leadership.

The bills reported out of committee are far along the way to passage. The committees assimilate the interests of the government and Parliament. Government proposals often undergo substantial revision in the committees, and relatively few changes occur on the floor of Parliament. The advice of committee members usually carries over to party positions in the full Bundestag. By the time a committee is through working, the fate of most legislative proposals has been determined.

When a bill is reported out of committee, it goes before the full Bundestag for a second reading. The proposed legislation is discussed in plenary session, and amendments may be offered. At this point in the legislative process, political positions already are well established. Leaders in the governing parties participated in the initial formulation of the legislation, and the party Fraktionen in the Bundestag have determined the official party position in caucus. Major revisions during the second reading are infrequent; the government generally is assured of the passage of its proposals as reported out of committee.

Bundestag debate on the merits of government proposals is thus mostly symbolic. Eberhard Schuett-Wetschky describes the major parliamentary debates as "political battles" fought with rhetorical weapons in which the parties and political leaders present their views to the German public.[11] The successful parties explain the merits of the new legislation and advertise the efforts they made in behalf of their supporters. The opposition parties use the debates to place their objections in the public record and draw public attention to the faults of the government. Although these debates seldom influence the outcome of a vote, they are nevertheless an important part of the Bundestag's informational function.

If a bill passes the second reading without amendment, it can immediately be considered for a third reading and final passage. If amendments are added, final consideration is delayed for at least a day to allow deputies and party Fraktionen to review the final proposal. After the third reading, a final vote is taken. Voting on most bills is done by a voice or standing vote. In cases of doubt, a formal division of the Bundestag occurs: The clerk counts deputies as yeas and nays as they file through separate doors, a procedure colorfully known as the sheep roundup (*Hammelsprung*). The request of at least fifty deputies is necessary to require a roll call, in which the name and vote of each Bundestag deputy is publicly recorded. Roll calls are infrequent, however; the early parliaments held about 150 per session, and recent parliaments have averaged only about 50 roll calls during an entire four-year term (compared to several thousand per two-year term in the U.S. Congress).

Deputies generally stick closely to party lines when voting. The party government model (Chapter IX) presumes that party deputies act as a single unit, casting their vote as a bloc. The parties formalize their position in Fraktion meetings that occur before the plenary sessions. Once party decisions are made, deputies closely follow their party's voting advice; the fluid voting patterns of the U.S. Congress are very different from the predictable party voting patterns of the Bundestag. The roll call votes in the first two years of the tenth Bundestag (1983–1984) show high levels of party cohesion. SPD deputies voted along with their party majority 98.9 percent of the time; the CDU/CSU Fraktion was in 99.9 agreement; FDP deputies supported their party majority on 98.5 percent of their votes; and the Greens displayed party cohesion 94.2 percent of the time. In most cases, it would be more accurate to say that Bundestag voting patterns are based on four party blocs, and not the votes of 496 separate deputies.

Partisan bonds are very strong, but at the same time the political values and principles of the Bundestag encourage cooperation across party lines. In the committees and in interparty negotiations, legislators try to work out compromises that both major parties can accept and support. Cooperation in most cases is simplified because the majority of the Parliament's work is passage of noncontroversial legislation: minor policy proposals or bills aimed at improving the administration of existing policies. In these cases, there is little debate in the plenary sessions and the legislation often receives bipartisan support from the CDU/CSU and SPD. Often, however, even legislation on major policy concerns—social policy, European integration, and foreign affairs—is supported by bipartisan coalitions. Over 80 percent of the legislation in the seventh (1972–1976) and eighth (1976–1980) sessions of the Bundestag passed with nearly unanimous majorities.[12] Klaus von Beyme has shown that this pattern of interparty agreement is nearly uniform across five different policy areas.[13] About two-thirds of all legislation in the five policy areas (1949–1976) was passed by a legislative majority that included a large percentage of the opposition parties.

The extent of partisan cooperation has ebbed and flowed over the past decade. In the early 1970s, the Christian Democrats routinely resisted the government's policy initiatives in an effort to undermine Brandt's bare majority in the legislature. After the failed constructive vote of no-confidence and subsequent SPD landslide in the 1972 elections, the Christian Democrats became more accommodating. The SPD has been somewhat more assertive after moving to the opposition benches in 1982, but compromise between the major parties still typifies most legislative proposals. In fact, only the Greens fail to cooperate, pursuing their course of fundamental opposition to the government's programs.[14]

A bill that successfully passes in the Bundestag goes to the Bundesrat, which represents the state governments in the federal policy process (Chapter II). The legislative authority of the Bundesrat is equal to that of the Bundestag in policy areas where the states share concurrent powers with the federal government or administer federal policies. In these areas, the approval of the Bundesrat is necessary for a bill to become law. In the policy areas that do not involve the states directly, such as defense or foreign affairs, the chamber's approval of legislation is not essential.

This sharing of legislative power between the state and federal governments is a mixed blessing for West German politics. The system introduces flexibility into the policy process. Through their influence on policy making and policy administration, state leaders can adapt legislation to local and regional needs. This division of power furnishes another check in the system of checks and balances by preventing the usurpation of political power by the national government.

The division of power between the two parliamentary bodies also contains some problems. The Bundesrat's voting procedures give disproportionate weight to the smaller states. The five smallest states control more than half the votes in the Bundesrat, even though they represent only one-fourth of the West German population. The Bundesrat thus cannot claim the same popular legitimacy as the proportionately represented and directly elected Bundestag. Moreover, the Bundesrat's voting system can foster parochialism by the states, because each state delegation votes as a bloc; this encourages each state delegation to view policy from the state's perspective rather than the national interest or party positions. The different electoral bases of the Bundestag and Bundesrat make such tensions over policy an inevitable part of the legislative process.

During the 1970s, the control of both legislative bodies was split between the SPD-FDP majority in the Bundestag and the CDU/CSU majority in the Bundesrat. Consequently, policy conflicts were frequent. In one sense, this division strengthened the power of the legislature, because the governing parties often were forced to negotiate with the opposition parties in the Bundesrat. Since the change in government in 1982, both the Bundestag and Bundesrat are controlled by the Christian-Liberal alliance, which may weaken the policy autonomy of Parliament but should produce greater cooperation between the legislative bodies. Parliamentary influence on policy making will continue to be important, but now Parliament works as part of the governing coalition.

As in the Bundestag, much of the Bundesrat's work occurs in specialized committees. State leaders or state civil servants scrutinize bills both for their policy content and their administrative implications for the state governments. After committee review, the bill and the committee's reactions are submitted to the full Bundesrat. If the Bundesrat approves of the measure as passed by the Bundestag, it is transmitted to the chancellor for his signature and promulgation by the federal president.

When the Bundestag and Bundesrat disagree on a legislative proposal, a complex process of negotiation and formal evaluation begins. First, representatives of both bodies attempt to resolve their differences in a Mediation Committee.[15] Unlike the varying membership of the Joint Conference committees of the U.S. Congress, the West German Mediation Committee has a permanent membership (11 Bundestag deputies and 11 Bundesrat representatives) that considers all legislative disagreements between the two chambers.

If the Mediation Committee reaches a compromise, the revised bill is sent first to the Bundestag for approval and then on to the Bundesrat. If the committee cannot agree on a compromise, the Bundesrat has two weeks to vote on the bill as originally passed by the Bundestag. On proposals that involve state responsibilities (which constitutionally require Bundesrat approval)—for example, a public health program that will be administered by the state governments—the Bundesrat may cast an *absolute* veto and the bill cannot become law. In the remaining policy areas, such as a defense policy initiative, the Bundesrat can only cast a *suspensive* veto, which the Bundestag may override. The West German Parliament contains an unusual procedure whereby the intensity of the Bundesrat's opposition determines the requirements for the Bundestag to override the upper chamber's suspensive veto. If the Bundesrat's suspensive veto was supported by a simple majority, a simple majority of the Bundestag is sufficient to overturn the veto and forward the bill to the chancellor. If two-thirds or more of the Bundesrat opposed the bill, then a two-thirds majority of the Bundestag is required.

The political stature of the Bundesrat has grown over the years as the chamber has become more assertive in championing states' rights. In the early parliaments, barely 10 percent of all legislation required Bundesrat approval; today this figure exceeds 60 percent. But the political authority of the Bundesrat is not based solely on its absolute veto. Bundesrat members can draw upon the extensive policy and administrative expertise of their state governments, which provides them with important information resources in evaluating and amending legislative proposals. The administrative responsibilities of the states (see below) give the Bundesrat additional leverage in negotiating with federal policy makers. The Bundesrat also uses the Mediation Committee as a vehicle for revising government proposals, and has been fairly successful with this tactic. The number of bills that the Bundesrat is ultimately forced to veto is almost negligible. In the 1976–1980 legislative session only nine of 354 laws failed passage as a result of Bundesrat opposition.

Throughout the legislative process, the executive branch is omnipresent.[16] After transmitting the government's proposal to the Bundestag, the federal ministries begin working to support the bill. Ministerial representatives participate in the deliberations of Bundestag and Bundesrat committees. Cabinet ministers lobby committee members and influential members of the parliament;

nearly all ministers are themselves Bundestag deputies. Ministers may propose amendments or negotiate policy compromises to resolve issues that arise during parliamentary consideration. Government representatives also are allowed to attend the meetings of the Mediation Committee; no other nonparliamentary participants are allowed.

Although the Parliament may substantially revise the government's proposals or even defeat them, the executive branch retains a dominant influence on the policy process. Figure X.3 shows the proportion of legislative proposals that are actually enacted into law according to their source. Nearly 90 percent of government initiatives eventually become laws, although many are amended in the process. Roughly one-third of the proposals originating in the Bundestag receive passage, and Bundesrat proposals have an even

FIGURE X.3 *The Percentage of Proposals Passed into Law, 1949–1986*

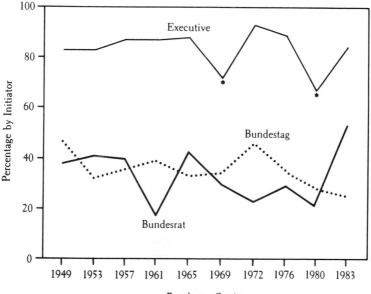

Source: *Statistisches Jahrbuch für die Bundesrepublik Deutschland 1987,* p. 92

*Percentages are exceptionally low in 1969–1972 and 1980–1983 because the legislative sessions were ended prematurely by early elections.

lower success rate. The vast majority of all successful legislation originates in the executive branch.

Our two policy examples—chemical regulations and abortion reform—provide concrete illustrations of the policy process at work. In 1979, the Interior Ministry drafted a bill on the regulation of new chemical products based on the existing statutes of the European Community. Chemical industry officials intensively lobbied the ministry during the drafting stage and had an appreciable impact on the content of the bill.

The ministry submitted the draft bill to the Bundesrat in August 1979. The Bundesrat made 104 recommendations on the proposal, most of which were suggested by representatives of the chemical companies or the BDI. The government accepted 56 of these recommendations and submitted the revised legislation to the Bundestag. The bill went to three committees, which coordinated their work through a subcommittee headed by the deputy from Leverkusen, the home town of the Bayer Corporation, the giant chemical firm. The bill reported out of committee was passed by the Bundestag with only a single SPD deputy dissenting. The revised version was agreed to by the Bundesrat, and thus the government enacted the Chemical Law of 1980.

Bulmer and Patterson conclude that, because of the specialized nature of the legislation and the substantial political clout of the chemical industry, the policy process in this case was dominated by the chemical interests and party political differences played no appreciable role.[17] The chemical lobby even was able to convince Helmut Schmidt to transfer responsibility for the management of the legislative process and the implementation of the law from the Interior Ministry, which normally handled environmental issues, to the Youth, Family and Health Ministry, which was more industry-friendly. This is an example of the extensive influence that established interest groups can wield.

Legislative efforts to reform government restrictions on abortion illustrate the atypical policy case. After the government failed to take the initiative during Brandt's first term in office, four separate pieces of legislation were proposed by groups of Bundestag deputies in 1973. Two proposals originated from the Social Democrats, and two from CDU/CSU deputies. The bills varied in the restrictions on abortions that they retained. The four proposals were referred to a committee, and a year-long set of hearings and deliberations followed. Unable to generate a majority in support of any of the proposals, the committee submitted all four to the Bundestag for its decision. The second reading of these bills sparked an intense debate in the Bundestag. Liberal members of the SPD and FDP argued that criminal penalties for abortion were counterproductive, citing the large number of illegal operations already being performed in the Federal Republic and the maternal deaths resulting from these procedures. Conservative members of the CDU/CSU countered by emphasizing that the right to life included unborn life. Prochoice and prolife groups lobbied parliament intensively.

In April 1974, the Bundestag narrowly passed (247:233:9) the SPD-FDP bill, which contained the most liberal provisions. Abortion during the first three months of pregnancy was permitted on mutual agreement of the doctor and the mother. Two weeks latter, the CDU/CSU-controlled Bundesrat rejected the bill and called for the joint Mediation Committee to consider the upper house's objections. The government maintained that the question of states' rights was not involved in this instance, and thus the Bundesrat could only pass a suspensive veto. Because of the intense political feelings, the Bundestag declined to have the bill reviewed before the Mediation Committee and overrode the Bundesrat's veto. The proposal was soon after enacted into law.

Many more legislative proposals resemble the case of the 1980 Chemicals Law than that of abortion reform. The policy process usually functions according to a consensual style; private negotiations and compromise smooth the road to enacting legislation. Policy conflicts do occur, however. Examples like abortion reform, the co-determination law of 1976, the deployment of NATO missiles in 1983, and more recent debates over revisions of the law on public demonstrations illustrate how intense political conflicts can be managed within the legislative arena.

POLICY ADMINISTRATION

Few federal ministries have the resources necessary to implement and monitor the policies enacted by the federal government. In areas where the federal government has exclusive authority, such as defense and communications, these policies are administered by the federal ministries. In other policy areas, the government has created federal administrative agencies that are responsible for policy administration. For instance, the Federal Labor Agency administers federal labor programs, including unemployment insurance. The agency works under the supervision of the Labor ministry but is not formally part of the ministry.

By and large, however, most domestic administrative responsibilities are assigned to the states. Article 30 of the Basic Law holds that "the exercise of governmental powers and the discharge of governmental functions shall be incumbent on the Länder in so far as this Basic Law does not otherwise prescribe or permit." The West German system of federalism is based on a horizontal division of political responsibilities. The federal government is the prime legislative arena, and the state governments administer policy—even the majority of the policies enacted at the federal level.

One indicator of the states' central administrative role is the distribution of public employees across the three levels of government. If one excludes employees of the post office and railways, barely 10 percent of all government workers in West Germany are employed at the federal level. More civil servants are employed by the state governments than by the federal and local governments combined. The federal government thus depends on the state and local bureaucracies for administration of most domestic programs.

In a limited number of policy areas, the states act as agents of the federal government, and therefore are subject to strict federal supervision. Highway construction is one example; federal funds were used to build the autobahnen, but the actual construction was administered by the Länder as agents of the federal government. In most instances, however, Article 30 grants the states substantial autonomy in how they administer legislation.

Because of this delegation of administrative responsibilities, federal legislation is often fairly detailed, so that the government's intent is followed in the actual application of a law. Federal agencies may review the actions of state agencies, and in cases of dispute apply sanctions or seek judicial review. Yet most legal attempts to restrict the actions of the states have been rebuffed by the courts; and legislative control of the states requires Bundesrat support, where claims for states' rights receive a sympathetic hearing. The Länder thus retain considerable discretion in applying most federal legislation. This decentralization of political authority provides additional flexibility for the West German political system.

JUDICIAL REVIEW

As in the United States, legislation in West Germany is subject to judicial review. A Constitutional Court has the authority to evaluate the constitutionality of legislation, and to void laws that violate the provisions of the Basic Law.

A distinctive feature of the West German judicial system is the open access to the judicial review process. Constitutional issues usually come before the court through one of three ways.[18] The most common way is through constitutional complaints filed by an individual. When citizens feel that their constitutional rights are violated by a government action, they may appeal directly to the Court. The alleged transgression might involve individual rights, those of a business interest, or a corporation. The issues range from complaints about "unconstitutional" taxes to petitions claiming that the government violated the individual's basic human rights. For example, the constitutionality of the 1983 census law was brought before the court by an individual petition, and the court agreed to invalidate parts of the law (and delay the census enumeration) because portions of the law violated the privacy guarantees of the Basic Law. More than 90 percent of the cases presented to the court arise from citizens' complaints, and citizens can file these cases without paying court costs and without a lawyer.

What originally began as a modest stream of citizen complaints has grown to a raging river in recent years. In the early 1950s, there were a few hundred constitutional complaints per year; in 1984, over 3000 separate petitions were filed with the court. To handle these complaints, the court established subcommittees that review submissions for their constitutional significance and decide whether the case should be considered further. Less than 5 percent of complaints are actually heard by the full court, but this still accounts for the majority of the court's decisions. The Constitutional Court is thus something of an ombudsman, assuring the average citizen that his or her fundamental rights are protected by the Basic Law and the Courts.

A second way in which cases reach the Constitutional Court is through the process of *concrete* judicial review. Concrete review is review of actual court cases that raise constitutional issues. Appeal to the Constitutional Court is not automatic, and is not requested by the litigants in a case, as in the U.S. court system. Instead, the lower court certifies that a case involves significant constitutional issues; this may happen even though neither the plaintiff nor the defendant raised the issue in the course of the trial. Once certified, the case goes to the Constitutional Court for review. The court case is merely the stimulus for constitutional review of legislation. The

Constitutional Court reviews the constitutional issues involved rather than acting as an appeal court for the case itself.

The third way in which the Constitutional Court can rule on legislation is through the process of *abstract* judicial review. The court can be asked to review the constitutionality of legislation as a general legal principle without reference to a specific court case. The federal government, a state government, or one-third of the Bundestag deputies can request the review of a law. This procedure is most often used by groups that failed to block a bill during the legislative process. During the 1970s, the CDU/CSU used this method to challenge the constitutionality of the Basic Agreement with East Germany and several other important pieces of legislation. Abstract judicial review substantially expands the constitutional protection of the Basic Law. At the same time, it directly involves the court in the policy process and at least partially politicizes the court as another agent of policy making.

This issue of abortion law reform provides one example of the court's impact on policy. As soon as the abortion legislation passed the Bundestag in 1974, an appeal for abstract judicial review was brought before the Constitutional Court by the CDU/CSU-governed Länder and 193 CDU/CSU Bundestag deputies. This appeal kept the law from going into effect until the constitutional issue was decided. In 1975 the Second Senate of the court overturned the reform law as unconstitutional. The court decided (5:3) that the right-to-life provisions of the Basic Law (Article 2) apply to the unborn and the state must protect this right through limitations on abortion. In issuing its finding, however, the court also declared that abortions would be constitutionally justified within twelve weeks of conception in instances where the condition of the woman is threatened by continuation of the pregnancy. New abortion legislation was then enacted by the Bundestag in 1976, following the guidelines provided by the court. In essence, policy was determined by the court according to its interpretation of the Basic Law.

The constitutional importance of the West German court may even exceed the influence of the U.S. Supreme Court. The two courts share the basic responsibilities of concrete judicial review and individual constitutional complaints, but judicial review is applied more broadly in the West German system. The West German court has the additional responsibility of abstract review, which considerably expands its powers.

The formal impact of the court on policy is consequently substantial. Between 1951 and 1980, the court declared 107 federal laws invalid and held that portions of 60 others were incompatible with the Basic Law.[19] Furthermore, the invalidation of legislation on constitutional grounds is only one aspect of the court's policy influence. The potential for abstract review also can produce an indirect influence on policy makers as they attempt to anticipate the court's reaction to legislation being drafted by Parliament. This sensitivity has even led to retired court justices being asked to testify before Bundestag committees on the likely response of the court. The court also influences policy when it interprets a law to ensure compatibility with the Basic Law. In these decisions, the West German court is not restricted by the common law principle of precedent (*stare decisis*). Each case is decided based on present legal understandings and future consequences, not on past decisions. This allows the court greater latitude in reaching its decisions.

The West German Constitutional Court also has more discretion in its handling of sensitive "political" cases. Historical and cultural forces militate against the U.S. Supreme Court's involving itself in political controversies, such as conflicts between political parties or the internal affairs of government. In contrast, the Basic Law calls on the German Constitutional Court to act as a guardian of the constitutional process, which encourages its active involvement in political disputes. On the one hand, this means that the West German court is more likely to accept jurisdiction on sensitive political issues or matters of political procedure. On the other hand, the judges on the court openly acknowledge that political consequences are relevant to the court's deliberations; this is seen as a legitimate part of the court's role in protecting the political bases of the state.[20] The court's opinion on the method of arranging for early Bundestag elections in 1983, for example, displayed a willingness to temper judicial reasoning with pragmatic political considerations.

The court's resolutions of such sensitive political issues as abortion reform and the Basic Agreement with East Germany give the court the image of a policy activist. The leading American specialist on the West German court, Donald Kommers, once concluded that by American standards the Constitutional Court exhibits "judicial activism absolutely running wild."[21] At the least, the extent of judicial action makes the Constitutional Court a significant participant in the overall policy process.

Separate from the Constitutional Court, the judicial system has many administrative courts that influence public policy through their decisions (see Chapter II). The Federal Social Court, for example, makes decisions that affect the distribution of unemployment compensation, health benefits, and other social services. The Federal Labor Court is the major arbitrator between business and the unions over matters of workers' rights and the application of federal labor laws (see Chapter VIII). Similarly, the administrative courts have become a major arena in the policy debate between the nuclear power industry and its critics, because the courts have the authority to decide issues involving the safety and technical feasibility of nuclear power plants.[22]

THE PROCESS IN REVIEW

The policy process in the Federal Republic is in many ways unusual for a parliamentary democracy. Compared to most other parliamentary systems in Western Europe, the West German system disperses much power to the various institutions of government. The federal structure of government provides important arenas for policy activity at both the federal and state levels. Even within the federal government, policy influence is distributed among the separate branches of government. In contrast to the normal fusion of executive and legislative branches that occurs in a parliamentary system, the framers of the Basic Law went to great lengths to maintain the autonomy and policy competency of both branches. The West German Parliament is undoubtedly the strongest national legislature in Western Europe, because of its bicameral organization and powerful committee structure. The Bundestag and Bundesrat review and revise government proposals, contributing their substantive concerns to the policy process. The U.S. Congress is probably the only democratic legislature that exercises a greater role in the making of public policy.

The innovative feature of the West German system is that the strength of the legislature has not come through a limitation of executive power. Within their domain of responsibility, the West German chancellor and the cabinet wield more policy influence than is normally the case in a parliamentary system. The chancellor possesses the formal authority to direct the affairs of government and the cabinet while also representing the majority of the Bundestag. Policies are primarily initiated by the executive branch, which is the major focus for pressure groups.

The potential policy influence of the West German courts is also more extensive than in most other West European democracies.

Access to judicial review is more sharply restricted in France, and the British courts cannot challenge the supremacy of the British Parliament. Intentionally or unintentionally, the West German courts regularly find themselves involved in matters affecting public policy.

This dispersion of power is one reason for the emphasis on a consensual style of policy making in the West German system.[23] With so many potential arenas for political conflict, in each of which a hostile minority could attempt to block a policy, cooperation and compromise enable the government to enact their program into law, even if modified. The government attempts to reach internal consensus before proposing new legislation, the major parties are willing to negotiate and compromise within the legislature, and the Bundesrat and Bundestag reconcile their differences in the Mediation Committee. In other words, the separation of powers not only balances the rivalry between contending political factions as political theory would suggest, but it also lessens the intensity of the rivalry.

The dispersion of power produces a more open policy process for the major national interest groups that seek to influence public policy, at least in comparison to what normally occurs in parliamentary systems. Not only can lobbying groups reach elected officials, but federal regulations require that the relevant groups be consulted as new policies are developed by the ministries. This situation is in sharp contrast to the closed nature of the British or French bureaucracy, for example. Yet the highly structured form of interest representation in the Federal Republic also has its drawbacks. Formalized consultations often lead to rigidity and a preference for the status quo; some government officials equate public input to a consultation process involving only a small number of special-interest organizations. A few large, well-established national organizations tend to exploit this formal process of interest representation, while other less-established groups find it difficult to gain access to closed ministerial consultations. Indeed, one of the major pressures on the policy process is to further expand access for new interest groups and interests that are not represented by an organized national lobby.

Another consequence of the consensual, bureaucratized style of policy making is the difficulty government has in actively responding to new policy challenges.[24] In a world of rapid technological change and uncertain international conditions, nations need to maximize the problem-solving capacity of their political systems. A consensual style of policy making may prove less adaptable to changing political demands. Under uncertain or changing social conditions, consensus may develop only after the opportunity for initiating successful new policies is past. Many critics claim that this slowness to react, combined with the lack of coordination and planning that also exist within the policy process results in an insufficiency in problem-solving capacity. How the policy process responds to these needs may determine the nation's future ability to compete with other industrial democracies.

NOTES

1. Peter Katzenstein, *Policy and Politics in West Germany* (Philadelphia: Temple University Press, 1987), ch. 1; Renate Mayntz, "Executive Leadership in Germany," in *Presidents and Prime Ministers*, eds. Richard Rose and Ezra Suleiman (Washington, D.C.: American Enterprise Institute, 1980).

2. In 1985, there were about 312,000 federal employees, excluding postal and railway workers; over 1.5 million full-time personnel were employed by the state governments.

3. Gerard Braunthal, *The Federation of German Industry in Politics* (Ithaca: Cornell University Press, 1965), p. 230.

4. Renate Mayntz and Fritz Scharpf, *Policy Making in the German Federal Bureaucracy* (Amsterdam: Elsevier, 1975), ch. 6.

5. In fact, policy making in the areas of finance and defense policy differ in significant ways from the general model elaborated here. See Helga Haftendorn, "West Germany and the Management of Security Relations," in *The Foreign Policy of West Germany*, eds. Ekkehart Krippendorff and Volker Rittberger (Beverly Hills: Sage Publications, 1980) and Nevil Johnson, *State and Government in the Federal Republic of Germany*, 2nd ed. (New York: Pergamon Press, 1983), pp. 113–114.

6. Renate Mayntz, "West Germany," in *Advising the Rulers*, William Plowed, ed. (Oxford: Basil Blackwell, 1987), pp. 3–18.

7. The material for this case study was drawn from Simon Bulmer and William Patterson, *The Federal Republic of Germany and the European Community* (London: Allen and Unwin, 1987), pp. 175–179.

8. Nevil Johnson, "Committees in the West German Bundestag," in *Committees in Legislatures*, eds. J. Less and M. Shaw (Durham: Duke University Press, 1979); Gerhard Loewenberg, *Parliament in the German Political System* (Ithaca: Cornell University Press, 1967), chap. 6; Winifried Steffani, "Parties, Parliamentary Groups and Committees in the German Bundestag," in *The Congress and the Bundestag*, eds. Robert Livingston and Uwe Thaysen (Boulder: Westview, 1988).

9. For an interesting comparison of legislative norms by a West German working in the U.S. Congress, see Werner Jann, "The Internal Workings of Congress and the Bundestag," *PS* 42 (Fall 1984): 901–906.

10. Ferdinand Müller-Rommel, "Interest Group Representatives in the German Bundestag," in *Congress and the Bundestag*, ed. R. Livingston and U. Thaysen.

11. Eberhard Schuett-Wetschky, *Grundtypen parlamentarischer Demokratie* (Munich: Karl Alber Verlag, 1984), pp. 68ff.

12. *Datenhandbuch zur Geschichte des Deutschen Bundestages 1949 bis 1982* (Bonn: Deutsches Bundestag, 1983), p. 686.

13. Klaus von Beyme, "Elite Input and Policy Output," in *Does Who Governs Matter?* ed. Moshe Czudnowski (DeKalb: Northern Illinois University Press, 1982); also see Hans-Joachim Veen, *Opposition im Bundestag* (Bonn: Eichholz, 1976).

14. E. Gene Frankland, "The Role of the Greens in West German Parliamentary Politics," *Review of Politics* 50 (Winter 1988): 99–122.

15. If the bill involves state constitutional rights and therefore requires Bundesrat passage, the Bundestag or government can require a meeting of the Mediation Committee; otherwise, the bill cannot become a law. If the bill does not involve state rights, the Bundesrat can only *request* review by the Mediation Committee.

16. The Basic Law grants the executive even more extensive formal powers in the area of fiscal policy. Parliament cannot revise the spending or taxation levels contained in legislation proposed by the cabinet. The Parliament cannot even reallocate expenditures in the budget without the approval of the finance minister and the cabinet.

17. Bulmer and Patterson, *The Federal Republic of Germany and the European Community*, p. 178.

18. The court also hears a fourth class of cases dealing with constitutional disagreements between units of government; for example, a state challenging the actions of the chancellor or the cabinet.

19. Christine Landfried, "The Impact of the German Federal Court on Politics and Policy Output," *Government and Opposition* 25 (1986): 522–541.

20. Donald Kommers, *Judicial Politics in West Germany* (Beverly Hills: Sage Publications, 1975), p. 184.

21. Donald Kommers, "The Federal Constitutional Court in the West German Political System," in *Frontiers of Judicial Research*, eds. J. Grossman and J. Tannenhaus (New York: Wilcy, 1969), p. 113; also see Landfried, "The Impact of the German Federal Constitutional Court on Politics and Policy Output."

22. Dorothy Nelkin and Michael Pollak, *The Atom Besieged* (Cambridge: MIT Press, 1981).

23. Kenneth Dyson, "West Germany: The Search for a Rationalist Consensus," in *Policy Styles in Western Europe*, ed. Jeremy Richardson (London: Allen and Unwin, 1982).

24. Renate Mayntz and Fritz Scharpf, *Policy Making in the German Federal Bureaucracy*.

CHAPTER XI

Policy Performance

BY MOST STANDARDS, the Federal Republic has one of the most successful policy records among postwar European governments. The economic advances of the 1950s and 1960s were truly phenomenal. Even today, in a world of economic uncertainty the West German economy is stronger than those of most of its neighbors. West German standards of living are now among the highest in the world, and nearly all indicators of material well-being have followed an upward trend. Social welfare provisions in the Federal Republic are among the most generous in Western Europe. Through its policies the government has improved the educational system, increased workers' participation in industrial management, extended civil liberties, and improved environmental quality.

Certainly the government is not solely responsible for the successes or failures of West German society; industry, labor, and other groups are crucial parts of the system. International influences, too, increasingly affect the domestic policies of all modern nations. Still, the government is a major guarantor of public welfare, both directly, through its own actions, and indirectly, through the actions it requires of others.

This chapter tracks the policies of government that have improved the social and economic conditions of West Germany. We examine the major policy successes of postwar governments and discuss the policy problems that remain unresolved.

THE SCOPE OF GOVERNMENT ACTION

Few would dispute the claim that modern democratic governments play a major role in protecting the social order and promoting individual well-being. Most people also agree that it is the government's responsibility to address the needs of its citizens. What sets the Federal Republic (and many other European democracies) apart from the United States is the extent to which these responsibilities involve the government in all manner of social and economic activities. The West German government has also grown substantially in the past 40 years, increasing its influence in many spheres of social and economic activity. In short, big government has grown bigger. The German citizen expects the government to actively address personal and societal needs, and the government has responded to these expectations and steadily expanded its societal responsibilities.

One of the most basic measures of the scope of government activity is the overall level of government expenditures. This statistic dramatically documents the trend of government growth over the past several decades (Figure XI.1).[1] In 1951, total public expenditures—federal, state, local government, and the social security system—accounted for just DM 37 billion. After two decades of con-

FIGURE XI.1 *The Trend in Total Public Expenditures, 1951–1985**

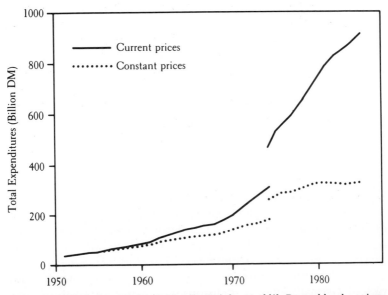

Source: *Statistisches Jahrbuch für die Bundesrepublik Deutschland,* various years.
*Accounting methods changed in 1974; see footnote 1.

servative rule by the CDU/CSU, public expenditures had grown to nearly DM 200 million. The most recent figure (1986) is over DM 900 million. Even after this statistic is adjusted for inflation rates, total public expenditures have increased more than eightfold in the past 35 years!

Almost any measure of the scope of government activity shows an upward trajectory paralleling total public expenditure trends. Per capita public expenditures increased from about DM 750 per person in 1950 to over DM 15,000 in 1986. Employment in the public sector accounts for a growing percentage of the work force. The number of people with jobs in the public sector has nearly doubled over the last 35 years, reaching almost four and a half million in 1985, or about one-sixth of the total labor force.

The statistics on government spending and employment are impressive, but they tell only part of the story. In addition to direct government expenditures, legislation and government regulations dictate additional activities and expenditures by the private sector. For instance, the government-mandated maternity benefits provided by employers are not counted as a government expenditure, but they are social benefits created by government legislation. Similarly, the costs that a business incurs in meeting government pollution standards are not expenditures by a public agency, but they are still outputs of the policy process. The time that individuals spend in preparing their tax returns is a government-mandated activity not represented in official expenditure figures. Another class of legislation determines what is socially and legally acceptable behavior: how guestworkers should be treated, what are the industrial safety standards, when are noise levels excessive, or how women's rights should be protected. Finally, government regulations directly influence everyday life in a multitude of ways; ask anyone who has tried shopping on Saturday afternoon (when the law requires that all shops close at 2 P.M.). Even the contents of the German's beloved beer are prescribed by government regulation.

Another measure of the government's reach is public ownership of key industries. In most West European democracies, the nationalization of major industries is seen as a leftist policy, proposed by socialist parties and their supporters. The West German experience is somewhat different. Reliance on the state is a longstanding feature of German political traditions. German political theory held that the state is the protector of individual welfare and the guarantor of societal interests. This philosophy was used to justify the

Kaiser's control over German society and the aristocratic rule of the Second Empire. Thus, when industrialization finally came to Germany, the Kaiser's government played a central role in developing new industries, such as steel production, coal mining, and the railroads. The authoritarian and paternalistic state of the Kaiser was also the first major European government to introduce extensive social welfare provisions to protect the working class from unemployment, sickness, and other economic hardships. The expenditures of the German government at the turn of the century thus exceeded those of many other European states.[2] Government ownership grew again at the end of World War II. After the collapse of Hitler's Reich, many major corporations that had collaborated with the Nazi state were nationalized. In effect, the nationalization of industry was expanded by the military occupation powers.

The early CDU governments attempted to decrease the government's ownership of industry in line with the party's conservative political principles. Government ownership in PREUSSAG, Volkswagen, and VEBA was reduced through innovative public stock offerings that gave the average citizen a chance to own shares in these corporations. When the SPD recanted its Marxist goal of nationalizing industry in the 1959 Godesberg Program, a political consensus was reached on the existing levels of government industrial ownership.

Present arrangements still leave the government deeply involved in several economic sectors. The government owns over a 25-percent share of more than 500 German companies, including three-fourths of the Lufthansa stock and large shareholdings in Volkswagen and the energy holding company, VEBA. The federal government owns and operates both the passenger and freight railway systems. The electronic media, radio and television, are owned by the government and managed by government-appointed supervisory bodies (see Chapter V). The postal and telephone systems are government monopolies, with strict restrictions on potential competitors. The Bundespost has the sole right to sell anything that connects to the nation's telephone system, whether it is a telephone, an answering machine, or a telephone connection for a computer. The government also possesses significant minority holdings in the steel, utilities, and banking industries. In overall terms, public ownership of German industry is not markedly less than in Sweden, pre-Thatcher Britain, or many other West European democracies.[3]

The tale of big government in West Germany and how it grew

has several different elements.[4] An obvious explanation for this growth is the expansion of the government's policy responsibilities. For example, in the 1950s the Federal Republic directed the postwar reconstruction of the economy and society and later developed a new German military force. In the 1960s, public attention turned to reforms, such as improving the educational system. The Brandt government expanded social programs throughout the early 1970s. These new programs, however, were not always responses to new needs; government policies often addressed previously existing needs. The educational system needed additional investment before funds were finally made available, and social programs merited expansion before the reforms of the 1970s. Simply put, the West German government grew not just because it chose to do more, but because it possessed the resources and support to do so.

The growth of government resources, and thus policy potential, is often described as a by-product of the Wirtschaftswunder and the expansion of government revenues along with the general growth of the economy. As personal incomes increased, government tax revenues also grew. Wages grew several-fold (adjusted for inflation) from the 1950s until the 1980s, providing a larger revenue base for government taxes. As the economic pie grew in size, government tax revenues inevitably increased. An expanding economy, however, is not a sufficient explanation of how the West German government grew so rapidly. The growth in the economy probably accounts for slightly more than half of the government's overall growth during the postwar period.

Not only was the government benefiting from the general growth in the size of the economic pie, it was also taking a larger and larger slice of that pie. Public-sector spending grew from under 30 percent of the Gross National Product (GNP) in the early 1950s to a peak of 52 percent in 1982. In other words, about one out of every two Deutschmarks in the economy was spent by public programs. And certainly, public expenditures are a conservative measure of the government's true impact on society.

This substantial expansion of government revenues did not cause heated political opposition for several reasons. The Wirtschafts-wunder lessened the financial burden of government expansion on the individual citizen. The economy was growing so rapidly that the take-home pay of the average worker was increasing even with the government deducting a growing share for itself. In short, both public and private incomes could increase simultaneously. Thus the growth of government was relatively painless to the average citizen; it did not lower private income but only slowed the rate of income growth.

A bipartisan consensus facilitated the growth in government. The Christian Democrats presided over a tremendous expansion of government activity during the 1950s and 1960s. Total public expenditures (in constant DM) increased by over threefold under their stewardship. Far from criticizing this activity, the opposition Social Democrats pressed for the government to do even more. When the Social Democrats assumed control of the government in 1969, their attempts to expand social programs often received bipartisan support. Many of the major social spending programs of the Brandt government passed the Bundestag with nearly unanimous support. During the decades of economic growth, few public figures criticized the government's expanding involvement in society.

Partisan acceptance of government growth was conditioned by general support for these activities in the German political culture. As was noted above (Chapter IV), the state has a special status in the German political culture; not only is the government responsible for the basic operation of the social and economic systems, but it is also the protector of individual welfare and the guarantor of societal interests. Sometimes this tendency is excessive. For instance, a Bundestag deputy recently noted that foreign music stars populated the top of the rock-and-roll charts in West Germany. His proposed solution called for the government to fund a research and training center for West German rock stars to better equip them for international competition. Most citizens have a more realistic view of reasonable government activity, but this attitude still works to make the government a prominent policy actor. If a legitimate need exists, Germans expect the government to deal with the problem. The state is viewed as the master problem-solver for all manner of personal and societal problems.

Public opinion polls document the public's belief that the state should actively address social and personal needs (Table XI.1). West Germans have high expectations of government; a majority think that correcting pollution, lessening unemployment, providing basic social services, fighting crime, and protecting the elderly are essential government responsibilities. Other studies confirm the impression that a large majority of the public supports government action to resolve social needs and promote individual well-being.[5] These sentiments are not unique to West Germany, but represent a com-

TABLE XI.1 *Public Perceptions of Government Responsibilities*

	West Germany	United States
Fighting crime	78%	53%
Fighting pollution	73	56
Providing good medical care	63	42
Guaranteeing jobs	60	34
Providing good education	55	47
Looking after old people	51	41
Providing adequate housing	39	25
Reducing income inequality	29	13
Ensuring equal rights for women	27	24
Ensuring equal rights for minorities	20	33
Average	49	37

Source: 1974 Political Action study. Table entries are the percentage of the public who think each problem is an essential government responsibility. These data are available from the Interuniversity Consortium for Political and Social Research in Ann Arbor.

mon preference among Europeans for more extensive government involvement in society. In contrast, U.S. citizens are much more reserved in their support for government action. Table XI.1 indicates that even in areas where the U.S. government is a primary actor, such as care for the elderly and civil rights, only a minority of Americans view these problems as essential government responsibilities.

Although the West German government has grown substantially, and almost steadily, over the past forty years, the inevitability of further increases became more questionable in recent years. The OPEC-induced economic shocks of 1973 and 1979 had a sharp effect on the West German economy. After the first economic recession, Helmut Schmidt's government was forced into a retrenchment on domestic policy reforms. Government deficits rose with the economic slowdown, and little money was available for new programs. These same temporizing policies were ineffective after the 1979 recession. Unemployed workers and struggling businesses turned to generous government programs for assistance, at the same time that government revenues dipped because of the economic downturn. The SPD-FDP governing coalition struggled to deal with these seemingly intractable problems, but these policy strains eventually became so great that the coalition failed, leading to the formation of a new, economically conservative government of the CDU/CSU and FDP in 1982.

Chancellor Kohl entered office promising a *"Wende,"* that is, a change from an expanding government toward less government involvement in society. Several different cost-cutting measures slowed the growth of government spending, at least at the federal level. The federal budget has increased at a fairly modest rate under Kohl's leadership (about 3 percent a year). Since 1980, the total level of public spending has remained relatively constant after adjustment for inflation. In line with Kohl's conservative economic philosophy, government shareholdings in private corporations have been reduced.

Despite promises of a fundamental policy shift, however, the pace of real policy change has been very slow. CSU members of the governing coalition delayed efforts to decrease government holdings in Lufthansa, for example, until the stock market crash in late 1987 put these plans on hold. Similarly, promises of deregulation and the break-up of government monopolies generate research studies and policy reports, but little government action. Some of the most glaring examples of economic inefficiency, such as government subsidy programs to uncompetitive industries, have been the most resistant to reform. Kohl has found that each government program exists because it has political supporters, often members of his own coalition. Moreover, general support for a strong state remains high. Kohl's conservative critics complain that this is the *"Wende ohne Winde"* (a change without any force). Thus it is unlikely that the present conservative government will fundamentally reduce the government's role in West German society, but it may ensure that government grows no larger.

THE GOVERNMENT BALANCE SHEET

It is difficult to describe precisely the activities of the government in terms of revenues and budgets. A major complicating factor is the extensive network of social service programs (see below). These programs are the largest single component of public expenditures; however, most of their revenues and expenditures are kept separate from the government's normal budgetary process.

Another complicating factor is West Germany's federal system of government. The Basic Law distributes public policy responsibilities among the three levels of government. The local communities (*Gemeinde*) are involved in policy outputs of two different types. On the one hand, the municipalities administer programs that are mandated and regulated by the federal or state governments. This includes the administration of youth, public health, and social assistance programs, as well as the maintenance of public records. On the other hand, the Basic Law (Article 28) also grants the local government responsibility for "all the affairs of the local community within the limits set by the law." This general declaration of competence justifies a broad range of activities by local government. Many municipalities develop the economic infrastructure of their community, for example, through the creation of industrial parks, transportation facilities, and other public services. Local governments also promote the cultural life of the community through the construction of cultural facilities and support for local artists. Finally, local authorities provide basic public utilities, such as gas, electricity, and public transport.

The distribution of policy responsibilities between the state and federal governments is more complex because they hold independent and concurrent powers (see Chapter II). In general terms, the states are chartered to manage educational and cultural policies. They also hold primary responsibility for public security and the administration of justice. Policies that are best handled at the national level are assigned to the federal government; this category includes foreign policy, defense, long-distance transportation, and communications.

The sharing of policy responsibilities means that all levels of government possess considerable resources for carrying out their assigned tasks. Public expenditures are distributed fairly evenly across the different institutions of government. In 1984, total federal expenditures (*Rechnungsmässige Ausgaben*) were DM 272 billion, an additional DM 293 billion was spent by the social security system, the combined state budgets were DM 198 billion, and local authorities spent more than 114 billion. The distribution of public employees also exemplifies the dispersion of government activity. Of the nearly three million public employees in 1986, over 50 percent worked for the state governments, about one-third were municipal employees, and about one-tenth were federal employees.

Because of these multiple levels of policy activity, the best overview of West German policy priorities comes from studying the combined expenditures from all public sources: the federal government, the state governments, local governments, and the social security system (Figure XI.2). The largest share of public expenditures, by far, is devoted to social programs: health care, pensions, unemployment, and similar programs. The extensive coverage and

FIGURE XI.2 *The Distribution of Total Public Expenditures, 1984**

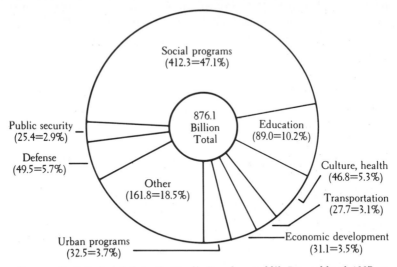

Source: *Statistisches Jahrbuch für die Bundesrepublik Deutschland 1987*, p. 428.

*In DM billions.

benefits of the various social programs account for nearly half of all government expenditures. It is easy to understand why the Federal Republic is sometimes described as a welfare state (see below). Exact estimates of how much social services spending has grown over the years are difficult to calculate because of changes in accounting practices, but it undoubtedly was one of the fastest growing sectors of public spending. Social service programs apart, public expenditures are distributed across a number of different policy areas. Education is an important concern of all three levels of government and accounts for about one-tenth of public spending. Educational spending increased at about twice the rate of overall government spending under the first two decades of CDU-led government, but since then has experienced about the same rate of increase as overall public expenditures. Defense and foreign policy expenditures constitute another significant share of the budget. Spending in this policy area has decreased from about 13 percent of all public expenditures in the early 1960s to today's level of about 6 percent of total public spending (or 3 percent of the Gross National Product). Other public spending is distributed over areas such as transportation, culture, urban planning, and economic development.

We can see how policy activities are assigned across the various levels of government by examining how these total expenditures distributed among federal, state, and local government (Table XI.2). Using 1984 public expenditures as an example, public spending in the areas of defense, foreign affairs, economic development, and transportation are predominantly allocated by the federal government. In the transportation area, for example, 45.7 percent of all public spending was done by the federal government, 31.5 percent by the ten state governments combined, and 22.8 percent by the various local governments. The Länder are the primary source of public funds for security, education, housing, and planning. Community development, sports, and cultural activities are primarily funded by local units of government. Apart from these three levels of government, a separate social security system, based largely on social insurance contributions, provides the largest single category of public expenditures. The DM 292.5 billion social security budget in 1984 was larger than all federal expenditures combined!

Budget expenditures indicate what the government is trying to do, but the actual results of these expenditures are difficult to assess. Most indicators of actual policy performance suggest that the government has been fairly successful in achieving past policy goals.[6] Standards of living have improved dramatically, as real wages increased by more than threefold between 1950 and 1980, and consumer goods such as color televisions and washing machines that were once luxuries are now widely available. Health statistics show similar improvement; for instance, the number of doctors per capita nearly doubled over the period from 1950 to 1980, and the average life expectancy lengthened by close to a full decade. Overall educational levels and access to higher education have dramatically improved over the past forty years. Although localized shortages of housing still appear, overall housing conditions display similar improvement. Even in new policy areas, such as energy conservation and the environment, the government has made substantial progress.

Perhaps the best overall assessment of the political system's policy performance comes from the evaluations of the citizens who are the consumers of government policy outputs. An opinion poll in 1984 found that most West Germans were satisfied with their job (90 percent), housing (85 percent), living standard (81 percent), and social security benefits (74 percent).[7] In fact, only two items in the poll failed to elicit satisfied responses from a majority of those inter-

TABLE XI.2 *Distribution of Public Expenditures by Level of Government and Policy Area*

	Federal Government	Social Security System	State Government	Local Government	Total
Primarily Federal Government					
Defense	49.5	0.0	0.0	0.0	49.5
Foreign affairs	17.1	0.0	0.0	0.0	17.1
Economic development	20.3	0.0	9.3	1.5	31.1
Transport/communications	12.6	0.0	8.7	6.3	27.6
Primarily State Government					
Security/Public order	1.7	0.0	19.5	4.2	25.4
Education	12.7	0.0	62.8	13.6	89.0
Housing/Planning	1.9	0.0	9.1	4.0	15.0
Primarily Local Government					
Community development	0.1	0.0	1.6	15.8	17.5
Sport	2.1	0.0	8.8	25.4	36.4
Culture	0.1	0.0	2.9	3.0	6.0
Other Areas					
Social security programs	81.8	291.3	15.2	24.1	412.3
Central administration	6.4	0.0	11.9	13.0	31.3
Miscellaneous	65.8	1.2	48.1	2.4	117.6
Total (billion DM)	272.1	292.5	198.0	112.2	874.8
Percentage of total expenditure	31.0	33.4	22.6	12.8	100%

Source: *Statistisches Jahrbuch für die Bundesrepublik Deutschland 1987*, pp. 438–439. Table entries are 1984 public expenditures in billions of DM.

viewed: public security and the fight against crime (only 47 percent satisfied), and environmental quality (22 percent). Certainly there is room for further improvement, but the West German policy record is marked by considerable success.

A TAXING PROPOSITION

The generous benefits of government programs are, of course, not due to the largess of government. The taxes and financial contributions of individuals and corporations provide the funds for these programs. Therefore, large government outlays inevitably mean an equally large collection of revenues by the government. These revenues are the real source of government programs.

Three different types of revenue provide the bulk of the resources for public policy programs. The largest share of public revenues comes from contributions to the social security system (Figure XI.3). The health, unemployment, disability, retirement and other social security funds are primarily self-financed by employer and employee contributions. The pension plan provides a typical example. Contributions to the pension plan amount to 18.5 percent of a worker's

FIGURE XI.3 *The Sources of Public Revenues, 1984**

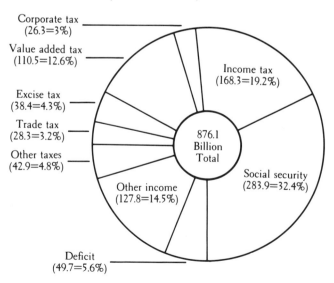

Source: *Statistisches Jahrbuch für die Bundesrepublik Deutschland 1987,* p. 436–438.

*In DM billions.

gross monthly wages, half being paid by the employee and half by the employer. All social insurance contributions combined—pensions, health, and unemployment—accounted for 14.9 percent of the average worker's income in 1986, with slightly larger matching contributions made by the employer. These insurance contributions are not taxes per se; the contributions are made to separate social security funds and used solely for this purpose. Still, these contributions support public policy activities, and in 1984 they amounted to DM 283.9 billion.

The next most important source of public revenues are direct taxes, that is, taxes directly assessed by the government and paid to a government office. One of the largest shares of public revenues comes from direct taxes on personal income (Figure XI.3). The rate of personal taxation rises with income level, from a base of 22 percent up to a maximum of 56 percent, although the CDU government has proposed a reduction in the top tax rate for the 1990s to spur economic growth. This tax system makes allowances for business expenses, private investments, and social security deductions, so the actual tax rate is lower than the official rate. The average worker pays about 18 percent of wages in direct income taxes. Corporate profits are also taxed, but at a much lower rate than personal income; tax policy encourages businesses to be profitable and to reinvest their profits in further economic development. Altogether, the income and corporate tax account for slightly less than one-fourth of all public revenues.

The third major source of government revenues is indirect taxes. Like sales and excise taxes, indirect taxes are based on the use of income, rather than wages and profits. The most common and lucrative indirect tax is the value added tax (VAT). A VAT charge is added at every stage in the manufacturing process that increases the value of a product. Between the raw lumber and a completed piece of furniture, for example, the VAT may be assessed several times. The cumulated VAT charges are included in the price of the final product, but not listed separately on the price slip. The standard VAT is 14 percent for most goods, with a lower rate (7 percent) for basic commodities such as food. Other indirect taxes include customs duties, an energy tax, and liquor and tobacco taxes. Indirect taxes now account for about 43 percent of all tax revenues.

Indirect taxes are one of the secrets to the dramatic growth of government revenues. Indirect taxes are usually "hidden" in the price of an item, rather than explicitly listed as a tax. Consumers therefore forget that they are paying taxes every time they purchase a product. At the same time, because the taxes are hidden, it is easier for policy makers to raise indirect taxes without evoking public awareness and opposition. The VAT on consumer durables has increased from 10 percent in the 1960s to its present level. Furthermore, revenues from indirect taxes rise automatically with inflation; as the price of goods rise, so does the indirect tax. Another aspect of indirect taxes is that they tend to be regressive; they weigh more heavily on low-income families, because a larger share of their income is used for consumer goods. Nevertheless, indirect taxes remain popular with political leaders because of their low visibility, and they are mandated by the European Community as one method of standardizing cost structures within the EEC.

Even with these multiple revenue sources, public expenditures repeatedly have exceeded public revenues in recent years. To finance this deficit, the government draws upon another source of "revenue"—loans and public borrowing—to maintain the level of government services. Although government borrowing originally was to be a temporary measure for dealing with an economic recession, the total public debt has more than doubled over the past decade. One of the primary goals of the CDU/CSU-FDP government is to halt this drain on the economy and bring the federal budget into balance (while maintaining government programs as much as possible). The growth in federal spending was held to under 3 percent per annum during the 1983–1986 term. This budgetary restraint and a small amount of new taxation sharply reduced the annual federal deficit from DM 37 billion in the 1982 fiscal year to DM 22 billion in 1985, although the deficit has begun creeping upward again; the projected 1988 deficit is DM 39 billion.

Sharing these various tax revenues is a basic element of the West German federal system of government. The federal government and the Länder each receive 42.5 percent of the income tax revenue, with the remaining 15 percent distributed to local government. About two-thirds of the VAT revenue is allocated to the federal government, with the other third distributed among the states. Other taxes are used exclusively or primarily by one level of government. For instance, the energy, tobacco, and liquor tax revenues go to the federal government. The revenues from the automobile, inheritance, and lottery taxes go to the state governments. The local communities primarily benefit from the property tax. The West German government, and other members of the European Community, also must send a portion of the VAT revenues to Brussels to fund the Community's activities.

The distribution of tax revenues through the federal system continues to be a sensitive issue. The division of taxes between the federal and state governments is subject to periodic review, as the distribution of responsibilities changes between the two levels of government. In addition, a policy of financial equalization between the Länder redistributes tax revenues from the more affluent to the less affluent states.

The average West German obviously has deep pockets to fund the extensive variety of public policy programs; U.S. taxation levels look quite modest by comparison, even though cries of a tax revolt are heard more often in the United States than in the Federal Republic. The marginal tax rate for the average German worker, including taxes and social security contributions, was 63 percent in 1986, compared to a marginal rate in America of just over 40 percent. When a German goes to the corner kiosk to buy a pack of cigarettes, 73 percent of the cost goes to taxes; taxes account for 66 percent of the cost of liquor and gasoline, 28 percent of the cost of a can of coffee, and 19 percent on a package of light bulbs.

It may seem like the West German taxpayer contributes an excessive amount to public coffers, and Germans are no more eager than other nationalities to pay taxes. Still, the operative question is not how much citizens pay, but how much value is returned by the government. In addition to normal government activities, German citizens are protected against sickness, unemployment, and disability; government pension plans furnish a livable retirement income. Moreover, the majority of the public expects the government to take an active role in most policy areas.

A CLOSER LOOK AT THE WELFARE STATE

The Federal Republic often is described as a welfare state, or more precisely a social services state, because of its extensive social services programs. The guarantee of basic social needs by the government dates back to the 1880s, when the Empire initiated innovative social insurance laws protecting workers against industrial accidents and sickness, and providing a retirement pension. This pioneering effort won not only worldwide attention, but also widespread imitation.[8] Although the government's motivation was less than altruistic (it hoped to lessen working-class support for the Social Democratic party and further legitimize the Kaiser's government), these policies identified the government as the protector of basic social needs and socioeconomic security.

The Federal Republic continued this tradition of state action and reinstituted the social insurance programs of the Weimar Republic. Compulsory social insurance programs include health care, accident insurance, unemployment compensation, and retirement benefits. In the health care area, for example, all wage earners are required to participate in a government-mandated health insurance program. Insurance protection also extends to students, farmers, and those receiving unemployment or pension benefits; individuals without an income of their own are insured by the government. Only employees with high salaries and self-employed persons are exempt from compulsory health insurance. This is not a system of socialized medicine such as exists in Britain and Scandinavia, in which the government employs the doctors and manages health care facilities. Instead, it is a self-financing insurance program mandated and regulated by the government. These insurance programs protect members of society against the major health and economic risks of life.

A second set of programs provides financial assistance for the needy and individuals who cannot support themselves. Residents of the Federal Republic who are unable to provide for themselves financially are entitled to a subsistence allowance. These cash allowances are quite modest, amounting to only a few hundred DM per month. In addition, however, recipients have access to other social service benefits, such as health insurance, applicable disability benefits, educational grants, and family allowances. Another program provides housing subsidies for low-income families to defray a part of their housing costs.

The early CDU-led governments also instituted a third set of programs that extended social services to the population at large without regard to economic need. The CDU initiated these programs as another method of legitimizing the new democratic system and integrating citizens into the new state. By directly providing benefits to a large number of people (even if these benefits were merely the return of the taxpayers' money), the government could more broadly advertise the advantages of the new political order. This investment yielded obvious returns as public attachments to the new political system developed.

One example of these broad-based social benefits is a program designed to lessen the economic burden of raising children by providing parents with a monthly payment for each child in the family (*Kindergeld*). By the end of the 1970s these child benefits amounted to DM 50 per month for the first child, DM 100 for the second child, and DM 200 for the third and each subsequent child. A family with three children thus received a tax-free check for DM 350 from the government each month, regardless of the family's income level. Another innovative CDU program encouraged savings and capital accumulation by working-class families. The government introduced tax-free savings plans and, later, special savings bonuses for participants in these plans. An employee can set aside up to DM 624 a year in a specially designated long-term savings account and receive a 30-percent matching contribution from the state (40-percent for families with two or more children). The significant aspect of all these programs was that the distribution of government benefits became generally available to all citizens, irrespective of economic need.

The combination of these various programs created the basis of the modern German welfare state. West German spending on social programs ranked among the highest of all Western industrial democracies from the early 1950s until the mid-1960s. As in the 1880s, a conservative German government had presided over a major extension of the welfare state.

Another round of program expansions began when the Social Democrats won control of the federal government in 1969. The benefits of the social insurance systems were improved, and the coverage of these programs was expanded. Accident insurance was extended to nonworking adults and children; vocational training was provided for the unemployed; minimum pension benefits were guaranteed for all workers; and new medical coverage was provided. The government enlarged the family allowance program to begin *Kindergeld* payments with the first child, nearly tripling the scope of this program in a single year. Total public spending on social programs nearly doubled between 1969 and 1975. Yet because most other Western democracies were expanding their own welfare systems at an even faster rate, Germany moved from a position as international leader in social programs to a level of social spending close to the European average.[9] Few people realize that the international ranking of the Federal Republic's social expenditures was highest under CDU governments and actually decreased during the Brandt administration.

The socioeconomic protections of the West German welfare state provide generous benefits for anyone who needs them. The unemployment program is a typical example of the range of benefits available. An unemployed worker receives insurance payments that provide about 68 percent of normal pay (63 percent for unmarried workers) for up to a year. After a year, unemployment assistance continues at about half of normal pay. Government labor offices will help the unemployed worker find new employment or obtain retraining for a new job. If a job is located in another city, the program partially reimburses travel and moving expenses. This is not an atypical example; benefits in most other programs are equally generous.

In one way or another—through retirement programs, family allowances, health care, or other social services—the welfare state has a direct effect on almost every German family. By one account, 80 percent of all families receive some type of direct financial payment from the state, either as retirement benefits, a family allowance, unemployment compensation, educational grants, or other social benefits. It is not a system intended to protect only the indigent; in fact, welfare payments to the financially unable are a very small and decreasing part of the social services budget. Instead, these programs are designed to guarantee broad social needs. Jens Alber calculated that in 1980 almost 12 million citizens drew a major part of their income from government social programs, making this group even larger than the number of blue-collar industrial workers in West Germany.[10]

The continuing growth of social service programs reflects the widespread support for these policies among the public. Most citizens feel that these programs fulfill basic social needs that must be protected by the government, even if tax bills increase. The West German system is also heavily based on compulsory insurance programs. Thus, program recipients are not seen as taking advantage of government handouts; they are receiving benefits they have "earned" through their contributions to these programs. Other programs (family assistance, savings plans, and educational assistance) are generally available to the entire public, which does not see them as welfare support. As a result of this consensus, social service expenditures grew under both the early CDU/CSU governments and the Social Democratic governments of the early 1970s.

Growing public demands for social benefits and expanding program coverage have steadily increased the cost of these policies. Total spending for social services was DM 63 billion in 1960; in

1986, the social service bill was DM 604 billion. The largest share of the social budget is devoted to the pension program for retirees, widows, and orphans, which amounted to DM 230 billion (Figure XI.4). Health services account for an almost equally large, and rapidly growing, share of social spending. The family allowance program is another substantial social investment. By comparison to these three main programs, unemployment compensation, housing programs, and incentives for savings account for a relatively modest share of social spending, and outright welfare payments are almost negligible. The social spending amounts in Figure XI.4 include not only direct public expenditures but also the indirect costs of social legislation, such as tax incentives (which are not usually counted as government spending) or government-mandated expenditures borne by private parties. Even if one considers only direct public expenditures for social services (as in Figure XI.2 above), these programs still account for the largest single share of public expenditures. The growth of these programs has been so extensive that they have consumed an ever-increasing share of the economy. In 1960, just over 20 percent of the GNP was spent on social services; by 1986, this share amounted to more than 32 percent.

FIGURE XI.4 *The Distribution of Social Services Spending, 1986**

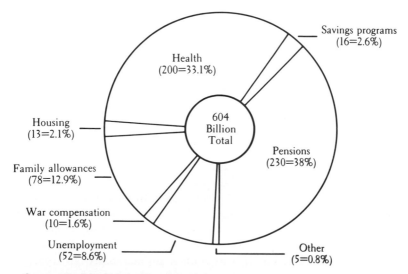

Source: *Sozialpolitische Umschau* (August 1986). no. 262.
*In DM billions.

In recent years the substantial costs of these social programs has stirred new problems and controversy.[11] Some critics claim that the social services network is overextended and its benefits are too generous. Immediate problems arose as the economic recession and high unemployment rates depleted the resources of the unemployment and assistance programs. The unemployment insurance fund, for example, ran into the red in 1975, 1979 and 1980. Only intervention by the federal government in the early 1980s maintained the viability of these programs.

With a weak economy, generous social programs will remain an expensive burden on the government. Moreover, some conservative economists maintain that liberal social programs undermine economic incentive and lessen the efficiency and international competitiveness of the German economy. Although they are not advocating a dismantling of the welfare state, these economists nevertheless favor making individuals and private institutions more responsible for their own economic security.

In the long term, demographic changes in the labor force may require a restructuring of the social insurance system. Today there are about three persons employed full time for every pensioner over age 60; that ratio will slip to two-to-one early in the next century. These population changes are producing an unfavorable balance of retirees drawing pensions and needing expensive health benefits versus active workers who are contributing to the social insurance funds. The financial weakness of the pension program has already become evident; benefits exceeded receipts from 1975 to 1979 and again in 1982 and 1983. The basic issue is whether the Federal Republic's extensive social services network can remain unaltered in the face of these changing economic and demographic conditions.

While the political parties continue to debate these issues, both SPD- and CDU-led governments have responded with a steady retrenchment in social programs over the past decade. A series of curtailment acts have restricted the benefits of nearly all programs and increased private cost-sharing. The series began with the Budget Consolidation Law of 1975, which limited unemployment benefits, transformed some university graduate student grants into loans, and reduced housing benefits. Legislation revised pension allotments downward in 1977 and 1978. Further restrictions on social benefits occurred on an almost annual basis. In 1981, a government reform package introduced cutbacks in every major government social program in order to balance social benefits against the government's strained resources. More significant than the fact that these reforms were implemented by a SPD-led government was the fact that social spending still continued to rise, reaching a postwar high (in constant DM) in 1981.

The SPD's inability to control social programs, and its reliance on budget deficits to finance revenue shortfalls, were factors that contributed to the downfall of the SPD-FDP government in 1982. The new conservative government enacted cutbacks in social programs almost immediately. In late 1982, the government reduced all major social programs in some manner. The starting age for pension benefits was moved back by six months at the same time that salary deductions were increased by half a percentage point. Copayments for medical care went up, and allowances for maternity leaves decreased. Stipends for university students were replaced by means-tested loans. Other programs suffered similar cuts: access to unemployment benefits was tightened by broadening the definition of acceptable alternative employment, unemployment benefits were reduced for unmarried workers, a family income limit was placed on Kindergeld allowances, and housing programs were cut. Total spending for social programs (after adjustment for inflation) actually decreased during Kohl's first term. Public spending on social services declined to just under 30 percent of the Gross National Product in 1987.

The limitation of social programs has provoked sharp opposition in at least some sectors of society. The SPD and the unions, for example, strongly protested the reduction of unemployment benefits at a time when two million people were out of work. Others complained that cuts in job training programs and family allowances occurred just when the real need for these programs increased. Still, most people seem to accept the conservative government's view that public accounts need to be brought into order to ensure the viability of the social security programs and the overall economy. Thus the CDU-led governing coalition won a major election victory in 1983, despite having sharply curtailed social programs a scant three months earlier. The coalition's continued strength in the 1987 elections further underscores this point.

Predictions of the end of the welfare state are clearly premature. Most political figures on both the Left and Right recognize that the benefits of the welfare state are a primary source of the "social peace" that has characterized political relations in postwar Germany.[12] The protections engendered by these programs have moderated the political competition between business and labor and provided a social climate in which economic and social progress could proceed hand in hand. Few politicians advocate the staunchly neoconservative views on social policy expressed by Ronald Reagan and Margaret Thatcher, and no one favors a return to the social Darwinism of the Weimar era and all that it implies. Thus it is not surprising that the government's attempts to limit social program have yielded only modest results. Public opinion polls indicate that most Germans still strongly support the basic tenets of the welfare state and want to preserve the present level of services as much as possible. Helmut Kohl's 1988 federal budget actually called for a slight increase (in real terms) in social spending. Although it is likely that the funding and benefit levels of social programs will continue to be a source of political debate, the basic structure of the welfare state will endure.

THE UNINTENDED CONSEQUENCES OF GROWTH

The Economic Miracle reaped amazing success in improving the living standard of the average German family. At the same time, however, economic growth brought some unintended consequences. Economic growth increased the burdens placed upon the land, water, air, and other natural resources. These burdens gradually showed in a deteriorating natural environment. The growth of auto ownership and the expansion of electricity production in postwar West Germany steadily increased the amount of pollutants released into the air. In Cologne, for example, automobile emissions cause so much damage to the cathedral in the city's center that a crew of stonemasons is employed to continuously restore the stone exterior. Water pollution worsened as a result of discharges from the dense concentration of industry along the banks of inland waterways. A massive fish kill along the Rhine in 1969 first drew widespread public attention to this worsening problem. West Germany's high population density and heavy urbanization magnified problems of noise pollution and the loss of natural areas. In short, the affluence of the Economic Miracle came at a substantial cost to the environment.

Environmental protection is generally described as a new issue in West German politics, but the first environmental legislation dates back to the beginning of the Second Empire.[13] Between 1870 and 1910, the Kaiser's government passed the first legislation dealing with industrial pollution, clean water, emission controls, and the protection of nature. But little new legislation was implemented over the next 50 years, and these early provisions grew more and more inadequate in dealing with the scale and technological complexity of modern environmental problems. Until the severe economic difficulties of the postwar period were addressed, Germans were not very concerned with the conditions of the natural environment. In 1961, for example, the SPD tried to emphasize environmental quality with the campaign slogan "Blue Skies over the Ruhr." Few voters were interested.

Environmental issues finally entered the political agenda in the early 1970s. Several dramatic environmental catastrophies and international policy studies drew public attention to ecological problems. Moreover, once affluence seemed secure, Germans were more willing to take steps to lessen the negative consequences of economic growth. In 1971 the SPD-FDP government laid out an agenda for environmental protection; environmental quality was a major goal of Brandt's reform-minded government and the FDP Minister of the Interior, Hans-Dietrich Genscher. The federal government revised the Basic Law in 1972 to grant itself jurisdiction on environmental matters, and then implemented 26 major pieces of legislation during the 1972–1976 session of Parliament—more environmental legislation than was passed in the first two decades of the Federal Republic.[14]

The government's commitment to environmental issues faded with the renewal of economic problems in the mid-1970s. Helmut Schmidt, who succeeded Brandt as chancellor in 1974, had a reputation as someone who could manage the nation's worsening economic situation; Schmidt was less concerned with Brandt's domestic policy reforms, such as the environmental program. The new Minister of the Interior also lacked his predecessor's enthusiasm for the environmental issue. Economic growth was again the government's top priority, and environmental legislation stagnated or was watered down by hostile amendments. Some of the strongest support for strict environmental standards came not from the SPD benches but from conservative CDU deputies such as Herbert Gruhl, who wrote a bestselling book on the growing environmental crisis. On the whole, the government and the established parties became unresponsive to the nation's environmental needs in reaction to the renewed problems of the economy and the mounting opposition of business and agricultural groups.

After a hiatus of a few years, attention to environmental issues began to grow again in the late 1970s and early 1980s. This time, however, the impetus for environmental reform did not come from within the party system but from outside. Citizen-action groups demonstrated against environmental problems in their respective locales. At the national level, lobbying groups such as the BBU, Greenpeace, and other New Left groups mobilized opposition to nuclear power, toxic wastes, and other environmental issues. The formation of the Greens in 1980 helped bring the issues of the environmental lobby into clearer focus, but still the government and the established parties were unresponsive.

The Greens' entry in the Bundestag provided a public forum to draw attention to the nation's worsening environmental problems. Soon thereafter, events seemed to confirm the Greens' worst claims. In the early 1980s, pollution was rapidly damaging the Germans' beloved forests; in a few short years nearly half of all trees had succumbed. This convinced many people that the Greens' claims were not just rhetoric; one could travel to the Black Forest and see the death of the forests (*Waldsterben*). Environmentalists then drew the public's attention to water pollution, toxic wastes, and the other environmental problems threatening the nation. In 1986, a chemical spill at a Swiss industrial firm killed millions of fish in the Rhine river and threatened local drinking water. The disaster at Chernobyl heightened the sense of an approaching environmental Armageddon. When the fallout spread to West Germany, government agencies told parents to keep their children indoors and to avoid certain foods. The government attempted to assure the public that a similar catastrophe could not occur in the German nuclear power industry, but a major scandal in 1987 eroded the government's efforts. A large nuclear fuel company, NUKEM, was accused of illegally transporting (and possibly disposing of) nuclear wastes. It seemed that with each morning's newspaper another hidden environmental problem suddenly became visible. In objective terms, West German environmental problems may not be substantially worse than those in other West European countries, but Germans became more concerned with issue.[15] In both the 1983 and 1987 Bundestag elections, environmental protection ranked near the top of the public's issue interests.

Helmut Kohl's government has, in fact, been more active than the prior Social Democratic administration on environmental issues. To cope with the worsening problems of acid rain, new regulations have significantly reduced air pollution from conventional power stations; another program offers tax incentives for automobiles that use lead-free gasoline. Several basic indicators of air and water quality show substantial improvement through the 1980s. The government also has initiated a series of conferences to protect the North Sea through international treaties. In 1986, Kohl created a new Ministry of the Environment; the Federal Republic was one of the last European democracies to do so.

Despite this progress, many pressing environmental questions remain unresolved. Growing public doubts about nuclear energy have not slackened the government's commitment to nuclear power. In the mid-1980s, about a third of all electricity was produced by nuclear power plants, and government projections call for this percentage to increase. Nearly fifteen years after American automobiles converted to lead-free gasoline and catalytic converters, these reforms still have not been implemented in the Federal Republic (in part because of opposition from other European countries). New exposés on toxic waste problems, forest death, waste management, and air and water quality appear in the media regularly. The public and political leaders are now more aware of these problems, but their solutions are still unclear.

BETWEEN EAST AND WEST

More than most other Europeans, West Germans are, and must be, attentive to foreign policy. In part, this necessity is a matter of geography; Germany is at the crossroads of Europe, especially since the postwar division of Germany into the Federal Republic and the Democratic Republic. Both Germanies are front-line states in any ideological or military conflict between the Western and Eastern blocs, and West Berlin remains a democratic island surrounded by East Germany. East and West meet at the intra-German border.

The importance of foreign affairs in underscored by the structure of the West German economy. The economy depends heavily on exports and foreign trade. About one-fourth of the active labor force produces goods for export, a percentage much higher than in most other industrial nations. As a result, harmonious diplomatic ties and liberal trade policies are essential for a healthy economy. Helmut Schmidt once said that, "for some years now . . . [West German] economic policy has simultaneously been our foreign policy"; this view is equally applicable to the present administration.

International matters have always been one of the major policy challenges of the Federal Republic, beginning immediately after the war with the questions of nation building and redefining the nation's role in postwar world affairs. The prewar Reich had been partitioned by the loss of territory in the east and the division of the remainder into two separate German states. The Allied powers retained the right to intervene in the domestic affairs of the Federal Republic even after 1949. To become an independent nation, the Federal Republic had to regain its sovereignty. This would be a difficult task, because Germany was still something of an outcast among the international community of nations, and opposition to the rebuilding of any German state was considerable.

Chancellor Adenauer's strategy for rehabilitating Germany's image and regaining national sovereignty was to integrate the Federal Republic into the Western Alliance. This decision inevitably reflected Adenauer's orientation toward Western culture and democratic institutions; he was the former mayor of Cologne during the Weimar Republic, a leader of the Zentrum party, and a strong Catholic. In addition, he believed that the West would eventually win its cold war struggle with the Soviet Union. In the long, run, therefore, the final resolution of Germany's status would be settled on Western (especially American) terms, and it was in the nation's best interests to pursue a close relationship with the West.

In his negotiations with the Allies, Adenauer did not insist on absolute autonomy for the Federal Republic. He wanted Germany to be a respected and equal partner in a strong Western Alliance, and realized that such a goal might not be compatible with absolute national sovereignty. Furthermore, he believed that West Germany's future influence in world politics would come through its association with other European nations, rather than as an individual nation-state. He therefore willingly handed over some of the independence granted to the Federal Republic by the Allied authorities to international organizations and institutions. Adenauer argued that "the age of the nation-state belongs to the past, a past full of jealousy and steeped in blood."[16] Adenauer's willingness to relinquish national sovereignty had an almost paradoxical effect, for it hastened the establishment of a sovereign West German state.

The international rehabilitation of the Federal Republic proceeded faster than most people would have predicted. By the end of 1949, West Germany was given a seat on the international boards that oversaw Ruhr development and the distribution of Marshall Plan aid. Adenauer supported the French plan for coordination of the French and German coal and steel industries, and in 1952 the

Federal Republic became a founding member of the European Coal and Steel Community (the predecessor of the Common Market). The major turning point was the U.S. proposal to strengthen the Western Alliance by rearming West Germany. Since the memories of German aggression in World War II were still very fresh, this proposal came as a considerable shock. Domestic opposition groups (the *Ohne mich* movement) attacked Adenauer's support for rearmament. The reaction of many West Europeans was equally negative. In debating the proposal for a rearmed Germany, one French parliamentarian summed up these sentiments: "I don't know if they would frighten the Russians, but, by God, they'd frighten me."

Adenauer agreed to a West German contribution to an international defense force—if Germany were treated as an equal ally and given its sovereignty. After temporary French recalcitrance on this issue, an agreement was finally reached which called for the Federal Republic to develop armed forces within the international command structure of the North Atlantic Treaty Organization (NATO). On May 5, 1955, the Federal Republic became a sovereign nation-state. The Western Allies recognized the Federal Republic as the only German government "freely and legitimately constituted and therefore entitled to speak for Germany as the representative of the German people in international affairs." In only six years, Adenauer led Germany from a position of political dependence to one of equality and acceptance within the Western Alliance.

In the early 1970s, Ostpolitik marked a broadening of West Germany's role in international affairs.[17] Even while strengthening its ties with the West, the Federal Republic attempted to normalize its relations with Eastern Europe. In place of the confrontational approach that had characterized earlier West German governments, Willy Brandt sought a reconciliation with the East. Treaties with the Soviet Union, Poland and Czechoslovakia resolved disagreements dating back to the end of the Second World War; a Basic Agreement with the German Democratic Republic began to normalize relations between the two Germanies. Public opinion surveys, and the results of the 1972 federal elections, demonstrated the popularity of these initiatives. With Ostpolitik, the Federal Republic defined for itself a new political role as a bridge between East and West.

The overall foreign policy objectives of the Federal Republic thus represent a complex mixture of goals. The Federal Republic is committed to the Western Alliance and identifies with Western values and interests. Indeed, the United States may have no stronger ally in Western Europe. These Western leanings are supplemented, however, by a belief in negotiation and compromise with Eastern Europe, even while maintaining a strong defense force. Since the 1960s, these concerns have produced a two-pronged foreign policy: defense and détente.

One example of the Federal Republic's integration into the Western Alliance is its participation in the North Atlantic Treaty Organization. West German troops are now a mainstay of West European defenses; a universal draft maintains a military force of almost 500,000, and these troops maintain forward positions on the borders with Eastern Europe. The Federal Republic makes one of the largest manpower and financial contributions to NATO forces, and the West German public strongly supports the NATO alliance.

Even though West Germany has rearmed, the role of the military is very limited in comparison to previous German regimes. The traditional officer corps was replaced by a military command dedicated to democratic values. The strict obedience to leadership that enabled Hitler to manipulate the military is now tempered by equal attention to personal conscience. Even the size of the armed forces is limited by international treaty to less than 500,000 troops, and the Federal Republic has renounced development of an independent nuclear force. Furthermore, Allied armies from six nations are permanently stationed on West German soil as NATO's front line of defense. In the event of war, these troops—including all West German combat forces—would be under the direction of NATO commanders.

The Federal Republic's commitment to Western cooperation also includes the process of European economic integration.[18] Nascent French-German economic and political cooperation first took institutional form in the European Coal and Steel Community (ECSC), which created an open market for coal and steel within the six member nations (West Germany, France, Italy, Belgium, the Netherlands, and Luxembourg) and assumed permanent responsibility for regulating these industries. The success of the ECSC led to the creation of the European Economic Community (EEC) in 1957. The immediate goal of the EEC was to provide a common market for commerce, industry, manufacturing, and agriculture in the six member states. Common taxes, customs duties, a common agricultural program, and economic regulations coordinated the economies of the member nations.

The process of European integration has continued since then. In 1973, the separate institutions were merged into a single organizational unit, the European Community (EC). The membership has expanded to include Britain, Ireland, Denmark, Greece, Spain, and Portugal in addition to the original six nations. Moreover, the policy responsibilities of the community have broadened to include social programs, regional development, monetary coordination, foreign aid, and other policy areas. With irregular steps, the EC has moved towards its goals of "ever closer union" spelled out in 1957 in the founding Treaty of Rome.

The Federal Republic was an initial advocate of the EC and remains one of its strongest supporters. This commitment includes substantial financial support for the EC, which receives a share of West German customs duties and VAT revenues, as well as political support for the principle of European integration. For instance, Helmut Schmidt was a primary figure in the initiation of a European Monetary System (EMS) in the late 1970s, and during the 1980s the German government has advocated reforms that would strengthen the supranational authority of the Community's institutions. Public opinion surveys generally find that West German support for the Community is among the highest of any member state.[19] In return, West Germany has benefited considerably from its EC membership. Free access to a large European market was essential to the success of the Economic Miracle and is a continuing basis of its export-oriented economy. Participation in Community decision making also has given the Federal Republic a major influence on the course of European development.

The Federal Republic's phoenixlike rebirth as an accepted member of the international community is a remarkable accomplishment, which can be traced to Adenauer's decision to "denationalize" West Germany's foreign policy.[20] Rather than pursuing foreign policy goals from the narrow perspective of national interests, West Germany developed a broader framework of international cooperation. The Republic pursued military and economic goals through international bodies, such as NATO and the EC. The public was, in fact, encouraged to think of themselves not as Germans but as Europeans. By cooperating with other governments in these international forums, the Federal Republic lessened lingering anxieties about German foreign policy goals.

Maintaining good relations with both East and West has required a fine balancing act. Perhaps the best illustration of this was the

West German reaction to the Soviet deployment of new intermediate range nuclear missiles in Eastern Europe.[21] NATO's response
was a "dual track" decision suggested by Helmut Schmidt: pursuing negotiations for the removal of Soviet SS-20 missiles while preparing for the deployment of NATO counterforces (Pershing and
cruise missiles) if negotiations were unproductive. As negotiations
failed to make significant progress and the date for a deployment
decision approached, the dual track policy became politically divisive. The peace movement, with the support of the Green party,
mobilized intense opposition in the Federal Republic and other
nations that would host the NATO weapons. At the same time,
conservatives pressed for a forceful response to the military build-up
in the East. In what must be one of the most ironic turns of European history, the French president spoke before the Bundestag to
encourage West Germany to strengthen its military forces by accepting the NATO weapons. The Bundestag approved deployment in
November 1983, culminating several years of intense politicking.

The NATO decision is symptomatic of a more general trend
affecting West German foreign policy. The partisan consensus that
characterized West German foreign policy since the late 1950s is
apparently weakening.[22] The Union parties continue to advocate a
strong defense posture, but the SPD and the Greens place a higher
priority on policies aimed at lessening East–West tensions. The
NATO dual-track decision was so contentious because it forced the
parties to choose between defense and détente. In the course of this
debate, the SPD shifted toward the left on defense and national
security issues, although it is still outflanked by the Greens. Green
policy papers claim that West Germany can defend itself through
massive civil disobedience against an aggressor army or with a citizen defense force patterned on the Swiss model. The extreme, fundamental criticism by the Greens has prompted the Social Democrats to become more critical of the government's defense policies.
Government proposals to increase defense spending or lengthen the
term of military service now provoke sharp partisan debate. Thus,
while a popular consensus still exists on the nation's Western orientations and the continuing need for the NATO alliance, the major
parties are diverging on the specific policies they propose to achieve
the Federal Republic's joint goals of defense and détente.

The growing partisan polarization on foreign policy issues is
especially problematic, because the Federal Republic faces a number
of difficult policy decisions in the near future.[23] The removal of

intermediate range missiles from Europe should increase pressures for an expansion of NATO's conventional forces. Any significant increase in German defense spending, however, would probably require cuts in social spending; this obviously would be politically divisive. Moreover, demographic trends indicate that in the late 1980s the number of available conscripts will begin to fall below the level necessary merely to maintain present troop levels. By the mid-1990s, the available pool of young males will equal only half of the military's annual manpower needs. A basic rethinking of present manpower policies is inevitable.

More fundamental than the questions of defense resources are the increasing debates on the Federal Republic's role in international politics. West Germany has functioned as a central pillar of the Western Alliance, bolstering Western affluence through the strength of its economy and ensuring Western security through its defense commitment. The Union parties, CDU and CSU, remain strongly committed to the West, and the majority of the German public endorse the nation's Western alignment. Yet as the traumatizing events that created the special United States–West German relationship fade into history, the Federal Republic's Western orientation has become a topic of partisan debate. The Greens and their supporters are aggressively challenging the strategic thinking underlying West German defense policy, calling for unconventional defense policies and even a withdrawal from the NATO alliance.[24] The radical foreign policy views of the Greens garner little support among the public at large, but they have won endorsement from some young SPD leaders. Moreover, the enmity toward the East that provided the basis of the NATO partnership has been attenuated by Gorbachev's success in creating a favorable image of the Soviet Union among West Europeans. In such an environment, it is easier for citizens and political leaders to question the Federal Republic's strong commitment to NATO and the alliance. In short, the consensus on foreign policy goals that has existed for two decades is, like the consensus on the welfare state, being called into question. This questioning is not a rejection of past goals but an attempt to rethink them and find a new balance in Germany's relations with East and West.

It is unlikely that the Western orientation of the Federal Republic will be seriously challenged. The social, cultural, and economic ties to the West are too strong. Few Germans hold neutralist or anti-American views, though those opinions are increasing.[25] It is more likely that the Federal Republic will pursue a more independent course while remaining within the Western Alliance, tending to its own national interests to a greater degree. Such sentiments can be heard in the electoral rhetoric of both the CDU and the SPD. Indeed, in more general terms, the Federal Republic is shedding its image as an economic giant but a political midget. This will likely lead to more contentiousness in West Germany's relations with its allies, and in this sense the unity of the Western Alliance will lessen. But in developing its own course the Federal Republic is also becoming a more equal member of the alliance, which should strengthen its integration into the West.

LOOKING TOWARD THE FUTURE

This book began by discussing how the "German question" initially dominated the study of West German politics. At the founding of the Federal Republic, there was widespread concern about whether the nation could rise above its cultural and political heritage. The frailties of Weimar democracy came from inherent weaknesses in German society and political traditions. Critics traced the political excesses of the Third Reich to negative national traits of intolerance and unquestioning acceptance of authority. The apolitical and undemocratic attitudes of postwar Germans appeared to be persistent features of the political culture. When these drawbacks were coupled with the severe economic conditions of the time, it was no wonder that many people speculated about whether the Federal Republic, and German democracy, would endure.

Over the course of the last forty years, these questions have been answered, almost always positively. Most of the major challenges that faced the nation at its creation were resolved within the span of a generation. Elites accepted and promulgated the new democratic order, and public support gradually developed for the democratic institutions and procedures of the Federal Republic. An apathetic and intolerant public became a sophisticated and participatory citizenry. The Federal Republic regained its national sovereignty more rapidly than anyone would have imagined in 1949, and has evolved into a respected member of the international community. The Economic Miracle fundamentally changed economic and social conditions. In short, as this book has described, West Germany made a remarkable transformation and successfully met these challenges from the past.

Despite this progress, the specter of the past probably will continue to influence Germany's future. Observers continue to voice doubts about the viability of German democracy, regardless of the preponderant evidence to the contrary. Similar questions simply do not arise about Britain, or even France, although surveys show that citizen support of democratic institutions is less certain in both instances. Germans themselves partake in this breast-beating, publicly lamenting over their condition. Sensitivity to the past and anxiety about the future are well established features of the West German political culture.

This eye to the past is important, less the lessons of history be forgotten, but it should not distort our image of the Federal Republic's current and future situation. The social and political forces driving West German society are no longer focused on the problems of the past, but on the emerging problems of an advanced industrial society. The "German question" has given way to the postindustrial debate common to other European democracies. Having addressed one set of challenges, West Germany faces a new set of political questions.

In discussing accomplishments, we outlined the policy challenges that lie ahead. The economic infrastructure that produced the Wirtschaftswunder is aging, which lessens the competitiveness of German industry in world markets. Compared to most other advanced industrial democracies, Germany's manufacturing and "rust belt" industries account for a larger share of the economy, and the service sector is relatively underdeveloped. A nation that was once a leader in research and technology now lags behind many of its competitors in the high technology fields (microelectronics, supercomputers, genetic engineering) that are likely to drive economic growth in the future. The Federal Republic faces new foreign policy questions about maintaining its defense committments in a changing international environment; and the unspoken issue of relations between the two German states cannot remain forever unresolved. In addition, the society is suffering from the unintended consequences of past economic growth, as seen in environmental pollution, overdevelopment, and the problems of urban life.

The Federal Republic's attempts to grapple with changing economic and political conditions have revived debates over the nation's long-term political goals. Renewed economic difficulties and changing demographic patterns reopened debate on the role of the welfare state in German society. The problem of balancing social needs against the resources of government sometimes appears intractable. Similarly, the shifting balance of international politics raises questions about which course the Federal Republic should follow in foreign affairs. Although a fundamental change in the welfare state or West Germany's international alignment is highly unlikely, the increased attention devoted to such questions indicates that the demand for policy change is high. Thus the programmatic alternatives presented by the political parties have begun to diverge, signalling an increased politicization of the policy process.

The policy challenges the Federal Republic now faces are not overwhelming when compared to the challenges of the immediate postwar years. These new policy problems are not even unique; many are shared by other advanced industrial democracies. It could even be said that West Germany's prospects are quite good. The crucial issue, however, is not the magnitude of these policy problems, but the ability of existing political and social structures to deal with these problems.

The highly bureaucratized and neo-corporatist style of West German politics was appropriate to the problems of the immediate postwar era, and this was partially the source of the Federal Republic's initial successes. The elite consensus on democratic politics enabled social and political institutions to combine their efforts to remake the political culture. Pressing economic needs and the trauma of the Third Reich led to the creation of a social partnership in which business and labor cooperated within a neo-corporatist system. The very success of this style of politics led to even more bureaucratization and the formalization of the policy process.

This same policy style may be less effective in dealing with the political challenges the Federal Republic faces as an advanced industrial society. The West German policy process emphasizes predictability and stability, in a time when flexibility and innovation are in increasing demand. A neo-corporatist system tends to perpetuate the status quo, as those groups who have won formal representation lobby to maintain their privileged position—even if they represent declining social forces. A neo-corporatist structure is ill-suited to accommodating the participatory demands of citizen-action groups and the other political groups spawned by the participatory revolution. In addition, this system discourages the representation of new social interests and the forces for social renewal that they represent. For instance, established interests acquire large subsidies to temporarily protect declining industries, such as agriculture and the steel industry, while the government ignores (at best) the entrepenuers who are creating the industries of the future. Regardless of whether one agrees with Helmut Kohl's proposed policy of "Wende," the government's inability to enact fundamental reform in a parliamentary system illustrates how the contemporary policy process discourages change. In other words, more than just paying attention to new issues, some reform in the structure or policy style of West German politics may also be required.

The apparent need for structural reform makes me somewhat cautious about the prospects for the West German political system. It is always difficult to get players to agree to change the rules in the middle of a game, especially when they are struggling with complex problems that lack simple answers. Still, the Federal Republic's past successes make the nation much better suited to this task. Moreover, challenges represent an opportunity for the political system to evolve—economically, socially, and politically. Rather than economic stagnation, innovation can lead to further economic growth. The attempt to risk more democracy and open access to the policy process can move the Federal Republic closer to its democratic ideals. And the willingness to attempt political change can continue the nation's political development. The political system's success in meeting these new challenges will determine the nation's future.

NOTES

1. Accounting practices have changed several times over this period. The Saarland was included in spending figures beginning in 1961 and in 1974 public spending statistics added substantial social security expenditures that previously were reported separately. The growth in expenditures in figure XI thus somewhat overestimates the actual growth in public spending.

2. Peter Flora, ed. *State, Economy and Society in Western Europe 1815–1975* (Frankfurt: Campus, 1983).

3. Charles Andrain, *Politics and Economic Policy in Western Democracies* (North Scituate, Mass.: Duxbury Press, 1980), chap. 2.

4. Jens Alber, "Germany," in *Growth to Limits*, ed. Peter Flora (Berlin: deGruyter, 1986), pp. 84–114.

5. Also see Arnold Heidenheimer et al., *Comparative Public Policy*, 2nd ed. (New York: St. Martin's Press, 1983), chap. 12; Edeltraud Roller und Bettina Westle, "Zur Politisierung und Depolitisierung von Wohlfahrtsansprüchen," *Soziale Welt* 38 (1987): 227–251.

6. Statistisches Bundesamt, *Datenreport 1985* (Bonn: Schriftenreihe der Bundeszentrale für politische Bildung, 1985); also see Alber, "Germany," pp. 52–83.

7. Statistisches Bundesamt, *Datenreport 1985*, p. 378.

8. Peter Flora and Arnold Heidenheimer, eds. *The Development of the Welfare State in Europe and America* (New Brunswick, N.J.: Transaction Books, 1979), ch. 1; H. P. Ullmann, "German Industry and Bismarck's Social Security

System," in *The Emergence of the Welfare State in Britain and Germany*, ed. W. Mommsen (London: Croom Helm, 1981).

9. Jens Alber, *Der Sozialstaat in der Bundesrepublik, 1950-1983.* (Frankfurt: Campus, 1988).

10. Alber, "Germany," p. 52.

11. Alber, "West Germany," pp. 114-132; Peter Katzenstein, *Policy and Politics in West Germany* (Philadelphia: Temple University Press, 1987), ch. 4; Klaus von Beyme and Manfred Schmidt, eds. *Politics and Policy in the Federal Republic of Germany* (London: Gower, 1985), chs. 3, 4, and 6.

12. Eric Willenz, "Why Europe Needs the Welfare State," *Foreign Policy* 63 (Summer 1986): 88-107.

13. See K. Wey, *Umweltpolitik in Deutschland* (Opladen: Westdeutscher Verlag, 1982); also Jochen Hucke, "Environmental Policy: The Development of a New Policy Area," in *Policy and Politics in the Federal Republic of Germany*, ed. von Beyme and Schmidt.

14. Hans-Dieter Klingemann, "Umweltproblematik in den Wahlprogrammen der etablierten politischen Parteien in der Bundesrepublik Deutschland," in *Umwelt, Wirtschaft, Gesellschaft—Wege zu einem neuen Grundverständnis*, ed. Rudolf Wildenmann (Stuttgart: Staatsministeriums Baden-Wurttemberg, 1985).

15. Commission of the European Communities, *The Europeans and their Environment in 1986* (Brussels: Commission of the European Communities, 1986); for additional information on public attitudes see, IPOS, *Einstellungen zu aktuellen Fragen der Innenpolitik 1987* (Mannheim: IPOS, 1987).

16. Quoted in Wolfram Hanreider, *The Stable Crisis* (New York: Harper and Row, 1970), p. 48.

17. Roger Tilford, *Ostpolitik and Political Change in Germany* (Lexington, Mass.: Heath, 1975); Michael Kreile, "Ostpolitik Reconsidered," in *The Foreign Policy of West Germany*, eds. Ekkehart Krippendorff and Volker Rittberger (Beverly Hills: Sage Publications, 1980).

18. Simon Bulmer and William Patterson, *The Federal Republic of Germany and the European Community* (London: Allen and Unwin, 1987).

19. See the series of *Eurobarometer Reports* (Brussels: Commission of the European Communities).

20. Wolfram Hanreider and Graeme Auton, *The Foreign Policies of West Germany, France, and Britain* (Englewood Cliffs, N.J.: Prentice-Hall, 1980).

21. Helga Haftendorn, "Germany and the Euromissile Debate," *International Journal* 40 (1986): 68-85.

22. Richard Eichenberg, *Public Opinion and National Security in Western Europe: Consensus Lost* (Ithaca: Cornell University Press, 1988).

23. Catherine Kelleher, "The Defense Policy of the Federal Republic of Germany," in *The Defense Policies of Nations*, eds. Norman Vig and Stephen Schier (New York: Holmes and Meier, 1985); James Cooney et al. *The Federal Republic of Germany and the United States* (Boulder: Westview Press, 1984).

24. Reinhard Stuth, "Die Aussen-und Deutschlandpolitik der Grünen," in *Die Grünen-Partei, wider willen*, eds. Klaus Gotto and Hans-Joachim Veen. Mainz, 1984.

25. H. Mueller et al. "Origins of Estrangement: The Peace Movement and the Changed Image of the America in West Germany," *International Security* 12 (1987): 52-83; Hans Rattinger, "Change versus Continuity in West German Public Attitudes on Nuclear Security and Nuclear Weapons in the Early 1980s," *Public Opinion Quarterly* 51 (1987): 495-521; Eichenberg, *Public Opinion and National Security in Western Europe.*

ADDITIONAL READINGS

CHAPTER I: THE LEGACY OF HISTORY

Bracher, Karl. *The German Dictatorship: The Origins, Structure, and Effects of National Socialism, 1919-1933.* New York: Praeger, 1970.

Broszat, Martin. *Hitler and the Collapse of Weimar Germany.* New York: St. Martin's Press, 1987.

Childers, Thomas. *The Nazi Voter: The Social Foundations of Fascism in Germany, 1919-1933.* Chapel Hill: University of North Carolina Press, 1983.

Craig, Gordon. *Germany, 1866-1945.* New York: Oxford University Press, 1978.

Fest, Joachim. *Hitler.* New York: Random House, 1975.

Halperin, S. William. *Germany Tried Democracy: A Political History of the Reich from 1918 to 1933.* Hamden, Conn.: Archon Book, 1963.

Hamilton, Richard. *Who Voted for Hitler.* Princeton: Princeton University Press, 1982.

Hilberg, Raul. *The Destruction of the European Jews,* revised ed. New York: Holmes and Meier, 1985.

Hoffmann, Peter. *The History of the German Resistance, 1933-1945.* Cambridge: Harvard University Press, 1977.

Holborn, Hajo. *A History of Modern Germany.* New York: Knopf, 1969.

Reinhardt, Kurt. *Germany: 2000 Years,* vols. 1 and 2. New York: Ungar, 1986.

Stern, Fritz. *Dreams and Delusions: The Drama of German History.* New York: Knopf, 1987.

Toland, John. *Adolf Hitler.* Garden City: Doubleday, 1976.

CHAPTER II: THE FORMATION OF THE FEDERAL REPUBLIC

Balfour, Michael. *West Germany: A Contemporary History.* London: Croom Helm, 1982.

Ellwein, Thomas. *Das Regierungssystem der Bundesrepublik Deutschland*, 6th ed. Opladen: Westdeutscher Verlag, 1983.

Gimbel, John. *The American Occupation of Germany: Politics and the Military 1945–1949*. Stanford: Stanford University Press, 1968.

Golay, John Ford. *The Founding of the Federal Republic of Germany*. Chicago: University of Chicago Press, 1958.

Grosser, Alfred. *Germany in our Time: A Political History of the Postwar Years*. New York: Praeger, 1970.

Gunlicks, Arthur. *Local Government in the German Federal System*. Durham: Duke University Press, 1986.

Hanrieder, Wolfram. *The Stable Crisis*. New York: Harper & Row, 1970.

Hoffmeister, Gerhardt, and Tubach, Frederic. *Germany: 2000 Years*, vol 3. New York: Ungar, 1986.

Jesse, Eckhard, *Die Demokratie der Bundesrepublik Deutschland*, 7th ed. Berlin: Colloquium Verlag, 1986.

Kommers, Donald. *Judicial Politics in West Germany*. Beverly Hills, Calif.: Sage Publications, 1975.

Livingston, Robert, and Thaysen, Uwe, eds. *The Congress and the Bundestag: A Comparison*. Boulder: Westview Press, 1988.

Loewenberg, Gerhard. *Parliament in the German Political System*. Ithaca, N.Y.: Cornell University Press, 1966.

Loewenberg, Gerhard, and Patterson, Samuel. *Comparing Legislatures*. Boston: Little, Brown, 1979.

Merkl, Peter. *The Origin of the West German Republic*. New York: Oxford University Press, 1963.

Presse- und Informationszentrum. *Datenhandbuch zur Geschichte des Deutschen Bundestages 1949 bis 1982*. Bonn: Deutscher Bundestag, 1983.

Tent, James. *Mission on the Rhine: Reeducation and Denazification in American-Occupied Germany*. Princeton: Princeton University Press, 1983.

CHAPTER III: THE TRANSFORMATION OF SOCIETY

Hardach, Karl. *The Political Economy of Germany in the Twentieth Century*. Berkeley: University of California Press, 1980.

Hartrich, Edwin. *The Fourth and Richest Reich*. New York: Macmillan, 1980.

Markovits, Andrei, ed. *The Political Economy of West Germany: Modell Deutschland.* New York: Praeger, 1982.

Rist, Ray. *Guestworkers in Germany.* New York: Praeger, 1978.

Smith, Owen. *The West German Economy.* London: Croom Helm, 1983.

Vogl, Frank. *German Business after the Economic Miracle.* New York: Wiley, 1973.

CHAPTER IV: A CHANGING POLITICAL CULTURE

Almond, Gabriel, and Verba, Sidney. *The Civic Culture.* Princeton: Princeton University Press, 1963.

Ardagh, John. *Germany and the Germans.* New York: Harper & Row, 1987.

Baker, Kendall; Dalton, Russell; and Hildebrandt, Kai. *Germany Transformed: Political Culture and the New Politics.* Cambridge: Harvard University Press, 1981.

Calleo, David. *The German Problem Reconsidered: Germany and the World Order, 1870 to the Present.* Cambridge: Cambridge University Press, 1978.

Conradt, David. "The Changing Political Culture," in *The Civic Culture Revisited,* eds. Gabriel Almond and Sidney Verba. Boston: Little, Brown, 1980.

Dahrendorf, Ralf. *Society and Democracy in Germany.* New York: Doubleday, 1967.

Greiffenhagen, Martin, and Greiffenhagen, Sylvia. *Ein schwieriges Vaterland: Zur Politischen Kultur Deutschlands.* Munich: List, 1979.

Hardin, Stephen, et al. *Contrasting Values in Western Europe: Unity, Diversity and Change.* London: MacMillan, 1986.

Inglehart, Ronald. *The Silent Revolution.* Princeton: Princeton University Press, 1977.

———. *Culture Shift in Advanced Industrial Society.* Princeton: Princeton University Press, 1989.

Lowenthal, Richard. *Social Change and Cultural Crisis.* New York: Columbia University Press, 1984.

Merritt, Anna, and Merritt, Richard. *Public Opinion in Occupied Germany: The OMGUS Surveys, 1945-1949.* Urbana: University of Illinois Press, 1970.

———. *Public Opinion in Semisovereign Germany: The HICOG Surveys, 1949-1955.* Urbana: University of Illinois Press, 1980.

Montgomery, John. *Forced to be Free: The Artificial Revolution in Germany and Japan.* Chicago: University of Chicago Press, 1957.

Noelle-Neumann, Elisabeth, and Köcher, Renate. *Die verletzte Nation.* Stuttgart: Deutsche Verlags-Anstalt, 1987.

Noelle-Neumann, Elisabeth, and Piel, Edgar, eds. *Eine Generation später: Bundesrepublik Deutschland 1953-1979.* Munich: Saur, 1983.

Offe, Claus. *Contradictions of the Welfare State.* Cambridge: MIT Press.

Piper Verlag. *Historikerstreit.* Munich: Piper Verlag, 1987.

Schweigler, Gerhard. *National Consciousness in Divided Germany.* Beverly Hills: Sage Publications, 1975.

CHAPTER V: PATTERNS IN POLITICAL LEARNING

Hearnden, Arthur. *Education in the Two Germanies.* New York: Oxford University Press, 1974.

———. *Education, Culture, and Politics in West Germany.* New York: Oxford University Press, 1976.

Max Planck Institute. *Between Elite and Mass Education.* Albany, NY: State University of New York Press, 1982.

Meyn, Hermann. *Massenmedien in der Bundesrepublik Deutschland.* Berlin: Colloquium Verlag, 1979.

Noelle-Neumann, Elisabeth. *Wahlentscheidung in der Fernsehdemokratie.* Würzburg: Verlage Ploetz, 1980.

———. *The Spiral of Silence: Public Opinion, Our Social Skin.* Chicago: University of Chicago Press, 1984.

Sandford, John. *The Media of the German-speaking Countries.* Ames, Iowa: Iowa State University Press, 1976.

Stahl, Walter ed. *Education for Democracy in West Germany.* New York: Praeger, 1961.

Torney, Judith; Oppenheim, A; and Farnen, Russell. *Civic Education in Ten Countries.* International Studies in Evaluation, vol 6. Stockholm: Almqvist and Wiksell, 1975.

Tydeman, John, and Kelm, Ellen. *New Media in Europe: Satellites, Cable, VCRs and Videotext.* New York: McGraw-Hill, 1986.

CHAPTER VI: CITIZEN ACTION

Barnes, Samuel; Kaase, Max, et al. *Political Action: Mass Participation in Five Western Democracies.* Beverly Hills: Sage Publications, 1979.

Dalton, Russell. *Citizen Politics in Western Democracies.* Chatham, N.J.: Chatham House Publishers, 1988.

Guggenberger, Bernd, and Kempf, Udo, eds. *Bürgerinitiativen und Repräsentatives System,* 2nd ed. Opladen: Westdeutscher Verlag, 1984.

Infratest. *Politischer Protest in der Bundesrepublik Deutschland.* Stuttgart: Kohlhammer, 1980.

Muller, Edward. *Aggressive Political Participation.* Princeton: Princeton University Press, 1979.

Powell, G. Bingham. *Contemporary Democracies.* Cambridge: Harvard University Press, 1982.

CHAPTER VII: POLITICS AT THE ELITE LEVEL

Aberbach, Joel; Putnam, Robert; and Rockman, Bert. *Bureaucrats and Politicians in Western Democracies.* Cambridge: Harvard University Press, 1981.

Adenauer, Konrad. *Memoirs,* 3 vol. Chicago: Henry Regnery Company, 1965.

Arzberger, Klaus. *Bürger und Eliten in der Kommunalpolitik.* Stuttgart: Kohlhammer, 1980.

Beyme, Klaus von. *Die Politische Elite in der Bundesrepublik Deutschland,* 2nd edition. Munich: Piper Verlag, 1974.

Brandt, Willy. *People and Politics: The Years 1960–1975.* Boston: Little, Brown, and Company, 1978.

Dahrendorf, Ralf. *Society and Democracy in Germany.* New York: Doubleday, 1967.

Deutsch, Karl, and Edinger, Lewis. *Germany Rejoins the Powers: Mass Opinion, Interest Groups, and Elites in Contemporary German Foreign Policy.* Stanford: Stanford University Press, 1959.

Herzog, Dietrich. *Politische Karrieren: Selektion und Professionalisierung politischer Führungsgruppen.* Opladen: Westdeutscher Verlag, 1975.

Hoffmann-Lange, Ursula; Neumann, Helga; and Steinkemper, Bärbel. *Konsens und Konflikt zwischen Führungsgruppen in der Bundesrepublik Deutschland: Eine empirische Analyse.* Frankfurt: Peter Lang, 1980. An abridged English language version appears in *Studies of the Structure of National Elite Groups,* ed. Gwen Moore. Greenwich, Conn.: JAI Press, 1984.

Reif, Karlheinz, and Cayrol, Roland, eds. *Party Conference Delegates in Western Europe.* Forthcoming.

Schmitt, Hermann., *Neue Politik in alten Parteien*. Opladen: Westdeutscher Verlag, 1987.

Wildenmann, Rudolf, et al., *Führungsschicht in der Bundesrepublik Deutschland 1981*. Mannheim: Lehrstuhl für politische Wissenschaft, 1982.

Zapf, Wolfgang. *Wandlungen der deutschen Elite: Ein Zirkulationsmodell deutscher Führungsgruppen*. Munich: Piper, 1966.

CHAPTER VIII: THE REPRESENTATION OF INTERESTS

Berger, Suzanne, ed. *Organizing Interests in Western Europe: Pluralism, Corporatism, and the Transformation of Politics*. New York: Cambridge University Press, 1981.

Beyme, Klaus von. *Challenge to Power: Trade Unions and Industrial Relations in Capitalist Countries*. Beverly Hills: Sage Publications, 1980.

Brand, Karl-Werner; Büsser, Detlef; and Rucht, Dieter, eds. *Aufbruch in eine andere Gesellschaft: Neue soziale Bewegungen in der Bundesrepublik*. Frankfurt: Campus, 1983.

Braunthal, Gerard. *The Federation of German Industry in Politics*. Ithaca: Cornell University Press, 1965.

Cullingford, E.C.M. *Trade Unions in West Germany*. Boulder: Westview Press, 1977.

Gress, David. *Peace and Survival: West Germany, the Peace Movement and European Security*. Stanford, Conn.: Hoover Institution, 1985.

Markovits, Andrei. *The Politics of the West German Trade Unions: Strategies of Class and Interest Representation in Growth and Crisis*. Cambridge: Cambridge University Press, 1986.

Nelkin, Dorothy, and Pollak, M. *The Atom Besieged: Antinuclear Movements in France and Germany*. Cambridge: MIT Press, 1981.

Papadakis, Elim. *The Green Movement in West Germany*. New York: St. Martin's Press, 1984.

Rochon, Thomas. *Mobilizing for Peace: Antinuclear Movements in Western Europe*. Princeton: Princeton University Press, 1988.

Roth, Roland, and Rucht, Dieter, eds. *Neue soziale Bewegungen in der Bundesrepublik Deutschland*. Frankfurt: Campus, 1987.

Schmitter, Philippe, and Lehmbruch, Gerhard. *Trends Toward Corporatist Intermediation*. Beverly Hills: Sage Publications, 1981.

Simon, Walter. *Macht und Herrschaft der Unternehmerverbände BDI, BDA und DIHT im ökonomischen und politischen System der BRD.* Cologne: Pahl-Rugenstein Verlag, 1976.

Spotts, Frederic. *The Churches and Politics in Germany.* Middletown, Conn.: Wesleyan University Press, 1974.

Weber, Juergen. *Die Interessengruppen im politischen System der Bundesrepublik Deutschland,* 2nd ed. Munich: Piper, 1980.

CHAPTER IX: THE PARTY SYSTEM AND ELECTORIAL POLITICS

Braunthal, Gerhard. *The West German Social Democrats, 1969–1982: Profile of a Party in Power.* Boulder: Westview Press, 1983.

Doring, Herbert, and Smith, Gordon, eds. *Party Government and Political Culture in Western Germany.* New York: St. Martin's Press, 1982.

Kitschelt, Herbert. *The Logic of Party Formation: The Structure and Strategy of the Belgian and West German Ecology Parties.* Ithaca: Cornell University Press, 1989.

Klingemann, Hans-Dieter, and Kaase, Max, eds. *Wahlen und politischer Prozess: Analysen aus Anlass der Bundestagswahl 1983.* Opladen: Westdeutscher Verlag, 1986.

Kolinsky, Eva. *Parties, Opposition and Society in West Germany.* New York: St. Martin's Press, 1984.

Langguth, Gerd. *The Green Factor in German Politics: From Protest Movement to Political Party.* Boulder: Westview Press, 1986.

Padgett, Stephen, and Burkett, Tony. *Political Parties and Elections in West Germany.* New York: St. Martin's Press, 1986.

Pridham, Geoffrey. *Christian Democracy in Western Germany.* New York: St. Martin's Press, 1977.

Soe, Christian. "The Free Democratic Party," in *West German Politics in the Mid-Eighties: Crisis and Continuity,* eds. H.G. Peter Wallach and George Romoser. New York: Praeger, 1985.

Smith, Gordon. *Democracy in West Germany,* 3rd ed. New York: Holmes and Meier, 1986.

Stöss, Richard, ed. *Parteien Handbuch: Die Parteien der Bundesrepublik Deutschland 1945–1980.* 4 volumes. Opladen: Westdeutscher Verlag, 1983.

CHAPTER X: POLICY AS A PROCESS

Blair, Philip. *Federalism and Judicial Review in West Germany.* Oxford: Clarendon Press, 1981.

Braunthal, Gerhard. *The West German Legislative Process: A Case Study of Two Transportation Bills.* Ithaca: Cornell University Press, 1972.

Dyson, Kenneth. *Party, State and Bureaucracy in Western Germany.* Beverly Hills: Sage Publications, 1977.

_____. "West Germany: The Search for a Rationalist Consensus," in *Policy Styles in Western Europe,* ed. Jeremy Richardson. London: Allen and Unwin, 1982.

Johnson, Nevil. *Government in the Federal Republic: The Executive at Work,* 2nd ed. Oxford: Pergammon, 1983.

Kommers, Donald. *Constitutional Jurisprudence of the Federal Republic.* Durham: Duke University Press, 1989.

Mayntz, Renate. "Executive Leadership in Germany: Dispersion of Power or Kanzlerdemokratie?" in *Presidents and Prime Ministers,* eds. Richard Rose and Ezra Suleiman. Washington: American Enterprise Institute, 1980.

Mayntz, Renate, and Scharpf, Fritz. *Policy Making in the German Federal Bureaucracy.* Amsterdam: Elsevier, 1975.

Safran, William. *Veto Group Politics: The Case of Health Insurance Reform in West Germany.* San Francisco: Chandler, 1967.

CHAPTER XI: POLICY PERFORMANCE

Alber, Jens. "Germany," in *Growth to Limits,* vol. 2, ed. Peter Flora. Berlin: deGruyter, 1986.

_____. *Der Sozialstaat in der Bundesrepublik, 1950–1983.* Frankfurt: Campus, 1988.

Beyme, Klaus von, and Schmidt, Manfred. *Policy and Politics in the Federal Republic of Germany.* London: Gower, 1985.

Bulmer, Simon, and Patterson, William. *The Federal Republic of Germany and the European Community.* London: Allen & Unwin, 1987.

Cooney, James, et al. *The Federal Republic of Germany and the United States: Changing Political, Social and Economic Relations.* Boulder: Westview Press, 1984.

Flora, Peter, and Heidenheimer, Arnold. *The Development of the Welfare State in Europe and America.* New Brunswick, N.J.: Transaction Books, 1981.

Hanrieder, Wolfram, ed. *West German Foreign Policy: 1949–1979.* Boulder: Westview Press, 1980.

Heidenheimer, Arnold; Heclo, Hugh; and Adams, Carolyn.

Comparative Public Policy, 2nd ed. New York: St. Martin's Press, 1983.

Katzenstein, Peter. *Policy and Politics in West Germany*. Philadelphia: Temple University Press, 1987.

Krippendorff, Ekkehart, and Rittberger, Volker, ed. *The Foreign Policy of West Germany: Formation and Content*. Beverly Hills: Sage Publications, 1980.

Merkl, Peter, ed. *The Federal Republic at Forty* New York: New York University Press, 1989.

Mommsen, Wolfgang, ed. *The Emergence of the Welfare State in Britain and Germany*. London: Croom Helm, 1981.

Schweigler, Gerhard. *West German Foreign Policy: The Domestic Setting*. New York: Praeger, 1984.

Smith, Gordon, et al. *Developments in West German Politics*. London: MacMillan, 1989.

Index